Reminiscences of Rosa Bonheur

THE HORSE FAIR

Reminiscences
of
Rosa
Bonheur

Edited by
Theodore Stanton

Hacker Art Books
New York 1976

First published 1910, New York.
Reissued 1976 by
Hacker Art Books, New York.

Library of Congress Catalogue Card Number 71-147039
ISBN 0-87817-096-0

Printed in the United States of America.

CONTENTS

CHAPTER I

EARLY LIFE

CHAPTER II

RAYMOND BONHEUR AND FAMILY

CHAPTER III

RAYMOND BONHEUR AND THE SAINT SIMONIANS

CHAPTER IV

THE MICAS FAMILY

CONTENTS

CHAPTER V

EARLY TRAVELS

CHAPTER VI

ROSA BONHEUR AS A LETTER WRITER

CHAPTER VII

FAMILY LETTERS

CHAPTER VIII

LETTERS TO FRIENDS

CONTENTS

CHAPTER IX

FONTAINEBLEAU

CHAPTER X

THE WAR OF 1870

CHAPTER XI

ROSA BONHEUR'S LOVE OF ANIMALS

CHAPTER XII

OTHER MENTAL AND PERSONAL TRAITS

LIST OF ILLUSTRATIONS WITH NOTES

LIST OF ILLUSTRATIONS WITH NOTES

LIST OF ILLUSTRATIONS WITH NOTES

greatly interested her and where she made many sketches of bison.—*Paul Chardin.*

It pleases me very much to succeed in a kind of painting that I had never cultivated, and the success is a sufficient reward.—*Rosa Bonheur to M. Chardin, By, July 9, 1897, àpropos of the Petit Gallery Exhibition.*

I made this sketch at By on December 27, 1872. This boar got so wild that Rosa Bonheur had to kill him. She had him stuffed and utilized him for sketching. In my drawing he is stuffed.—*Paul Chardin.*

This picture was made for Mr. Gambart, as a pendant to his "King of the Forest," that splendid work of Rosa Bonheur where the stag stands boldly facing you. The artist then had at By a live boar, which was used for this picture, but which had to be killed a few years later because he became too savage. This is one of the few pictures of boars made by Rosa Bonheur. She never took a great fancy to this animal, considering him "heavy and uncouth," as she once said.—*Hippolyte Peyrol, Jr.*

The first two belong to my wife and the third to my brother. The first is a spirited conception of the miraculous stag, with a luminous cross between his antlers, which appeared to St. Hubert, the huntsman's patron. The second contains three portraits of my dog Tobey. The third is a fanciful and graceful group of sheep, which gentle animals Rosa Bonheur loved so much to paint. By the way, she made but few fans.—*Georges Cain.*

A lighter and frivolous style of work to which I have not been trained and which is not in my nature.—*Rosa Bonheur.*

I reply post haste.—*Rosa Bonheur to Mme. Cain.*

A good example of one of those little drawings with which Rosa Bonheur hastily adorned her letters now and then. A postilion of the olden time is hastening along the route, letter in hand.—*Paul Chardin.*

By, January 14, 1894: I have not been able to answer your letter before, because I am sitting to Mme. de Grasse for my portrait, so that your old artist companion is not free except in the evenings, and then, after a day's sitting, she is not much disposed to write.—*Rosa Bonheur to Paul Chardin.*

LIST OF ILLUSTRATIONS WITH NOTES

In 1892, I made a portrait-sketch of Rosa Bonheur, which she pronounced to be a good likeness; and a year later, her London publisher engaged me to paint her portrait, which was to be engraved for her Works and be a pendant to the well-known portrait by Dubufe, done forty years before and now seen in the Louvre. When the work was finished, Rosa Bonheur painted in the dog's head, so that the canvas bears two signatures— hers and my own.—*Consuélo Fould.*

November 26, 1893: When once the portrait is finished, or even before, if you prefer, you can send me the canvas and I will paint the dog.—May 19, 1894: I have just unpacked my portrait, or, rather, your portrait. At last it is dry, and I am going to set to work on the dog's head.—*Rosa Bonheur to Consuélo Fould.*

This, one of the many preliminary studies. is notable as being elegantly tinted, and is found reproduced in the middle of the final picture.—*Hippolyte Peyrol, Jr.*

As Rosa Bonheur admired my bust, "Modern Comedy," I made her an exact copy of it in marble, and by way of acknowledgment of this gift, she painted for me a pretty picture of a stag, which she sent me with some verses—an odd composition—both of which I still possess.—*Princess Georges Stirbey.*

> When the fair goddess of the day
> Half drew the welkin's veil away,
> The stag as yet in slumber lay,
> Basking his limbs in sunny ray,
>   Within a fern-deckt, bushy clump.
>   —*Rosa Bonheur.*

Rosa Bonheur was about sixty years old when this was taken. All her friends consider it an excellent likeness and I think it one of the best that exists.—*Georges Cain.*

The fine large studio was worthy of Rosa Bonheur's fame, and is a touching spot to visit to-day, filled as it is with so many interesting souvenirs of the dead artist and left just as it was when she passed away, almost brush in hand. It adjoins the house, and towers above the wall at the corner of the Rue des Arts and the Rue de la Gare, to employ the pompous names which the municipality of Thomery has had the bad taste to give to the rustic lanes of its village suburb.—*Theodore Stanton.*

The Castle of By—villa or country house would be a more exact designation —which Rosa Bonheur and the Micases bought in 1860, is very ancient, its history going back for at least a century before the discovery of America. During her long residence there, the artist made many changes in the old edifice, which was finally rendered fairly comfortable. There is even a touch of spaciousness about the place.—*Theodore Stanton.*

This is where Mlle. Rosa Bonheur and I used to lunch when we were out sketching from nature in Fontainebleau forest.—*Paul Chardin.*

By, October 15, 1869: I will tell you, my dear Rapin, what I was saying to myself just now. Since All Saints' Day is near at hand, I was thinking that about this time a year the famous Rapin used to come and call on his old General, in order to go and sketch with her on the melancholy Long Rocher, both shivering with cold; then, in order to warm themselves at lunch time, they would descend into the Grotto, lighting a big fire that their varlet had gleaned wood for among the firs, at the expense of the State, and there toast their poor trembling bodies and blue faces; next, they would stuff themselves with enormous hunks of bread seasoned with good victuals and an agreeable cup of coffee boiled over the big fire; and finally, they would smoke an exquisite cigarette while chattering about everything that passed through their heads, before returning each to his seat to go on daubing masterpieces.—*Rosa Bonheur to Paul Chardin.*

A drawing made in 1846, when Rosa Bonheur was visiting Auvergne, where she obtained materials for several pictures, especially that of the "Red Oxen of Cantal."—*Anna E. Klumpke.*

Souvenir of a Deer of Ten. To her friend Paul Louis Léger Chardin, a very immodest young man, who is of course disliked, as he merits—this scapegrace who was long ago found out.—*Rosa Bonheur.*

The above is the dedication written under this drawing, which is dated April 26, 1870, and which was sent to M. Chardin. A letter of Rosa Bonheur—see page 308 of this volume—to M. Antoine Passy, wittily describes this incident.—*Theodore Stanton.*

LIST OF ILLUSTRATIONS WITH NOTES

xvi

Monval, the Police Commissioner of her ward, whom she requested to aid her to obtain a regularly authorized permit to wear men's clothes. He made the necessary application to the Prefect of Police and it was granted. Thereafter, Rosa dressed as a man almost continuously at home and when she went out on horseback, though in the streets of Paris she wore a gown. —*Hippolyte Peyrol, Sr.*

When reading Ossian in 1868, Rosa Bonheur produced this curious composition while under the spell of the mystic bard. Apart from its own beauty, this drawing is remarkable as being, if not the only one, at least a very rare example of a picture by Rosa Bonheur in which she has put no animal.— *Hippolyte Peyrol, Jr.*

From out-of-the-way books, Rosa Bonheur now and then drew inspiration. This was notably the case with Ossian, who suggested a picture quite in the Ossian style.—*Paul Chardin.*

This portrait of one of Rosa Bonheur's favourite Scotch greyhounds was drawn by her in pencil and given to me many years ago.—*Paul Chardin.*

A good specimen of one of those many drawings which Rosa Bonheur was continually throwing off as a pretext for her signature. It is simply an autograph.—*Hipployte Peyrol, Jr.*

My worthy old and good Friend: I have just received your portrait of my little Wasp. Nothing could give me more pleasure. You are indeed the nicest of men and of friends. I suppose you know that I have lost the poor little original, whose body I have laid away in a corner of the garden. So does everything pass away. I have kept one of her pups. But it is not the same thing, my friend, it is not the same thing. So your gift becomes doubly precious, and on account of its pretty dedication, too.—*Rosa Bonheur to M. Mène, January 2, 1861.*

M. Antoine Passy, deputy and member of the Institute, wore in the country cravats covered with flowers. He had sent us, while I was visiting By in the autumn of 1864, a rhyme on one of my adventures in the Fontainebleau forest. "Let us give him some nonsense in return," exclaimed Rosa Bonheur. The idea was immediately taken up and agreed to. Thereupon, she went to a closet and got a large piece of sheeting, which she stretched over a table and marked off in lozenge-shaped spaces. Then, all those present at

2

the house were invited, during the following evenings, to fill up the spaces with original caricatures. So we set to work—Rosa and Isidore Bonheur, Mlle. Micas and I—to daub the future cravat with pictures in water-colour.—*Paul Chardin.*

PLOUGHING IN THE NIVERNAIS. *By Rosa Bonheur.* . Facing 400

This painting, so true to nature, so well drawn, so carefully modelled and so harmonious in colour, at once established her reputation as a great artist.—*William Bouguereau.*

Rosa Bonheur's first great success in Paris was, of course, her "Ploughing in the Nivernais." Its beauty lies in its absolute truth. The artist did not seek a strange, unusual landscape. Everything is very simple; just the men and the oxen occupied with their ordinary every-day work. It is all so natural. You feel that the men are tired, that the oxen, too, are tired. Everybody was stuck by the truth and simplicity of this picture, and this it was which gave her this first success.—*Prince Georges Stirbey.*

Rosa Bonheur's "Ploughing in the Nivernais" has always been my artist's joy, and I remember when, as a child, I used to visit the Luxembourg Gallery, it was this picture which most appealed to my imagination.—*Julien Dupré.*

Paul Potter's "Bull," which may be seen at The Hague, is a remarkable picture, but not a masterpiece. The animal stands out against too hard a sky; he has no relation to the circumambient atmosphere. Contrast this canvas with Rosa Bonheur's ploughing scene at the Luxembourg. There the very earth smokes, the oxen are lowing; you see the men toiling, and the emotion is perfect. In a word, the painting is alive.—*Georges Cain.*

Reminiscences of Rosa Bonheur

REMINISCENCES OF ROSA BONHEUR

CHAPTER I

EARLY LIFE

ALL available information respecting the Bonheur ancestors represents them as having cultivated the culinary art from father to son. Jean Bonheur, who lived in the time of Louis XIV, was a cook at Toulouse, then the cultured capital of Languedoc, the finest province of southern France. His son, Guillaume, exercised the same functions in the grand establishment of Mme. de Cazalès, one of the aristocratic ladies of the period. Guillaume's son, François, mounted a step higher in the quality of his employer, though still remaining faithful to his sauces and his sauce-pans. He became head cook of the celebrated Cambacérès family, whose members have made a reputation in pulpit oratory, law, and statesmanship. Here, however, the tradition was interrupted, for the next descent was destined to produce the head of a race of artists.

François Bonheur, who lived from 1753 till 1829, married the daughter of an old invalided soldier that had warred in Germany under Louis XV. Her name was Eléonore Marie Pérard. By her he had two children, the aunt and the father of Rosa Bonheur. The aunt, Elisabeth, better known in Rosa's letters, as we shall see, as "Tatan," was probably born in 1780, although the lack of careful registration in those days makes the date somewhat uncertain. "Tatan," it may be added, never married and lived to a good old age, dying only in 1873. "She was a woman of lively imagination, of energetic character, and not always easy to get on with," writes her grand nephew, Hippolyte Peyrol, the sculptor, who was a boy of seventeen at the time of her death.

1

The second child, Rosa Bonheur's father, was christened Oscar Raymond. His mother, herself a woman of some education, remarked her son's natural abilities, and did her best to cultivate and develop them. The young Raymond showed his first aptitude for drawing by imitating the ornaments in butter and sugar which his father executed in the Toulouse kitchen for the dining table of the Cambacérès family, a curious example of Taine's favourite doctrine of the influence of surroundings on budding intellect. His parents then sent him to the drawing school at Bordeaux, where, under the clever tuition of Lacour, of whom more will be said farther on in this biography, he quickly became a distinguished pupil; and, after completing his studies, he began, while still young, to teach in his turn. It was a modest existence that he entered upon; for, at that time, artists did not enjoy the favour accorded them to-day.

Among Raymond Bonheur's pupils was a young orphan girl, who was being brought up in a well-to-do Bordeaux family, that of M. Dublan de Lahet, son of a royal treasurer under Louis XV, and who had been a page of Queen Marie Antoinette. Her name was Sophie Marquis; and she had been born at Altona, near Hamburg, in 1797. Soon the professor and his pupil fell in love with each other, and on May 21, 1821, they were married. In the following year, on March 16th, a daughter was born of this union, and was baptised by the name of Marie Rosalie. This babe was the future artist, Rosa Bonheur.

It will be noted that the maiden name of Raymond Bonheur's bride was Marquis, which is, perhaps, the origin of the statement which has often been made that Rosa Bonheur sprang from a titled family. On this point she used to say proudly: " The only thing noble about my parents was their character, which is more than many so-called aristocrats can boast."

The foregoing information concerning the mother of Rosa Bonheur was communicated to me by M. Peyrol, and he thinks that this is all that is sure. But Miss Klumpke, the friend and confidante of Rosa Bonheur during the closing months of the latter's life, gives a more mysterious account of the origin of the artist's mother. " A veil hangs over her birth," Rosa Bonheur is declared to have stated, " which I have never been able to lift. The marks of esteem which I have received at different epochs from several crowned heads are such that I cannot, in conscience, attribute them uniquely to my talent." Yet the birth register of the Altona Catholic church mentions Rosa Bonheur's mother as " a legitimate daughter," though her marriage certificate describes her as " the daughter of an unknown father and mother." But on his death-bed, M. Dublan, who had always called her his niece and ward, and had brought her up with his own children, informed her that he was her father. When she asked for the name of her mother, he replied: " My child, I promised never to reveal it, but you will find in my writing-desk papers which will tell you." After the funeral, when she went to open the drawer of the desk, she found that the lock had been broken, so that she had no claim on the estate and was left in total ignorance of her maternal origin. The Duchess of Saxe-Coburg-Gotha, who died in 1904, was a warm friend of Rosa Bonheur, and Miss Klumpke reports the artist as saying: " Perhaps this noble woman knew the secret of the birth of my mother."

At the time of Rosa's birth the position of the young couple was fairly comfortable. Raymond earned about enough to pay his way; his wife, who was a good musician, added to their income by giving piano lessons, one of the accomplishments which she brought with her from her life in musical Germany; and, though the aged François Bonheur had to be helped by his son, his wife was able to requite this pecuniary aid by relieving Sophie of much of the housework. But with each fresh year of married life the burden to be supported grew heavier. A second child, Auguste, was born in 1824; a third, Isidore, in 1827; the grandfather needed more and more assistance, the grandmother was less and less able to look after the house.

It was the embarrassment resulting from this state of things which led Raymond Bonheur to form the plan of leaving Bordeaux for Paris, where his elder sister Elisabeth—though " Tatan " in the family was nicknamed " Ophélie " by Rosa Bonheur—had been settled since 1823, and was engaged in teaching.   He hoped that in the capital there would be greater facilities for earning money, and more scope for developing his own artistic talent.   Nor was he mistaken in this.   Though money never flowed into the Bonheur household, the art development of himself and his gifted children owed everything to this change of residence.   If Raymond Bonheur had continued to vegetate in a provincial city, the genius of Rosa Bonheur might never have ripened.

Raymond Bonheur, therefore, quitted Bordeaux toward the end of March, 1828; and, leaving his wife, children, and parents until he could make a new home for them, he arrived in Paris at the beginning of April, where he was kindly received by the Silvelas, members of the celebrated literary and political Spanish family of that name, this branch of which had once resided in Bordeaux, but was now keeping a boys' boarding school at the French capital.   They hospitably invited him to stay with them, pending his future arrangements, and did much to accustom him to his new and rather lonely surroundings.   What these surroundings were and what Raymond Bonheur's feelings were at this time are tenderly revealed in the correspondence then exchanged between husband and wife.

In a letter addressed to Mme. Bonheur and dated from Paris on April 1, 1828, occurs this passage:

I have just arrived after an excellent journey.   I went first to my sister's lodging, where I deposited my trunk, and am now with the Silvelas, who are most kind to me.   But neither their kindness nor the noise of Paris can fill the void I feel away from you and all my loved ones.

In a second letter, on the morrow, he wrote:

I have had a glimpse of the Tuileries.   It is quite fairy-like. But how much more fairy-like it would seem to be transported to

4

your side, dear one, and to be with poor mother and father and my darlings, Rosalie and Auguste. Kiss them for me.

It was, in fact, a hard trial for Raymond Bonheur to bear the absence of his family. In most of his letters at this time he alludes to the separation, and in his wife's replies the allusion finds an echo. Week after week passed by without there appearing any likelihood of his being able to establish a permanent home in Paris. It was the inevitable struggle in a new place. He was compelled to observe the strictest economy. " Sixty-nine francs per month for board," he writes to his wife, " and nine francs sixteen sous for lodging," a total of seventy-eight francs and sixteen sous, an exceedingly low figure, though under the Restoration and Louis Philippe living in Paris was much cheaper than it is to-day. Lessons were few and poorly paid; and for some months his wife remained with the children at Bordeaux, receiving all the money her husband could spare, after paying his own expenses, and supplementing the resources he furnished by whatever she could earn with her music teaching. Thus a year passed away, when, at last, Raymond was able to write announcing that a home was prepared. The old grandfather—" Pépé " little Rosalie called him—was left behind in charge of a trustworthy person, being too infirm to undertake the journey; and the rest of the family started. Just before their departure, Raymond Bonheur, on the 16th of April, 1829, sent them a letter containing the following lines:

Be sure, dear mother, to take every precaution during your three days' journey. Here, we will try to forget our troubles. And you, dear Sophie—I think of your present fatigue. Try not to be too sad in leaving the old place. Think of my having been alone so long, and of our meeting again. And you, my little ones, try to be good. Look round and fix in your memory the spot you are leaving, for many years may go by before you see it again. At last you are about to become Parisians!

5

REMINISCENCES OF ROSA BONHEUR

The new home was in the Rue St. Antoine, that broad, dusty, and rather shabby and populous thoroughfare, the continuation of the Rue de Rivoli and the link between the somewhat better quarters of Les Halles and the Châtelet and the old revolutionary district of the Faubourg St. Antoine. This part of Paris is much the same to-day as it was at the epoch when the young Rosa Bonheur inhabited it. The surroundings were not uncongenial to artists. On the opposite side of the street and almost visible from the very windows of the Bonheur apartment is the striking old front of the church of St. Paul, built back at the very beginning of the seventeenth century, with its handsome Renaissance portal, and into which the child Rosa may have more than once strolled to gaze at the numerous paintings hanging in the dimly lighted chapels, among which is an early work of Delacroix. On the same side of the street with the Bonheurs and but four or five numbers away stands the ancient Hôtel de Béthune, the former residence of the famous minister of Henry IV, the great Duke de Sully. The elaborate sculptures in the court, the vaulted roof of the entrance, and the imposing street-front were before the eyes of Rosa every time she went out into the city. In fact, historical buildings, picturesque effects, and glorious memories abound in this part of Paris. They are known to have had their influence on Raymond Bonheur, susceptible to a degree, who must have transmitted his impressions and his enthusiasm to his equally impressionable children, whose art education he directed and inspired.

In 1897 Rosa Bonheur related some of her souvenirs of this time, which her nephew has revised for this chapter. "Our apartment in the Rue St. Antoine," she writes, "was over a private bath establishment. The house still stands. I shall always remember the pork butcher's shop that was opposite our windows, because of its sign, a boar in painted wood. More than once when I went out I stopped to caress the poor animal! This was, perhaps, one of my earliest manifestations of a love for the dumb world!"

This house not only still stands, a good example of the un-

STUDY OF A BULL.

THE SIGN AT NO. 49 RUE ST. ANTOINE.

changeableness of the quarter—it is No. 50—but the bathing business is still carried on there, though transferred to the portion of the edifice at the back of the court, where, probably, was held the school mentioned farther on in these souvenirs. The pork shop over the way—No. 49—is also still there, and the wooden boar, too, a formidable-looking animal that might well have awakened the wonder and admiration of a sturdy child, such as was Rosa Bonheur at five or six.

The souvenirs continue:

The change from Bordeaux to Paris was at first hard to bear. I didn't like the great capital. Even the bread seemed insipid when compared to our southern loaves, which were salty and so to my taste. Moreover, I yearned for the sun of my native town, especially as the early spring days of that year were cloudy and chilly.

In the same building where we lived was a school kept by a M. Antin, who was a Jansenist, and who became a good friend of ours, my father showing thus early a tendency to break with established things in spiritual matters, a tendency which grew with the years and which has always left its stamp on me. Old Father Antin, as we all called him reverentially, remarking that I was unoccupied, proposed to my father to take me as a pupil; so I entered the little boys' class with my brothers Auguste and Isidore. This was, I believe, the first pronounced step in a course which my father always pursued with us children and which in modern times has been named co-education. The influence which it had on my lifework cannot be exaggerated. It emancipated me before I knew what emancipation meant and left me free to develop naturally and untrammelled. I well remember that I was not at all shy because my only companions were boys. When, during the recess, we went to play in the garden of the Place Royale— to-day, Place des Vosges—I was generally the leader in all the games, and I did not hesitate now and again to use my fists. So from the very start, a masculine bent was given to my existence. This school life, which did so much for me in so short a time, continued till 1830.

7

REMINISCENCES OF ROSA BONHEUR

The cannons of the Revolution of July were thundering at the moment my sister Juliette was born. I do not exaggerate in employing this expression; for in front of our door a piece of artillery had been stationed, which opened fire on the Place de la Bastille, not far away. Indeed, I had a narrow escape from being a victim. My father had climbed on to the big street entrance door of our house so as to get a better view of the cannonade operations; and at the first discharge the door was so shaken that he fell off close by me. I recollect very well the charge of the royal guard, the shouts of the victorious combatants who drove them back; then, we heard that the king had quitted Paris.

After 1830 we found it more difficult to live. My father could get no lessons, and in 1832 the cholera came to make things worse. It was dreadful. Carts filled with corpses were continually in the streets. Every one was terror-stricken. But just before this—in October, 1830—we went to live in the Rue des Tournelles, in the same quarter, in an old house dating back to the time of Louis XIII. A big stone staircase gave access to our apartment. It was so gloomy that I was frightened to go up it alone, especially as underneath us lived an undertaker's man. His wife made shuttle-cocks and other children's toys. She bought the skin from a Mme. Micas, who had a little girl whom I had met in the garden of the Place Royale. We often used to come across the poor, pale-looking child with her comical hat that made us laugh, and with a green shade over her eyes to protect them. All the pupils of M. Antin's school were just at the age, as La Fontaine says, that knows no pity. We made fun of her on account of her weakly, sickly air. And yet this small suffering creature was Nathalie Micas, fated to become later my dearest and best friend!

It was about this time that Saint Simonianism was flourishing. My father, whose nature was impressionable and enthusiastic, hastened to adopt the new doctrine. He was so carried away with it that he even partially separated himself from us in order to take up his abode with the brethren at Ménilmontant. But my mother was heart and hand with him in this effort to " regenerate humanity," as they used to say. Every Sunday we all went to pay him a visit at " the convent." The street boys would sometimes mock at my Saint Simonian cap with its big tassel. Some of them even threw stones at us. This touch of persecution made us all the more ardent supporters of the sect, where my father made the acquaintance of such men as the Péreires, Arlès-Dufour, Carnot, father of the future President, Le Verrier, Talabot, d'Eichthal, Enfantin, Michel Chevalier, Stéphane Flachat, Olinde Rodrigues, Bazard, Auguste Comte, and Félicien David, the composer, all superior minds in different fields and most of whom were open supporters of the young faith. We children came to know the children of many of them, and we were all—parents and children—elevated by these choice associations. This Saint Simonian episode in our life had influences that I now perceive were much more far-reaching than any of us imagined at the time. Reforms and reformers are a fine atmosphere for young people to grow up in. There was of course " no money in it " ; but the money came later. The moral brace which I received from Saint Simonian connections has remained with me to this day.

In 1833 Raymond Bonheur had the misfortune to lose his wife, " my dear Sophie," prematurely worn out by the trials of a precarious life. He had lost his father in 1829 and his mother in 1831 ; so that he was now left alone with his four little children, Rosa, the eldest, being still under twelve. For some time, being unable, on account of his enforced absence from the house, teaching every day, to look after them properly, he confided them to a friend of his sister's, Mme. Pélérin, who lived in the same street where he then lived—the Allée des Veuves, in the Champs Elysées of those days—and who also took charge of some other children. This arrangement was finally modified by another change of residence—" in my early youth we used to migrate with the birds," Rosa Bonheur once remarked—and Raymond Bonheur, who had gone to live on the whilom Quai de l'Ecole, had his children back home again, much to his own and their delight.

Rosa Bonheur in her revised souvenirs writes:

This new home was a few yards from " The Parnassus," the well-known café of that time, kept by the old carpenter whose

9

daughter had married the famous Danton. Here my father met Fabre Palaprat, grand master of the Templars. This Palaprat had in his house the helmet and breast-plate of Jacques de Molay, the famous grand master of the order, who was burnt by Philippe le Bel on the Pont Neuf in 1314. I need hardly say that my father took up with the order formerly so severely persecuted by the cruel king of France. It was always his nature to be with " the under dog." He carried his enthusiasm so far that I was baptised by the Knights of the Temple, whose lodge was in the Cour des Miracles, which spot, however, no longer exists. Among the souvenirs of their ancient glory, they had preserved their altar, their pulpit, and their baptismal font. The ceremony was performed in their sort of chapel, under a canopy of steel formed by the drawn swords of the knights in costume, and, full of solemnity, it appealed eloquently to my imagination, so that for a time I believed myself a knight in reality.

Hippolyte Carnot and several other of the ablest of the original Saint Simonians entered the sect via the Templars. " The Order of the Temple," writes Carnot, " continued to be a secret society after the death of Molay and remained faithful to doctrines which explained, up to a certain point, the energy of its persecutors. We found in these doctrines enough to satisfy our curiosity, but nothing more; while we soon discovered that the members of the order were no more accessible to progress than Roman cardinals." So these liberal-minded young men resigned from the organisation in 1827 and eagerly took up Saint Simonianism with all its promise of regeneration. In this group was Raymond Bonheur.

My knighthood notwithstanding, I was subsequently apprenticed to a dressmaker, Mme. Gendorf. But I had no taste for sewing, and, instead of sitting in the work-room of Mme. Gendorf, I used to go into that of her husband, who was a maker of percussion caps for fowling pieces. I turned the wheel, which suited me much better than stitching and hemming. Consequently, my stay with the dressmaker was a short one.

As my father's time was monopolised by his lessons, I was left a good deal to myself. But soon after this, two friends of his, M. and Mme. Bisson, who were engaged in heraldic painting and who coloured plates of every kind, took pity on my idling faculties; and, remarking that I was interested in their work, gave me some easy drawings and kaleidoscope views to colour. Whenever I think of the pence I earned in this work, it makes my heart beat more quickly, for it was the first money I ever made in art, such as it was. Mme. Bisson, by the way, was an amusing original. Mother of three boys and inconsolable at having no girls, she had rebaptised her sons with girls' names. The youngest, who was my friend, was called Eleanor.

As I grew older, my father not wishing me to remain ignorant, I was sent to a boarding school kept by Mme. Gibert in the Rue de Reuilly. Here I became an element of discord. My tomboy manners had an unfortunate influence on my companions, who soon grew turbulent. One day I proposed as a game a sham fight in the garden. We procured some wooden sabres and I ordered a cavalry charge. The result was the destruction of Mme. Gibert's fine rose-bed which was her pride. This exploit was the last hair on the camel's back. The Giberts refused to harbour any longer such a noisy creature as I, and sent me back home in disgrace. But my good father did not take a tragic view of the affair and I quickly recovered from the untoward episode. The worst of it all was that it rather discouraged his well-meant efforts to improve my mind conventionally, and I fear, for example, that my knowledge of French spelling, which has always been one of the weak points of my education, then and there got a bad set-back. If I am not mistaken, this Gibert experiment was the last attempt to " polish me off."

These joust-like frolics were always a favourite sort of amusement with the youthful Rosa Bonheur, and the Giberts and flower-beds were not the only sufferers therefrom. M. Hippolyte Peyrol, Sr., writes:

Though Rosa worked with ardour, she was no less fond of play. Whenever opportunity offered, she joined in the games of her brothers, although younger than herself; and nothing pleased her better than to dress up and create an illusion of the Troubadour days when ladies mounted behind horsed knights in armour. More than once, when the family lived in the Rue de la Bienfaisance, during the father's absence from the house, the easels and pictures of the studio were utilised for a sham fight between Rosa and her brothers and one of their companions, Edmond Dérvas. The palettes served as shields and the maulsticks for lances, while the little Juliette was seated in the midst of all the tinsel finery they could find, and represented the lady of their choice. Occasionally the canvases were damaged, and the catastrophe brought them back to real life, and the repairing of the damage.

The souvenirs continue:

We were now back in the Rue des Tournelles, but at No. 6, instead of No 30, as before. I am not sure, however, that these are the numbers to-day. The first story of the house had been transformed into a painter's studio; and while my father was away giving lessons, I was doing my best to study painting alone at home. One evening, after a tiring day, he returned and surprised me putting the finishing touches to my first picture, painted from nature. It represented a bunch of cherries.

"Why, that's quite pretty," he said; "you must now go to work in earnest."

"To tell the truth," writes M. Peyrol, "Rosa Bonheur's father had tried up to this moment to turn his daughter from her evident inclination for an artist's career, knowing from his own experience the trials it involved for any one obliged to gain a livelihood. However, seeing that she persisted in her endeavours, he at last yielded, in spite of his own fears and the remonstrances of his friends, and thenceforth did all in his power to help her."

His other children were at school, the two boys in an institution where the drawing lessons he gave paid for their tuition, and Juliette in the Rue de Reuilly establishment which Rosa had been obliged to leave. Raymond Bonheur, therefore, was able to devote himself more to his elder daughter, and did so with both a father's and an artist's love.

That Rosa Bonheur's aptitude for art was a born one would appear from a letter written by Raymond Bonheur to his sister, when his first child was only two years old. This letter, dated February 8, 1824, runs as follows:

Rosalie is a dear little thing; and I must tell you that already she has begun to show a taste for the arts. She often seizes my crayon and scrawls on the door and then calls to me: "Papa, papa, Lalie (Rosalie) makes picture." And she draws rounds and strokes innumerable.

During the year which Raymond Bonheur spent in Paris before his family arrived, Rosa's mother frequently mentioned in her letters to him the little girl's artistic proclivities. Thus, on June 1, 1828, she wrote:

Rosalie asks every day when you are coming back. She longs to see you again. She is painting you some little men to send.

Again, on August 14th:

Rosalie is sending you in the box her first tooth which has come out, and a picture, with the promise of nicer ones in the future.

And in the beginning of 1829 this excellent prognostic:

I don't know what Rosalie will be, but I have a conviction that she will be no ordinary woman.

"Thus, from her earliest years," are M. Peyrol's comments on these extracts given above, "Rosa Bonheur's vocation showed itself clearly, and with increasing intensity; and when her father left her free to follow her bent, she began to work with passionate

13

ardour, rejoicing in the toil which later was to produce such magnificent results. From the age of thirteen she studied regularly in her father's studio, receiving from him every morning a daily task to perform; now, a plaster cast to copy; now, engravings, or again, subjects of still life; and when her father came home in the evening, he inspected and criticised the results achieved, sparing no pains and enabling her to profit fully by the fruits of his long experience. Being convinced that the method then in vogue of copying engravings and designs was less stimulating than the eye's contact with the objects themselves, Raymond Bonheur encouraged his daughter to paint from nature, and as soon as she had mastered the first difficulties, he set her to study landscapes and animals and birds."

Another member of the family writes me:

Every Sunday she used to accompany her father through the environs of Paris in long walks, which were all the more profitable to her as a third companion was Justin Mathieu, a sculptor of much talent, and her father's inseparable friend.[1] Under such influences, Rosa Bonheur's progress was rapid; and before long she was allowed to go to the Louvre, in order to make studies of the masterpieces. Here her assiduity caused her to be remarked by the attendants, who nicknamed her, from the style of her dress, the little hussar. Generally, she stayed there the whole day, lunching on bread and fried potatoes, with a draught of water from the hydrant in the court-yard.

So the years of her childhood rolled on. In the meanwhile, at the end of 1838, the nomadic Raymond Bonheur set up his household goods in the little suburb of Roule, at No. 157 Rue du Faubourg St. Honoré, which quaint old house still stands in the midst of a rapidly transforming quarter of the city. We have already seen that some time before, the Bonheurs had left the

---

[1] For a biographical note on Justin Mathieu see page 286

ancient St. Antoine district and were moving westward. They had reluctantly abandoned the picturesque Place Royale, with its low arcades, its steep-pointed roofs, and its spacious garden, all so in keeping even now with the distant days of Lous XIII. " Sometimes when I have a free hour in Paris," Rosa Bonheur used to say in the closing years of her life, I revisit this old spot, not only because it takes me back to those early hours when everything was before me, but because, in the midst of the rebuilding of modern Paris, it chimes in with an artist's temperament to feast one's eyes on this æsthetic souvenir of the grand past."

The new home not only brought the children nearer the Bois de Boulogne and the more open spaces of this then unbuilt-over part of the growing city, but in the same house with them dwelt a man who was very useful in a social way to Raymond Bonheur and who remained a fast friend of his distinguished daughter when he had attained eminence. St. Germain Leduc, the son of a sculptor, was a well-known man of letters of that day, who wrote on agriculture and domestic animals, and who had been a friend of Balzac's. He was able to introduce his co-tenant to several people of position, among others to Baron Feuillet de Conches, the prolific writer of the Second Empire who directed all the court ceremonies of the Tuileries and who, in after years, remembered the Bonheur artists on several occasions when his functions could be useful to them. In this connection Rosa Bonheur once said: " Several of these early acquaintances of my father—and they were not a few and not undistinguished—proved helpful to us children in our later career, though he who made them possible unfortunately passed away before they had come to full fruition. In some instances, the sons and daughters of these old friends continued to be our friends—a strong evidence of the high esteem their families had for him."

This change of residence also brought Raymond Bonheur nearer to the school attended by his sons, among whose companions were the sons of Princess Czartoryska, whose grandsons still occupy the famous Hôtel Lambert on the Ile St. Louis, Paris. It is of this noble Pole, noble in both senses of the word, that Rosa Bonheur writes as follows:

She often used to come in the afternoon and spend some time in our studio. Her favourite pastime was fine embroidery work which she sold to help those of her Polish countrymen who, exiled like herself, happened to be in distress. She was very kind-hearted and procured my father several good-paying pupils, so that our circumstances improved. Our modest studio even became gradually a most agreeable social rendezvous. I remember in particular one little English lady, rather eccentric, the wife of the admiral who was in command of the fleet that conveyed Napoleon to St. Helena. She one day pressed me to accompany her to Versailles, and it was to her that I owed my first white dress. Some time after, I gave drawing lessons to Princess Ida Czartoryska. But I am now bound to confess that we did little else than slide up and down the highly-polished floor of the big gallery of the Hôtel Lambert. When I recall all this, I confess that I fear my grandfather was about right when he said to my mother on one occasion: " You imagine you have a daughter. It is a mistake. Rosalie is a boy in petticoats! "

Count Rusteyko, the venerable private secretary of the two brothers, the Princes Czartoryski, the representative to-day of the family, and himself a Polish patriot who fought in 1848–49 and in 1863, writes me as follows concerning this distinguished house and Rosa Bonheur's relations thereto:

That remarkable lady and able business woman, Princess Anna Sapieha, the mother of Princess Adam Czartoryska, made the acquaintance of Rosa Bonheur somewhere between 1834 and 1840. The celebrated painter was in constant relation with the family for a long period of years. Very friendly to the Polish cause, then regarded with so much sympathy by France, she annually sent some of her sketches to the public fair then held in the historical Hôtel Lambert for the benefit of Poland. Several of these may be seen to-day in the collections at Goluchow Castle, in Prussian

Poland, which belongs to the heirs of Countess Dzialynska, the last child of the grand Polish patriot, Prince Adam Czartoryski, and with whom Rosa Bonheur kept up relations to the end of the countess's life. But she never knew the surviving members of the family.

The paternal studio at length became a real art academy. Auguste and Isidore, who had now left school, had also taken up art, the elder, painting, the younger, sculpture; and they either worked with Rosa at home, or accompanied her in her excursions in search of material for study. Rosa's predilection for animal painting was now beginning to show itself more strongly. In spite of the pleasure she found in copying the great masters— and some of these reproductions were noteworthy, as, for instance, the " Henry IV " of Porbus, the " Arcadian Shepherds " of Poussin, and the " Reapers " of Léopold Robert—her keenest delight was to escape into the country. The first definite result of this preference was a picture, " Rabbits Nibbling Carrots," which was exhibited at the Salon of 1841, together with a sketch of some goats and sheep. The first-mentioned canvas is now in the possession of Rosa Bonheur's surviving relatives.

Toward the end of the year 1841 Raymond Bonheur left the Faubourg du Roule and went to live at No. 13 Rue Rumford. This street, which no longer exists, having been swallowed up by the piercing of the Boulevard Malesherbes, was close to the present Quartier de l'Europe and near the Plaine Monceau. At that time all the part of Paris now traversed by the Avenue de Villiers was nothing but fields and farms; so that Rosa was easily able to meet with animals to paint. " I discovered a delightfully rustic spot at Villiers," she wrote at a later period, " near the park of Neuilly, where I lodged with a worthy peasant woman. I spent several months with her, off and on, at different times. I had here a good opportunity to study animals in their natural surroundings, which was of great advantage to my budding art development. I have always retained a warm place in my heart for

17

the once pretty village of Villiers, though it is now simply a shabby suburb of the great city."

This growing love of the animal creation gradually transformed the Rue Rumford studio into a sort of Noah's ark. There were rabbits, fowls, and ducks in it, and some tame quails which Rosa took into her own room after barring the window and arranging a grotto in one corner with heather and other plants. She even went so far as to introduce some canaries, finches, and other birds into the same room, leaving them free to fly about. But, on account of the dirt they made, she was finally compelled to banish them. An interesting allusion is made to this menagerie in the following letter, written in 1842 by her father to Rosa, who had gone to spend a few days at Annet, near Claye:

We are very glad you can study as you like with the worthy Mesdames Hébres. But be careful that you do not take cold this damp weather. You know that it is dangerous to sit on the ground after a rain storm. We are all well and all the live stock, too. The little goat is very tiring with its bleating, and smells strong. The squirrel has shut itself up like a hermit in Diana's head, but comes down regularly morning and evening to beg and play its tricks. The canaries are singing the " Gloria Tibi, Domine," and the finch is getting steadier on its legs. The rats are off wandering somewhere or other, and the butterflies, transfixed by a pin in your box with the other insects, have not budged since their martyrdom. So you see that all those you care about are thriving.

The squirrel mentioned in this letter was the cause of an accident which might have had fatal consequences. It gnawed through the cord of a framed picture, large and heavy, which hung over the place where Raymond Bonheur usually worked when painting. The picture fell and crushed the artist's easel, with a commenced canvas on it. This exploit caused the little rodent to be confined. But Rosa, to whom the sight of its imprisonment was painful, soon restored its liberty.

18

M. Hippolyte Peyrol, Sr., writes me as follows concerning this period of Rosa Bonheur's life:

When I came to Paris in 1842, after the marriage of my mother with Raymond Bonheur, the Bonheur family lived at 13 Rue Rumford. There is nothing particular to be said about the

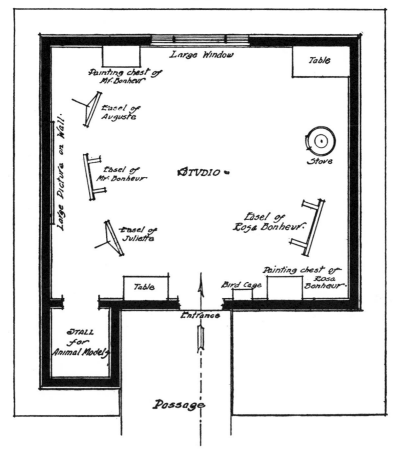

STUDIO IN THE RUE RUMFORD.

apartment occupied by the Bonheurs, but, as regards the studio on the floor above, something interesting may be written, for there it was that Rosa Bonheur, working side by side with her father,

19

painted the earlier canvases, which won for her those first salon honours and began to attract public attention.

This studio was a good-sized rectangular room, some five yards by six, lighted by a large vertical window. When the busy father had a few free moments from his lessons, here he would work, surrounded by his children who were also busy with their art. To the right of M. Bonheur, Auguste had his easel; to his left sat Juliette, while behind him was Rosa. Isidore had no fixed place but would draw or model wherever he liked.

Here is the way the time passed in the Rue Rumford. Rosa worked steadily with her brothers or sister. During the day the father was generally out, engaged in giving the lessons which kept the wolf from the door. With the evening, all came together, and after dinner, by lamplight, each one busied himself or herself, either by making lead-pencil drawings or sepia sketches, giving free play to their imaginations, while one member of the family read aloud. Thus it happened that the pencil of father or child often created a picture suggested by some passage in the book which was being read. I recall, for instance, a mass of drawings based on the tales of Walter Scott, who was the rage in France at that moment. When, later, Rosa Bonheur visited England, it was this early passion for the great novelist that had much to do with pushing her steps to North Britain. In fact, she once said to me: " Sir Walter's ardent love for animals drew me more closely to him and even increased my fondness for the dumb world, if this were possible."

In summer, when the days were long and it was still light out of doors after dinner, instead of drawing by lamplight, the family would go out for a stroll over the Monceau Plain, which then extended from the present Rue de la Bienfaisance to the fortifications, and which was a succession of vacant lots, unfenced for the most part.

Although Rosa was at this time some twenty years old, she took part in all our games. Sometimes she played horse with Isidore. She would put into his mouth, as bit, a big drawing pencil, with a cord attached to either end, and thus harnessed, horse and driver would go rushing wildly about over the Monceau Plain and finally return home covered with dust and in a dripping

ROSA BONHEUR AT TWENTY–TWO.
By Auguste Bonheur.

perspiration. I very well recall Rosa and Isidore coming into the house in this state one evening in the year 1844. The former was then twenty-two years old! But, after a whole day passed in sedentary work, it is easily understood that Rosa needed to expend some muscular energy.

Rosa Bonheur was always a great walker and did not at all resemble those young women who never want to move. On Sunday, in the summer time, the whole family would go for a long promenade, generally to the Boulogne Wood, where our favourite game was fox and hound. Rosa would enter into this play with the greatest ardour. In winter, the afternoon was spent in the Monceau Park, which could then be entered only by those holding cards, which favour M. Bonheur owed to the kindness of a friend.

Notwithstanding her assiduous labour at the studio, Rosa never lost an occasion to make outdoor animal studies. Our milk came from Clichy, the village just north-west from Paris, between the city and the Seine. At this milkman's she made several studies of this kind; especially one representing a young boy on a horse, which she afterward utilised in a canvas of two horses ploughing. The milkman's son was the boy. For these same good folk she painted a sign, a cow, which was sold later at a good price to a picture dealer named Vail or Weil.

Subsequently she went to Villiers, where she would spend the whole day drawing at a little farm on the banks of the Seine not far from the village of Levallois-Perret. As this place was some distance from the Rue Rumford, Isidore used to accompany his sister and draw at her side.

Toward 1845 Rosa Bonheur, who was then about twenty-two or twenty-three years old, began going to the slaughter-houses, which at that time occupied a large tract of ground bordering the Rue de Miromesnil. There, as has often been related, the young woman had sometmes to put up with the scurrility of the butcher boys, who seemed to take keen pleasure in saying rough things in her presence. Finally, this annoyance reached such a point that it required all her energetic force of character to continue to work under such conditions. One·day a tall fat man of some forty years of age, noticing the unhappy expression of the girl's face, asked her in a kindly tone of voice what was the matter with her. Reassured by his manner, Rosa briefly explained the situation. " Well, my child," he said, " you may feel at ease for the future, on this score. It is I, ' Father Emile,' who says so "; and then, turning toward a bevy of her persecutors who had gathered around during the conversation, he continued: " The first one of you who troubles this young woman will hear from me. You all know who I am and you also know that I always mean what I say. So remember, I am this girl's protector, and don't you forget it! " When Rosa returned home that evening she told her father what had happened, and M. Bonheur went and thanked " Father Emile " personally.

This " Father Emile," whose real name was Emile Gravel, was one of the slaughter-house scalders, who also prepared and sold, wholesale, calves' heads, calves' and sheeps' feet, etc. It was from him that the tripemen of the quarter made their purchases. Though not rich at this time, he was in easy circumstances, and, later, became quite well off through real-estate speculations at Levallois-Perret. One of the streets of this Paris suburb bears his name. He was an excellent fellow, and though he did not possess much book-learning, was endowed with great good sense and considerable intellectual shrewdness. He loved the arts by instinct, and when he got better acquainted with the Bonheurs, he invited the father to paint the portraits of the different members of the family. He enjoyed angling and was a most expert rodster, being especially clever in up-stream fishing. Whenever he drew the river, he was sure to send the Bonheurs a fine jack.

The protection of " Father Emile " was not an idle promise. From that moment Rosa Bonheur was able to work at ease in the slaughter-houses of Paris. She made a long series of studies of the dumb beasts as they stood attached at the doors of the sheds. These sketches even sold easily and brought in not a little money. One of her first buyers was a wholesale grocer named Bovy, whose shop was in the Faubourg St. Martin and who paid in kind for the pictures which he purchased from Rosa, Auguste, and their father. A wholesale shirtmaker, named Bourges,[1] did the same and furnished in exchange all the canvas which the family

---

[1] The father and daughter are mentioned several times further on in this book.

needed for their art work. Later, this Bourges became a picture dealer and had a shop in the Rue St. Georges. But at this moment he did not handle Rosa's paintings.

Rosa Bonheur, and all of us for that matter, were good walkers. I recall how, very early one summer morning in 1846 or the year following, we all started off for a day's outing in the Meudon forest, near Paris. The weather was very fine at first. But later we were caught in a drenching thunder-storm, far from any habitation. Rosa sought shelter in an earth hut at the roadside, and when she came forth after the downpour she was a sight to behold. Her green dress was covered with yellow and red spots, and, taken all in all, she looked like a zebra. She shared our fun at her expense, and finally we all got home, late in the afternoon, as wet as rats.

In 1855 Rosa Bonheur let at Chevilly, near Bourg-la-Reine, not far from Paris, a sort of old barn belonging to a large farm and fitted it up as a studio. There she had, almost under her eyes, all the animals she needed—lambs, goats, horses, cows, etc. The place served her as a kind of country villa. She used to go out there from her Rue d'Assas studio either on horseback or in her tilbury. She bought for this purpose a mare named Margot, which she kept for a long time and which carried her quickly from Chevilly to Paris, and *vice versa.*

Two of the friends of Rosa Bonheur have given me descriptions of her as she appeared on horseback at this time, which may be inserted here. M. Paul Chardin writes:

I first met Rosa Bonheur at the Gisors home of the Passy family. On my return to town, I went one morning to pay my respects to the great artist at her studio in the Rue d'Assas. She was just getting down from her horse, and was attired in a sort of masculine costume that was really grotesque. It consisted of a frock-coat, loose gray trousers with understraps, boots with spurs, and a queer hat. She held a riding whip in her hand, and the effect, as a whole, was that of a girl dressed as a man. It is the only time I ever saw her in such a fantastic get-up.

When she rode out at By, where I used to see much more of

her than at Paris, Rosa Bonheur wore a masculine habit that was much less absurd. Her jacket, which was of brown velvet, reminded me a little of that seen among certain Brittany peasants. On her head was a broad-brimmed hat, sometimes of felt, sometimes of straw, with a black velvet band whose ends hung down behind and were fastened together with a silver buckle. Baggy knee-breeches of the same material as the jacket and black leather leggings, a sort of Brittany spatterdashes, which she bought at Pleyben, a Finistère burg, whose shape pleased her very much, though they were really very ugly—this completed her riding-costume. In fact, I always saw her so attired at By whether she went out driving, walking, or riding.

Here is the description of M. Robert David d'Angers, son of the celebrated sculptor, and himself a sculptor:

At one period Rosa Bonheur's studio was near the home and studios of my father, in the Rue d'Assas, which were blotted out when the Rue de Rennes was cut through. She was often in my father's studio, but the most vivid recollection I have of her was seeing her from time to time on horseback in our street. She was in masculine dress. Her trousers had boot-straps, the last pair of the kind, along with my father's, that I remember seeing. Her cap was the queerest part of her odd get-up. It reminds me of those sometimes worn by "lady bicyclists" of the present day. She was naturally short and the cut of her jacket made her look still shorter, when in the saddle. The ensemble of this costume was not happy. She sat her sorrel astride and her short legs stuck out at a pronounced angle, which was all the more noticeable when you looked at her from behind. This shortness of the legs caused the stirrups to be pulled up high, so that Rosa Bonheur on horseback makes me think to-day of Frémiet's " Joan of Arc " in the Place des Pyramides!

And yet it would appear that Rosa Bonheur did not hesitate to ride in the Bois and even in the Champs-Elysées. Thus, we read in a letter dated April 9, 1855, and addressed to that notable thinker and writer, the late Gustave d'Eichthal, father of the present member of the Institute of the same name:

I don't know what we did to miss one another. It is true that I was a little late at the rendezvous. I waited some minutes at the Dauphine Gate, scrutinizing each horseman who came up. I made a mistake not to go as far as the Auteuil Gate. But as I didn't see you anywhere, I finally started off on a chase after all the riders in view, and when I made the grand tour of the Wood, I returned home by the Dauphine Gate and the Champs-Elysées.

Perhaps it should be added in explanation that if a man of Gustave d'Eichthal's position did not hesitate to gallop through the most fashionable part of Paris with so eccentric an equestrian as Rosa Bonheur must have been, this was due in large measure to his early life among the Saint Simonians, where unconventionalism was carried to its utmost limits.

At this date, Raymond Bonheur had, as we have already seen, a second wife, having married in 1842 a widow whose maiden name was Marguerite Picard. Her first husband had been a M. Peyrol, and her eldest son by this marriage, Hippolyte, whose souvenirs were just given above, became later the husband of Juliette, Raymond Bonheur's youngest child, by his first wife, who, by the way, was brought up for the most part at Bordeaux, in the house of Mme. Aymé, an old friend of the first Mme. Bonheur.

With the advent of " Mamiche," as the children called their stepmother, Raymond Bonheur's household of boys—for Rosa could hardly count as a girl—regained its order and tidiness; and gradually, by the united efforts of all, the position of the family grew to be more comfortable. Rosa was beginning to earn money and Auguste also was now able to contribute to the common fund. His initial attempt at gaining a livelihood had been made in a boarding school kept by a M. Leclerc at Pithiviers, a small town about half-way between Paris and Orleans. This absence called forth the following touching letter from Raymond Bonheur, which shows that Auguste was not contented in his new calling, and which contains besides some slight revelation of the father's philosophy of life:

MY DEAR PIPON: You are as self-denying as a little sage, and patient resignation dwells beneath your cap. In Paris, your daddy is striving to plough his furrow in the somewhat too stony soil that God has given him. He, too, is compelled to abandon his dreams, meditations, and studies, in order to succeed in avoiding pitfalls while providing for present urgent needs. And you, my dear boy, are surrounded by brawling children, who worry you from morning till night and who rob you of your best hours, without themselves much profiting thereby. It is my youth over again; for, like you, I have wept in secret far from my unhappy home, which I left, as you, through duty at an age when I was only half fledged. But there I learnt to ponder on many ideas that in other situations can only be superficially considered, and later I came to realise that the greatest thoughts have their origin in the most painful experiences of our existence.

Fortunately for his future, Auguste Bonheur gave up teaching before the close of the year, and returned home with the firm resolution of devoting himself to art and of succeeding in it. He set about painting portraits, and among the early commissions he received was one for the counterfeit presentment of M. and Mme. Micas, whose acquaintance Raymond Bonheur had made while giving lessons at the Mondolot Institution to their daughter Jeanne, familiarly called Nathalie, who was a boarder at this school. This was the same little girl with a green shade over her eyes whom Rosa had met in 1830 playing in the garden of the Place Royale. The two quondam acquaintances now struck up a friendship which was destined, in spite of some occasional quarrelling, to last until Nathalie's death in 1889.

As Mme. Aymé was unwilling to part with Juliette, although Raymond Bonheur, since the visit he paid to Bordeaux in 1844 to see his daughter, had been pressing to get her back, Rosa obtained her father's permission in 1845 to go down and stay

JULIETTE BONHEUR.

with her sister for a short time. While there she received from her father the following letter, dated June 14, 1845, which, a conscious or unconscious imitation of a famous epistle of Mme. de Sevigné, works the expectation up to a climax:

Let me tell you first of all a piece of news that will please you very much. Yesterday evening we received a big envelope from the director of the museums, M. de Cailleux. The envelope was a large one with a big royal seal on it, and was brought by a tall attendant from the Louvre, who had a huge smiling face. Tatan was just at dinner and—" But, dear papa, you haven't told me what was in the envelope; be quick, for I am burning to know." I can fancy you scanning the lines hurriedly in order to get the explanation. Can't you guess? Try. Perhaps it is an order. But then it isn't. That's just what Tatan asked the attendant, who was laughing all over his broad face. Tatan had got it into her head that the attendant was a man from the bank, who had come to receive payment of a bill, and she talked all sorts of nonsense, while her green peas remained uneaten on her plate, awaiting the opening of the envelope. As for me, I had not come home, being at the Fine Arts with Isidore, painting a fine crown for his Majesty Louis Philippe, whose portrait, as you know, we are executing for Toulouse. Toulouse! Now that I think of it, your pictures must already be there on exhibition. In short, to come back to what I wanted to tell you, you must know, don't you know? and France shall know! Anyway, it is not the devil! However, let us thank divine providence who grants us the good health we are all enjoying; at least I trust it is the same with you all at Bordeaux, for which let us thank God, and the saints, and the tall attendant from the Louvre, and the writer of what was inside the envelope, and M. de Cailleux, and M. de Montalivet,[1] and, in fine, his Majesty Louis Philippe.

ROSA BONHEUR HAS RECEIVED THE GOLD MEDAL!

Good-bye, my dear daughter. Kisses from all. Your joyful Papiche.

---

[1] Minister of the Interior and the Fine Arts.

Rosa's return to Paris was a happy one. She had satisfied her longing to see her sister; and this recognition of her talent by the Salon jury gave her renewed ardour in her work. During her stay in Bordeaux she had overrun the moors, and now brought back with her an ample provision of sketches from nature. Every day her reputation was growing; and, notwithstanding her youth, she found herself more and more in possession of a real mastery of her art.

In the following year, 1846, she undertook an excursion for the purpose of study into the Auvergne country, where her stepmother had been brought up. Several pictures were produced from materials gathered on this journey, notably the " Red Oxen of Cantal," which was exhibited in 1848, and definitely established her fame. Indeed, in this year she obtained the first medal and was chosen by her fellow artists a member of the hanging committee of the Fine Arts Society. But she declined the honour with thanks on the ground that her absence from Paris made it impossible for her to perform the duties attached thereto. This is, perhaps, the earliest example of Rosa Bonheur's excessive modesty and disinclination to accept honours, a disposition which grew with the years, until she became a veritable recluse, and which somewhat checked the full recognition of her genius not only by her brother artists, but by the world at large. But she could not be moved on this point, for Rosa Bonheur would neither heck nor ree, as the old phrase goes. Yet on this occasion, as on so many others later, several of the great painters of the day seized the opportunity to congratulate her on her success, among them being Horace Vernet, Paul Delaroche, Brascassat, and Léon Coignet, who rivalled one another in their compliments.

About this time Juliette Bonheur came home again to live. In 1846 Auguste, following on Rosa's visit of the preceding year, had gone down to Bordeaux; and when he returned, Juliette came with him. No doubt this event was partly hastened by some premonitions that Raymond Bonheur had of the disease which three years later was to terminate his life. Writing to Auguste in Bordeaux, on April, 1846, he said: " To tell the truth, I have grown old, and my heart is affected. I cannot walk as quickly as formerly, or run upstairs. I am forbidden to allow myself to get in a state of excitement, and so am very careful to let nothing put me out."

Attracted by the general example, Juliette was not long in beginning to paint, although her age did not allow her to be one of the family group that exhibited at the Salon of 1848. The four whose names figured on the list were the father and his three children, Rosa, Auguste, and Isidore.

The family was now complete, for, about the same time, Raymond Bonheur had sent for the son of his second wife, Hippolyte Peyrol, who was living in Auvergne, and had apprenticed him to the celebrated animal sculptor Barye, with whom he learned all the art of bronze work. This stepson Raymond Bonheur treated exactly as if he had been his own child; and the affection thus lavished was warmly returned. Nothing is more interesting than to listen to this modest, alert grandfather, clad in his overalls, calling up memories of the Bonheurs and their group, standing in the show-room of his Paris bronze manufactory, in the midst of the scores of beautiful sculptures, all the creations of two generations of this wonderful family; for the elder Peyrol was, and is still, the link between the trade and Isidore Bonheur, the younger Peyrol and Rosa Bonheur herself, who has left a few specimens of her chisel, which show conclusively that she could have succeeded in both branches of art.

Here may be placed some souvenirs of this period, contributed by early friends of Rosa Bonheur, and among which are these glimpses of the daily life of the artist, by Princess Stirbey.[1]

I saw Rosa Bonheur for the first time in the studio of Mathieu Meusnier, a sculptor of talent, whose " Viala " adorns the park at Versailes, and the " Death of Laïs " the garden of the Tuileries. M. Meusnier's parents, who were ardent art lovers and had a

---

[1] A biographical note on Princess Stirbey will be found on page 249.

special affection for artists, possessed a spacious dwelling and a large garden between the Rue Notre Dame des Champs and the Rue d'Assas, where they had built three studios separate from the house, one for their son, another for the painter of military scenes, Adolphe Yvon, and the third for Rosa Bonheur, to whom also they gave a stable and the space necessary for keeping the animals used as models.

At this time the Odéon Theatre was scoring a success with a play entitled " Honour and Money," the liberal ideas of which had provoked a burst of enthusiasm among the students of the University. I made my début on the stage in a charming girl's part in this piece. Rosa Bonheur saw my performance and from that moment she seemed to have a warm affection for me. Being intimate with M. Meusnier, who was just then modelling my medallion bust, she asked him to bring me to her studio, which he did. When she saw me enter, she got down from the high stool on which she was perched, painting her fine picture, the " Horse Fair," in order to greet me. How well I remember her appearance. Her hair was short and curly; her eyes were black, keen, and merry; merry, too, her mouth, which was rather large, with well-formed lips and dazzling white teeth. Her stature was small, and she wore trousers, surmounted by a woman's short jacket. For the trousers, she made a slight apology. She then complimented me on my acting and returned to the theatre several times to see the piece, her friendship for me seeming to increase after each of these occasions. As I was then only a beginner and she already an artist of established reputation, this generosity made a deep impression on me.

M. Meusnier eventually sold his property and the convent of Notre Dame de Sion took up its quarters on the premises. In the houses which M. Meusnier proceeded to build opposite his former residence, he fitted up studios for his son and Yvon. But there was no room for a garden, so that Rosa Bonheur was obliged to leave. A ball was given to celebrate the house-warming in the new building, and, in memory of her association with the other two artists, she was invited. She was present, dressed as a negro, accompanied by Mlle. Micas, who was disguised as a clown—" an arrangement in black and white," remarked Rosa Bonheur wittily.

This dancing party is believed to be the only one at which she was ever present.

M. Georges Meusnier, the art expert and son of Mathieu Meusnier (1824–96), writes me as follows concerning this studio life in the Notre Dame des Champs quarter:

Four or five years before her death, Rosa Bonheur, who had complained of their not going to see her, succeeded in getting my father and mother, both of whom were then over seventy, to go out to By. Rosa was full of recollections of her youth and reminded my father of how he and Adolphe Yvon had once decorated the flower beds of her little garden. " I remember," she said, " Yvon was then painting a big battle picture and was using large brushes. Some of these he stuck, handle down, in the earth while you cut out some little French flags, which you gummed to your sculptor's tools and then stood them up in the beds. The first were meant for trees, and the second for flag-poles, and my garden looked like a wood with soldiers camping in it."

M. Du Pays, a distinguished art critic of the middle of the last century, gives in the *Illustration* of May 1, 1852, this description of Rosa Bonheur's personal appearance, which supplements that of Princess Stirbey: " A young woman, small and delicate-looking, with straight, strong lines in her features, a large square forehead, framed in heavy hair cut short like a young man's, and with black, lively, flashing eyes."

Théophile Thoré, an eccentric art critic also of this period, has left an interesting estimate of Rosa Bonheur's talents. This note by M. Paul Chardin on the curious mien of this nondescript Thoré deserves transcription here. " In my childhood I often met him, and his queer attire has left an indelible impression on my memory. He was always dressed in black from head to foot; his felt hat had a broad brim; the skirts of his long frock-coat were plaited, and his baggy trousers came together at the ankle like gaiters. I believe he had been a Saint Simonian, where he probably got this taste for odd dress. In politics he leaned toward the

4

socialists of 1849, and I think he was exiled after the *coup d'état*."
Thoré had the habit of writing criticisms of the annual Salon, and
four of these, covering the years 1844, 1845, 1846, and 1847,
have appeared in book form under the title, "Les Salons de Thoré."
These appreciations were penned at the very beginning of Rosa
Bonheur's artistic career, and hence it is peculiarly valuable to
know what this competent judge thought of the budding painter.
Speaking of her " Grazing Bulls " of the Salon of 1845, he says:
" They are better than the bulls of Brascassat," who was very
much admired at this epoch as an animal painter, and who still
stands high among the artists of France. " He painted cows and
sheep," writes M. Paul Chardin; " and his work was very studied,
but cold and dry in colouration." " The flock of sheep of Mlle.
Rosa Bonheur," Thoré writes of the Salon of 1846, " makes one·
wish to become a shepherd, with a crook, a silk vest, and ribbons."
In the Salon of 1847: " Mlle. Rosa Bonheur, who, before the
French Revolution, would have been a member of the Academy of
Fine Arts, has brought oxen under the yoke and has her sheep rest
in the meadows of Cantal. Mlle. Rosa paints almost like a man.
What a pity her strong brush is not held also by M. Verboeck-
hoven and other *précieux*, who paint like young ladies." The
phrase " oxen under the yoke " refers to the celebrated canvas of
the " Ploughing in the Nivernais " in the Luxembourg Gallery, on
which she got a medal at this Salon.

This further pen-and-ink sketch of Rosa Bonheur's physiognomy and demeanour may be added to the two given above. It is
from the skilful hand of M. Paul Chardin:

She was of medium height, if anything under it, and toward
middle life grew stout. She had a round face, a high forehead,
and an abundance of silky, chestnut hair, cut short and parted at
the side. Her features were regular, her nose thin and slightly
aquiline. Her mouth was large, and the lips, which were somewhat
thick, were often compressed by reflection. Whenever they opened
in a smile, two white, regular rows of teeth became visible. Her
hands were small and supple, her fingers long and slender, with

a tapering form that showed the skill they possessed. The most striking characteristic was, however, the expression of the eyes, which were of a warm dark-brown colour. This expression was frank, loyal, and scrutinising, always on the alert to observe and investigate. Her manners were quick, lively and easy, even somewhat blunt. Her temperament, especially earnest and meditative, could yet yield to mirth, and would suddenly pass from grave to gay, from melancholy to laughter. Her voice, clear and sonorous, would then re-echo throughout the house, and her imagination indulge in a thousand playful tricks, stooping from the woman to the child. Her studio costume helped the illusion that she might be of the male sex, it being invariably a blue peasant's smock and a man's trousers. When she received company or when she went to Paris, she resumed her woman's dress, a black skirt and a sort of black velvet cloak, half cassock, with a rather masculine cut, beneath which showed a kind of waistcoat which was buttoned straight up.

All the friends of Rosa Bonheur dwell, like M. Chardin, on the remarkable daintiness of her hands. Thus, Mlle. Léonide Bourges writes: " I always admired her hands, which were extraordinarily delicate and finely shaped, with an energetic thumb. It is a pity the model of these hands could not have been preserved for posterity." And the faithful old servant, Céline Rey, who lives right opposite the By house, and whose physiognomy grows more and more like that of her former mistress, is always enthusiastic over these " wonderfully delicate small hands." Nor are such hands an unimportant equipment of a good painter; for who can say how much of the fine, highly finished work of Rosa Bonheur's remarkably gossamery brush was not largely due to these slender, sensitive digits?

I am indebted to the late Venancio Deslandes, formerly head of the National Printing Office of Lisbon, for a very original and characteristic bit of Rosa Bonheur autobiography, in the form of a short Life of her, written by Eugène de Mirecourt, and annotated by the artist herself. This pamphlet appeared in 1856, when Rosa Bonheur was but thirty-four, and her fame, as we have seen, had only just begun. It forms one of a series called " Les Contemporains," published by Gustave Havard, 15 Rue Guéné-gaud, Paris. M. Deslandes came across this little book in 1897 and sent it to Rosa Bonheur with a request that she would indicate to him how far it was trustworthy. On November 13th, in this same year, she returned it with copious corrections and comments scribbled with lead-pencil in the margins, adding: " If you find them rather free, you may keep them for yourself."

The pamphlet opens with a description of the Bois de Boulogne in 1831, when, says the author, Rosa used to go there, instead of going to school. " The Bois had not yet charmed me," corrects Rosa, " and as regards school, it was not till after my mother's death that my aunt had us placed at Mme. Pélérin's and paid almost the entire amount of the tuition, since my father could not. My poor mother's death occurred in 1833, at the age of thirty-five, or perhaps a little more. My father at this time was still with the Saint Simonians at Ménilmontant, and came down only a few days before her death, she hiding from him her dire poverty. The Bois was, in 1838, finer than now " (the author had affirmed the contrary, and spoken of the Cossacks cutting down the trees in 1815) " and less a park. There were grand old oaks of more than three hundred years' growth, and the smart lady and gentlemen riders drew my admiration. The Cossacks did not cut down the trees, for they had had no time. But I have remarked that after each revolution our rulers have thinned out our forests in order to make money. I was not fond of nosegays " (the author had enlarged on the way she spent her time in the Bois, among other things, gathering huge posies of buttercups and daisies), " but was especially interested in the effects produced by the light filtering through the leaves. Nor was I ever dreamy, but rather matter-of-fact in everything—American style."

Commenting on M. de Mirecourt's references to their early life at Bordeaux, Rosa says: " Our garden was large. We lived, in fact, in the open country on the banks of the Garonne, and its influence on my nature was great." Accused by the author of chastising a parrot which they then had, when he called her, imitating her mother's voice, she affirms: " I never beat this parrot; on the contrary, I respected him very much."

An acquaintance of Raymond Bonheur at Bordeaux, says M. de Mirecourt, was the distinguished Spanish poet Leonardo de Moratin (1760–1828), son of an equally well-known poet, Nicolas de Moratin (1737–80). He had lived there in exile since 1808. Rosa Bonheur makes the following comments on this passage:

M. Moratin was especially the friend of the families Silvela and Figuera. While at Bordeaux, my mother used to go to the country house of Mme. Figuera, who was a school friend of hers, and stay there some time. M. Moratin was also a visitor at this same house. He would sometimes play hide-and-seek with me and call me his little ball. It was through the Silvelas, by the way, that my father obtained some pupils at Paris and art work at the Garden of Plants, having been introduced by M. Silvela to the great Geoffroy Saint-Hilaire (1772–1844).

This paragraph well illustrates a fact that frequently appears in the life of Raymond Bonheur, and that has already been noted in this chapter—his acquaintance with people of intellectual and moral prominence, and proves that he possessed marked mental and spiritual worth of his own, which was fully recognised by men of parts. This circumstance particularly interests us, for it shows that the Bonheur children were also early brought into direct contact with celebrities, which always produces a deep impression on young people in their formative period that abides with them throughout life. Thus, this introduction to the founder of the fame of the Geoffroy Saint-Hilaire family was continued with the scarcely less famous son Isidore (1805–61) and with his son, formerly director of the zoölogical garden founded by his father in the Bois de Boulogne, and who writes me: " I was long acquainted with the eminent artist, who was frequently at our house, for, from her earliest youth, she assiduously frequented the menagerie of the natural history museum of which my father was the director."

But to return to M. de Mirecourt's biography. Charged by the author with resenting, through pride, her apprenticeship to the dressmaker, Mme. Gendorf, she writes: " I can boast of never having been proud, or jealous of any one, and am incapable of being so. In my humble opinion, there is no inferiority of position when one earns one's living honestly." " Humbug," she inscribes opposite the paragraph speaking of her pale features as proving how deeply she felt the humiliation, and then she continues: " I was in excellent health, only I should have better liked being with my kind father. True, I made percussion caps with goodman Gendorf, rather than dresses with his wife; but I loved being with my father more than either of these occupations, and, above all, I preferred my liberty."

She admits what the author says of her ignorance in grammar, spelling, etc., but advances some defence: " It's true. My geography wasn't worth much either, though it was I who did the maps for prizes. History I thought little of." Continuing to speak of her school experiences at Mme. Gibert's, to which we have already referred, she affixes " quite true " to the story of her cutting out grotesque figures in paper, tying them with a bit of thread to a lump of chewed bread, and then throwing them up to the ceiling, where they dangled and cut capers to the delight of the class and the scandal of the principal. Here is Rosa Bonheur's other account of how she left this school: " It was in consequence of my having, one night, made a battle-field of M. Gibert's hollyhocks, with the help of a wooden sword. Never did French or Russians see such deeds of courage! By the Lord, I took them in good faith for phantoms; and when, later, I came to read ' Don Quixote ' and the story of Joan of Arc, I found I had more than one point of resemblance to these two mortals, one of whom, by the way, wore breeches! "

M. de Mirecourt, proceeding to speak of her studying at the Louvre, asserts that she copied Rubens, Poussin, and Lesueur,

But she crosses out the name of Rubens and adds that of Leopold Robert. " I was never so foolish as to disdain the Dutch painters, my fathers," she says, contradicting her biographer, " and I admired Karl Dujardin." Of these artists, Dujardin (1635–78) was Dutch, Poussin (1594–1665) and Lesueur (1617–55), French, and Leopold Robert (1794–1835), Swiss. She confirms the story that English-speaking tourists used to stop in front of her easel and exclaim in lame French: " Very well, very well indeed." " But she did not seem to hear their further praise," continues M. de Mirecourt; " she was too modest." " Modesty had nothing to do with it. How could I know what they said? I didn't understand English! "

Commenting on the author's assertion that even at this period she aimed at reproducing " the great passions and thoughts of man," she sensibly remarks: " At this time I understood very little about the great passions, which I was indeed quite indifferent to. I was busy with ' the lower animals,' which are no great shakes at the passions."

Referring to the sheep kept in the Rue Rumford apartment, she writes between the lines: " It was a ewe, Jocrisse by name. My brother Isidore ought to know something about this animal, for it was he who carried Jocrisse on his shoulders up the six stories."

At the end of the paragraph relating to her sketching at the slaughter-houses she writes: " Finding our species most unfortunate to have to live on blood."

" Youth must have its day," is her note on the mention of two of her pictures exhibited at the Salon of 1843. In 1846 she exhibited five canvases, one of them, the " Three Musketeers," being different from her usual style. She confesses: " Without importance, my ' Three Musketeers.' But it was the fault of Papa Dumas, the Elder, whom I liked, by the way, more than the son."

In pompous style M. de Mirecourt exclaims: " More fortunate than many others, Rosa Bonheur was not obliged to dance attendance at the gates of glory." Whereupon she adds: " So I took the lady by the hair, like Fortune herself!" And then she continues farther on: "My dear and venerated father never thought of himself. At the moment when my 'Ploughing in the Nivernais' was giving me a more permanent position in the field of art, he was near his death, and he passed away happy and tranquil as to my future, having armed me with a strong breast-plate."

She does not admit the author's criticism that "each of her personages alone does admirably, but they do not concord to form a whole." "This is an assertion, my dear sir, in which you are not in agreement with the art critic, M. Debois Gallais. You two ought to reconcile your statements." "In Rosa Bonheur," he goes on, "this absence of logic is an extra charm." "And yet," retorts Rosa, "I have never lacked logic, which I find very useful."

"It is not very flattering to appear a man when one is a woman," she subscribes to an allusion on the subject of her male attire. M. de Mirecourt, in registering the astonishment of the public, assures them that Rosa Bonheur's motive was quite different from that of George Sand. But as he does not indicate what the motive of Mme. Sand was, and as Rosa Bonheur always stood up stoutly for the celebrated novelist, she exclaims: "What the deuce, then, could Mme. Sand be doing when she put on breeches, which, any way, were most useful to the Virgin of Belleville? After all, perhaps, it was simply so as to be the better able to gad about!" In another place the biographer notes that George Sand is Rosa Bonheur's favourite author, and is astonished, deeming her books immoral. She writes between the lines: "I don't think so. I venerate Mme. Sand, and have only one reproach to make against her. She was too womanly, too kind, and dropped the treasures of her noble heart and the pearls of her soul on the dung-heap, where cocks found the pearls and swallowed them without being able to digest them."

M. de Mirecourt touches on other peculiarities of Rosa Bonheur's dress. We are told, for instance, that she never wore lace or embroidery, whereupon Rosa says: "In my old age, I reproach myself for it." We are further informed that her hats were curious, generally too large and unsuitable. She confesses that she was " once insulted by a parrot which called after her: ' Ha, ha, that hat!' " In the street, he says, it is impossible to tell that she is a woman. " Very lucky for her," comments Rosa. And yet

ROSA BONHEUR'S HEADGEAR.

he states that " two big dogs, one on the right and other on the left, escort her whenever she goes out." " Like Bismarck," she pencils.

The story of Rosa Bonheur going to the theatre in a blouse, through absent-mindedness, has been variously related. By M. de Mirecourt it is wonderfully embellished. But the artist crosses out half the details which he gives, though she admits the fact, and adds: " It was at the Opéra Comique. The usher stupidly placed me on a flap-seat, in full view of a staircase, and, but for fear of attracting still greater attention, I would have slipped out. I thought I should be put in a box where nobody would be able to see what I had on. I had left home without having time to change."

M. de Mirecourt goes into details on how Rosa Bonheur spent her day, when she continues the list with: "She also rides every morning on a broomstick, flying off up the chimney like a witch, especially going out on Saturday night, which is the hobgoblins' frightful hour of orgies."

"Decided not to contract marriage," M. de Mirecourt goes on, "Rosa Bonheur pitilessly turns away the suitors for her hand." "I was never asked in marriage except on one occasion by an apothecary at whose shop I used to stuff my pockets with a provision of cocoa. We soon got tired of one another. The courtship lasted a week! An apothecary's cannula did not inspire me with high respect!" Continuing the same subject, the author accuses women of playing with men's affections and of being coquettes. While condemning the jilting of an honourable man—"it is cruel," she says—Rosa Bonheur, in the following lines, defends her sex:

I have remarked that if a woman is not a little coquettish, she comes near being a virago. If she is virtuous, and, at the same time, graceful, handsome, and kind, she is sure to have many admirers; and each of them, through pique, will try to blacken her reputation and to take advantage of her. While studying animals, I have, like Molière and La Fontaine, studied my human brothers, just as they have studied their sisters.

One of Rosa Bonheur's artist friends, Consuélo Fould [1] (the Marchioness de Grasse), writes:

When asked why she had never married, she always answered: "Nobody ever fell in love with me; I have never been truly loved." More than one man, however, really worshipped her. But she inspired such deep respect that no man seems to have dared to reveal his feelings to her. There is a curious example of this fact, taken from the humble walks of life and which came under the special notice of my own family. On several occasions Rosa Bonheur had

---

[1] For a biographical note on Consuélo Fould see page 250.

40

MME. BONHEUR AND FAMILY.
By Raymond Bonheur.

done a service for a workingman, who, throughout his life, spent his savings in buying engravings of her principal pictures and photographs of herself. His simple dwelling was a temple to her kindness. He described himself as " the earth-worm in love with a star." The person here referred to—Mr. E. A. Gautray, of Clermont-Ferrand—tells me that Rosa Bonheur once asked him why he was not married, and he replied by asking her the same question. Here was her answer: " Well, sir, it is not because I am an enemy of marriage; but I assure you I have never had the time to consider the subject."

I return to the pamphlet. Rosa Bonheur rectifies as follows the list of animals possessed by her when she lived in the Rue d'Assas: " One horse, one he-goat, one otter, seven lapwings, two hoopoes, one monkey, one sheep, one donkey, two dogs, and my neighbour Mme. Foucault, mother of the famous physicist,[1] who used to get on the wall to see me practise mounting on my mare Margot,"—which reminds one of Shelley's description of the Palazzo Guiccioli: " Lord Byron's establishment consists, besides servants, of ten horses, eight enormous dogs, three monkeys, five cats, an eagle, a crow, and a falcon; "[2] and of Lady Hesketh's account of Cowper's home: " He had at one time five rabbits, three hares, two guinea pigs, a magpie, a jay, and a starling; besides two goldfinches, two canary birds, and two dogs; I forgot to enumerate a squirrel."[3]

M. de Mirecourt devotes some space to Rosa Bonheur's early labour as a teacher of art. " Her natural history class was interesting to attend," he says, and she adds: " I even had the confidence of Geoffroy Saint-Hilaire." Referring to her Girls' Drawing School, the author declares that her opinions were received as from an oracle; whereupon Rosa writes: " You couldn't have

---

[1] Léon Foucault (1819–1868). The house at the north-west corner of the Rue d'Assas and the Rue de Vaugirard has an inscription on its front stating that on that site stood the former home of the Foucault family, which fact fixes the spot where was the studio of Rosa Bonheur.

[2] Dowden's " Life of Shelley," ii, 430.   [3] Wright's " Life of Cowper," 218.

heard a fly on the wing." Even the pupils who pleased her, we are told, never heard her say: "That is good." "This is a mistake," Rosa corrects, who admits, however, that she scolded the careless girls and told the weeping ones "to wipe their noses."

Referring to the famous "Horse Fair," M. de Mirecourt says: "The French Government bought it." Rosa adds in the margin: "The Government, on the contrary, had no confidence in my horses before their exhibition."

M. de Mirecourt, writing in 1856, says: "Rosa Bonheur has in her portfolios between seven and eight hundred sketches and studies." Rosa Bonheur, writing in 1897, about a year and a half before her death, puts the figures at 3,570. "In England," asserts the author, "even a bit of paper sketched on by Rosa Bonheur would fetch 500 francs." Rosa exclaims: "That proves the good taste of the British Isles!"

At the end of his biography M. de Mirecourt relates several anecdotes to illustrate the artist's generosity, and asserts that twenty times she pledged things at the pawnshop in order to aid her fellow artists when in trouble. "If only that could procure me canonisation after my death!" writes Rosa in the margin, and then adds at the bottom of the page: "It was my poor mother and my aunt who used to have recourse to 'my uncle's'; but I must own that I never did so myself."

On the last page of the pamphlet Rosa Bonheur pencils this concluding note: "It's not bad. M. de Mirecourt is evidently a good sort of man; only he has made the mistake of swallowing a great many fairy-tales. Rectified by Rosa Bonheur herself, this biography not being intended to be read by children. R. Bonheur, November 12, 1897."

The following letter, written from By, to Venancio Deslandes, about eight months after the above notes, may be regarded as an epilogue to her comments on M. de Mirecourt's biography:

I am a painter. I have earned my living honestly. My private life is nobody's concern. I have only to thank God for the protection he has always granted me by giving me a guardian angel in my friend and keeping alive in me the remembrance of my mother, who suffered so much and who was the noblest of creatures as she was the proudest.

When sending me a copy of the foregoing letter, M. Deslandes wrote me, *à propos* of the sturdy, independent spirit which it reveals and which was always so characteristic of his friend:

It has been said of somebody that he was better fitted to shine at a tea party than to stand in his own shoes. Rosa Bonheur was just the contrary of this. She was never more herself and better than when in her own shoes, especially if they happened to be *sabots*.

Such was Rosa Bonheur on the threshold of her artistic career. "Perfection in art is perhaps more sudden sometimes than we think," says Tennyson; "but then the long preparation for it, that unseen germination, *that* is what we ignore and forget." And Aubrey de Vere has said of Tennyson and his admirers: "Friends could but raise the sail high enough to catch what breeze might be stirring. The rest depended on the boat." Both of these remarks are pertinent, as the reader will perceive, if he has not already done so, on closing this volume.

CHAPTER II

FRANCIS GALTON says in his " Hereditary Genius " (American edition of 1884, p. 247) : " The Bonheur family consists of four painters, Rosa, Juliette, Jules [this name should be Isidore, who was, furthermore, not a painter, but a sculptor], and Auguste, and they are the children of an artist of some merit." But the genealogical table of the Bonheur family given on the following page shows that Galton's contention that " artistic talent is, in some degree, hereditary," is much more strongly supported in the case of the Bonheurs than he seems to imagine; for, beginning with Raymond Bonheur, and including him and his fourteen lineal descendants, we find twelve persons, who have displayed a decided taste for some branch of the fine arts. In fact, the history of French art is very remarkable in instances of this kind among the contemporaries of the Bonheurs, especially conspicuous in this respect being the Dubufes, one of whom painted a famous portrait of Rosa Bonheur, and the Alaux family, with its five generations of artists.

Professor Ribot in his work on " Heredity " (American edition of 1884, p. 147 *et seq.*), in formulating the laws on the subject, says that " which occurs more frequently is where heredity occurs between different sexes—from father to daughter, from mother to son." This principle is well exemplified in the case of Rosa Bonheur and her father; for from him she inherited not only her artistic temperament, but many other mental characteristics, which, though overshadowed by her art genius, will reveal themselves not infrequently in the course of the following pages.

44

GENEALOGICAL TABLE OF THE BONHEUR FAMILY

Jean Bonheur, cook at Toulouse, *married* Françoise Depigeron.

Guillaume Bonheur, cook, b. 1714, Toulouse, *married* Marie Dussaut.

François Bonheur ("Pépé"), cook, b. 1753, d. 1829, Bordeaux, *married* Eléanore Marie Pérard ("Mémé"), b. 1753, d. 1831, Paris.

1. Elisabeth Bonheur ("Tatan" and "Ophélie"), teacher of writing and French, b. 1780, d. 1873, Paris.

2. Raymond Bonheur, PAINTER, b. 1796, Bordeaux, d. 1849, Paris.

1. Sophie Marquis, 1821, b. 1797, Altona; d. 1833, Paris.

2. Marguerite Picard ("Mamiche"), 1842; b. 1813, d. 1887, Paris.

1. Rosa Bonheur ("Zaza") PAINTER; b. March 16, 1822, Bordeaux; d. May 25, 1899.

2. Auguste Bonheur ("Pipon"), PAINTER; b. 1824, Bordeaux; d. 1884, Paris. Married 1851, Marie Fanché.

3. Isidore Bonheur ("Dodore"), SCULPTOR; b. 1827, Bordeaux; d. 1901, Paris.

4. Juliette Bonheur ("Juju"), PAINTER; b. 1830, Paris; d. 1891, Paris. Married 1852, Hippolyte Peyrol, ARTIST IN BRONZE.

Germain Bonheur, PAINTER; b. 1848, Paris; d. 1880, Blois.

5. Hélène Bonheur.

4. Raymond Bonheur, COMPOSER.

1. Marguerite Bonheur, married Edouard Launay.

2. Marie Bonheur; d., 1874, at 19.

3. Juliette Bonheur, PAINTER.

1. Hippolyte Peyrol, SCULPTOR. b. 1856, Paris.

2. René Peyrol, PAINTER; b. 1860; d. 1899.

Pierre Peyrol, b. 1896. SHOWS REMARKABLE TALENT IN LINEAR DRAWING.

Jean Launay, ARCHITECT; b. 1883.

REMINISCENCES OF ROSA BONHEUR

Raymond Bonheur owed much of his art education to an able teacher mentioned in the preceding chapter, Pierre Lacour (1778–1859), painter and archæologist, who was for many years director of the Bordeaux School of Design, as had been his father before him, and curator of the Museum of Painting and Sculpture of the same city. His son, also named Pierre Lacour, was likewise a painter, but especially an engraver, and succeeded his father as curator, which post he held for a long period. If the Bordeaux collection of paintings is one of the best in the French provinces, and if the municipality has always been generous in its treatment of the fine arts, this wise policy is due in no small measure to the influence of the Lacours, excellent specimens of whose work are found in this gallery.

There are several proofs of the deep impression made on Raymond Bonheur by the art instruction and the moral worth of Pierre Lacour. Thus, when the former became a Saint Simonian, as we will see in the next chapter, and he thought that the millennium was at hand, one of the first persons whom he wished to convert to the new religion and to admit to the joys of this nascent resurrection was his old master.

Raymond Bonheur's æsthetic gifts were not confined exclusively to the painter's art. He enjoyed poetry and even wrote verses himself. "On Sundays," Prince Georges Stirbey [1] informs me, "he would gather his neighbours and friends about him, when he would recite these rhymes, while the children would sing the chorus." Similar testimony comes to me from Mlle. Léonide Bourges, who writes me à propos of entertainments at her father's house: "The Bonheur-Bourges dinners were exceedingly gay and merry. Raymond Bonheur, whom I remember as a fine, handsome man, contributed no little by his wit and conversation to their success. On these occasions, he would sometimes recite verses, while Rosa would sing some of the popular songs of the day, or old ballads." This proclivity to the courting of the Muses,

---

[1] For a biographical note on Prince Stirbey, see page 249.

which also showed itself in **Raymond Bonheur's** sister, he transmitted to his children, and references to it and examples of it will be found in subsequent pages of this volume, its manifestation in the daughter Rosa being one of the most curious features of her correspondence.

But perhaps the most pronounced trait in the many-sided character of Raymond Bonheur was a bigness and tenderness of heart that made life hard for him and singled him out from the ordinary run of humanity. This element of his make-up was well summarised by Gustave d'Eichthal in the pathetic words pronounced at his grave, when he referred to " his touching devotion to his family, to his self-denial, his talent, his courage, and to his deeply imbibed ideas of emancipation and of pacific progress for the human race." It comes out frequently in the few letters we have from him, as, when writing from Paris to his wife, in 1828, he says:

The lack of friendship, which is such an imperious need of my nature, would make me altogether melancholy and deprive me of all energy, if I had not you, dear Sophie, to know and love me. Perhaps my outward defects, my impulsiveness, my bluntness, may prejudice people against me and conceal my real nature. So, continue to love me, since your love consoles me for all troubles; nor should I be happy without it, had I all other advantages.

Or in a letter to Justin Mathieu, where he writes:

When you left, I felt a great blank. But I comforted myself with the thought that you would write to me and that this would be some compensation for what was lacking to us, especially to you who are more lonely than I as regards these outpourings of the artist and philosopher, and who must feel the need of opening yourself to some one; for it is very sad to have to keep everything to one's self and to be understood by no one. The aim of life is attained when one has procured one's self a little satisfaction and has shared it with some friends; for, on lonely days, all that we can both of us appreciate is the melancholy joy of musing to one's self, either abroad in the sun or by the household ingle.

I am no longer living in the Rue des Tournelles. I have gone quite away from the Faubourg Saint Antoine, and am now living at the other end of Paris, in the junction of the Roule and the Chaussée d'Antin quarters. I occupy a first floor in a nice house —5 Rue de la Bienfaisance—where there is a wide view and a fine garden. The rent is 450 francs, which is apparently dear. But in the same house are two young ladies who, by the lessons they take, are worth 200 francs to me, and the relations I have formed in the house are good. I have a charwoman who keeps the rooms clean, and I am getting my eatables and cooking from outside until I shall have procured some kitchen utensils. Rosa is well. She is doing nothing but work at her painting. My children are boarding near me, and if work does not come in as I should like, I can always earn enough to have bread and cheese, either through the dealers or through lessons. I try, however, to avoid this poverty, for my past experience of it has much injured me. At present, I have orders to last.

And you, my dear friend? Until something better happens, you must keep your head to the wind and make the best of opportunities. Your good, meek wife is with you no doubt. But I fear she will fret over the change of place and will find it difficult to get accustomed to provincial life. If it were Bordeaux, it would be different and supportable. But where you are, the women must be mostly stuck-up, proud of their empty-headedness, while among the men there are doubtless pedants not a few, perhaps a philosopher or two, but none to whom you care to unbosom yourself. In fact, what with the out-and-out Royalists and the Liberals, it must be hard for you to find protection on either side without offending the other. It is a dangerous thing for a poor artist to have enemies.

However, there is in your part of the country, as here, a kind nature, even more beautiful and warmer than here, which to your good heart is a book that has its own charms; and you have, besides, your pencil, your colours, your child and your wife. You

have time, too, and the power to usefully employ it. And let me
tell you, my dear friend, it is something to have one's daily bread
and some time to one's self. If either is really lacking, then adieu
to life according to nature, to God, to the fine arts. The wise
man loves retirement. Learn how to conform yourself to it in
peace; and let me hear from you. Speak to me of yourself, your
mother, your plans. As for me, I desire nothing so much as to
know that you are happy.

A few brief words may now be devoted to the careers of Raymond Bonheur's children and their descendants in order to complete the picture of this remarkable family of artists and place
Rosa Bonheur, the most famous of the group, in the brilliant
setting where she shone so conspicuously.

Auguste Bonheur, who stood next to Rosa in age, was born
at Bordeaux on November 4, 1824. His father gave him as good
an education as the straitened means of the family would permit,
with the purpose of making him a teacher, and at about eighteen
he became, as we have already seen, an usher in a boys' boarding-
school. But as he had carefully studied drawing under his father,
a love for the art of painting gradually took possession of him,
and at twenty-one he exhibited, for the first time, in the Salon of
1845. From that year on he was represented at almost every
annual Salon. In 1848 he sent a portrait of his sister Rosa, and
in the following year one of his father. In 1852 he was represented by three pictures, and was awarded a third-class medal.
In 1853 he exhibited three canvases whose subjects were taken
from Auvergne. One of these—the " Ruins at the Castle of
Apchon "—was bought by the Duke de Morny, the half-brother
of the Emperor and a great personage during the Second Empire.
In 1859 came his second-class medal; in 1861 his first-class medal,
and in 1867, the year of the international exhibition, he was made
a chevalier of the Legion of Honour.

In 1865 Auguste Bonheur left Paris, with an established reputation and a growing family, and took up his residence on the edge

49

of the little village of Magny-les-Hameaux, picturesquely situated some six miles south-west from Versailles. The house, the old home of Brascassat, the animal painter, is surrounded by meadows and woods, so that the artist could work out of doors, with his models in the fields or under the trees. His neat studio, where Brascassat also did some of his best work, is at the top of the house, and is piously kept just as he left it. Here he painted nearly all of his pictures,—the "Dormoir," which was much remarked at the Salon of 1886, and that in the New York Metropolitan Museum, being among them. On the easel, in the centre of the room, is one of his last canvases, a charming landscape with cattle. From the big window can be had a rather extensive view over a valley, with a wooded hill on the horizon, and in the little churchyard, a stone's throw away, Auguste Bonheur lies buried with the immediate members of his family. The death in 1874 of a favourite daughter, one of five children, was a great blow to him, and weakened still further his health, which had suffered by the war of 1870. He died suddenly on February 22, 1884, while on the train near Paris.

Isidore Bonheur was born at Bordeaux on May 15, 1827, and, like the rest of the family, studied drawing under his father, and began painting. But a taste for sculpture soon mastered him, and he made his *début* at the Salon of 1848 with a group in plaster— a negro horseman attacked by a lioness. From that date he continued to exhibit at nearly every Salon. In 1853 he sent a group representing a zebra attacked by a panther, which was in plaster, and which reappeared two years later, put into bronze by the State. It now adorns the garden of the Castle of Fontainebleau. In 1865 he was given the unique medal at that time awarded for sculpture, and in 1869 he again secured this medal, which made him a non-competitor at subsequent Salons. He sent three groups to the international exhibition of 1889 and was awarded a gold medal. In 1894 he was admitted to the Legion of Honour, and died, without having been married, on November 19, 1901.

RAYMOND BONHEUR AND FAMILY

To Mme. Passy,[1] her " Dear Adoptive Mother," Rosa Bonheur writes from By, June 24, 1861:

Thanks for the kind praise of my brothers. Auguste has now secured an acknowledged position, which is a great source of satisfaction to me. His talent is young and I hope it will develop

ISIDORE BONHEUR SKETCHING.

still further, notwithstanding the fact that he is already full-grown. And, dear Mme. Passy, the product of this talent is all his own, in spite of the deceitful rumours whose origin I am ignorant of. Believe me, the studies and pictures of my brother

---

[1] Wife of the Deputy and Member of the Institute (1792–1873), and mother of Louis Passy, also Deputy and Member of the Institute, whose souvenirs of Rosa Bonheur are given elsewhere in this volume. "She was a superior woman," writes Paul Chardin, "both as regards mind and heart. She wrote a great deal, and her style was easy, original, and full of charm."

are as much his own as mine are my own. Our father was our only master, both in matters of art and matters of honour; and he also taught us how to keep the latter untarnished. As regards Isidore, he, too, has much talent, only, like his sister, he is more a builder of castles than a doer of deeds.

Rosa Bonheur's only sister, Juliette, was, as has already been stated, born in Paris at the end of July, 1830. When she took up art, she at first devoted herself to still life. Her *début* at the Salon was in 1853, and in 1855 she was given her first honourable mention, which was followed by several others at subsequent Salons. Her highest honour was a third-class medal, which was awarded to her at the international exhibition of 1889. From 1849 to 1860 she aided her sister in the Girls' Drawing School at 7 Rue Dupuytren, and in 1852 married the son of the widow who became the second wife of Raymond Bonheur, by whom she had two artist sons.

Germain Bonheur, who was the last child of Raymond Bonheur and by this second marriage, was born in June, 1848, at 13 Rue Rumford, Paris. His father dying the following year, Germain was brought up by his mother and his half-brothers and sisters. He was sent to the well-known college of Sainte Barbe, and having taken his degree, he, too, began to study art, entering Gérôme's studio at the School of Fine Arts. In 1870, though exempt from military service on account of his rather diminutive stature, he entered the army, took part in the battle of Sedan, was made prisoner, escaped, returned to Paris, and again became a soldier. At the close of the war he resumed his painting, and between the years 1872 and 1875 exhibited several pictures at the Salon. In 1877 he married the daughter of Ulysse Besnard, the Blois painter on porcelain. But his health had been irretrievably shaken by the campaign of 1870, and he finally died in Blois in 1880, at the age of thirty-two, without issue.

Hippolyte Peyrol, the eldest son of Juliette Bonheur, was born in Paris on June 10, 1856, and was graduated from the college

A SHE–CAT.

A COW'S HEAD.

SHORECK AND PUPS.
By Juliette Bonheur.

BONIFACE.

of Sainte Barbe with the degrees of bachelor of letters and bachelor of sciences, when he entered the National School of Decorative Arts, where he remained a year. He then took up the study of sculpture under the guidance of his uncle, Isidore Bonheur, and exhibited for the first time in the Salon of 1880, continuing to send to almost every Salon figures of animals, several of which have attracted considerable attention. In 1883, 1884, and in 1886 he received honourable mentions, in 1888 a third-class medal, in 1892 a second-class medal, and in 1894 a first-class medal, since which year he has been a non-competitor. Since 1897 he has been a member of the Salon jury, and in January, 1898, was appointed professor at the National School of Decorative Arts. His only child, Pierre, born in 1896, just a century after his great-grandfather, Raymond Bonheur, already shows a taste for the arts.

René Peyrol, the second son of Juliette Bonheur, was born at Paris on July 4, 1860, and, in due season, was graduated from the college of Sainte Barbe. He studied painting with Jules Lefebvre and Boulanger, and under their influence produced a certain number of canvases representing a figure in a landscape. But soon, following the example set by his family, he specialised little by little, and gave his chief attention to animals. Thus, to the Salon of 1898 he sent a flock of sheep, and the next year cows at the watering-place. But this was his last exhibit. Full of artistic promise, he was suddenly taken ill of a cold at the beginning of 1899, and died on January 29th of this same year at the age of thirty-nine.

There remains a word to be said in this connection concerning the only other descendants of Raymond Bonheur, the children of Auguste Bonheur. One of the three daughters is an artist. The only son, Raymond, is a composer of acknowledged ability, whose talents would receive wider recognition if his modest and retiring disposition did not keep him confined to his country home. He comes up to the busy city only at rare intervals, and never lifts a finger to advance his own musical or material interests in which particular he resembles all the Bonheurs, especially those of the generation that immediately preceded him. He has been engaged for some time on a musical drama entitled " Malva," suggested by Gorki's tale of that name. His most recent production is the music which accompanied " Polyphème," the piece of M. Albert Samain, given at the Comédie Française a year or two ago.

Here may be placed some souvenirs and appreciations of the Bonheurs by old friends of the family. Thus, M. Paul Chardin writes:

Auguste Bonheur I saw only three or four times. His pictures were much remarked at the various exhibitions, and he certainly had talent; but, in my opinion, he lacked personality. Both his subjects and his style of painting resembled those of Rosa. He was a man of grave, even melancholy aspect, and was devoted to his work. He was a tall, pale, blond-complexioned man; in fact, more like his sister Mme. Peyrol than like his sister Rosa.

Isidore Bonheur was much more of Rosa's type, being shorter than Auguste, and was light-complexioned, with a reddish beard. Him I knew better than Auguste. He too was grave, even taciturn, but exceedingly good-hearted, and devoted to his friends, whom he was always ready to oblige. He possessed much talent and more individuality than his brother Auguste. In his artistic work as a sculptor of animals, he showed great correctness of design and a skilled hand that recalled his sister's so far as the execution of details was concerned. Moreover, he had the ability to give amplitude to his execution, a good example of this being the greyhounds that support the mantelpiece in the By studio, which are carved with a large simplicity that gives to them a most impressive appearance. He produced a great number of art objects, small or medium-sized, which his brother-in-law, Hippolyte Peyrol, Sr., cast in bronze. The animals he most often fashioned were horses and cows: He modelled but few thoroughbred horses, preferring cross-bred and cart-horses. In the former, by the way, he was inferior to the young Cuvelier, whose talent was nipped in the bud, he being one of the first killed at the siege of Paris. Like his sister Rosa, he was an indefatigable worker and had a keen observing eye. In fact, most of Rosa's moral qualities and idiosyncrasies were found in both brothers, though neither of them possessed their sister's dash and intermittent mirth.

THE MANTELPIECE IN THE BY STUDIO.

I met Juliette Bonheur but two or three times. She was certainly a pupil of her sister, seeking to imitate Rosa's manner of painting, in the sheep which she generally chose as the subject for her pictures.

Rosa Mathieu, daughter of the sculptor to whom Raymond Bonheur addressed the letter given a few pages back, has said to me:

I remember Rosa Bonheur as long ago as I can recall anything. Among my earliest recollections is being seated on one of her father's knees while Germain, her half-brother, was seated on the other. All the members of the family had marked individuality. Elisabeth, the sister of Raymond Bonheur, was essentially a southerner, with a large share of meridional exuberance and emphasis. She possessed something of the artist in her nature, had a touch of the tragic in her manners, and an excitable temperament. Auguste was rather peculiar in character, a good fellow at bottom, but somewhat difficult to get on with. Isidore was more like Rosa, and there existed between these two, all their life, a genuine sympathy and mutual understanding.

Isidore Bonheur seems to have left the warmest memories in the old friends of the family. Thus Bouguereau, when engaged on one of the last pictures that left his easel, said to me with considerable feeling:

Though I met Rosa Bonheur from time to time, it was her brother Isidore whom I knew the best of the family. In fact, he was an intimate friend of mine at one period of my life. We were both bachelors and we once lived in the same house in the Rue Bréda. The first time I saw Rosa Bonheur was when Isidore took me to her studio in the Rue d'Assas *à propos* of a goat which she had, and which I wanted as a model for the goat in my picture, " The Return from the Field." She very kindly lent me the animal and he appears in my painting. Isidore was a charming man.

Princess Stirbey writes:

Isidore Bonheur was an exceedingly able sculptor, far superior to Frémiet,[1] in my opinion. Although a man of high artistic attainment, his extreme timidity kept him from reaping all the honours due to his talent. He should have been a member of the Institute. But the Bonheurs all shone by their passivity; they would do nothing to push themselves to the fore. Rosa was tenderly attached to him, and he had an equal affection for her; so when she died, he didn't long survive her.

---

[1] The distinguished French animal sculptor and nephew of Rude, born in 1824 and member of the Institute.

RAYMOND BONHEUR AND FAMILY

These souvenirs may close with this anecdote concerning the Peyrol Brothers furnished me by Mme. Bouguereau:

Desirous of saving her children from the harassing uncertainties of an artist's life, Mme. Juliette Peyrol, whose husband once told me this story, made known to them the wish of their father as well as herself, that they should enter upon a commercial career. But as the two boys had inherited a passion for art, this decision came as a death-blow to their fondest dreams. How could they avert so cruel a fate? They turned to their great aunt for comfort, and Rosa Bonheur readily made herself an accomplice in a little intrigue whose aim was to defeat parental authority. Though very busy at the time on some of her own work, she complacently sat as a model to the elder of the boys for a plaster study of her head, which, when done, revealed marked talent. Taking it to his mother, he besought her to let him be a sculptor. By his side stood his brother, with a forcibly sketched landscape in his hand, who declared that he must be a painter. Of course, maternal affection and pride could not resist such appeals, and two new artists were added to the Bonheur galaxy.

This chapter will be supplemented by the collection of Rosa Bonheur's letters given farther on in this volume, and especially by those addressed to the various members of her family, which contain many intimate touches that throw much light on the thoughts, aspirations, and acts of the whole Bonheur home circle during a long period of years.

CHAPTER III

Two persons had a particularly strong influence on the life of Rosa Bonheur. One of these was Nathalie Micas, as we shall frequently see, especially in the next chapter, and the other was Raymond Bonheur, glimpses of whose ascendency have been caught in the preceding pages. But the impress of the father was not wholly of an artistic nature. It had also a peculiar ethical character; and the moral stamp which he transmitted to the daughter came to him largely from a really extraordinary source, from his early association with a remarkable religio-socialistic sect, the celebrated Saint Simonians, and from his ardent belief in their curious and original doctrines. When we know who were the Saint Simonians, and what were their teachings, and when, on closing this volume, we shall have perceived the whole personality of Rosa Bonheur, then it will be strikingly evident that these noble-minded but erratic reformers of 1830 did indeed do much, both through the father and directly, in moulding her individuality and in shaping her life-work.

"The three chief aspects of France at the moment of the advent of Saint Simonianism were, in the social order, competition; in the moral order, scepticism; in the political order, anarchy." So writes Louis Blanc in his interesting chapter on the sect in his "History of Ten Years." He continues: "This school rehabilitated the principle of authority in the midst of the triumphs of liberalism; proclaimed the necessity of a social religion at a moment when the laws themselves were atheistic; and advocated the organisation of industry and co-operative ideas at an

58

epoch when the deceptive success of competition had attained its highest point. With an intrepidity which has never been equalled and with a vigour well seconded by lofty talent and profound study, this school laid bare all the sores of the century and opened up to the intelligent a vast and new vista."

The teachings of the Count of St. Simon, the founder of French socialism, produced but little effect during his lifetime (1760–1825). But at the very start he won over to his views some of the most brilliant young men of the day, such as Auguste Comte and Augustin Thierry, and during the two years which followed the revolution of 1830 Saint Simonianism became a power in the intellectual world of France, to become later a power also in the industrial world and even to exercise a certain influence in the political world.

Perhaps the best way to enable modern readers to understand the intellectual side of Saint Simonianism is to point out that many of its tenets and acts resembled those of the American Transcendental movement of the middle of the last century. What Emerson said of a certain meeting of the Transcendental Club, that it was like " going to heaven in a swing," might be repeated of many of the Sunday lectures in the Rue Taitbout or of the gatherings of " The Family " in the Rue Monsigny. We are told, for instance, that at some of the lectures or sermons the congregation was often so moved by an appeal, for example, to the privileged classes to help the working classes, that tears were shed, while, amidst applause, the listeners began to embrace one another and scenes occurred that remind one of a Methodist revival or an American camp-meeting. This Family, which consisted of seventy-nine members, exclusive of the catechumens, and included the two Supreme Fathers, sixteen Fathers of the College, two of whom were women, and Raymond Bonheur, who was among the faithful of the third degree, took their meals in common, when all the principles of Saint Simonianism were discussed, while a deep spirit of fraternity prevailed; all of which reminds one of the atmosphere and conversation which characterized the plain dining-room of Brook

Farm. The comparison holds good in almost every particular. Just as the monks of Ménilmontant—the Saint Simonians, for a season, led a monastic life—sought to organise a regular religion, so there was a tendency of this same kind at Brook Farm, with William H. Channing as a sort of embryonic Enfantin. In the department of music, John S. Dwight was the Félicien David of Brook Farm, and in the field of journalism, *The Harbinger* was *Le Globe.* George William Curtis, who hovered on the outskirts of the farm, just as did several choice spirits of France on the heights of Ménilmontant, speaks of " this effort at practical Christianity," while St. Simon's doctrine was often described as " the new Christianity." In a general way Transcendentalism has been defined as the doctrine that the principles of reality are to be discovered by the study of the processes of thought, while the Transcendentalists themselves preferred to call themselves " the Disciples of the Newness," though a less reverent observer dubbed them " a race who drove into the infinite, soared into the illimitable, and never paid cash." " Its most systematic historian," as Higginson styles Lindsay Swift, says of Brook Farm, which experiment lasted from 1841 to 1847, that " there was a distinct beginning, a fairly coherent progress, but a vague termination," which also well describes the history of Saint Simonianism, as, in fact, all these socialistic attempts in general. Curtis said in one of his " Easy Chair " essays of 1869: " It is to the Transcendentalism, that seemed to so many good souls both wicked and absurd, that some of the best influences of American life to-day are due. The spirit that was concentrated at Brook Farm is diffused, but it is not lost." Professor Charléty, in his excellent " Essai sur l'Histoire du Saint-Simonisme," makes much the same remark concerning Ménilmontant: " These apostles had many friends, who, while lamenting their foolishness, admired their talents," and Georges Weil, in the latest and one of the best studies of the sect, " L'Ecole Saint-Simonienne," points out that it is a mistake to imagine, as most people do, that Saint Simonianism ended with the famous trial of 1832. " Up to the time of the death of Enfantin, in 1864, and even later," he says, " though there was no longer a Saint Simonian sect, there was a group of Saint Simonians, and there was especially a Saint Simonian state of mind. Its remarkable influence did not even disappear with the extinction of the last of the disciples." And, finally, the superiority of the individual character of so many of the original Saint Simonians—for, taken as a body, they were a grand lot of men and women,—also finds its counterpart in their American pendants— in Hawthorne, Ripley, Dana, and others. But curiously enough, it may be said in passing, I do not find that the Transcendentalists remarked, either before or after their dispersion, this resemblance between themselves and their French precursors.

Both of these observations are true of Saint Simonianism and the woman's rights movement in America. Not only had they many points in common, but the American reformers do not appear to have been aware of this fact. John Stuart Mill, in his " Autobiography," was, perhaps, the first in the Anglo-American world to call prominent attention to the Saint Simonians " proclaiming the perfect equality of men and women, and an entirely new order of things in regard to their relations with one another," which has " entitled themselves to the grateful remembrance of future generations." But the " Autobiography " was not printed until 1870. " Enfantin proclaimed as a religious necessity," says Louis Blanc, " the enfranchisement of woman and her participation in the supreme power alongside of himself in the religious system, when would be established what he called the Dual Priesthood." In fact, the Saint Simonian belief in a female element in the godhead exactly resembles a latter-day phase of the American woman's rights creed, which startled the more old-fashioned wing of the reformers and shocked the Church. In reading various writings of the Saint Simonians you are continually encountering ideas and even phrases which you find in almost exactly the same words in the publications of Elizabeth Cady Stanton during the closing years of her life. Thus, in the Saint Simonian profession of faith occur such passages as these:

" I believe in God, Father and Mother of us all, man and woman."
" I believe that God has raised up Father Enfantin in order that
he may call to his side the Woman Messiah, who, by the equality
of man and woman, will consecrate the union of humanity and the
world." Holstein, a distinguished Saint Simonian, declared almost
in his last breath: " I believe in God, Father and Mother." Michel
Chevalier thus states the credo of the sect: " I believe in social
regeneration based on the equality of man and woman, and I await
the coming of the woman who will bring this about." One of the
songs of the Saint Simonian poet, Vincard, contains this line:

"Let us cause to reign our God, Father and Mother."
(Faisons régner notre Dieu, Père et Mère.)

An article in *Le Globe* has this sentence: " There is being
prepared in the moral world something that is unexpected and
unheard of; we anticipate the coming of a Woman Messiah." In
the calendar drawn up especially for the sect, several days each
month were sacred to " the Father and the Mother." Charléty
declares that these dreamers " turned their whole attention toward
the coming of the Woman; it was their fixed idea." For a moment it was even thought that she might be at hand in the person
of George Sand! Enfantin had repeatedly and confidently announced her advent, and when she did not appear he lost influence,
and it was the beginning of his discredit and the fall of the sect.

Saint Simonian ideas are also reproduced in a more general
way in the American woman's rights movement. The Ménilmontant thinkers did not overlook the educational and political claims
of their female co-workers, nor forget their promises when the
day for fulfillment seemed at hand. When the second Carnot, an
old Saint Simonian, became minister of public instruction under
the republic of 1848, he authorized at the College of France the
opening of a series of lectures especially devoted to woman, while
Olinde Rodrigues, one of the ablest of the early Saint Simonian
leaders, gives women their political rights in the constitution

which he drew up for consideration at this same crisis. Even female dress was reformed. The Saint Simonian women wore a sort of Bloomer costume—a kind of riding hat, black veil, short black skirt, leather belt, and trousers. Though it is true that Rosa Bonheur first put on male attire in order to facilitate her art work in the Paris slaughter-houses, it must also be true that having seen, as a child, the Saint Simonian women dressed in this way, and her own mother, possibly, among them, it became very easy and natural for her to don a somewhat similar costume when necessity called for it.

No wonder then that Rosa Bonheur, the favourite child of an ardent Saint Simonian, brought up in such surroundings, with eye, mind, and heart under such influences, should have been " almost born an emancipated female," as some one has remarked. It would have been odd if it had been otherwise. " She was a believer in woman's rights in this sense," Mme. Virginie Demont-Breton, the distinguished painter, writes me, " that she desired the development of woman's artistic faculties to be carried as far as possible. ' If physical force is greater in man,' she once said to me, ' it is because he is the natural defender of woman against the material dangers of life. But in all that is moral and intellectual, she contributes as well as he to the security and happiness of the family. Consequently, there is no reason why her judgment, thought, in a word, her moral strength, should be inferior. Is not intelligence, especially as regards the artistic sense, to be found first of all in the heart? ' Writing to me on the subject of ' our colleagues of the palette,' as she called them, she said in a letter dated By, January 12, 1899, speaking of the earnest workers: ' They prove that the Creator has made woman the noble companion of man, and that He has differentiated them only for the purpose of reproducing a noble race in this world.' "

On another occasion Rosa Bonheur said: " I have no patience with women who ask permission to think. Let women establish their claims by great and good works, and not by conventions."

Touching on this same subject in a more general way, M.

REMINISCENCES OF ROSA BONHEUR

Léonce Bénédite, conservator of the Luxembourg Picture Gallery, says:

It was the naturalist movement that produced the greatest artistic personality in the feminine world of recent times, Rosa Bonheur. The part played by Rosa Bonheur is important from the point of view of the New Woman, for she broke away from the old ideas concerning her sex, and showed the world what women could do in the matter of energy, continuity of purpose, methodical and intelligent labour, and, in a word, in that indispensable quality, inspiration, which gives an impetus to art. Before her day, the woman painter had been looked upon rather as a phenomenon, and was grudgingly given a place in the domain of art on the ground that she was indulging in an elevating and tasteful pastime which might be classed under the head of ' accomplishments.' But Rosa Bonheur put woman on the same footing as man in art, and, at the same time, won for herself wide admiration, based, not on any singularity of life, not on looseness in morals, not on social triumphs, not on having friends at court, but on her own unaided, robust, virile, observing, and well-trained talent, which, in its turn, was based on a preliminary study of anatomy and osteology, and further developed by continued observation of the habits and ways of the animal kingdom. Her long career was crowned with success, and she attained an exceptional place in art, akin to that of George Sand in the field of letters." [1]

The remarkable industrial talent of the Saint Simonians has rightfully excited wonder. St. Simon himself, when in the New World at the time of the American Revolution, proposed to the Viceroy of Mexico to make a canal between the two oceans, and half a century later his disciples went still farther in this same direction, when, in August, 1833, Enfantin wrote: " It is left to us to make, between ancient Egypt and old Judea, one of the new routes from Europe to India and China; later we will dig the other

---

[1] These same observations, sent me by the author for this work, have appeared in a slightly modified form in "Women Painters of the World," edited by Mr. Shaw Sparrow.

COMING FROM THE FAIR.

(By permission of Messrs. L. H. Lefèvre and Son, 1a King Street, St. James's, London, England, proprietors of the copyright, and publishers of the large engraving.)

at Panama." Professor Charléty says: "Enfantin was the pro-
moter, inspirer, and the first engineer of the Suez Canal. The
glory of the enterprise rightfully belongs to the Saint Simonians
and the Polytechnic School." Nor did the sect confine its efforts
in this field to interoceanic canals. The first railway built in
France, that from Paris to Saint Germain, which was opened in
1837, was the work of these remarkable men. In fact, they were
the very soul of the whole early railway construction of the country, and several of their sons and grandsons now hold high posts
in the management of the chief lines. Indeed, these old friends in
high places were a help to Raymond Bonheur in more ways than
one in his struggle with the hardships of life, and a curious example of the manner in which Rosa Bonheur utilised these railway
relations will be given in the next chapter. A director of one of
the great French railways, who is also a member of the Institute,
and whose father was one of the most prominent leaders of the
sect, has said to me: " At the very beginning of her artistic career
my father used to buy Rosa Bonheur's pictures, and we still have
some charming ones painted, I believe, as early as in 1849." This
is but one of many similar examples that I might give of the aid
which the Bonheurs owed to this spirit of comradery.

Politically, too, Saint Simonianism presents a striking interest.
St. Simon himself was a friend of the first revolution, but when
he saw that the republicans were incapable of governing, he accepted Bonaparte and put all his faith in him. In 1848 his followers did the same thing in respect to Napoleon III. During
the reign of Louis Philippe almost all of the Saint Simonians
were republicans, and some even conspired against the government. So when the revolution of 1848 broke out they were much
stirred. But a letter from the Father urged the disciples not to
take part in the uprising. This is why we saw Raymond Bonheur simply an onlooker during the stormy days of February.
In a word, the Saint Simonian school welcomed the advent of the
Second Empire, for to most of them political liberty was a secondary consideration. What they desired above all was a gov-

ernment strong enough to preserve order and assure progress. What they had looked for in vain in a parliamentary republic, a despotic government gave them; and so they rallied to its support. M. Weil says: "Napoleon III was, for a period at least, Saint Simonianism crowned. . . . If we follow Napoleon III in his speeches and his letters, we will find him continually in accord with the Saint Simonians. . . . It was not only the ideas, but the men of the Saint Simonian school who triumphed under the Empire; several even lived in the immediate circle of Napoleon III." In fact, the folly of the democrats was equalled only by the selfishness of the conservative burgher class in 1848. Under these circumstances " the conduct of the Saint Simonians was remarkable," a close observer has pointed out. They stood almost alone between two extremes, and, though they approved of the change, they strove to draw from it only practical results, such as primary schools for all, a better banking system, and large appropriations for public improvements.

This inclination of the Saint Simonians toward the Empire made it easier in after years for the Fontainebleau court and the By recluse to exchange civilities, as we shall see farther on in this volume. Princess Stirbey writes me as follows on this point:

What especially struck me in Rosa Bonheur, over and above her great artistic talent, was her philosophic mind, which judged everything with originality and independence. Up to a certain point, her intelligence had received the impression of her father's ideas. Brought up in the midst of the Saint Simonians and mixing with many of the remarkable men of the day, she all her life preserved a most lively sympathy for democratic and socialistic aspirations. But this feeling did not prevent her from appreciating the work of Napoleon III. Perhaps the marks of favour which the Emperor and especially the Empress showered upon her may have had also their influence. At any rate, she recognised and acknowledged Napoleon's efforts to increase the prosperity of France and to improve the lot of the working classes by raising their wages and spreading abroad more generous ideas.

RAYMOND BONHEUR AND THE SAINT SIMONIANS

The socialistic side of the new doctrine was indeed very pronounced. "Two forms of modern thought," writes Professor Charléty, "which are closely allied, though not necessarily confounded in the same men, positivism and socialism, really spring from Saint Simonianism." Though the reform failed, "it prepared the way both for socialistic rhetoric and sociological studies." It should be remembered that, at the moment of the revolution of 1848, it was a Saint Simonian who, first in France and in Europe, proposed to solve the difficulties between capital and labour by the system of the sharing of profits. It is a common mistake, however, to think that the social question was introduced into French politics by the revolution of 1848, whereas it was precipitated into the arena by the outburst of 1830. Pierre Leroux, a distinguished Saint Simonian, who, by the way, once blamed Victor Hugo to his face for never having made a verse in honour of the founder of the sect, was the first, in 1834, to employ the word socialism; while the new socialists, Cabet, Louis Blanc, and Proudhon, were very much in evidence throughout the reign of Louis Philippe, though highly distasteful to the advocates of pacific progress, the peculiar characteristic of the Saint Simonians after they had come to their senses and were dispersed.

During the Days of July the people of Paris came generously to the support of the sorely pressed liberal burgher class, and when the victory was won the working classes naturally felt that they should share in the consequent benefits. During the Restoration the burgher class had alone been on the scene. But the Orleans monarchy brought the people into politics, and the Saint Simonians, who were quick to perceive the innovation and immediately took advantage of it, owed much of their early success to this fact. Some of the more sanguine leaders even thought for a moment that they might get control of the new situation and bring about a complete social revolution in accordance with their ideas. Lafayette, who for a short period was the arbiter of France, was even approached with this end in view; in fact, so carried away were the most ardent, that they did not hesitate to turn their eyes toward the Tuileries, and Louis Philippe himself was summoned to yield his place to the apostles of the new sect!

The Saint Simonian doctrine may be stated briefly as follows: Saint Simon divided society into workers and non-workers, and held that the future belonged exclusively to the first, which he strove to classify as exactly as possible, finally concluding that as man feels, thinks, and acts, all human work can be done by those who address themselves to our sensibilities, who cultivate our intelligence, and who set in motion our activities. Consequently, the three social functions consist in moving, enlightening, and enriching men; and hence there are three classes of workers—artists, teachers in the broadest sense, and manufacturers. Under the name of neo-Christianity, Saint Simon brought together all his scattered ideas and reduced them to three dicta, viz., universal co-operation based on love, and consequently subversive of competition; the formula " to each man according to his capacity, to each capacity according to its works," which destroyed the principle of inheritance; and, lastly, the thorough organisation of industry, so that war is put an end to. In a word, Saint Simon attacked every privilege of birth and declared all armed conflicts impious. " The golden age," he said, " which a blind tradition has always placed in the past, is really in front of us." " Like all reformers," says Louis Blanc, " he started from the perfectibility of humanity." But his disciples who followed were not always so precise in their definitions. " The Saint Simonian doctrine," says one of them, " was neither a Koran nor a Leviticus; it was a conception with a frame, a preface with a table of contents." Lerminier's definition is somewhat similar—" a vast and confused table of contents, a hasty prospectus of the French philosophy of the nineteenth century "—while another declares that it is simply " a new reform of Christianity—nothing more, nothing less."

Saint Simon died in 1825. The journal which he was bent on founding at the moment of his death, the *Producteur*, appeared from October, 1825, to October, 1826. Then followed two years,

1826 to 1828, of "the silent expansion" of Saint Simonianism. It was in April of this latter year that Raymond Bonheur arrived in Paris, where, alone and sad for a twelve-month, as we have already seen, he was in the very mood to take up with the new sect. Toward the end of this same year, the little group of Saint Simonians instituted a series of sermons concerning the religious side of the doctrine. This went on for nearly two years, when these sermons were eventually published in two volumes, and constitute the chief philosophical work of the sect. These public lectures were followed up by private talks, when conversions to the new faith were accomplished. Each believer was expected to bring a friend or two to these evening reunions, who were argued with and their objections refuted, with the result that a new adherent was generally secured. Among the early apostles were many young and brilliant graduates of the famous Paris State Polytechnic School, which has always played such a prominent part in the liberal movements of France. They were one of the chief sources of strength of the reform. To these were added sentimentalists, mystics, and persons troubled by religious anxiety and who hoped to find rest for their weary souls in this new haven. "Many of the neophytes," writes Gustave d'Eichthal, "sought here consolation of some sort; others hoped thus to escape from the state of vague melancholy into which they had been plunged by Romanticism, while still others were fleeing family troubles, or seeking rest from the fatigues of a wild and misspent youth." Professor Charléty says: "The Saint Simonians poured into the hearts of the young of both sexes a generous spirit of enthusiasm. To their minds was offered the elevated pleasure, the joy of possessing the truth. The appeal was heard. All those whose souls were unsettled, who were looking for a belief or impatient to do something; all those who, weary of the commonplaceness of received opinion, longed for 'something else,' who, tired of the inaction in which some insufficient calling left their souls asleep, were ambitious—all such persons flew to the Saint Simonians, as in other times they sought out literary circles or political clubs."

The youthfulness of the Saint Simonians was very notable, and explains much of the attractiveness of the reform. So immature were several of them that nature refused to second the rule of the sect that all its members should wear full beards! The principal apostles were indeed a very young body of men. Only one of them had reached forty, and he remained but a short time. Thirteen were in their thirties, one of these being Raymond Bonheur, who was thirty-six; while eighteen were under thirty, and three of these, youths of twenty. No wonder, then, that Charléty declares that " the retreat of the apostles to Ménilmontant was not infecund, for it filled their old age with pleasant memories and gave strength to their middle life, Ménilmontant, where they had loved one another so dearly, where, in the exuberancy of youth, they had entertained such wild but sublime hopes, such noble joy, which appeared, through the flight of memory, purified from all dross; " which reminds one of Renan's remark: " It is almost always a principle with great lives that during some months they feel God, and the perfume suffices to fill whole years with energy and suavity."

That Raymond Bonheur on his arrival in Paris should have been immediately attracted to this group and that he quickly took an honourable position among the disciples of the new philosophy is another evidence that he was far from being a commonplace man. That he was highly respected at Ménilmontant, I have found several proofs in the curious and voluminous archives of the Saint Simonians recently thrown open to consultation at the Arsenal Library in Paris. Though Professor Charléty tells me that " Raymond Bonheur played but a secondary and rather obscure part in the Saint Simonian movement," he admits that he has " met his name quite often between 1829 and 1833," and that he cites " him a good many times " in his book. Michel Chevalier wrote to a friend on July 2, 1832, from the retreat on the heights back of Père Lachaise, of " Raymond Bonheur, an artist endowed with facility, who will probably paint the fronts of the buildings and the walls surrounding the grounds," while Father Enfantin, nearly twenty years after the dissolution of the community, in an open letter to Lamartine, dated September 15, 1849, in which he was enumerating the celebrities of the sect, referred to " that poor Raymond Bonheur to whom the *Moniteur* yesterday paid such a touching tribute, and who has left in his daughter one of the greatest artists of the epoch."   Furthermore, M. Henry D'Allemagne, one of the best living authorities on Saint Simonianism and the Saint Simonians, tells me that it is generally believed that it was Raymond Bonheur who designed the peculiar costume of the order— a short tight-fitting violet-blue frock-coat, without a collar; a red waistcoat fastened up the back with hooks and eyes; white trousers and a black leather belt with a brass buckle.   " White is considered to signify love; red, work; and violet-blue, faith," wrote Raymond Bonheur to Lacour; " and the whole costume symbolises, therefore, that Saint Simonianism is based on love, is fortified by labour, and is enveloped by faith."   Furthermore, in the words of Father Enfantin, " the waistcoat is the sign of fraternity, for you cannot button it alone "; and, lastly, as each one of the faithful assumed the responsibility of his own conduct, his name was written in large letters across his breast.

Several dicta of the new doctrine appealed strongly to Raymond Bonheur.   It was declared at the very start, as we have already seen, that humanity was to have a triple governing power —knowledge, industry, and the fine arts—and when the sect was definitely founded, a large part was reserved to artists.   It was pointed out in the *Producteur* that art was too individualistic, at the mercy of the caprice of each artist, " the symbol of the moral anarchy in which we live."   " But the moment is doubtless at hand," continue the Saint Simonian journalists, " when the painter, the musician, the poet, who shall have attained to the complete development of his faculty to feel, will possess the power of pleasing and moving in as certain a manner as the mathematician now possesses the power of solving a geometrical problem, or the chemist the power of separating a body into its elements.   Then will the moral side of society be definitively constituted."   Art has its

71

social side; " it should move the masses." This was the germ of the theory which certain of the leaders soon pushed to an extreme. It was taught that the religious side of the sect would be directed by the man of the most artistic nature, who would be the supreme priest. Raymond Bonheur, like everybody else, was drawn to the reform by the fine presence and attractive manners and language of Enfantin, whom all agreed in pronouncing " a real charmer." Of course, knowledge would have its head and industry, too, but the religious head would be he of the most artistic temperament. So the artist became the prophet, and when Saint Simonianism assumed the garb of religion, and killed itself thereby, the artist became the high priest. No wonder, then, that Raymond Bonheur and other young painters, that Félicien David, Liszt, and Halévy, that sculptors and architects, either coquetted for a moment with, or openly and ardently embraced, the new faith that gave them the place of honour in the society which it was to organise. But it was more to be wondered at that a whole group of young men, intelligent, and most all of them endowed with a strong personality, should shut themselves up in Enfantin's house and submit to the severest rule which had no other sanction than the praises or the reproaches of the Father; many of them having to break with family ties that were very dear to them. And yet not one of them hesitating an instant to do so—this was indeed the triumph of art!

In his enthusiasm for the new tenets Raymond Bonheur did not limit his activity to the purely art side of the work, which was rather humdrum. He was also an ardent propagandist. Paris was divided into four " sections," and Raymond Bonheur was named " co-director " of the second section, with headquarters at No. 70 Rue Contrescarpe St. Antoine, a street which no longer exists; and to further extend Saint Simonian influence among the working classes of the capital, a committee of three, composed of a physician, a director, and a directress, was appointed for each of the twelve wards which then formed the city. In the eighth ward Raymond Bonheur and his wife held the last two positions, and their followers, men and women, numbered twenty-one.

But then occurred an unfortunate departure in the movement. After the funeral of Enfantin's mother, on April 22, 1832, all the friends, several hundred in number, who went to the cemetery, returned with the Father to his home at Ménilmontant, where he pronounced a short address. Then all departed except the forty apostles, who were henceforth to abide with him. Among these chosen ones was Raymond Bonheur.

The daily life at Ménilmontant resembled that of a convent. The brothers rose at five, breakfasted at seven, dined at one, supped at seven, and were in bed by ten. There were no domestics, and each apostle had certain menial duties to perform. Thus the cultivated Gustave d'Eichthal cleaned plates, while the Father Superior presided over the garden, and among the brothers who aided him in these horticultural tasks was Raymond Bonheur, of whom there exists a picture, spade in hand.

At this moment the Saint Simonians were one of the chief centres of curiosity of the proverbial inquisitive Parisians. The gates of the convent were thrown open twice each week, on Sundays to all comers, and on Wednesdays to privileged persons. On Sundays as many as 10,000 persons would sometimes walk out from Paris to see the Saint Simonians go through their ceremonies, to look at them eat, and to listen to their songs. So great was the crowd that the government sometimes surrounded the spot with soldiers for fear of disorder.

One of the rules of this peculiar sort of monastery was that requiring the apostles not to leave its gates. It was the hardest one for Raymond Bonheur to conform to, for it meant his separation from wife and children; and there were those, even among his friends and relatives, who blamed him for this course, though, as has already been stated, it was unhesitatingly followed by several of the other apostles, some of whom were in a much higher social and intellectual position than this plain, struggling drawing teacher. It should be remembered, also, that one of the

73

fundamental principles of Saint Simonianism was that family, caste, city, nation were synonymous with antagonism; that all social forms made for war. The idea of association, however, had peace as its aim. When Raymond Bonheur accepted the new doctrine, he accepted, too, this "revelation." Indeed, this episode of her father's life was generally passed over in silence by Rosa

RAYMOND BONHEUR AS A SAINT SIMONIAN.

Bonheur, and is seldom referred to willingly by the living members of the family. But this feeling of disapproval is not wholly due to a quasi-desertion of the domestic hearth for a few months. It was largely caused by two other incidents.

On August 27 and 28, 1832, the Saint Simonians were tried before the courts for immorality, though the impartial historian must admit that the charge, if partly true in the case of Enfantin, was wholly false concerning his faithful followers. The truth of the matter is that the sect had become troublesome, not to say more, to the powers that were; and in over-centralised France, especially in the time of the July monarchy, this was a grave political crime. So loose morals was seized upon as the pretext and article 291 of the criminal code as the real means of suppressing these *enfants terribles.* At 7 A.M., on the first day, Enfantin and the apostles, in full Saint Simonian dress, with Raymond Bonheur among them, marched down from Ménilmontant, through the whole breadth of Paris, to the court-house, where several of the leaders were condemned to fine and imprisonment, in accordance with the article just mentioned, which reads as follows: "No association numbering more than twenty persons, which meets daily or on certain fixed dates, and whose aim is of a religious, literary, political, or other nature, can be formed without the consent of the government, or under conditions other than those which it pleases the public authorities to impose upon it." The application of this article in the case of the Saint Simonians was not approved by several of the liberal organs of the time, and it was finally abrogated seventy years afterward, in July, 1901.

In the month of October following the first trial the Saint Simonians were again arraigned, accused this time of dishonesty in money matters. But there was no ground for the charge, and all the accused were acquitted. After the first trial the sustaining fund of the monastery began to diminish, and the faithful had grown weary of a life of almost nothing to do. After the second trial the financial situation got still worse. Thereupon the Father divided the apostles into two groups, one, the smaller, remaining with him at Ménilmontant, while the other group was to go forth and preach the good word. Among the latter was Raymond Bonheur. But once having breathed again the free air of the everyday world none ever returned to the restraints of Ménilmontant. This happened in the late autumn of 1832.

It is in his letters of this period, four of which I have been able to discover in the Arsenal Library, that the noble and generous character of Raymond Bonheur comes out strongly and in its true light.   No sooner had he become a Saint Simonian and believed that he had found on earth the peace of soul and mind so earnestly desired than he longs to share his supreme happiness with his friends, and thereupon displays a characteristic tenderness of sentiment by turning first to his old teacher at Bordeaux, Pierre Lacour.   The printed letterhead reads: " St. Simonian Religion," and the letter is dated " Paris, March 1, 1831."   It begins as follows, to his " dear and former master ":

I little ever imagined that I, moved by a religious sentiment, would address myself to you.   But, unbeknown to you, I received from you other benefits than those of learning the arts of painting and drawing—arts to-day so poor and unreligious.   You will pardon my confidence, my hope, that I may be able to give you something in exchange for your lessons, and as it was due to you that I turned my back on the dangerous doctrines of Boulanger [1] and company, I like to believe that you will at least permit me to thank you and proclaim the wisdom of your course.

The writer then goes on, in a closely-written, four-page, commercial-size sheet, to develop the doctrines of Saint Simonianism, the aim being to convert Lacour; and the wordy and rather wandering epistle ends with this postscriptum: " You may communicate this letter to the members of the Philanthropic Society, of which I have the honour to be a corresponding member, bearing in mind the purpose of the letter and overlooking its shortcomings."

On the same day and on the same large-size paper he writes another letter, this time six pages in length, addressed to a former fellow pupil of Lacour.   He tells how he was converted to Saint Simonianism and paints a dark picture of the society of the time, " where neither kings nor presidents, congresses nor ministers,

---

[1] The reference is doubtless to Clément Boulanger or Louis Boulanger, probably the latter, who was a friend of Victor Hugo, and both of whom took part in the Romantic Movement.

deputies nor journals, nobody, either of the Right or the Left, knows what remedy to propose." He then continues:

Like you, my dear Durand, and with the greatest energy, I have cried in the desert—cries of imprecation and sorrow against a blind power which seems cruelly to conduct everything into the yawning mouth of fatality, the fiend of ruin and destruction, which tears us to pieces all the more unmercifully because we are generous and tender! I revolted and strongly protested against every belief except that of my own individual conscience. But consolation could I find nowhere. I was in a state of despairing scepticism, when a friendly voice having directed my attention to the doctrines of Saint Simon, I soon found my hopes the more thoroughly realised because, at first, I was wrong in thinking myself deceived at the reunions in counting on the sympathies of those who acted on impulses like my own. Well, my dear friend, I read much, I meditated long on the works explaining the doctrine, and I attended lectures on the subject. One evening I argued with all my force against everything which appeared to me Utopian, or dreamy, or anarchical, or Jesuitical; for it seemed to me that I saw on all sides contradictory tendencies. But I finally came to recognise that the apparent confusion emanated from myself. I perceived it in the strongest opponent of the doctrine, who, like myself, in the end honestly surrendered.

This letter is signed " James Raimond Bonheur," being the only instance I have found of Raymond Bonheur using the name James. Later, he spelt Raimond with a y.

In a fourth letter from Ménilmontant, Raymond Bonheur refers to " this society which is dissolved by individualism," and thus disposes of the criticism that the Saint Simonians were intolerant: " Scepticism, doubt, can alone tolerate. To tolerate is to abandon, to be indifferent. The man who loves virtue, can he tolerate brigandage? "

The language of Raymond Bonheur's letters written from Ménilmontant is not always clear. But this was peculiar to the writings of the whole sect, the printed and spoken speech of the

Father being especially so; in which respect they again resembled our own Transcendentalists. Both these French and New England illuminati had an exasperating way of twisting words away from their ordinary meaning. Curiously enough, this same defect stands out glaringly in many of the letters of Rosa Bonheur, where it is often impossible to guess what she means. A friend once showed her one of her letters and asked her what an obscure passage signified, when she replied: "In the first place, I can't read it, and even if I could, I probably would not know now what I was driving at then. In fact, perhaps I did not know even then!" But probably it is too much to attribute this singularity to Saint Simonian influence.

But in moulding her religious belief, Saint Simonianism unquestionably had an influence on Rosa Bonheur, both direct and through her father; an influence that frequently manifested itself throughout her life and remained with her to the end.

On November 13, 1897, about a year and a half before her death, Rosa Bonheur wrote as follows from By to her friend Venancio Deslandes of Lisbon:

I have the honour to hold the same views as Mme. George Sand concerning the brief sojourn we make in this world, and, though I never enjoyed the personal acquaintance of, nor saw, this genius, I have read with pleasure the extract herewith enclosed. It was copied out by a distinguished woman well known in the world of art and a friend of one of my men-friends to whom she sent it from New York. Please read it.

The extract referred to above is stated by the copyist to be taken from "an exquisite philosophical book by George Sand," and is a rather remarkable presentation of the novelist's belief in reincarnation; remarkable inasmuch as it anticipates in form much of what is taught to-day by the accredited leaders of Theosophy. The salient passage of the extract is the following:

We are allowed by reason and we are bidden by the heart to count on a series of progressive existences proportioned to our good desires. And certainly the first of all our legitimate aspirations, since it is noble, is to find in this future life the faculty of recollecting in a certain measure our previous lives. It would not be very agreeable to trace back all our pains and sorrows in detail. Even in the present life, such a remembrance would be a nightmare. But the luminous points, the salutary trials wherein we have triumphed, would be a reward, and the celestial crown would be the embracing of our friends and their recognising us in their turn.

Another proof that such was Rosa Bonheur's acknowledged view of the future life is furnished in these lines sent me by M. Henri Cain: [1]

Rosa was always glad to have my brother and me bring her books. She read rather advanced ones. I am interested in occultism and she shared my interest. The doctrine must not be confounded, however, with modern spiritualism or magnetism. The occultism which held our attention was a philosophical form of the conception of the migration of souls, of the survival of the spirit in us after death. Towards the end of her life, Rosa Bonheur gave much thought to these questions and read all she could find on the subject. She began with the volumes of Figuier and Flammarion, and did not hesitate to tackle more solid works, if I may so express myself; treatises that went into the details of the whole complex question. Though she may have had a leaning toward spiritualism, I can affirm only that she believed thoroughly in our occult theory.

It should be pointed out that many of these ideas, such, for example, as that of the migration of the soul, are found in the metaphysical speculations of the Saint Simonians, where Rosa Bonheur probably first made their acquaintance.

All her friends agree in the essential facts which show that Rosa Bonheur was a free thinker in the right acceptance of the

---

[1] For a biographical note on M. Cain, see page 216.

term. In proof of this assertion I may give these further attestations from some of those who knew her best and longest.

Alexandre Jacob has said to me:

Of religion, Rosa Bonheur rarely spoke. She was not a member of the Church, never attended mass and probably inherited from her father her thoroughly independent attitude toward catholicism. Yet, while so little attached to ordinary religious observance, she was punctilious as regards the rites of marriage, baptism and burial, and when her friend Nathalie Micas died, she was careful to have performed all the Church requires from the devout.

M. Louis Passy, Deputy and Member of the Institute, has said to me, and I noted down his statement in his presence:

As regards Rosa Bonheur's religious convictions, my opinion is that she was an agnostic. I do not think she ever gave her mind to an examination of those questions. She worked from morning till night, and had no time to study such serious matters. Why, even when on visits, she was sketching all the time. This is my view of the religious mentality of Rosa Bonheur.

Princess Stirbey has written me:

To hear Rosa Bonheur talk, some people would have considered her an enemy of religion. She certainly did fulminate against many tenets of Catholicism, criticising the Church with a frankness and, at the same time, with a popular colouring of expression and a vigour that one would have expected rather in a man. And yet, when Nathalie Micas died, she consented to all the funeral rites being celebrated without a single omission, and was herself present at the whole of them both at the church near By and at the Père Lachaise cemetery, in Paris, where Nathalie was buried. During all this sad day I was with Rosa, who, amid her sobs, kept repeating: " What will become of me? " She was quite prostrated by the blow, but yet remained devout.

BRITTANY SHEEP.

(Reproduced by permission from the engraving published by Messrs. Henry Graves and Company, London.)

RAYMOND BONHEUR AND THE SAINT SIMONIANS

In a conversation with Prince Georges Stirbey, I made these notes while with him:

When Mlle. Micas died, Rosa Bonheur suffered great grief. It was as if she had been struck by a thunderbolt. She was so upset by her great loss that she could not work. The cruel blow awakened in her thoughts of religion. One day she turned suddenly on me and put this question:

"Do you believe in a future life? The thought has troubled me a great deal of late. My spirit is refractory to all ideas of the life to come, and the immortality of the soul. I do not understand these things; but my heart seems to tell me that I will see again my Nathalie."

And as I talked with her, I saw that she had a certain sense of religion. Hers was the religion of the artists who see God everywhere and in all nature. But if you spoke to her of complex dogmas, she was no longer able to follow you. It was her heart rather than her mind which governed her in these matters.

In a letter written in April, 1867, to M. Paul Chardin, occurs this passage: "To my mind, my good Rapin, death does not exist. It is a transformation in the physical as in the moral world." M. Chardin makes the following comment thereon:

It is quite true that Rosa Bonheur was not a practising Catholic, and her religious ideas were, I think, very vague. But it is certain from this letter that she believed in the immortality of the soul, that she held that there is another life and that there is a moral transformation of the spiritual part of our being tending toward perfection.

These attestations from old friends may close with these lines from M. Georges Cain:

Rosa Bonheur was a philosopher and of pantheistic leanings. These ideas she was able to reconcile with a deep reverence for the Divine and a hatred for what she called "the Jesuits." By birth

81

a Catholic, she neglected all outward religious observance. Her reading was very general, the Bible and La Fontaine being two of her favourites. The Gospels she thought to be incomparable.

Rosa Bonheur's will, dated November 9, 1898, directed that she be buried without the presence of clergy, and no priest was at her death-bed. However, a few weeks before she passed away, she said to Miss Klumpke: " Personally, I prefer a civil funeral. But as I wish to be interred with the Micas family, I cannot do so decently unless I pass by the church. Yet, though I make this concession as to my body, my philosophical belief remains unalterable."

Rosa Bonheur's pantheistic conception of the unknown was well expressed in these words of Tennyson, which she warmly approved when they were translated to her by a dear friend: " It is inconceivable that the whole universe was merely created for us who live in this third-rate planet of a third-rate sun." But she was not one of those " persons who are afraid of holy water while they are living and of the devil when they are dying." [1]

---

[1] Gente che ha paura dell' acqua santa quando vive e del diavolo quando muroe. Antonio Fogazzaro, "Piccolo Mondo Moderno," p. 67.

CHAPTER IV

THE MICAS FAMILY

WE have already seen in Raymond Bonheur a never-satisfied craving for love and affection. Forced by cruel circumstances to pass much of his life in poverty and isolation, he sought comfort wherever he thought he could find it, whether among the visionary monks of Ménilmontant or among the more commonplace friends of the poorer quarters of the great city. Rosa Bonheur showed these same tastes, especially both at the very beginning and at the very end of her life, and also at various periods between these two extremes. At the threshold of her career she formed a peculiar friendship, as has already been said, for Nathalie Micas, which lasted, midst storm and sunshine, till the two friends were finally parted many years later by death. The story of Rosa Bonheur's existence would be very incomplete unless the reader were properly introduced to the Micas family, mother and daughter. So I give place here to the souvenirs of Rosa Bonheur's friends and to some letters of Rosa Bonheur herself, which throw light on this phase of her career. Further references to these two original women—Mlle. and Mme. Micas—are scattered through the pages which follow this chapter, and will complete the picture whose main outlines are given below.

Of all the old friends of Rosa Bonheur who have spoken to me of the Micas family, Paul Chardin, I think, has produced the best likeness, as regards detail and humour. He says in this connection in one of his many charming contributions to this volume:

Nathalie Micas, who was gifted with an imagination of the romantic kind, claimed to be of Iberian origin, and her friend,

83

Rosa Bonheur, had surnamed her Inés dellas Sierras, or, as she freely translated it, the Great Agnes, from a story by Charles Nodier. Her gaudy dress contrasted strangely with the artist's plain painting blouse and somewhat masculine coat. She was especially fond of red and black in her toilet, and generally wore hats turned up in the Spanish fashion, trimmed with plumes in the same diabolical colours, which accentuated the disagreeable sallowness of her complexion.

She was a woman of action, was Nathalie, most enterprising and energetic, and always ready to oblige her neighbours. She pretended to possess medical knowledge and even surgical skill. She acted as veterinary surgeon when any of the animals were sick in the menagerie at By, and was soon on the spot if any inhabitant of the village met with an accident, carrying with her drugs and instruments, the latter for real use in case of need.

Her imagination was always at work, with the result that she was continually inventing something or other. Among a hundred marvels, there was a famous brake warranted to prevent railway accidents. In order to illustrate its grand qualities, she had a miniature tramway laid down in the private grounds at By, where small platform cars provided with this wonderful mechanism might be seen running; and she sent for engineers, railway directors, and all the big-wigs she could hunt up, to come and see it work. The invention appears to have been patented, but no company adopted it.

As Rosa Bonheur's friend, Nathalie Micas conceived a taste for painting. She used in preference to paint cats, one picture in particular, I remember, representing some kittens playing with a ball of wool. It was an awful daub; yet Rosa Bonheur, with that naïve goodness so characteristic of her, took the trouble to advise Nathalie and even to add a few touches to the wretched canvas. At times, she would even encourage her and say: " Well, my old Inés, and what have you done to-day? Come, that's not bad." Whereupon, Nathalie, greedily swallowing the flattering words, would return the compliment, and, sticking herself in front of Rosa's easel, would launch into congratulations and critical remarks, quite like a connoisseur.

Moreover, Nathalie Micas had a strong dash of sentimentality in her nature. Whenever she spoke of her mother, it was with a tremolo in her throat that smacked of melodrama; and yet there was really no affectation. She was naturally tragic, both in her waxen-coloured face and her majestic gestures, and every word that issued from her lips seemed solemn and prophetic. When a dreamy fit came on her and she went to air her melancholy in a solitary walk, her head surmounted with the red and black plumed hat, it was almost impossible for a person meeting her to help bursting into laughter. I recall having surprised her in one of these moods, and having made a sketch of her as Hamlet, holding in her hands a skull, which was mine, and exclaiming: " To By or not to By." My bad pun she did not understand, but being very good-natured, she never lost her temper over a joke made at her expense.

The elder M. Passy enjoyed immensely Mlle. Micas's letters and used to get much fun out of them. He once said to me: " Nathalie spoke as she wrote, always employing high-sounding words and absurd comparisons, and both her attire and physical appearance were in harmony with her style. Nothing was more comical than seeing this couple together, Rosa Bonheur, who, in her blouse, looked like a lad, and that tall, lank, pale woman, with her head crowned by a big hat with black and red plumes, who pronounced with a prophetic and dramatic tone pompous periods which had neither head nor tail."

Here is M. Chardin's sketch of Nathalie's mother:

Mme. Micas, although at bottom a very good-hearted woman, could not take a joke, and it would have been a risky matter to make her a butt. She was a stout dame, of imperturbable solemnity, having probably caught the Hispano-Portuguese gravity of the hidalgo who had been her spouse. I never saw her laugh. She spoke rarely, and each word that dropped from her lips seemed an oracle. She no doubt fancied that her position as housekeeper to a great artist (artiss, she pronounced it) rendered this dignity of attitude necessary.

On Sundays, I often beheld amusing scenes at By. As it was a holiday, Mme. Micas and Nathalie used frequently to invite their former neighbours and friends, small shopkeepers from the Faubourg du Temple, to come out to By. Some of them had known Rosa Bonheur when she was a girl, and she always welcomed them with her frank cordiality. These good people, much flattered to be on visiting terms with so celebrated a personage and emboldened by her simple and affable manners, expressed their opinions freely about the pictures that were being painted, their remarks being often most grotesque. Rosa Bonheur, far from treating them

MME. MICAS.

with disdain, replied to them and discussed her work just as if they had been experts. I recollect that at one of the dinners given to these half-educated nobodies, Rosa Bonheur happened to allude to the massacres of St. Bartholomew's Day, when one of the guests exclaimed, with a desire to show off: " Oh, yes; that took place in the time of Charles X." You mean Charles IX," I corrected. " Charles X or Charles IX, it's about the same thing," was the answer. There were only 258 years between the two reigns!

Mme. Micas especially prided herself on her cooking and you had to be careful never to ruffle her in this domain. I remember once, when I was invited to dine at the château, I arrived after a long ride on horseback, which had wonderfully sharpened my appetite; and I was imprudent enough, as it turned out, to mention to Mme. Micas that I was ravenously hungry. After the soup, we were told to expect a savoury dish, a superb carp caught out of the Seine and presented to Mlle. Bonheur by one of her country neighbours. Just before the fish was brought in, my nostrils were assailed by a sickly odour, and in proportion as it approached the table my stomach began to rise. Really, when the coachman, who was waiting on the table, put it before us, it stank!

" Since you are so hungry," said Mme. Micas, addressing me, " I will give you a large slice."

I protested my inability to eat any, owing to a sudden indisposition.

" But how can you refuse this fine fish just fresh from the river? " exclaimed Mme. Micas, looking much hurt.

In spite of my hunger, I declined again, while Rosa Bonheur, who didn't seem to mind the smell, partook of the dish with evident relish, and Mme. Micas helped herself twice.

The good lady's menus sometimes comprised most unusual mixtures. Thus, I recall that at one dinner roasted pigeons were served on a dish of sorrel. I ventured to express my astonishment, but I should have done better to hold my tongue. Mme. Micas was quite offended. Looking me up and down, she disdainfully observed:

" I, sir, have never seen pigeons served otherwise than on sorrel."

That settled it, at least for Mme. Micas. Even a Brillat-Savarin could not have changed her mind on this point.

M. Louis Passy adds these further details to the picture drawn by his old friend, M. Chardin:

I was the first of my family to make the acquaintance, about 1857 or 1858, of Rosa Bonheur, who was then at the height of her fame. I went to By two or three times, and, as she appeared to take a fancy to me, she visited us at our country home, at Gisors, in Normandy. My father entertained there many interesting persons, and my mother and he, who were of exceptional character and culture, became quite intimate with the distinguished painter. The first time Rosa Bonheur came, it was, she said, " to see the apple trees in bloom, one of the most beautiful sights of nature." This remark made a curious impression on me. Having been brought up largely in the country, I had never given particular attention to the superb vernal display of our apple trees, so many and so gorgeous in Normandy, " the land of cider." But to-day, when charmed by this brilliant spectacle, I always recall Rosa Bonheur and her enthusiasm for this delicate combination of variegated colours.

We also knew the Micases and were especially interested in the famous brake of Mlle. Micas. As my father was in a position to do so, he tried to aid Mlle. Micas to gain recognition for her invention. We interested in the affair M. Combes,[1] who was a colleague of my father at the Institute, and also the Péreires, who were then creating the railway system of France. Rosa Bonheur also helped in every way she could, and we were given to understand, at one moment, that the invention was a success. But I believe that it eventually turned out to be a failure.

Nathalie Micas imagined herself capable of doing great things for humanity. She was convinced of her own importance, took herself very seriously, and was amusing for the very reason that she thought she possessed exceptional talents, which made her equal to anything. For instance, I always supposed she knew how to play the guitar. But a common friend, who was better acquainted with her than I was, told me that I got this impression simply because Rosa Bonheur, who was always ready to poke fun at " dear Nathalie's foibles," used to pronounce her " a Spanish beauty " and would sometimes draw her with a guitar in her hands. In a word, Mlle. Micas was odd, original, and devoted.

Mme. Micas was a woman of little culture, who was not even sure of her French when she spoke. But she was an excellent housekeeper, who put order in Rosa's home. She could cook well and often did so. Rosa Bonheur sometimes dubbed her, but to her back, " Madame Vatel." My father used to say : " While Nathalie played the lady, Mme. Micas made the soup ! "

Though Rosa Bonheur had a strong affection for the Micases, mother and daughter, she was never " taken in " by the superior airs of the latter, and enjoyed the absurd side of her character as much as anybody else. She once remarked : " Sometimes I think

---

[1] Charles Combes (1801–72) was a distinguished engineer.

Nathalie would have made a fine wife for one of the court jesters of the olden time!" And yet, these two women certainly dominated Rosa Bonheur and partially separated her from her family. But she seemed to accept the situation, though she always showed, especially in the early years of her life, a marked love for kith and kin.

This episode of the railway brake is one of the most curious incidents in the joint relations of Rosa Bonheur and Nathalie Micas, and is so characteristic of the latter that it calls for some attention.

On April 2, 1863, four engineers of the Belgian Sambre and Meuse Railway, in whose shops the Micas brake was made, experimented with the invention on an inclined plane, and did not hesitate to sign a formal document which declared that, " after the trials which were made in our presence, the results obtained are very satisfactory, and we are convinced that if a few slight improvements are made in the invention it will be nearly perfect." At the first trial the train carried a load of 12,000 kilogrammes, and was moving at a speed of 25 to 30 kilometres per hour, but was stopped within a distance of about 12 metres. Several other trials were made with a load of 115,000 kilogrammes, the train moving at the same rate as before, with the result that it was brought to a standstill within a distance of about 200 metres " without the least shock or difficulty." Furthermore, these engineers do not hesitate to affirm that " the Micas brake is far superior to the Cabry brake, since, while the first stopped the train within 200 metres, the second, under similar conditions, only brought the train to a complete standstill within a distance of from 400 to 500 metres." Nor was this all. " We also believe that wear and tear of the rails and road-bed will be less than with the Cabry brake, and that there is less danger of derailing."

The foregoing document I found in the archives of the Paris, Lyons, and Mediterranean Railway Company, and is a reply to certain strictures made by an engineer of this company, who, in an official report dated August 12, 1862, gives the following description of the brake and an account of its trial:

The aim of this invention is to transform, momentarily, a car into a sort of sledge by introducing under the wheel a wedge which slips along the rail. There are eight wedges for each car, four for use when the train is moving forward and four when it is backing.

In accordance with orders, I went on July 23d to the château of By to see the model made by the inventor. I found there a little tramway about a hundred or more yards long, which began with a strong incline and ended with a level and a slight incline. The brakes were attached to three little platform cars about a yard long and two feet wide, which were several times started down the incline and stopped by means of the brakes. There was a person on each car. At these trials the brake worked well and the wedge under the wheel was easily freed. But I do not think it should be concluded therefrom that in actual practice the result would be the same. Everything of this kind is easy when weight and speed do not have to be reckoned with. My opinion is that if the Micas brake were applied to a real train, the experiment would simply bring out its mechanical defects, its cost and its problematical resistance.

The following letter from Mlle. Micas, addressed to P. J. Mène,[1] the animal sculptor, and his wife, was written from By at this moment:

It is a long time since you have heard from the two friends, and you must have thought them dead or forgetful. But they are neither the one nor the other. Rosa and the grand Pierrot are as busy as ever. But what the deuce do you think? The latter has gone and joined the band of poor mad inventors! Well, with the help of God, things are not going on too badly, though just now I am in great perplexity, having to undergo the visit of the engineers. I had one here yesterday, Friday, and am expect-

[1] For a biographical note on M. Mène, see page 215.

ing another on Wednesday. How the thing will go off, I cannot say. But this is certain—I shall not lose all the money I have put into my invention; for the visit of each one of these gentlemen acts like a medicine on me. You will see at the end of the year how my doctor's bill has decreased! As I don't want my friends to run the risk of a disappointment, I haven't asked them to come and see the first experiments. Moreover, I have still on my conscience the trouble I have given Rosa in making tiresome journeys for me in this connection. But, after all, I think everything is now going on all right, both as regards my invention and my health. I hope to get the government to appoint a commission to report on the former and as soon as this is accomplished, I mean to give all my friends a ride on my railway. If everything comes up to my expectation, I will be able to stop a train, at whatever speed it is going, within a distance of fifty meters without there being any shock at all. But there is great competition, and it is more difficult to convince than to invent. I must, therefore, wait, but I cannot say, patiently. I have been waiting so long that my stock of patience was exhausted some time ago.

To which letter Rosa Bonheur adds this postscriptum:

I am but a pygmy alongside of the great inventor, my friend Nana, who has put a brake on the fury of the trains. I hope you will soon come and see this curious piece of mechanism.

M. Hippolyte Peyrol, the sculptor, gives me this description of one of these rides, which probably followed close upon this letter:

On one occasion, when Mlle. Micas was experimenting, she got a half dozen of her lady friends, Mmes. Bourdon, Mène, Cain, Gauthier, etc., to mount on to her little platform cars, which were then started down the incline of the tramway at the end of the grounds. But when the party got to the bottom, either the brake would not work or it brought the train to a too sudden standstill—I cannot now remember which—with the result that these good ladies were all thrown off on to the grass and into the air, and though no bones were broken, there was a conspicuous display of white nether garments that made me, boy as I was, smile audibly.

Two more letters bearing on this affair may be given here, not so much for the light which they throw on it as for the light which they throw on the strange personality of Mlle. Micas. In 1862 Mlle. Micas wrote from By to M. Paul Chardin:

Notwithstanding all my fine successes, the difficulties remain the same. I beg of you, therefore, my good friend, to get M. Passy to write to the engineer Chimay. All those gentlemen who were here the day of the trial were enthusiastic about the result. But as we made the big mistake of not getting them to sign then and there a written statement to that effect, now no one of them dares to be the first to move in the matter. Though they are perfectly honourable men, as the inventor is not an engineer, they feel that they are in a hole and don't want to confess that they were surprised at the result.

This is much like what happens to one of those unfortunate natural children who comes into the world endowed by God only with distinction and intelligence. He is at first taken for a marquis or a duke, and all the best houses are thrown open to him. But when it is discovered that this genius has neither father nor mother, that he is worse than an orphan and that his only ancestry is his fortune, then everybody turns their back on him. Such is the conduct of the fashionable world. So do what you can for this pariah, my dear friend.

A little later we find her writing to M. Antoine Passy:

I learn from a letter of M. Chardin to my friend that you were kind enough to try and get me some help among your friends, and, although you did not succeed, I feel myself none the less under obligations to you and hasten to express to you all my gratitude.

It is a hard thing even to do good. Though I laboured with a humanitarian aim in view, I couldn't make anybody believe it. I found that it is uphill work to disturb vested interests, and my invention had the misfortune to intrench upon more than one. So, much against my will, I was forced to seek help from foreigners. It often happens thus that one cannot work for one's own country. But this should not deter us from doing what lies before one. I tried everything I could here in France before turning elsewhere. And my friend did the same. She went and saw, for example, the elder Péreire,[1] and asked him to have my brake tried on a half dozen cars. She agreed to pay the cost, either cash down or with a picture. They would probably have preferred the latter. The whole expense could not have exceeded four hundred dollars. But they didn't even take the trouble to answer her request, though they seemed happy to see her again, these people who drew her father into Saint Simonianism.[2] They have invited her to call this winter in a social way, for it is very nice to have a great artist in one's drawing-room! But it isn't worth while to lose time saying " Yes " or " No " to this same artist.

Such is man, my dear sir; and yet there are those who are surprised that people become misanthropical.[3] We must live like a rat in her hole. But I see that a wish to unbosom myself is causing me to digress. Please excuse me and believe me, with renewed thanks, yours very sincerely.

The real trouble which lay in the way of Mlle. Micas is best expressed, perhaps, by Mr. E. A. Gautray, mentioned towards the end of Chapter I., a retired foreman of the railway shops of the Paris, Lyons and Mediterranean Company, at Clermont-Ferrand, who writes me as follows:

Hundreds of such inventions are presented. Attention is paid to those that come from the railway shops; for, after a little modification, the chief engineer can get the credit for them. But an invention sent in by an outsider, especially if this outsider be a woman, is looked upon as a sort of intrusion and does not receive

---

[1] Emile Péreire (1800–75) and his brother Isaac (1806–80) were ardent Saint Simonians and active in introducing railways into France.

[2] Spelt "sinsimonisme" by Mlle. Micas.   [3] Spelt "misantrope."

a warm welcome. So it was fatal to Mlle. Micas's hopes that her brake had to combat this prejudice.

I now take up a disappointment of quite another kind which came to Mlle. Micas a year or two later. It is described rather humorously, and not perfectly exactly, in these paragraphs from the manuscript memoirs of the late Joseph Verdier [1]:

One day Rosa Bonheur was painting with her usual ardour, while Nathalie Micas was taking a bath in a room opening into the studio, when, suddenly, a noise outside reached their ears, and soon the head of a scared servant appeared in the doorway.

"I thought I told you to let no one in," said Rosa angrily, before he could speak; "who is it?"

"It is the Empress, Miss, with a lot of ladies and gentlemen," replied the man.

"The Empress!"

"Yes, Miss; she asked me if you could receive her. They are coming upstairs now."

After rushing to close the bath-room door, Rosa glanced at her own attire.

"Well," she exclaimed with a laugh, "I do look a sight for receiving visitors, and such visitors!"

Quickly laying aside her palette and brush, she tried to pull off her blouse. But just as it was being wiggled over her head, the door creaked and she heard a voice say:

"Oh, Mademoiselle, I am so sorry to have disturbed you. Let me at least help you."

The Empress showed great cordiality, said she would come again, and invited the artist to visit the Emperor and herself at Fontainebleau. Lastly, before going away, she took from one of her officers a small box containing the cross and red ribbon of the Legion of Honour, and pinned it with her own hands on to Rosa Bonheur's bodice.

Nathalie Micas was enraged at being compelled to remain in her bath-room and miss the introduction to royalty. Nor did she recover from her disappointment for some time.

---

[1] For a biographical note on M. Verdier, see page 273.

SHEEP UNDER A SHADE TREE.
By Auguste Bonheur.

The Empress Eugénie called twice on Rosa Bonheur in her studio. The two visits were about a year apart. The first, which occurred in the summer of 1864, is thus described by M. Hippolyte Peyrol, Sr.:

One afternoon, when Rosa Bonheur and I were quite alone at By, the Court came for the first time to the studio. We were smoking our after-luncheon cigarettes, when we heard out on the highroad the tinkle of carriage bells and the clatter of horses' hoofs. Listening for a moment, Rosa said:

" I feel in my bones that this is Madame ——, coming to bother me. She herself isn't bad; but she always brings with her a lot of uninteresting folk. She ought to see that this disturbs me dreadfully. Do go and tell Félicité to say that I am out."

I was just starting to carry out my sister-in-law's instructions, when the door suddenly opened and the maid, all in a fluster, rushed in exclaiming:

" Mademoiselle, Mademoiselle, it's the Court, the Empress!"

When this announcement was made, Rosa was attired in her blue working blouse, which she immediately started to take off. But in her haste and the excitement of the moment she had forgotten to undo the top button of the garment and, consequently, her head wouldn't go through! For an instant, we both feared she might be caught in this ludicrous position by the imperial party. Finally, however, she succeeded in extricating herself from the plaguey blouse and getting into a sort of jacket which she wore indoors, just as the Empress, accompanied by a dozen ladies and gentlemen of the Court circle, swept into the studio. Rosa, who quickly recovered her composure, to which the Empress's charming manner contributed not a little, showed the distinguished company some of her work, I aiding as best I could. After a pretty long stay, the Empress, who seemed much pleased, retired, leaving Rosa and myself somewhat stunned by this kind but unexpected visit.

At the second call of the Empress, it was my wife who happened to be with Rosa at the moment. But they had been informed the night before of the intended visit. It was on this occasion that the cross of the Legion of Honour was bestowed on

Rosa, the Empress herself attaching the decoration to the lapel of Rosa's jacket.

One or two letters of Rosa Bonheur bearing on this incident may be given here. Thus, she writes from By June 15, 1864, to her brother Auguste and her sister:

MY DEAREST PIPON AND JULIETTE:

I am happy to announce to you that yesterday I received the most gracious visit that a sovereign can pay to an artist, and that I am most deeply touched by it. Her Majesty came with all her Court to surprise me. You may fancy, my Juliette, how gladly I would, at first, have hidden myself in any mouse-hole. Fortunately, I only had to pull off my blouse and put on a jacket, but, in my confusion and haste, I couldn't get my head out of my blouse collar. But at last I freed myself, just in time to make my appearance, and somehow or other welcome her very gracious, very good and charming Majesty. Luckily, Hippolyte happened to be in the studio, and he helped me, quite simply and nicely, to exhibit my dust-covered sketches.

The Empress spoke to me of you, my dear old Pipon, in the most flattering manner. Isidore's name also came up, which gives me great hope for the next exhibition. I expect to see you, my dear Auguste, on Saturday in Paris, and will then give you further details about the high favour shown your sister.

I am going to paint a picture for the Empress. She gave me the order in the most charming manner, and I intend to do my best to execute it in a creditable fashion. As I was taking her to her carriage, she held out her hand to me, and I thought it my duty to kiss it. Thereupon, with the greatest kindness, this sovereign, whose simplicity and affability add to her distinction, did me the honour to embrace me. I don't think a higher mark of esteem and favour could have been shown me. Yet I must not forget to mention the invitation I have received to the Castle at Fontainebleau and the announcement of a possible visit of the Emperor himself.

There, my dear brother and sister, my dear Marie,[1] is the piece

---

[1] The wife of Auguste Bonheur.

of news I wanted to tell you. I will write about it to Dodore [1] and to Tatan,[2] who will no doubt do a weep and ask if I was not very stupid in the midst of it all.

Rosa, still at By, writes the following year concerning the second visit of the Empress:

DEAR MONSIEUR CHARDIN, MY ESTEEMED RAPIN [3]:

Subjects are not wanting, forsooth, for illustration, referable to the great day when Nathalie shared my glory. Just at the critical moment of the entrance, she was taking a Barèges bath. She got out hurridly, with a slipper on one foot and a buskin on the other; for, in moments of embarrassment, it is a case of putting on whatever is handy. A white dressing-gown, together with a feather-trimmed hat, completed her attire in this instance! But instead of writing you all about it, I prefer to keep the rest of the narration for the first favourable occasion when we meet, especially as I am counting upon you as my partner in the lancers at no distant day.

Here may be placed the reminiscences of some of the friends of Rosa Bonheur which bear upon her relations with the Micases.

Princess Stirbey writes:

Mlle. Micas, herself a painter, lived, so to speak, under the shadow of the great artist. She played in Rosa Bonheur's life an important part which did not count in the esteem of ordinary people. On the whole, it was a necessary and beneficent part. Rosa Bonheur could never have remained the celebrated artist she was without some one beside her, at each instant, to spare her the material cares of the household, the daily worries of existence, and to help her also with moral and physical support, as well as with advice in many things relating to her art. Nathalie made

---

[1] Nickname of Isidore Bonheur.
[2] Nickname of the aunt of Rosa Bonheur.
[3] The French word for a young and inexperienced student of painting. It was Rosa Bonheur's favourite nickname for M. Chardin.

herself small, ungrudgingly, so that Rosa might become greater. She surrounded her with attention and affection throughout the years that she was her companion.

This exclusive, sisterly love had, doubtless, its inconveniences, at least for others. Nathalie Micas kept people away from Rosa Bonheur in order that the latter might work without being exposed to the disturbances and importunities from which celebrities have to suffer so much. It may be, too, that she showed herself jealous of certain persons whom Rosa Bonheur numbered among her friends. However, I never had to complain of this myself. Nathalie Micas always welcomed me with pleasure and I owe this testimony to her memory.

Prince Stirbey has said to me:

Three persons, or groups of persons, outside of her own family, had an influence on the development of Rosa Bonheur.

She came up to Paris at the moment when a grand school of landscape painting was in full sway there, when Troyon, Daubigny and Corot were captivating the world. It was a splendid epoch and she was dazzled by its splendour. Her admiration centered especially in Troyon, whom she admired and considered as a sort of god. She owed much also to the father-in-law of Auguste Cain, Mène, both animal sculptors. The latter often corrected her work, and to the end of her life she remained on intimate terms with the Cain-Mène families.

Ernest Gambart had also something to do with the art development of Rosa Bonheur. This may sound strange, at first blush. It was not due wholly to the fact that Gambart was a remarkable connoisseur in pictures, but chiefly to the fact that he was a Jew, by which remark I do not mean to cast a reflection on his race, but simply wish to say that when he found talent, he knew how to trade on it. He had Rosa Bonheur go over to England and visit Scotland, that she might make the acquaintance of those lands, see the strange little Scotch ponies, study the cattle and note the particular type of its inhabitants. This made her popular in Great Britain, where Gambart resided. She immediately began to sell pictures there and the number grew steadily in importance, which was good for her purse and her artistic morale, and which gave Gambart a fortune. In a word, he monopolised her, both to his own and to her material advantage; and this excellent state of things continued to the end.

The third influence was that of Mlle. Micas, and it was a beneficent one. She saw in Rosa Bonheur an admirably gifted woman. She was able to judge her nature, and made it the business of life to render her friend's work easy. She and her mother freed Rosa Bonheur from all household worries, from all the details concerning the sale of the pictures, from all kinds of business correspondence, so that she had all her time for her art work and for letter-writing to her friends and family. This is the chief reason why Rosa Bonheur's epistolary product is remarkably large.

Mlle. Rosa Mathieu has said to me:

The long companionship that existed between my godmother and Nathalie Micas was, I may say, more than beneficial to both. Of the two, Nathalie possessed the better education and instruction, and her constant presence certainly did much to polish Rosa Bonheur, who, however, remained even to the end somewhat of a diamond in the rough. Nathalie had enough artistic appreciation in her composition to understand Rosa's perfection in art, but her own character and aptitudes were more those of the pedagogue. In fact, she was never so happy as when administering correction of some kind or another, unless, perhaps, when she varied the correction with medical dosing and amateur surgery. These pedagogic activities, however, did not disturb Rosa's equanimity, probably because she realised the deep affection that lay between them. Nathalie Micas literally worshipped Rosa Bonheur. The latter had her painting as well as having Nathalie; but Nathalie had only Rosa, which will explain why she was sometimes jealous of Rosa Bonheur's other friendships. Many examples might be given of my godmother's affection for Nathalie. But the following one will suffice:

One day Rosa Bonheur had just finished a picture which was still wet, and was standing before it, brush in hand, absorbed in

99

her last examination and desire to be quite sure that there were no further touches to be added. At this moment Nathalie came with a biscuit for Rosa, and not daring to interrupt, lightly placed it on the top of the frame. This movement was executed, however, somewhat awkwardly, so that some of the sugar and fine crumb of the biscuit fell down on the canvas and adhered to the wet paint. The damage was not irremediable but was sufficiently serious to necessitate a tedious labour of picking off almost individually each grain of sugar and crumb. Nathalie was naturally in the greatest distress, but my godmother took the matter very philosophically and seemed more concerned to reassure her friend than about the injury to her picture.

Rosa Bonheur's meeting with Madame and Nathalie Micas was an event in her early life the importance of which can hardly be over-estimated. It occurred at a time when she was wasting her artistic talent in painting pot-boilers, fans, signs even, anything that would sell, in order to live and increase the resources of the family. The home which Mme. Micas offered her enabled her to complete her artistic studies without further anxiety as to ways and means.

Mme. Micas was a woman of great mental capacity and sterling character, who had amassed a very decent fortune in the manufacture of spectacle-cases, carrying on, though a widow, a business that occupied twenty work-women. She spared no money to give Nathalie an education, sending her to a boarding school in Paris where Raymond Bonheur gave drawing lessons. When Rosa Bonheur went to live with her, Mme. Micas had already retired from business and had taken a house in the Rue d'Assas, which was given up only when the By property was bought a few years later, partly with her own money, partly with Rosa Bonheur's.

Nathalie Micas possessed her mother's capacity of mind, but intensified and capable of embracing many branches of knowledge. A tolerable artist, as a picture I have of hers proves, she also dabbled in science, was fond of mechanics, and had considerable literary ability, as her letters relating her and Rosa's early journeys abundantly show. Her special hobby was medicine and amateur surgery, which she indulged by operating on Rosa's pets;

one amusing sketch by the great artist representing a young lion with Nathalie administering an enema to him.

In any attempt to appreciate Rosa Bonheur's work as a whole, and the success which so early crowned her artistic efforts, the share of the two Micases, both mother and daughter, should be adequately acknowledged. They supplied the fostering influence of atmosphere, so essential in the development of art, and as long as they lived they made it possible for Rosa to live with her painting and for her painting without any outside interference or disturbance that might have made its expression less perfect.

M. Henri Cain says much the same thing, but more briefly:

From early womanhood, Rosa Bonheur and Nathalie Micas were closely united. Their affections, well-being, and occupations were one. Mme. Micas was, in fact, her guardian angel, relieving her from all material worries, taking care of the house, and thus making it possible for Rosa to live her beautiful dream of an artist. Rosa Bonheur often felt a real admiration for Nathalie Micas. Everything the latter did, the former was disposed to approve of; and as regards Mlle. Micas's feelings toward Rosa Bonheur, why, she simply worshipped her.

The warm attachment between the two young women gave rise to more than one fantastic and unauthentic statement. Thus, Mme. Paul Le Bret, Gustave d'Eichthal's daughter, who, as a child, saw Rosa Bonheur frequently, has said to me:

One of the reasons why Rosa Bonheur was so attached to Mlle. Micas is to be found in the power which the latter pretended to possess of hypnotising animals. By looking them firmly in the eyes, she could keep them still while her friend Rosa transferred them to paper or canvas, with pencil or brush.

On the margin of one of the pages of M. de Mirecourt's pamphlet mentioned in a previous chapter, Rosa Bonheur wrote:

As to Nathalie's power of subduing by her gaze any animal I wished to paint, this is another tall story served to the public.

101

She was not my amanuensis, as M. de Mirecourt says; she was my well-beloved friend. She was my equal in everything, and my superior in many things. She preserved me from being spotted by the mud that was thrown at me. Her mother helped me to pay the debts due at my father's death. The only reward of both was that they received the mud meant for me.

Some of the shadows on the picture have been referred to in the foregoing pages. "Rosa Bonheur's friendship with Nathalie Micas," writes Joseph Verdier in his manuscript memoirs, "was not without its inconveniences both for herself and her other friends. The latter's jealousy of any other affection than her own led her to sow discord on more than one occasion between Rosa and those who were attached to her." Céline Rey, the faithful old servant of Rosa Bonheur, once said to me: "When Mme. Carvalho [1] made a visit to By, Mlle. Micas went out of one door as Mme. Carvalho came in the other, and remained in Fontainebleau throughout the visit." These jealousies and the very decided character of Rosa Bonheur sometimes strained the relations between the two friends to the point of an open rupture. Rosa Bonheur's correspondence with her family and friends occasionally shows traces of this, as will be seen farther on in this volume. But these storms quickly blew over, and when Nathalie Micas passed away, June 22, 1889, it was the severest blow of Rosa Bonheur's life. We find her writing from By, July 7, 1889, to Mme. Auguste Cain:

My health is very good. I am like iron in that respect. As for my mind, my dear friend, you can very well understand how hard it is to be separated from a friend like my Nathalie, whom I loved more and more as we advanced in life; for she had borne, with me, the mortifications and stupidities inflicted on us by silly, ignorant, low-minded people, who form the majority on this terrestrial ball, called the earth. She alone knew me, and I, her only friend, knew what she was worth. We both of us made ourselves

---

[1] Miolan-Carvalho (1827–95), the well-known prima donna.

humble, so as not to hurt the feelings of other people, while we were too proud to seek the confidence of idiots who doubted us. Keep this outpouring of my heart for yourselves alone, my old friends. I should be very sorry to pain anybody.

If, for the moment, I desire to be a little quiet and to remain at home, it is in order to get ready to resume work, to put my affairs in order, to pay my debts, to see what the State is going to charge for my inheritance,[1] and to conform to the law.

Several letters somewhat similar to the foregoing one will be found in this volume, under the year 1889, in the two chapters devoted exclusively to Rosa Bonheur's correspondence with her relatives and friends, and which place in a still stronger and nobler light the deep and pure attachment which these two women had for each other.

---

[1] There was a tacit understanding between the two friends that the first to die should leave her fortune to the other.

CHAPTER V

At the beginning of June, 1850, Rosa Bonheur and Nathalie Micas started for the south of France on a journey which lasted until the latter part of September. Both of them were in poor health, Nathalie appearing to have got into a low nervous state accompanied by a good deal of intermittent fever. As a remedy, they were advised to drink the waters and to frequent the baths of one or two celebrated places in the region of the Pyrenees; and acting on the recommendation, they proceeded to Eaux-Bonnes, later to St. Sauveur, and finally to Barèges, all famous for the sulphurous properties of their waters.

As a record of this trip we have a series of long letters written by Nathalie to her mother, with some few written by Rosa. Nathalie's letters are largely made up of the tender effusions an affectionate daughter, separated from a mother she loves, knows so well how to write. There are, besides, a certain number of passages descriptive of the scenery, which have considerable merit, and reveal in Mlle. Micas a power of words and of eye that show her to have possessed artistic faculties of no common order. They also serve to illustrate the qualities and sentiments which made this young woman a fit companion for Rosa Bonheur, and fully explain the terrible void which her subsequent death left in the life of the latter.

The two girls found Eaux-Bonnes to be a fashionable place, very dear, where the inhabitants excelled in fleecing visitors with the most amiable manners and looks imaginable. The women were pretty, black-haired, white-teethed, but dirty. The snow-

104

clad mountains in the distance assumed the strangest forms, the snow itself seeming like ghosts climbing up the soaring heights. " We have been some beautiful walks," Rosa writes, " but done no real work, which is beginning to bore us, for one cannot be in the presence of these lovely mountains without longing to get a picture of them in one's portfolio."

Of course Rosa Bonheur donned man's attire most of the time, and it appears that Nathalie Micas did the same, at least during certain parts of this trip. They tell how the gendarmes of Pau took Rosa at first for a young man, and had a good laugh on recognising their error. Notwithstanding her masculine dress, Nathalie informs us that Rosa was a most skilful and delicate-handed nurse. The former was suffering, among other things, from an affection of the eyes, which required a daily dressing, and it was the latter who applied the lotion in such a way as to avoid giving pain. They could not afford the luxury of trained nurses, for their resources were not great, and Mme. Micas was in part their banker. They contented themselves with rooms that were anything but palatial. The bed was hardly two feet wide, the mattress was a sorry one, and the bolster so low that Rosa raised it a little higher with a paint box. Most of the furniture was rickety, and there were so many mice in the room that the two occupants were obliged to bribe the little rodents with bread to prevent them from attacking the clothing.

If, however, the inside was not very comfortable, the outdoor charms of the region were a compensation. When the weather allowed, for the year was a wet one, the two companions were always abroad, now going to drink the waters at the Hontalade, when they were at St. Sauveur, whither the blessing of an old beggar, to whom they had given their mite, followed them with its good augury; now meeting with a handsome shepherd who played on his flute a mountain air that was full of poetry.

One of their amusements was a vulture-shooting expedition organised by a gentleman who admired Rosa's artistic talent. Nathalie explains the method adopted with a view to get the bird within gunshot. " A sheep is killed and is placed on the plateau of a mountain, the intestines being scattered in various directions and the animal's blood poured on the ground some distance away. The vulture is attracted either by the smell or the object, and, advancing with precaution toward the spot, pounces upon the prey, if it sees no one near." We are further told that during the expedition that preceded this one no fewer than twenty-three vultures were seen.

It appears that vultures were not the only game to be found in the neighbourhood of the Pyrenean watering places half a century ago. While Rosa and Nathalie were at Eaux-Bonnes a huge bear was killed not far from where they were lodging. No wonder the good mother at Paris was nervous when she read the letters containing these accounts. Nor were all her fears removed when Rosa wrote her: " Don't worry; the roads are quite safe, and we don't go where there is the least danger." Nor was the excellent housewife probably less perturbed when she learned that the girls had bought a big dog. Fearing that Mme. Micas would object to receiving the animal in a pent-up city house, Rosa wrote to apologise for what she had done. " Nathalie will have told you that I have allowed myself to be led into temptation. It is true, I confess. But what a dog he is! A mountain-dog who will become as big as a donkey. But how, after all, can one help doing things of this sort, when one is so apt as I am to fall into the besetting sin? There is one good excuse, however, in this instance, for this creature will be a protection, belonging to a breed that knows only his master, and will attach himself to no other person. I intend to accustom him to watch inside my studio at night, and, I assure you, I shall be able to leave my key in the door with a fellow of this sort behind it."

Another amusement which they indulged in occasionally was horseback riding, which was considerably facilitated by their male attire. " Both Nathalie and I are pretty well; we tuck in a good deal," writes Rosa in her usual offhand style, " and in addition to this, we are gaining quite a reputation as horsewomen." It was probably astride of horses that they twice made the grandiose excursion to Gabas, through the famous Ossau Valley, which Nathalie describes quite graphically in one of her letters. " The road is hewn out of huge mountains in granite, and the way lies over several bridges which overhang a dreadful torrent that rumbles still more dreadfully. Here several cascades meet, and after travelling for some distance, the granite mountains give place to pine forests that flank the torrent on either side. These forests themselves grow on the mountain sides or in gorges of colossal size. Nothing can be more imposing than this vast spectacle of nature. The only thing I regret is that the spot is too far for us to go there often enough to paint it."

The journey to St. Sauveur was made in company with an abbot and his sister, presumably in a carriage, which cost Rosa and Nathalie less by sharing the expenses with the others. Following the chain of the lower Pyrenees, with its charming landscape, they again entered the Ossau Valley round which rose mountains on every side. It was a change from a region of copses and groves to find themselves in the midst of the Bearn country, the earlier home of Henry of Navarre. Here they struck the torrent once more, and winding along its banks, passed between natural grottoes offering the most fantastic shapes. Soon they came to the magnificent valley of Lourdes, bordered with gigantic-treed forests, whose branches spread themselves with majestic sweeps seldom seen elsewhere. " The valley," writes Nathalie, " is not content to possess a fertility of the richest kind; it rejoices also in its historic monument. This monument is an old fortified castle that commands the whole plain, being built on a huge rock. Nothing can be finer or more imposing than this ancient pile which has withstood time and weather for perhaps two thousand years." Nathalie probably refers to the famous château at Lourdes.

The travellers were disappointed with the appearance of Bétharram, where they stopped for lunch. This place is a favourite resort for pilgrims and possesses a calvary which Nathalie would have liked to ascend, but was prevented by weakness. Tall houses with low black marble doors and small windows of the same material gave to the streets a melancholy air and an atmosphere from which they were glad to escape. Happily the plains along which they continued their journey were in bright contrast; maize and wheat fields, fruit-laden orchards, with a mellow sun overhead, welcomed them on their way. The vines especially attracted Nathalie's attention. "They are not stunted ones," she writes, " like those that make your back ache when you gather the grapes. Their supports are trees—oaks, walnuts, cherry-trees, and even pear-trees." Nothing could be more charming than this " intermingling of vine-branches with those of the trees, together coquettishly forming bowers that would tempt for a second time our mother Eve." She continues:

At half past seven in the evening we reached the road leading into St. Sauveur, where a new landscape awaited us. Instead of plain and fertile vales, we were again among the mountains, not, however, the granite heights of the Gabas Valley, with the warm waters of Eaux-Chaudes, but the loftier peaks, cultivated for the most part half-way up, which gives to the surroundings a less wild aspect yet without detracting from the grandeur.

This journey, as a set-off to its agreeable side, was the cause of one small annoyance. During the change of carriages at Bétharram, Rosa's and Nathalie's paint-boxes were mislaid so that, on arriving at destination, the young artists were minus their working materials. Nor could their hotel accommodations hardly be called an improvement on those of Eaux-Bonnes. Their room, we are told, was nothing more than a decent-sized closet, some eight feet by six, with a wretched little centre-table and an old green shawl of check pattern for a carpet. The bed was in keeping, and they had to supply their own candles. Even the physician's science consisted " mostly in long words," and the water treatment, whatever its efficacies, involved a continual tipping of attendants, not to speak of hotel waiters, which was most potent in lightening the girls' purses. Luckily, Rosa was able to announce, almost immediately after their arrival, that the baths, which they rose as early as four o'clock in the morning to take, were doing them more good than those of Eaux-Bonnes. " The country, too," she adds, " is more admirable than that we have just left."

But the wet weather pursued them still and the fuel was at times so damp that they had difficulty in lighting a fire. One day, after trying in vain to make the wood ignite, a bright idea struck them. They rummaged out some of the stuffing of their mattress, and, with this novel combustible, managed to obtain a blaze. Among other things they had to do for themselves was occasionally a little cooking. In one of her letters Nathalie writes: " You know what funny tastes dear Rosa has. For instance, for some days she has been clamouring for maize gruel; so I have made her some. I don't know whether she will go into ecstasies over my attempt, but I do know that I myself find it a very nasty mixture."

This tender care of Nathalie for Rosa, examples of which are scattered all through this correspondence, was fully reciprocated by the latter. About this time, for instance, Rosa was solicited by some of her pupils to return to Paris. She refused, however, not being willing to abandon Nathalie, who appears to have had a slight relapse. A change of room, which carried them to a higher floor, gave them better accommodation than the uncomfortable closet they had been inhabiting, and Nathalie soon improved in health. In a letter to Mme. Micas, alluding to this removal, Rosa writes:

At present we can at least breathe, and Nathalie has got over her attack. She has suffered a good deal, poor girl; but at this moment she is asleep and quite easy again. I shall let her take a long nap. I am so glad she can sleep. I could never leave her alone, she is so weak and has so much need of some one to love her and make up for the physical pain she has gone through. Ah! she has just woke up; sooner than I wished. But never mind; the worst is now over. By the way, Nathalie has no doubt told you

109

that we don't need more money, though the poor girl is quite in a way to be spending while her mother is working. But when she gets better, she, too, is intending to work, in which she takes after you, for you know she is not of an idle nature. As for myself, I am better and hope these waters will give me back my strength. Then I will paint some fine pictures and earn a good deal of money, so as not to be always a burden to you, as I am at present. Yet I know that what you do is done with pleasure because you love me as your own child. On my side, I love you just as much, and am your number two daughter.

The last part of this letter throws a flood of light on Rosa Bonheur's relations with the Micas family; explains why there was a tacit understanding between the two girls, which was afterward carried out, to the effect that the first to die should bequeath her earthly possessions to the other; largely accounts for Rosa Bonheur's partial separation from the members of her own family, her deep love for Nathalie, her poignant sorrow at her death, and the great comfort which she found in the closing months of her life by discovering in the American artist, Miss Klumpke, a congenial substitute for her earlier confidante.

The finest description Nathalie's letters afford was occasioned by a visit to one of the magnificent natural spectacles near St. Sauveur, which Rosa announced as follows in a short note to Mme. Micas, before starting: " We are mounting on horseback to go to the famous Cirque de Gavarnie. I warrant you it is a son you have at present." Nathalie continues the narration in these words:

The weather is fine and the mountains stood out majestically against the azure firmament, so that everything could be clearly distinguished. Our horses were noble steeds, capable of doing fifteen miles in three hours. At eight o'clock we mounted, to the great amazement of the onlookers. The guide cracks his whip and away we gallop in triumph. After half an hour, we come upon the most fascinating panorama, even to our eyes, by this time accustomed to see vast landscapes. To the left of our road are huge mountains, not like those of Gabas, in granite. Here they

GOATS ON THE MOUNTAIN.

By Auguste Bonheur.

have a warmer appearance to the eye, for these rocks contain a ferruginous ore which gives them a reddish tint. In addition, there is the glinting of the sun's rays which diffuse a dazzling light over all. Many of the stones are crystallised so that at times you are able to imagine yourself transported into some region of the " Arabian Nights." These various scintillating ores so take up your attention that you momentarily forget the huge precipice you have on the right, a precipice you are unable to fathom with the eye.

At last we come to the Ladder Bridge. It is a bridge constructed on top of another. Over this we pass and from it we see on either side of us the Gave, formidably great, a frightful abyss in which foaming waters swirl and rage in a manner impossible to describe. It is not water; it is a mass of snow-white froth resembling soapsuds. Farther distant from the waterfall, you find a calmer spot where the running stream regains its purity and reflects the azure blue of the sky. After admiring this magnificent spectacle, we resume our journey with the Gave now on our left, and passing by several poor hamlets composed of a few little houses nestling among the rocks, we reach the great chaos. Great is the proper word, for a greater pell-mell could not be conceived. There are boulders as big as a house which seem to have been broken off from the mountain in some cataclysm, and to have rolled down into the valley. Nothing more terrible can be imagined than these huge blocks of granite that hang suspended over your head. You fear that the slipping of a little pebble would suffice to set them a-falling, and instinctively your heart begins to beat faster while you hasten your steps. Yet this sort of nightmare has stood there for centuries, and, right in the midst of these boulders, human hands have cut a road. You perceive when you get near to them how shaky the base is. You fancy that an accidental kick could displace one of these boulders, which, furthermore, appear dwarfed to the size of an ordinary stone by the colossal dimensions of those that are above. Nor is this the only cause of anxiety. Under these rocks one might often fear to encounter wild beasts or brigands, these natural caves being well adapted for lairs or dens.

At length we catch sight of the snows of Gavarnie, and the

guide points out to us the breach made by Rolland, Charlemagne's Roland. By eleven o'clock we arrive at the immense circus or amphitheatre which is animated only by the presence of occasional flocks and wild birds, and where we find a few wild iris lilies and daisies. From the plain, we go on climbing still, up a mountain which rises to a height of two thousand feet and which is the source of eight waterfalls. The water has so far to tumble that it looks like a fine dust studded with precious stones, an effect produced by the sun's rays. This mountain is called the Marboré, from the marble of which it is composed. Nearly half way up, the sides of the mountain form tiers which are in regular order and are covered with snow. After lunch we went to the foot of the cascade which I have just mentioned, where the violence of the falling water created such a far-reaching fine rain that we were obliged to keep at a respectful distance. Here, amid the rocks, we gathered a little white flower resembling a forget-me-not, and another small blue flower, which Rosa and I send you. At three o'clock, we remount our horses and return to St. Sauveur.

Another mountain excursion, this time to the Pic de Bergons, enabled the travellers to get a glimpse of the whole chain of the Pyrenees, right away to Spain. Four large eagles hovering above their heads increased the wildness of the prospect. Nathalie writes:

We again see the superb Marboré and the lovely cascade; but what we took for tiers of snow, we now perceive to be immense inaccessible glaciers. Once more we behold the huge plateau that goes by the name of Roland's Breach. The guides relate you quite seriously the story as to how it was produced. They tell you without a quiver that Roland made the breach with his sword, though, in the same breath, they declare this breach to be at least six hundred feet in width! And they themselves appear to fully believe what they are saying. In speaking of the prints of the horses' hoofs, which are in-proportion to the rest, they are just as credulous.

This excursion was made on donkeys, " which cost quite as dear as horses; but, then, Rosa wished to study these queer little animals. 'One of the best ways to get acquainted with a beast,' she says, ' is to get on his back.' " At the summit of the mountain, Rosa and Nathalie made each a rough sketch of the landscape and enjoyed a rustic lunch by the side of a spring, " while the asses browsed near us." Both of them were struck by " the harmonious symphonies produced in the mountain air by the lowing of oxen, the bleating of ewes, and by the voices of other animals that all seemed to be in possession of the purest happiness." Among the other charms of such rambling were the amateur botanising and geologising they did. Now it was a magnificent rhododendron they discovered, now some mineralised stones in which Rosa found a curious mixture of copper, silver, and iron. They also came across a village wedding-party, " not too young," since the bridegroom was forty-five, the bride thirty, and the husband's mother eighty-one. This, however, did not exclude mirth and Rosa and Nathalie danced with the guests.

These touches of the comic are scattered through the letters of both of the girls, who thus early, and especially in the case of Rosa, had a considerable sense of humour, which was, in fact, one of the points of contact between their characters. " I have managed to get nicely sunburnt," writes Nathalie at this time; " my forehead and nose are a fine craw-fish red. When I go back to Paris I shall be able to earn my living, if other means fail, by exhibiting myself as a red-skin." Rosa writes: " Nathalie is combing her pigtail. She is titivating in preparation to see the doctor, and has a weakness for this sort of mammiferous animal. Your children, furthermore, are not idle in the mountains. By the side of a poetic torrent we have washed some of our linen. I soap very well. In fact, Nathalie is quite pleased with my labour and has complimented me highly."

Rosa Bonheur visited the Pyrenees on several other occasions. References to these excursions are found scattered through her correspondence with her family and friends. Thus, to Mme. Verdier she writes from Cauterets, on August 18, 1853, three years after the tour just described:

REMINISCENCES OF ROSA BONHEUR

Three days ago a splendid bear was killed close to here. I saw it brought in in triumph. It was a female and the little ones were with her in the same mountain. I am sorry I could not take part in the hunt. By the way, speaking of animals, I may tell you that I have an otter which was caught in one of the lakes hereabouts. You can't imagine how intelligent the little creature is. I am trying to train it to bring me what it catches in fishing.

The extracts from the following letters were all written from Cauterets in this same year, 1853. To her sister, Mme. Peyrol, she wrote on September 3d:

I am now less charmed with my excursion than when I began it. Rain has been coming down ever since the wind has ceased blowing from Spain, though thereby we no longer get its insupportable heat. I fret, for there are so many fine studies I want to make and can't; so much material I could utilise, flocks and herds so picturesque. In order not to lose my time altogether, I am making some rough sketches of Spanish people. You would so like the men's manly faces. How I should enjoy admiring, in your company, my own Juju, the fine landscapes here. But it is only a pleasure deferred, I hope. I mean to earn a good deal of the "filthy lucre," for it is only with that that you can do what you like. If I had had enough this year, you should have come with me.

Fame is not without its inconveniences as well as its agreeable side. Up to now I had succeeded in keeping my incognito; but at present I am receiving cards from all quarters, and my hotel landlord, who is an artist of his kind, is so proud to have me in his house that he walks about the streets singing my praises. Yesterday, just as I was preparing to go and dine with Princess Kourakine, an excellent woman and lady-in-waiting to the Russian Empress, M. Pradet, the landlord in question, presented me with a missive on a salver, politely informing me that it was prepaid. I opened it and read:

Ode Addressed by J. Pradet,
Landlord of the Hôtel de l'Europe, Cauterets,
To the Great Mademoiselle Rosa Bonheur.

I am keeping the poem for you, it being really worth reading. We enjoyed it yesterday at the Princess's, and you may imagine our dessert was a merry one. The Princess, by the way, is intending to call on us in Paris and wants to know us all. Her children she is bringing up with the utmost simplicity, and tells them they are the brothers and sisters of the poor little peasant children. This is sensible and noble.

Such are the honours that attend your sister everywhere, and they are sometimes useful. All the country people like me and the Spanish men look at me with a favourable eye. Mariano, a famous smuggler, whom it is impossible to capture, he is so clever and so much dreaded, and who says he has never sat for his portrait to any one but me—what an honour for me! —has been to lunch with me at the hotel. In spite of the distrust which he inspires in me, he appears to have taken a fancy to me, and goes about the country saying he would give his life for me.

I have tamed a still wilder specimen; a man who never remains here more than an hour at a time. Like a bear, he is always in the mountains. I refer to the famous Navarros, who has had so many fights with the customs officers. You would hardly believe it, but we get on capitally together. He has sat to me, and allowed me to become acquainted with his tiger's smile—a thing rare enough. During an excursion which I am planning with some friends, he wants to carry me on his back, saying he would be so proud to do this and that he would find the burden light. However, I should not care to trust him; and if I go to Panticosa— the wretched village and famous springs just over the Spanish frontier from here—as I feel inclined to do, I shall take Jean Marie, who is a sure and faithful guide.

To her brother Isidore she writes on September 4th:

I have been making a rough sketch of some smugglers, and have managed also to get you a few Havana cigars—smuggled ones. This time they will not do you any harm, old boy. I can smoke them myself and enjoy them. They are not steeped in nicotine.

To the same she writes eight days later:

If I hadn't been ill, I should have written to you first, my dearest Isidore. However, none of you must be anxious about me, as it is nothing dangerous. For the last week I have had a constant headache, with violent arterial pulsations in the temples; and I have no appetite. Even soup doesn't digest. The doctor says it is fatigue and gives me bitters. The people here are very kind, and have done all they could for me. To-day I am rather better; so, no doubt, the attack will soon pass. Of course this has prevented me from getting on with my work, which makes me fume. And then, when it isn't warm, it's cold; and when it rains, one gets wet; and when one is at home, it isn't possible to be out. That's Dame Truth's own truth. If this is the lady who is the cause of all that has happened this year, may she and the deuce take us rather than recommence.

Later in the same month she writes to the same:

I am seeing a good many things, Isidore, my old boy. There is here a big mountain with lots of animals on the top, where the cows do wonderful things when the fancy takes them. For instance, they will set off and gallop like mad, executing twists and turns, and carrying their tails high in the air when they have a fly behind them. The sheep of this country have a more lively way of wagging their caudal appendage than those I have seen elsewhere; and the result of all this is that the poor creatures let themselves tumble down what painters would call splendid, but the shepherds, frightful precipices, where they are dissected by vultures.

I have seen and admired the superb Gavarnie Circus for the second time; the cascade that has a fall of two hundred feet, the Marboré, the Lost Mountain, some exquisite Spanish costumes, some handsome mules, and a fine pair of wild goat's horns, which I bought for four francs. I shall also bring back a Basque shepherd's costume, and if I were richer, I should add to my artistic paraphernalia a superb Spanish one, too. All this is magnificent! What a pity it is so far away! This is an artist's country. I intend to come back here and push over into Spain.

116

My dog is getting enormous. I don't know how I shall manage to convey him from here, for he will be as big as a donkey. Dear me! What an unfortunate hobby mine is! What would you say if I were to confess what efforts I have made to resist the desire to bring back a sheep and a goat? I really can't help it. I have my failings as well as my virtues. I am so fond of little sheep. However, this dog is quite enough for the journey.

I have not done much work; but the time has not been wasted, since I have got a whole host of ideas. My health is better. For several days I have had no fever, and the odour of cabbage soup again delights my nostrils. Remember me to silly old Tatan. I am very fond of her all the same and in spite of her sins. Who doesn't sin more or less in this world? Tell me how she is, and give me news of her dowdy hat and her reactionary umbrella. Good Lord! I am getting silly myself! I must have inherited my share.

At Borce, " at 11 A.M., July 28, 1855," she addressed the following letter to " My dear Everybody ":

As I promised, I send you a few lines to announce my safe arrival. The journey was long, for between Bordeaux and Pau there is no regular week service. From Pau I went to Eaux-Bonnes to see Dr. Tarras, who received me kindly and committed me to his brother, who brought me on here. This place is quite wild and there are neither bathers nor tourists. The country round is a regular eagle's nest. There are just enough corn fields to feed the modest peasant folk. The Gave flows just below us, and above are well-wooded mountain peaks. I intend to do some good sketching here—mules, sheep, and shepherds. To-morrow being Sunday, we are going up to the frontier, at the top of the Pyrenees, whence we shall see Spain and France at one and the same time. I shall bring back good souvenirs of all I see. I am with some very nice people, so simple and hospitable. The children of the family are so pretty, sweet, and artless. Their aunt is a veritable Genevieve after the fashion of Lamartine, with a distinguished air to boot. I thought such types were to be

117

found only in novels. Their house is most rustic, and the few others that are in the neighbourhood are picturesque.

To M. Gustave d'Eichthal, dated August 2, 1855:

Here I am, dear M. d'Eichthal, on the very frontier, with one foot in France and the other in Spain, on the mountain tops, in a real, quite out of the way, Spanish inn, where usually only mule-drivers, smugglers, and the shepherds of the region lodge, with meagre fare, plenty of fleas and wine that stinks of tar. So much for creature comforts. But then what an admirable wilderness, what a splendid solitude! The stillness is disturbed only by the mountain torrents and the sheep-bells on the snow-covered summits. We have a fair number of bears in the environs, so that I hope to be able to study their habits. The shepherd costumes are most becoming. So you see I lack nothing in the way of material for painting and I intend to profit by the opportunity. I may add that I am with the best people in the world. An abbot, an acquaintance of mine, gave me a letter to them. I have two native boys as attendants, two big mountain dogs, that have taken a liking to me and follow me everywhere, as companions, while the gendarmery of Urdos, the nearest French town, protect me. So I could not be better situated.

To her sister, Mme. Peyrol, written from St. Sauveur, September 12th of this same year:

I hope, my dearest Juju, that, notwithstanding my fiery-red complexion, I will not seem to you to have grown too thin. As you anticipated, the sight of Spain has not done me any harm, in spite of Tatan's opinion that one should not indulge too much in the beverage that excites persons of our temperament. As a matter of fact, my quaint countenance, with my white silk waistcoat and my gaudy dress, won't look bad when prize-day comes at our drawing school. I shall look like a Mauriac [1] mock-virgin, with just a touch of fine breeding thrown in. We shall make a big hit, thanks to this Spanish dash.

---

[1] An old Auvergne town whose church has a celebrated black Virgin.

Last evening all St. Sauveur was illuminated in celebration of the Malakoff victory. I burnt my pound of candles like any other good French person. If that brigand Lemercier had paid me, I should have profited by the rise in the funds which this news is bound to produce. You see, my Juju, I have financial anxieties at present—savings which bear interest.

Hippolyte tells me you are painting something. I long to see your little cottage, where I shall have time to make a sketch for a hunting picture which I have in mind. I have not done much yet in the artistic line; but I have got some inspirations that are up to the knocker. I am going to visit Roland's Breach, and there I will soar above all low ambitions. I shall conceive there some grand and noble ideas, and invoke the grand Roland to grant me an artistic power worthy of his own arm and courage. There! How is that to end with?

To M. Mène, the sculptor, and his wife, she wrote as follows from Eaux-Bonnes on July 6, 1864:

Here I am, my dear friends, in the most admirable country imaginable. How beautiful it is, my dear M. Mène, how beautiful it is! Why aren't you here, too? How much we should have to talk about! The mountains are still covered with snow, whereas in the valley it is hot enough to roast one alive. Our journey hither tired us a good deal—three days and three nights without rest. You can judge of our condition from that. Here we are settled down at last, but not without having had some trouble, for there is a host of people taking the waters this year.

Nathalie adds in a badly-spelled postscriptum:

Nothing can equal the view of these mountains. But I am sure you will get a better idea of them from Rosa's studies than by all the descriptions in the world. Oh, M. Mène, if you were only with us, what a fine lot of tadpoles you could catch! We have a great quantity of them.

Toward the end of August, 1850, the two travellers began to think of returning from their first visit to the Pyrenees. So the correspondence from the south during this tour ceases at about this date, and is replaced by letters from Ems, whither the doctors sent the invalids. This is the first, written in September, 1850, to Juliette Bonheur:

Here I am at last, and I can assure you I am not sorry to get to the end of the journey, for this has not been accomplished without experiencing adventures quite as interesting to relate as those which befell Telemachus. I am going to tell you all this out under the trees, where I will be better than here in the hotel.

My Juliette, I thought I was going to sit down under the trees and have a nice chat with you, but I got started drawing some oxen that were ploughing; however, I am now back to you again. But before giving you a description of this country where I find myself, let me begin at the beginning and tell you briefly how we got here.

Well, as you know, we left Paris Thursday evening and, after spending the night on the train, reached the Belgian frontier at noon the next day, and at four o'clock the same afternoon were in Brussels.[1] We asked to be taken to a hotel as near as possible to the station for Cologne, for, you know, the trains in Belgium do not run at night. But, on the whole, I was glad to get the rest. The next morning at five we started for Cologne.

On leaving the Belgian capital, the road passes through fine big meadows where were grazing thousands of animals nearly all spotted black and white, which is not pretty, as they all appear to be in half mourning. Finally we reached the German frontier, where, as had already happened at the Belgian frontier, we had to change cars and show our passports. Then, passing over a pretty country of wooded hills and châteaux built in the midst of meadows, going through numerous tunnels, we emerged into a broad plain, whence we eventually began to catch glimpses through the mist of the spires of the Cologne churches.

Arrived at Cologne, our poor luggage had to be re-examined; but fortunately it is handled here in a much more orderly way than in France. An obliging gentleman who knew a little French

---

[1] The journey from Paris to Brussels now takes a little over four hours!

told us of a good hotel. We got into a superb omnibus all decorated with mirrors and gold embossed work, and displaying the
royal Prussian arms. Then I caught sight of the Rhine, a wide,
rapidly-flowing river, and we entered the city by passing over
drawbridges, through a wall fortified with two forts armed with
cannon whose black mouths are turned toward the passer-by; and
all this guarded by Prussian soldiers who appear very savage,
attired in their feudal-looking uniforms which give them a rather
striking exterior.

Having reached the hotel, we sat down to dinner. We found
wine scarcer here than in Belgium. I asked for beer, as water is
too weak a drink during a journey. But I was told that beer was
too common a beverage to be served in a hotel. Then, thinking it
would cost less than wine, which is three francs a bottle, the
cheapest kind, I asked for porter and was surprised to learn that
it was three francs and twelve sous. So we decided to content
ourselves with water. The dinner was quite dear and very bad.

The next morning we left Cologne at seven o'clock for Bonn
by train, where we took boat on the Rhine for Coblentz, a fortified
city with a military guard as at Cologne. The banks of the Rhine
are very beautiful, but it is not just what I expected. Nevertheless, the river is majestic, and rising from its shores here and there
are high hills whose rocky summits are generally crowned with
old castles. The view at Coblentz is fine. The city is curious and
its fortifications are reflected in the water. A bridge of boats,
doubtless ready to be broken up in case of danger, crosses the
Rhine here. In this city resides our dear Henry V,[1] who, out of
regard for his health, would do well not to take a change of air.
The boat we came down on was a fine one belonging to the state.
We reached Coblentz at three in the afternoon, where we took an
omnibus for Ems, six leagues away.

Here at Ems the only thing we cannot stand is the cooking,
with its devilish sauces. These awful Germans concoct disgusting
mixtures. For instance, you are served strawberries along with
fat meat, oil, potatoes, and pears, and then, to crown all, you are
given water to drink. I don't know if it is due to the food, but I

---

[1] Count de Chambord (1820–83), Bourbon pretender to the French throne.

have been upset ever since I got here. The beds are very narrow
even for one person and so short that, though I get my head well
up against the board, my feet stick out at the foot. But all these
things count for nothing in comparison with the discomforts of
the journey from Paris here. However, you are compensated by
the pretty scenery in the midst of which Ems is built, situated as
it is on the banks of a nice little river, surrounded by wooded and
cultivated hills. The environs must be beautiful. It is a charming place to live in, but there is, perhaps, a little too much of the
English garden style about it for my tastes. But if I hunt about,
I think I may find some good things to sketch.

I am told the waters have wonderful medicinal properties, but
I can't imagine anything worse to drink. It is a flat and warm
liquid. To get it down gives you a wry face, and you have a
strong wish to throw it up again. The physician has ordered me
to take it, though I should like very much to disobey the command.

By way of amusement I regale myself with the laughable
spectacle of the fashionable set here. There are flirts here as
everywhere, and lots of sentimentalists, especially among the English. There is a British matron whom we have nicknamed " the
giraffe." You can't imagine anything more comical than all this.

But I must wind up this gossipy epistle. I shall not write as
often as I should like, for I learn that postage rates are very high.
Embrace old Isidore for me. I kiss you once again, and remain,
your sister and devoted friend.

About the same time Rosa writes to Mme. Micas, whom she
addresses as " My Dear Mother Micas ":

At last we are here, but not without trouble, I assure you,
for Prussia is a sorry country. First I must tell you that it is
melancholy enough to be always hearing a jargon one cannot
understand, so that to ask for the least thing you have to go
through a veritable pantomime. In the second place, I may add
that it took us from eleven till six the next evening to get from
Paris to Brussels. At the Belgian frontier we had to unpack all
our boxes; the same thing at the Prussian frontier. In Belgium,
however, it was easy enough, as everybody spoke French. At
Cologne, on the contrary, it was enough to make you lose your

head, one speaking English, another Russian, a third Flemish, and a fourth Polish. In short, we were obliged to shift for ourselves, and what was still more bothersome, we had to change our nice little French gold pieces for wretched coins, half copper, half silver, with values difficult to get accustomed to, especially when you do not understand the language. In exchange for four hundred francs we had a whole bag filled with this ironmongery which looks much like a domestic's buttons. I do believe the king of Prussia coins money out of the buttons of his old suits of livery. Anyhow, Nathalie and I looked at it for a long time without knowing what to do with it. As the bag was very heavy, we were forced to carry it between us.

There is much more luxury here than in the Pyrenees because there is a much greater number of visitors. Yesterday evening we had a short walk in the Promenade, which is a flower garden at the extremity of a pretty little river surrounded on all sides with well-wooded mountains or meadows. There is music every evening, I think. Anyway, a band played yesterday in a small stand in the open air. It is a good idea to have this music in the midst of pretty landscapes. We sat down and laughed to our heart's content at all the caricatures we saw. I assure you there is plenty to laugh at here. French women are blamed for their coquetry, but you should come here if you want to see the pretentious airs put on by both women and men. There are old flirts in the sere and yellow leaf seeking adventures. In short, most are very elegant and very ridiculous, and I see that we shall be able to enjoy more than one amusing spectacle without trouble. Good gracious, what noodles, and worse than that, society people are! I begin to think that simplicity of heart is an exceptionally rare thing and good sense a still rarer. Really there is not much progress in this respect.

As Nathalie is just on the point of putting my letter into the envelope, it occurs to me to give you on this bit of paper an idea of the king of Prussia's soldiers. I don't know why, but this little king or emperor [1] of Prussia interests me a great deal. Per-

---

[1] Frederick William IV, who had been elected the previous year hereditary emperor of the Germans, an honour which he declined, however. These were revolutionary times in Germany.

haps it is because he suffers our pretender to reside in one of his fortified and well-fortified towns, for fear they should rob him of the dear Henry V. May God grant that the Count always remains in a country where the laws are in such harmony with the monarchic spirit. That will be better for his health!

The rainy weather seems to have followed the travellers to Germany, which may have contributed to shorten their stay, for they appear to have left Ems toward the middle of September. "We received your last letter this morning while we were cosy in bed," wrote Rosa Bonheur at this time to Mme. Micas; "for what else can we do? It rains here day and night, so that it is impossible to get out. Consequently, I shall bring back to Paris nothing but an unbounded desire to begin my great picture" ("The Horse Fair"). They were glad to leave Prussia and set foot on French soil again, with "hearts content and purses light," as Nathalie Micas wrote, at the same time launching a parting anathema at this celebrated watering-place: "To the deuce Ems and all its jargon-speaking people. What a joy to see human faces once more! France and its friends forever! My happiness just now is unequalled, and if I were not afraid of passing for a lunatic, I should find strength enough in my legs to dance a polka."

After the success of her picture, "The Horse Fair," Rosa Bonheur, in August, 1856, left France on a visit to England and Scotland. She was away about five weeks, returning home in the middle of September. Certain details of this journey have been preserved in letters written by Mlle. Micas, who, as usual, accompanied her friend, and addressed to her mother. Occasional postscriptums were, as was her custom, added by Rosa Bonheur, whose deep affection for the "grosse bonne mère" showed itself again repeatedly. As neither of the travellers spoke English, they were fortunate to be under the guidance of Mr. Gambart, who suggested and planned the expedition, and who piloted them throughout the various excursions in England and Scotland.

Reaching Dover just as the troops, returning from the Crimean

War, were camped on the Southern Downs, and continuing their journey, they soon found themselves in the midst of a society of artists and literary men who frequented Mr. Gambart's house. Both Rosa and Nathalie easily accustomed themselves to the numerous repasts which kept them eating " from morning till evening," and were rather astonished to discover that the English were by no means the melancholy people they were represented to be.

One of their first visits was to Windsor, where some herds of deer, several hundred in number and different from anything they had seen in France, delighted Rosa's eyes, and at once set her to work on a small female destined to figure in a future painting.

But Rosa Bonheur was all impatience to begin the journey northward. " My kind big mother," she writes to Mme. Micas, " just a line or two to say that I am longing for Gambart to have finished his preparations and to be off on our way to Scotland. We are going to London to-day, for I want to see what they are doing with the engraving of my ' Horse Fair.' We start for Scotland to-morrow, but we shall take three days to get there, as we are to visit three English towns on the way. Gambart says we must not tire ourselves too much. For my part, however, I should have preferred travelling more quickly."

Nathalie's letter of August 13th informs her mother of their arrival at Birmingham, " the capital of the midlands." She adds: " Reaching here at mid-day, we had only just time enough to dress in order to go and lunch with a celebrated picture amateur who had come to meet us. At this gentleman's house a most agreeable reception awaited us. All the most eminent artists and men of letters in Birmingham had assembled to pay their respects to Rosa and to offer her, in the name of the inhabitants, the expression of their sincere admiration for her talents. Her picture is on view here and has obtained a marked success."

Nathalie again alludes to the abundance of good cheer in England. " In this country people are always eating," she says. After the first lunch, they went to another house where a sort of " Balthazar's banquet " had been prepared for them and where

"SEE HOW WE DRIVE WHEN WE GO TO MAKE A CALL."

the ladies of the house had arranged over the entrance-door a French flag encircling the initials R. B. At the end of this letter Rosa adds a few words, announcing their departure on the morrow for Glasgow, and gives a pen-and-ink sketch of how they drove to pay these visits." (See the sketch on page 126.)

Glasgow was reached on August 14th, after a journey through scenery which excited the admiration of the two travellers. "Whoever does not know England cannot speak of it," writes Nathalie; " it is an admirably fine country." In the great industrial town they made the acquaintance of the Anglo-Irish painter, Daniel Maclise (1811–70), and went to visit what Nathalie affirms to be the oldest iron foundry in the world. " Only to see it was worth the journey hither. Just fancy blast-furnaces that have burned for two hundred years, day and night, without ever being allowed to go out. In this foundry is metal worth twenty-five million of francs. Everything was explained to us with the greatest care and a pot was cast for us in which we are to have our soup made this evening."

Their arrival in Edinburgh brought with it a new and not altogether pleasant experience—that of a Scotch Sunday. If they had stayed at home with their Scotch host and hostess they would have been obliged to " look into the whites of each other's eyes all day without talking or stirring." Rosa joined with her friend in bewailing Scotland's two drawbacks—its Sabbath and its rain. " We are spending a nice sort of Sunday," she adds in a postscriptum; " it is pouring without, and in this country the Lord's day is sanctified to such good purpose that there is not even a cat in the streets and you can't visit the castle, either. We are in the big drawing-room engaged in dozing or studying the tips of each other's nose."

While in Edinburgh a little adventure marked their first excursion. They had set out to visit the island of Bass Rock, at the entrance of the Firth of Forth, in company with Mr. Maclise and several other gentlemen. A monster lunch had been packed up; but alas! the waves were in a bad temper and seasickness put in its appearance, so that the pleasure party was somewhat interfered with. But a little later, on their return visit tó Edinburgh, they again made the sail to Bass Rock, under more favourable conditions, and before she left Scotland Rosa Bonheur could write: " Nathalie and I are becoming perfect sailors—real feminine jacktars."

From Edinburgh the two travellers went to the Trosachs, which Scott has made famous, and whose scenery carried their enthusiasm to its highest point. Nathalie pronounces the beauties of Scotland " a veritable gold-mine for artists," and Rosa was laying up in her memory mental pictures of the charms which tourists at that time but little understood. In the Trosachs they were comfortably lodged in a hotel where the foreground was the Loch and the background the soaring hills. They enjoyed to the full the lovely effects produced by the sun in its rising and setting. Frequent short trips were made on the water, and Rosa did a fair amount of sketching. They had difficulty in getting any one to carry their painting materials, and now and again Mr. Gambart had to load himself like " a veritable beast of burden."

They finally retraced their steps to Glasgow, where they embarked for Arran Island in the Firth of Clyde, and after a short stay there, went on by sea to Liverpool, a nineteen hours' voyage. Thence they proceed to Mr. Gambart's country house, where they were glad to get a little rest after journeying over hill and dale and on the tossing water for five weeks. The animals Rosa Bonheur had bought at the Falkirk Fair, a bull, two cows, and a calf being among the number, had been forwarded to Mr. Gambart's residence, and the eager artist was soon at work on some new pictures in which these latest acquisitions to her live stock were to be represented.

Both Rosa Bonheur and Nathalie Micas seem to have brought back from Scotland the happiest souvenirs, and their friendship was, if possible, rendered closer by their common enjoyment and appreciation of Scotch scenery. Nathalie found even the drawing-room of their Highland inn " poetic," though the names of places sorely tried their organs of speech, Ballachulish, on Loch Leven, where Nathalie dated some of her letters, being considered by both of them quite unpronounceable. She remarked " the melancholy voice of the wind, the pert little birds that came and tapped at the casement window, and, above all, the lochs." She noted that even in the wilds of Scotland Rosa Bonheur's celebrity procured her the honour of being followed about by admiring crowds. In fact, at the Falkirk Fair, the artist complained a little of her movements being watched. We are not told whether she wore male attire during this Scottish tour. But she probably did, especially in the Highlands and on the occasion when she and Mr. Gambart went out shooting. This would account for much of this popular curiosity.

Nathalie Micas also dwells with great satisfaction on the material advantages sure to result from this journey. The enthusiasm of the English for Rosa Bonheur's work had grown to such a point, she says, that even if the French should quarrel with her and refuse to buy her pictures, she could spend the rest of her life in executing the overwhelming orders of these British customers. And Mlle. Micas was not wrong in this judgment. From this date on, during nearly half a century, the English public, and later the American public, continued to be the warmest admirers of Rosa Bonheur's talents and the largest buyers of her productions, which proves that Mr. Gambart was well inspired when he proposed this visit. Rosa Bonheur never forgot his early interest in her, and his affection for her did not cease when the end came. A year or two after her death and not many months before he followed her to the tomb, in 1903, he raised to her memory, as we shall see farther on, a handsome monument in one of the public squares of Fontainebleau.

Here may be inserted the following extract from the manuscript memoirs of Mr. Gambart, where he speaks of this visit to Great Britain. It supplements the account just given and adds some new details.

REMINISCENCES OF ROSA BONHEUR

On Rosa Bonheur's visit to London, in 1856, Sir Charles Eastlake,[1] President of the Royal Academy, gave a grand dinner in her honour, at which she made the acquaintance of Sir Edwin Landseer,[2] whom she was delighted to meet, having the highest admiration for his great talent and his numerous pictures, which she knew through engravings.

After a couple of weeks spent between London and Wexham, we started for Scotland, but stopped at Birmingham on our way, where I had accepted an invitation to dinner from the picture amateurs of this town. A great surprise awaited us. These gentlemen had prepared a triumphal reception for us, the children of the schools being massed round the station, while bouquets were presented to the ladies, and an address of welcome handed to us. After a large dinner, at which the municipal authorities were present, we at length started northward and embarked at Liverpool, making the rest of the journey, as far as Greenock, by sea.

Rosa Bonheur was very happy to reach the country of Ossian, and when, on the morrow following our arrival, we took the Inveraray road toward Loch Eck, she was able to make her first sketch of a herd of Scottish oxen. This sketch and the studies based on it resulted in a picture entitled " Morning in the Highlands," which was engraved by Charles Lewis.[3] Toward evening a fresh encounter of cattle furnished the subject of a second sketch, which was likewise the beginning of a picture, subsequently painted and sold under the title of " Denizens of the Highlands." The engraver of this was Thomas Landseer.[4]

From Oban we went to Ballachulish, intending to spend some time there. Indeed, it would have been difficult to find a spot more conducive to work and scenery more picturesque. It was not the tourist season, and we had no one to interrupt us, except the midges. These little insects were indeed a torment. But Rosa Bonheur, in the ardour and excitement of work, seemed not to notice them, and bore their bites with a resignation that aston-

---

[1] The distinguished historical painter and writer on art (1793–1865).
[2] The celebrated animal painter (1802–73).
[3] 1808–80.   [4] Brother of Sir Edwin (1795–1880).

DENIZENS OF THE HIGHLANDS.

(By permission of Messrs. L. H. Lefèvre and Son, 1a King Street, St. James's, London, England, proprietors of the copyright, and publishers of the large engraving.)

ished me. Many of the sketches made at this time still preserve numbers of these little pests caught in the wet paint, and thus fixed on the canvas. The artist's forehead was marked all over by their bites.

The annual fair at Falkirk was close at hand, and every day at low tide herds of oxen, coming thither from the north, crossed the firth swimming, escorted by two or three boats with shepherds in them and drovers, who guided the animals to the farther bank and now and again upheld them by their horns, if they were in danger of drowning. These picturesque sights attracted Rosa Bonheur's attention, as offering an interesting subject for a picture, so that she made numerous sketches in view of it.

Another subject for a picture presented itself in the ferrying of flocks of sheep from one island to another when the pasture of one island was all eaten. Some years after the artist painted a picture based on what she had seen here. In it two shepherds are seen rowing across the water a boat full of sheep. The title was " Changing Pastures," and an engraving of it was made by H. T. Ryall.[1]

In the valley of Glencoe we were overtaken by a bad storm, during which we came across a shepherd sheltering with his flock in the hollow of a rock. This experience furnished the material of a superb painting entitled " After a Storm in the Highlands." It was engraved in 1886 by Joseph B. Pratt.

When we visited the Falkirk Fair we drove from a friend's house in a waggonette. Our arrival created quite a sensation, for, besides our own party, there were two distinguished members of the Royal Academy and one or two other guests. This sensation was increased when Rosa Bonheur pointed out from her carriage six animals, a young bull and five splendid oxen, which she wanted to buy and take away with her. Instead of separating them quietly from the herd, the drovers began to strike right and left in order to get them out more quickly. This caused a panic, during which the cattle crushed several sheep of a flock that was in the vicinity. On reaching Paris, Rosa Bonheur made a sketch of this scene. But it was only years later that the picture was

---

[1] 1811–67.

painted, or rather, drawn in crayons. Begun in 1867, it was finished in 1870. Even then the picture was not quite to the artist's mind, so that she began a fresh work which received its last touches in 1873, when the completed drawing, in black and white and sepia, was delivered to me under the title " A Stampede," together with another entitled " The Straits of Ballachulish." Both were engraved by Thomas Landseer.

On our return from Scotland to Wexham, where my guest stayed for a short time to sketch, Mr. Ruskin, the eminent art critic, was invited to meet her at dinner. His arrival turned the little village upside down. Two days before, his servant came to hire rooms for him, and as the furniture was not considered suitable, some better had to be fetched from Windsor. A cook came down also, in order to prepare his breakfast, and when Mr. Ruskin himself entered the village it was with his own carriage and domestics, the railway being disdained. After dinner his conversation with Rosa Bonheur gave rise to some interesting discussion. I remember that at one moment, his antagonist's arguments seeming more weighty than his own, Ruskin cried out:

" I don't yield; to vanquish me, you would have to crush me."

" I wouldn't like to go so far as that," answered Rosa Bonheur.

Another guest at Wexham at the time of his visit was Frederick Goodall,[1] who painted Rosa Bonheur's portrait, in which she is represented making a study of two of her oxen, the one lying down and the other eating some hay.

Here may be given in full a few of Rosa Bonheur's letters bearing on this same journey to England and Scotland, one of which, to Mme. Peyrol, dated Wexham, England, August 8, 1856, is first quoted.

After a good crossing, during which no one was sick, here I am at Gambart's country house. England is really a fine country, though rather trim. The vegetation is admirable, with magnificent trees. The oaks are almost black, which gives an imposing character to the landscape. I went yesterday and visited the park and

---

[1] An English painter of history and genre (1822–1904).

forest of Windsor. People talk of the trees at Fontainebleau. But here you have the same ancient forest monarchs.

In the Windsor park I saw a very pretty subject for a picture. Under some gigantic oaks was a herd of two hundred deer. So I stopped the carriage and Gambart and I began to approach them stealthily in order to see them close to. To my astonishment, however, instead of taking to flight, they executed a most interesting piece of manœuvring. All the males formed themselves into a close battalion and showed us a front of splendid antlers carried with the utmost grace and pride. Meanwhile, all the females and the young ones ran and took up their position behind this advanced guard. Then, to amuse ourselves, we deviated to the left, when the band of female deer immediately ran to the right, while the males looked at us with a martial air. You may imagine how we enjoyed the spectacle of these military tactics in the presence of danger. It was so pretty. It appears, however, that it doesn't do to stay too long teasing them, especially in the month of September.

I have also visited the camp of the Highland soldiers returning from the Crimea. The Scotch costume is charming when seen in the mass, with the band in front of them, just as it is all described in Walter Scott's novels. The bagpipes and drums give to the whole a most original appearance, which is half warlike, half pastoral, and to which an odd something is added by the bare legs of these superb soldiers.

It seems that it often rains in this country, and especially in Scotland. So I am preparing to paint some rain effects in order to get my hand in. But just at this present moment I am engaged in sketching a little deer.

Gambart is the best travelling companion imaginable. He looks after everything, so that his little wife is the most spoilt of females. He is always running about and coming to tell us something about the journey, so that he generally seems as if he were about to fly away by the aid of the skirts of his frock-coat, which go ever floating in the wind behind him.

I will write to Pipon to-morrow. Remember me to the old silly, although he isn't worth the devil's slipper. Love to all and much to yourself.

A week later Rosa wrote to Auguste Bonheur, " My dear Pipon ":

When I received your last welcome letter I was in the Island of Arran and just on the point of leaving. That's why I have delayed so long in replying. I am now back at Mr. Gambart's with the animals I bought at the famous Falkirk Fair. They are so picturesque and have such nice colours, for in Scotland, where the animals are left in a state of nature, this good dame gives them fine coats to protect them against the climate.

Besides Arran, we visited also Glencoe and the Black Mountain. In Arran we climbed to the top of the highest peak, whence a view is obtained simultaneously of the north of Scotland, of Ireland, of England, and of Wales. And such beautiful sea tints and skies! It made me want to go and visit all the little spots where tourists don't go, but which are always the finest and wildest. I enjoyed myself immensely.

Mrs. Gambart insisted on going to the summit of Ben Avon, so as to be able to say like other ladies: " Oh! bioutifoull! veri-goud! " [1] And it was her poor husband who had to take her in tow. By the way, nothing is more comical than Gambart on his travels.

Well! I am not sorry to be back from my trip, though I bring with me only souvenirs. I might compose an album entitled, " Souvenirs and Regrets," just like the good Lamartine. I think he wrote something of the kind.

You are no doubt glad to be in your Auvergne, where there are so many fine studies to be made. At least, that's my opinion. In Auvergne is a charm of temperature which lends to objects both intensity and colour.

I mean to work hard this winter, so as to be able to go to Brittany with you in the spring.

On the same day she sent the following letter to Mme. Peyrol:

Here I am back from my gad about the Highlands. For just a month we have been climbing mountains and crossing waters

---

[1] So written in the original.

without resting. I am about tired. Ah! why can't I show you, my dear Juju, all the fine things I have seen? I must, at any rate, tell you about them by word of mouth. I have seen all the places Walter Scott has chosen for the characters he has created, especially those of the " Legend of Montrose," which I have just been reading. I have been to Argyll Castle where Mary Stuart was born, and I visited it from top to bottom; Edinburgh also, a most picturesque town where it rains too often. At present, I know Scotland pretty well. You meet with nothing but MacGeorges, Macdonalds, and Macs of all sorts, real bare-legged mountaineers, and big Englishmen who travel in opera costumes in order to pose as heroes. In fine, I will relate you my excursions and tell you my stories by Mammy's fireside, while smoking cigarettes, which I am longing to do.

I arrived yesterday at Mr. Gambart's country house, after a twenty-hours' sea voyage. You see that I am quite experienced, and shall be able one of these days to go sketching to America or China. I am bringing back a cargo, not of studies, but of living animals, of which I intend to make some fine pictures, if I can. I have a bull, two cows, two young bulls, four sheep, and a calf. They are so picturesque and their colour so beautiful that I should like to paint them all at the same time. I mean to peg away as if my life depended on it. In fact, I have all I want, except sufficient time. In a word, I am in ecstasies over what I have seen. But a rolling stone gathers no moss, and I haven't collected much in the way of studies. I must make it up with the animals, which have cost me dear, although I bought them cheaper than in France. I shouldn't like to fail with a single one, they are so beautiful to paint.

Kiss your little brat [1] for me. I wanted to buy him a little Highland costume, it suits children so well. But this shall be for next time.

Writing from By, November 26, 1897, to M. Venancio Deslandes, Rosa Bonheur says:

----

[1] Hippolyte Peyrol, the sculptor.

REMINISCENCES OF ROSA BONHEUR

I have your kind letter of the 20th inst., asking me for my impressions of my journey to England and Scotland, Anno Domini 1856, a date already far back in the flight of time.

I found England, and especially Scotland, a superb country in spite of its melancholy mists; for I prefer what is green to what is scorched. The Pyrenees, Auvergne, and Brittany are also to my taste. This, alas! is the extent of my travels. Life is too short; otherwise, I should have liked to voyage more than it has been in my power to do. I have had to paint pictures for a living; and when one works, one cannot gad about. For this it was that I quitted landscapes for animals. But on this head I have nothing to complain of.

Now, to comply with your request, this is what I think of Sir Edwin Landseer. I consider him the greatest painter of animals and I believe that he will remain the greatest of his kind, for he has left the most admirable canvases, such as " The Sanctuary," " The Challenge," " The Battle of the Stags," and " After the Battle," not to mention many other masterpieces which are full of poetic grandeur and rare intelligence. In art, as in all creative things, we should admire first the creative faculty; execution is secondary. In creative power, Landseer certainly stands in the first rank. His colouring has been criticised; it has been found somewhat sombre. But I do not share this opinion, for I love the Scotch mists, the cloud-swept mountains, and the dark heather —I love them with all my heart.

Sincerely yours, my dear doctor and kind chevalier.

After this letter, in which Rosa Bonheur pays such a high tribute to the great animal painter of England, it may be interesting to give the opinions, concerning her own genius, of some of the leading living animal painters, as expressed in letters addressed to the editor of this volume, the first coming in 1904 from H. W. B. Davis, R.A., of Glaslyn, Rhayader, Radnorshire:

You ask for my opinion in a few lines of the art of Rosa Bonheur. I can, of course, but add my own high appreciation to the almost universal admiration felt for the talent of that distinguished artist. Perhaps the most distinctive charm of her work

136

lies in the perfect naturalness of her subjects—her animals, painted with wonderful vigour and solidity, being admirable in their un-exaggerated and life-like character, generally placed, too, in a simple unaffected landscape equally suggestive of reality. And I am not sure that French modern art is not indebted to her for having drawn attention, with such emphasis, to the quiet charm of unconventional rural scenes as subjects for pictorial treatment. She was certainly one of the very first to do so. Though then but a mere boy, I can recollect the sensation produced at the time by her picture of the ploughing oxen. Nothing, quite of its nature, had been seen before in art.

My remarks must be understood to apply more particularly to her earlier and, as I think, most successful work, and especially to her rural subjects of horses, cattle, and sheep. Her rendering of other animals, particularly in later years, was not, I think, so happy; and though they were always treated with great vigour and effect, they displayed a certain clumsiness, were defective even in drawing sometimes and generally lacking in the characteristic expressions of the various creatures depicted. Her figures were always weak, this being the one point, perhaps, revealing the woman, in her otherwise extraordinarily virile work. She was the first painter of animals, certainly in France, who combined these qualities of vivid and simple realism in animal subject and landscape background.

Troyon, so erroneously referred to sometimes as an animal painter (animalier), was a great landscape painter assuredly, who introduced animals indeed in his pictures, and most effectively, but rather as accessories and foils, so to say—and how fine they are as such—to his scheme of composition. But except for those valuable qualities of colour and light and shade so readily found in rustic animals, Troyon's were wanting in the essential char-acteristic of animals as distinguishing them from vegetation—viz., the look of life, both in action and expression. To how many animal painters, so called, would such remarks apply!

The art of Rosa Bonheur was never, I believe, so enthusias-tically hailed and esteemed in France as it unquestionably was in England; and in later years but little was heard of it there. Her reputation in the latter country, fanned as it was by the exertions of the chief picture-dealers of the day, who had introduced her works into England, where public taste is, possibly, less discriminating, more easily led, and a keen judgment less general in matters of art than on the Continent, was immediate, and possibly a little in excess of what was due. Under these auspices, however, her works, beginning with the celebrated " Horse Fair," were in great vogue in England, became highly popular, and her fame was assured.

M. Julien Dupré, writing from Paris, on December 6, 1903, expresses his admiration in these words:

I greatly admire and venerate the talent of Rosa Bonheur. Her " Ploughing in the Nivernais " has always been my artist's joy, and I remember when, as a child, I used to visit the Luxembourg Gallery, it was the picture that most appealed to my imagination.

Unfortunately, I have never seen many of Rosa Bonheur's works, never having travelled in England where her talent, I know, is much appreciated. But I can speak of the exhibition of her pictures which was organised after her death. There I realised what she had accomplished by her arduous labour, and admired the fine sketches which had served her during her artistic career.

Quite recently, I had an opportunity of seeing at the Luxembourg other studies she had made, and in the presence of these examples of such accurate and faithful work my admiration grew stronger and stronger.

M. Edouard Debat-Ponsan wrote in 1903:

Although from temperament, I am more inclined to undergo my impressions than to analyse them, I will try to sum up in a few lines my ideas on our animal painter, Rosa Bonheur.

In the first place, it seems to me that her works prove that she painted animals because she loved them. She painted them for themselves, and, generally, as apart from any accompanying action. She considered them to be integral parts of country life, bathed in the light and clothed in the cheerfulness of nature. She mingled them with the toil of the fields, or, if wild, represented them in solitude. She never painted them in a situation of a violent or dramatic character.

In the second place, Rosa Bonheur was fond of detail, and dwelt with lingering touch on the animal's hair or wool. Gentle movements were what suited her brush best. Her " Horse Fair," with its greater animation, was an exception to the rule; and she can hardly be said to have produced another canvas like that. She found all the parts of her models interesting and was unwilling to sacrifice any one of these parts. Realising that, in rapid movement, it is impossible to avoid such sacrifice, she preferred not to cultivate it. In the effort to produce an effect, she followed a similar simple plan. Thus, most of her animals were painted with a full light on them, so that the interest might be concentrated upon them. The landscape is more often a mere background. Here again the same rule is observed. This landscape is made very simple, lest it should interfere with the main subject. The consequence is that you can look for a long time at one of Rosa Bonheur's pictures without being fatigued. The quiet and calm of a summer's day seem to be distilled from the canvas. We experience none of the emotions that would be aroused by the sight of stronger artistic effects.

In fine, Rosa Bonheur may be said to have kept the womanly instincts in her painting. Correct in her drawing, scrupulous in detail, sober in execution, she offers us a striking contrast to such vigorous animal painters as Landseer and Troyon, to such landscape painters as Constable and Theodore Rousseau.

M. Léon Barillot wrote from Paris in 1904:

In her drawing, at once exact and delicate, Rosa Bonheur reveals the love she felt for our brothers of the lower creation.

Professor Hermann Hartwich sent these lines from Munich, on February 1, 1904:

I can only acquiesce in the general verdict of artists and connoisseurs the world over that Rosa Bonheur had genius of a high order, and that she was one of the greatest artists as well was one of the most remarkable women of her time.

Here, too, may best be printed letters from other artists, not, strictly speaking, animal painters, giving a more general appreciation of Rosa Bonheur's genius.

In her letter from Paris, December, 1903, Mlle. Louise Abbema speaks thus of Rosa Bonheur:

While still a little girl, I heard Rosa Bonheur much spoken of, and it was her talent and her fame that decided me to become an artist. I began drawing with ardour, yearning for the time when I too should be a celebrated woman painter, a prospect which seemed to me, and indeed which still seems, one of the finest attainable. Later, I was better able to understand and appreciate the powerful yet tender genius of the woman who had aroused my enthusiasm in childhood, and I became one of her worshippers. However, I never dared to get introduced to her, and it was not until she received the rosette of an officer in the Legion of Honour that I ventured to express to her in writing my deep and respectful admiration for her. To this letter she replied by a few lines which I have since treasured and which I regard with pride as one of the rewards of my artistic career. The note contained this phrase: " If you have become an artist through admiration for Rosa Bonheur, I am very proud of it. I have a sincere admiration for you and cannot tell you all my fraternal gratitude."

During the same year Mme. Virginie Demont-Breton, then at Le Typhonium, Wissant, near Boulogne, showed her appreciation in these words:

Among ancient and modern painters who have devoted themselves to the study of animals and who, in this field, have produced lasting masterpieces, are some who, by this means, have, so to speak, symbolised country life. They have utilised all the various elements—sun, earth, clouds—and so have enwrapped their living subjects in mist and light, thus embracing within a narrow limit, which is, however, enlarged by the ideal, a part of great nature. The animal is there, important by the position it occupies, but the picture is first and foremost " An Evening," " A Morning," " A Southern Landscape," poetically perceived and rendered.

140

These artists are landscape painters, since they have always subordinated the living creature to the general harmony of effect.

But the artist who penetrated most deeply and with the greatest tenderness and conscientiousness into the intimate being, or what may be called the sentiment, the soul of the animal, and interpreted it as a figure-painter; the artist who best rendered the look of a lambkin pressed against its mother's warm wool, the goodness of the suckling mother caressing her little one, the proud strength of the male, the family relations of these creatures to each other; the artist who most simply and touchingly related all the episodes of the life of ruminants in the open air, was Rosa Bonheur.

From Paul Chardin comes this tribute written at Paris, January 20, 1903:

Among the painters forming what was known as the Barbizon school were three who, like Rosa Bonheur, devoted their artistic talent to depicting animals. These three were Troyon, whose favourite subject was the cow; Karl Bodmer, who painted mostly deer; and Jacques, famous for his sheep. Compared with her, the first and third were much more ample and powerful in their execution, and excelled also by their colouring and sentiment of harmony. On the other hand, her drawing was more precise and correct, her touch more wonderfully skilful. Troyon, who painted so many masterpieces and deserves a first place among modern artists, was especially struck by the whole of what he saw rather than by the detail. Rosa Bonheur, on the contrary, saw the exact outline, the minute parts, much more than the harmony of the whole. She took pleasure in reproducing a horse, a cow, a sheep, hair by hair, so to speak; and could interpret with fairy-like perfection the moors where heather and flowering gorse mingle and are browsed by flocks. There are pictures of hers that are like embroidery, or delicate work in gold, a manner of execution hardly calculated to please such a painter as Troyon.

Of the three painters just mentioned, Bodmer is the most similar to Rosa Bonheur, although his execution is not so delicate as hers.

141

REMINISCENCES OF ROSA BONHEUR

Rosa Bonheur especially admired Landseer, whose touch is so delicate and so amorous of detail and form, and she had quite a quantity of superb engravings from the canvases of this artist, many of which were superior to the originals. In her folios were also many other English engravings representing animals, a kind of painting in which the English excel.

Venancio Deslandes wrote on September 14, 1904:

I hold that Rosa Bonheur should be classed among those artists, of whatever age or school, who have devoted their talents to the painting of animals and who, in this department of art, have left so many immortal canvases; as the one who has shown herself to have the rarest acquaintance with nature and who has known how to most truthfully reflect it in them. In my opinion, the work of this splendid master places her forever among the most famous animal painters, whether ancient or modern.

This Scottish experience—to return to Rosa Bonheur's travels —always remained green in her memory, and on more than one occasion she thought of repeating it. The following letter, written from By to Paul Chardin in 1863, is evidence of this:

As I guessed—not seeing Auguste arrive nor a letter from him, which I had been expecting for some time—our trip has fallen through for this year. This is because my brother having his son ill, but out of danger, can't go. Also, it would be a little late to start for Scotland now, when we ought to be there at this writing. I am quite vexed about it, dear M. Chardin; but what is to be done? It is simply a pleasure postponed, if you will. And the forest will do its best to make up for the loss, if you are not detained elsewhere. As for myself, I must confess that I am only half vexed at this disappointment, for now I can finish my shepherd, which is not so well advanced as I would like and which I would have had to leave standing, though heaven knows that I am impatient to finish it. For three mortal years I have been struggling to keep my promise concerning it, while the devil bewitches me, rendering the days so short for work, or for loaf-

142

ing either. So don't blame me for this failure, my worthy Rapin, but, on the contrary, believe that I regret the frustration of this nice little trip, which would have done me a world of good, for I begin to weary of turning ever in this same spot. At moments I am seized with a burning desire to go to the ends of the earth, having at the bottom of my make-up vagabond tastes. But I have been foolish enough to get a house on my hands, like a snail, and wisdom demands that I stay here quietly for at least another year, so as to get ahead in my work, and thus have leisure for our journey.

M. Chardin makes this comment on this letter: " Rosa Bonheur had told me that Lord Breadalbane had offered her a shooting-box ·connected with one of his castles. The trip was never taken."

In fact, except brief journeys to Nice and a few other parts of France, an occasional run to the Swiss mountains, and a business trip to Brussels in connection with the Micas brake, what is related in this chapter seems to be the extent of Rosa Bonheur's travels. During nearly forty years, she seldom left Fontainebleau, though Paris, where she even had a *pied à terre*, was so near.

CHAPTER VI

WHATEVER may be the success of a translator in transferring from one tongue to another the language of a writer who has large individuality and genius, he will always fail to convey the full effect of the original. Style and idiom are sensitive leaves that shrink and droop under any other than nature's first handling; and the diminution has to be accepted.

No apology is needed for placing Rosa Bonheur's letters before the public. Although it was her brush, not her pen, which gave to her name the right to be handed down to posterity, yet in the simple outpourings of her mind and heart, written without any literary intention, there are such abundant revelations of temperament and character, such touches of pathos and humour, such outbursts of artistic enthusiasm, and, withal, such generous and many-sided humanity, that they become of the highest interest to us, especially when they are thrown into proper relief by the souvenirs of those to whom they were addressed and who for long years enjoyed her intimacy.

The deciphering of Rosa Bonheur's letters is often difficult even to those accustomed to her chirography. Not that she wrote badly or that the characters lack form. Except in some rare instances where agitation of mind interfered, the strokes, with their bold, firm lines and certain peculiar flourishes, have rather a pleasing appearance and invite attention. The difficulty is mainly caused by three particularities. First, the almost absolute identity of shape in her initial j's, g's, f's, and s's; secondly, the insertion,

144

FACSIMILE OF ROSA BONHEUR'S CHIROGRAPHY.

through writing rapidly, of numerous little loops resembling an e, and easily confused with this vowel; and, lastly, the tendency to slur the end of the word, so that a necessary consonant or vowel is frequently omitted and the last syllable has to be guessed from the preceding ones. Then there are minor perplexities caused by numerous examples of wrong spelling and incorrect grammar.

Perhaps too much has been made of these last-mentioned defects by those who have been cognisant of them, for, in reality, Rosa Bonheur's slips in writing were far more wilful than inevitable. Though her early instruction suffered from her juvenile devotion to art, yet her mature reading and habit of the pen were such as to largely remedy youthful shortcomings of this sort. The truth is that she found the subtleties of French concords too troublesome to observe in the rapid flow of her thought, and, as a rule, cared little whether she were expressing herself grammatically. Her nephew, Hippolyte Peyrol, tells me that on one occasion his aunt, when writing an epistle in his presence, asked:

" Are there two p's or is there only one in *apercevoir?* "

" One, aunt," answered the young man.

" Oh, the deuce; I've gone and stuffed in two," exclaimed the artist with a gesture that showed her indifference.

Writing to Princess Stirbey as late as 1897, Rosa Bonheur confesses: " I am obliged, I am ashamed to say, to consult the French dictionary from time to time, which admission may amuse you a little." The fact is that Rosa Bonheur might have repeated, concerning the French, what somebody said of the Basque language, that " the devil himself never could learn it."

While some of her mistakes are ludicrous, as, for instance, *s'est* for *c'est*, *cources* for *courses*, *viendrons* for *viendront*, etc., others belong more to the category of slips that may be made in French by almost any one through inattention. But neither in the one kind nor in the other can they, in this instance, be interpreted as mere illiteracy, since none are inveterate. Some of them are of common occurrence, it is true; but then, again, she will at times avoid them. Flinging her words on to the paper with the

145

same freedom of movement as in the handling of her brush, the phonetic temptation would seem to have been too strong for her just as it is for children, who make the same mistakes day after day, although corrected by their teachers. The reason is that logical reflection has not yet succeeded in making itself felt between the uttered sound or the thought and the written expression of it. This reflection comes with age; and yet there are some who lack it till the end of their lives.

Rosa Bonheur was one of these. She reached the three-score years and ten, in fact, the twilight period of her career, before the juvenile, impulsive tones partially fade out of her character, and a somewhat slower movement of her mind replaces them; and even then it was more the death of her old friend and companion, Nathalie Micas, which produced the change. "In every man of genius," Balzac has well said, "there is a child."

To the persistence of this juvenile and this impulsive element in her, from which indeed her letters derive some of their charm, is also due Rosa Bonheur's habit of using slang. It was a slang of the studio, a slang of the young, and was employed not through vulgarity, but from a desire, commonly manifest in children, to find a more personal language than serves as current exchange among the elders. The pet names conferred on all her family and friends, as that by which she dubbed herself, are one phase of it; and while some of these remain constant throughout, such as Pipon for Auguste, Dodore for Isidore, Juju for Juliette, Zaza for Rosa, Tatan for Tante, Rapin for M. Paul Chardin, etc., they do not hinder others being chosen for occasional service, as the letters abundantly show.

In this peculiarity Rosa Bonheur reminds one of Cowper, whose letters to his cousin, Lady Hesketh, often open with a "My dearest Coswoz" or a "My dearest Cuzzy-wuzzy," etc., and like Cowper, too, she liked to indulge in hop-o'-my-thumb rhyming letters. Here and there the nicknames are embellished with snatches of doggerel, while some of the epistles are an attempt at serious or at humorous versification rather more ambitious

146

both in form and matter. " Rosa Bonheur had a passion for verse," Princess Stirbey has written me, " and she would send me from time to time lines that were charming as regards the thought, though lacking in classical correction." One short example of this sort of macaronic verse tendency in Rosa Bonheur's correspondence may be given here and others will be found in the two chapters which follow this one. The author's system of rhymes has been preserved in translation, and also her carelessness of rhythm in the middle lines. It runs as follows:

> Young gentleman of noble fame,
> > Paul Chardin!
> Whom I accustomed am to name
> > My Rapin!
> I am glad you can assert
> You were not too much hurt,
> When your horse tumbled you into the dirt,
> And you got up perky and pert.
> Come down to By and with me dine;
> Share my brown bread, good though not fine;
> You'll eat my radishes divine,
> And drink of my black currant wine.

It is possible that this rhyming habit was caught from Rosa Bonheur's custom of reading ancient French authors whose fondness for assonance even in prose is well known. M. Chardin seems to hold this view, for he writes me: " Rosa Bonheur perhaps thought she was writing poetry when she accumulated in a number of phrases a series of words which, as regards rhyme, were simply assonant. She enjoyed our old writers, some of whom indulged in this practice. There it is that she may have got this fancy; or, which is much more probable, perhaps it was simply a whim of hers when she wished to joke."

It is probable, too, that Rosa Bonheur's epistolary style, with its colloquial energy, was somewhat influenced by her practice of wearing male attire and her unconscious fidelity to the assumed

147

rôle. More than one of the many bold epithets thickly scattered throughout her correspondence, as, for instance, " sacré bâton de Dodore," translated in the text as " Dodore, you old cuss," must have slipped off her pen when her mind, through contemplation of its outward vesture, blouse and trousers included, had dreamed itself into the sterner sex, and spoke and acted accordingly. She signs one of her letters to M. Georges Cain: " Your old General Leather Breeches " (*Votre vieille culotte de peau de Général*).

And this transmogrification was all the easier for Rosa Bonheur, as she certainly possessed the humourist's power of detaching herself from the trammels of ordinary experience and of regarding life under the angle in which philosophy is begotten, or caricature, or both. The philosophy in her case is fragmentary; both the natural bent of her mind and the cultivation of her art kept her from much treading the paths leading into the arcana of abstract thought. Instead of this, she willingly deviates into caricature that frequently takes the picturesque form. Quite as often as not she turns the laugh against herself, and the letters abound in passages in which this attitude is brought out. As regards the caricature drawings, some in pencil, some in pen and ink, a few are given here and there in the pages of this book, and best illustrate this side of her mind and talent. It would be a mistake, however, to imagine that caricature was the normal tendency of Rosa Bonheur's genius. As her friend M. Chardin remarks, " she was too serious and too meditative, and had too lofty a conception of art to deliberately seek in nature the ridiculous side of things." These frequent deviations spoken of above were caprices of the moment, and, consequently, when she indulges in them, there is a certain exaggeration and a lack of typical presentation which are not found in the professional caricaturist.

M. Paul Chardin makes these general remarks on Rosa Bonheur as a letter writer:

Rosa Bonheur's fashion of composition was to pile one fancy on top of another without any order, just as the ideas happened to come into her head, so that it is sometimes impossible to know

148

what she means to say. She gives you simply a profusion of confused thoughts. The style is frequently incorrect, but this defect is surpassed by the exuberancy and hodge-podge of the topics touched upon, which really crowd one upon the other. She liked to go off into philosophy and history, without having the slightest knowledge of those subjects. Often the fancy took her to treat with her pencil historical or legendary subjects, when her sketches were guilty of many anachronisms because of faulty documentation. She too often formed a very false opinion of persons and things, and she would express this opinion with an assurance characteristic of those who think they know what they are talking about but who really do not know. But everywhere are evidences of the warm and generous heart of the great artist, of her frank, true, devoted nature.

The number of letters that Rosa Bonheur wrote was so considerable as to be remarkable. And what astonishes also is that she seems to have replied to all her correspondents of whatever category with her own hand, even when Mlle. Micas might have relieved her more often of the less important tasks. More than one member of her circle has written me in words similar to these from her god-daughter, Mlle. Rosa Mathieu:

Rosa Bonheur's habit was to reply in person to the many communications which she received not only from her numerous friends but also from a large body of admirers. I should not have thought it unkind if my letters to her had sometimes remained unanswered. But in this respect I could not have wished for more. Often apologising for being, as she said, late in answering, she was really most assiduous, and accused herself when there was no cause. It is true I occasionally could not read the letters when I got them, hurriedly scrawled, as they generally were, on half a sheet of paper, with some kind message which I was able to make out only in its general bearing.

Georges Cain adds these touches:

At no time of her life did Rosa Bonheur seek for many friends. To the few she had she was constant, as shown by her correspond-

149

ence. Though, perhaps, she did not care for letter-writing in itself, as it was a way of meeting these friends, she would write charming epistles, merry and mad, sometimes, and always witty. If she had not had warm attachments, her letters would have been far fewer.

The truth is Rosa Bonheur was fond of using her pen. It was another kind of painting; and in nearly all her epistles the painter's mind can be seen. In fact, the whole very contradictory nature of Rosa Bonheur's complex character comes out clearly in her correspondence. It is the "*Te totum in literis vidi*" of Cicero or the comment of Rousseau on the letters of one of his female acquaintances—"in going over them, I see again my old friend with all her goodness and her petulance." Rosa Bonheur's petulance was indeed notable and stands out so conspicuously here that we may well repeat what Rogers said of Southey: "The Laureate has two inkstands always at hand; the one is filled with gall and the other with milk."

Although in selecting for publication it has often been necessary to omit those of the letters in which the same incidents are related to different people and those in which the matter is too exclusively private, both the published and the unpublished generally bear a stamp as peculiarly Rosa Bonheurian as the pictures which more fully reveal her genius. The guiding principle of the choice has been twofold. It has been sought to retain, in the first place, all that can help to throw light on the artist's life and work, and, in the second place, all that can bring out idiosyncrasy and character. To this double object, the souvenirs concerning her of Rosa Bonheur's friends, in which this volume abounds, will also, it is hoped, contribute by completing and interpreting the letters.

CHAPTER VII

In 1848 Isidore Bonheur, who was then twenty-one years old, was compelled by the conscription law to go and serve in the army, the drawing of lots not having been so favourable to him as to his brother Auguste. When he started, the resources of the family were not sufficient to enable him to find a substitute. The series of six letters which follow relates to this incident and shows Rosa Bonheur's warm affection for this, her favourite brother, as well as her constant readiness to spend her money in behalf of the family. Rosa Bonheur was then twenty-six years old.

Writing from Paris, November 2, 1848, and addressing her brother as a " Fusilier, 5th Company, 2d Battalion of the 22d Line, near Grenoble," she says:

I have several times meant to write you; but either there was no room in the family letter or else it was sent off before night, and as I am at my studio all day long, I could never manage it. So I have decided to make up a separate epistle, especially as I have a good deal to tell you.

And first, M. and Mme. Vernet [1] are interesting themselves in your behalf. They intend to try and get you an unlimited furlough or have you put on the staff of hospital assistants at Versailles. You could then have more leisure to work. I have been to see the Vernets two or three times, and his wife has called to see me, and invited me to dine with them.

I really have great hopes about the furlough. How glad we should all be and what a great jollification we would make, my

---

[1] Horace Vernet (1789-1863), the celebrated French painter of battles.

poor Isidore! In spite of my earning pretty well of money this year, we have not been able to buy you off, neither I nor the poor pater. Never mind! Perhaps the money would have been lost, for almost all the insurance companies have failed. So don't let us complain, since Providence has been good to us amidst the general distress.

We are lodged like ministers and have our firing on the same scale, gratis. Papa's salary is 3,000 francs. When you come back, you shall have a fine sculptor's studio, near the one you had in the Rue Rumford, and, moreover, near all the public works of art worth studying, which is also agreeable.

I may tell you now that I have a superb studio, where I display all my sketches and work, and, besides, that one of my recent acquisitions in the way of friends is Mène, who is a very good sort of fellow. He has presented me with his " Boar Hunt," his " Merino Ram," and his " Sheep." We struck up acquaintance at the ceremony of awarding the State Art Prizes, on which occasion, too, Horace Vernet came and shook hands with me, and when I called to see him, he offered to lend me some Arab costumes. I saw his Russian horses and he showed me all over his house. We will go and thank him together for all he is trying to do for you, and you shall see his studio.

My poor brother, I should have written all these little things to you sooner, for I know they please you. But sometimes I am so disgusted with everything that it seems they must have no importance for other people. And then, why talk to you about the good things that happen to me while you, poor lad, are carrying the knapsack? But the good news is not all.

We have had an anxious time with Papa, who was very ill for a while. Happily, he is better now, and on Sunday next his pupils that have succeeded at the competitive examination are to receive their prizes. So he will be on his throne and I on mine. Just imagine, my dear lad, the Pater and Rosa on a public platform, distributing laurel wreaths to great ninnies that execute drawings in dotted lines! And to decide on their merits, we have called in David d'Angers [1] and Heim. [2]

---

[1] The famous sculptor (1789–1856). [2] The French historical painter (1785–1865).

By the way, if your captain could use his influence in your behalf, and a small picture of mine were likely to predispose him favourably, I will send you one for him. Let me know about this. I would, if advisable, address it to him.

Hippolyte[1] is still engaged in chiselling bulls, which Papa has had cast, as well as the largest of your horses. As for myself, I have done no modelling for some considerable time. You will find everything pretty much as when you went away.

I dare say I am forgetting some particulars I ought to mention. But I have no more room. So it will be for another letter. Much love to you, my dear Isidore. I trust we shall soon see each other again. We all—both family and friends —send loving greetings, and my dog offers his paw. He is a shepherd's dog, and a handsome one, I assure you. When the day arrives, he will make one of the party to go and meet you. Once again my love to you, and believe me, your devoted sister.

October, 1849, from La Cave, a country place belonging to the Mathieu family, near Nevers:

MY POOR ISIDORE,

How grieved I was to read your letter! What can I do? I do not think I could find time to return to Paris, at present. And yet I should like to, in spite of the work I want to finish. It is true, you are going away again only for a month; but it is annoying all the same. Can anything be done? You ought to have gone to an insurance agent, with Mammy, and seen if some arrangement could not be made. It was stupid of me not to have done so myself, as I first thought of doing. But any way, my Isidore, if you are obliged to leave us, it won't be more than going there and coming back. Answer my letter directly. I will go back to Paris, if you think I can be useful. I was so relying on Mme. Vernet.

My dear Isidore, will you go into my studio, where you will find, on the left side of my desk, the drawing of a cow's skeleton,

---

[1] Hippolyte Peyrol, Sr.

153

among the other drawings? Please give it to M. St. Germain Leduc for me.

Oh! my dear old boy, I am so upset. Much love to you and good-bye.

The next three letters are written from Paris. On October 27, 1849:

My Dear Old Isidore,

I have just been to M. Genty de Bussy's.[1] You will get his letter before this. Go, without losing any time, to Châlons and hand the letter to your colonel. It is only fifteen leagues, and you must have money enough. So don't delay showing M. de Bussy's missive. Now I have something better to announce. To-day I was assured that you would soon get your discharge. Fancy our joy! You see, therefore, everything is turning out for the best. You will be able, my dear old boy, to go back to the school, and this time without fear of any further interruptions to your studies. Cheer up then, my Isidore. What remains to be done can't take long. I got back to Paris from La Cave to-day, where I had good sport and feasted well. All the menagerie are in good health. Good-bye and fondest love from your devoted and affectionate sister.

May 7, 1850:

We were glad to get your letter, as we had begun to be anxious. Thank your captain from me. I will send him my little sketch for his album in a few days, together with a few lines expressing my gratitude. This will no doubt induce him to take more interest in you. You will do well to wait for his advice. But it is difficult to know what may happen between now and the month of July. The foreign powers are still arming and the newspapers seem to think war inevitable. Of course, it is only a rumour; so don't repeat what I say. But judging from appearances, I earnestly hope you won't remain long in the army. You see, it wouldn't be easy to find a substitute later on. So

---

[1] Deputy (1793-1867).

take your steps in time, and don't hesitate to pay 1,200, 1,300, or even 1,400 francs. It will be better to sacrifice a little more now and be sure of your man.

June 16, 1850:

I am sending off to-day, by stage-coach, the box for your captain. You will be able to get it at the post-office. The carriage on it is paid. I am just going to post you your money for the substitute. So now, my dear old boy, at last, everything is finished, and I shall see you soon, I trust. I shall wait till you come before going to see David d'Angers. All send love, and I in particular. Your affectionate sister who loves her Isidore dearly.

P.S.—In this letter I enclose the order to be cashed at your post-office, for 1,100 francs. I have handed over the money here.

St. Sauveur, June 30, 1850:

At last you are free to do what you like. This thought makes me feel happy. At present, our Pipon is in the country. It will do him good. Your task must be to encourage him, since, if he likes, he can show talent, the same as I and you. Indeed, he has already enough to enable him to gain a reputation as a landscape painter. What I want is for us to be known as the three Bonheurs. As for Juliette, she has too much of the motherly instinct in her for my taste, and I am afraid she will get less happiness out of having children than from an artistic career.

I must confess to you that I have not been able to resist the desire to buy a mountain dog, which, I may add, cost me only eighteen francs.

I feel much better since I have taken two of these St. Sauveur baths.

Writing to her aunt, Mlle. Elisabeth Bonheur, from Pleyben, a town in Brittany, which province Rosa Bonheur was visiting with her brother Auguste in 1887, she says:

We have been knocking about ever since our departure, and have rarely spent more than three days in the same place; whence

155

my difficulty in keeping up a correspondence. You understand, one must wander about to see and know a region. For the last fortnight we have beheld Bretons of all kinds. I will tell you everything when I come back, and we shan't stay much longer, now. I will show you a lot of old trumpery I have bought, and, this next winter, I shall dress you up in all the Breton costumes. You shall stick, on one side, the big hat I've got, when we have emptied our glasses together. I don't give you an address, because I am not sure where we are going. If we stay somewhere for four or five days, I will send you our address.

Again, in 1860, Rosa, now at By, writes to " My dear Isidore, alias Dodore ":

I want to see your ploughmen and Juju's dog. Poor Juju! What a lot of spirit there is in that poor little woman's carcass! If only the head could do everything in a picture, things would go swimmingly with her. I always advise her not to work on too big a canvas. From what I saw, when I was last over, that dog will look very well. I trust your chimney-piece will produce a good effect at the Salon. If you get your group of ploughmen done in time, I feel pretty sure it will please, too. So try and finish it, you old dilly-dally, and then come and have a good day or two with your old Sis. We will go for some nice walks in the forest, and you can touch up your dogs. I will go to Paris and fetch you, and we can bring back some clay and wax. Thanks for your po-osy.[1] That's how you must pronounce it!

I saw Paul Chardin to-day and he told me you had written him a letter in verse. Accept my compliments. When are you coming over here to spend a few days at work with your old Sis? It would be such a pleasure to have you, old boy. You must work hard, my Isidore. Let me see you produce something new and beautiful. I know well enough what an unremunerative thing sculpture is. But it seems to me that there are still some pretty models to be executed. If you are in need of a little cash, make no bones about the matter, and confide in your old Sis, who is

---

[1] Her aunt Elisabeth used to pronounce the word "bouquet" as bookiay.

ready to supply you. I hope it won't be long before we meet. Much love to you, dear old hermit.

A year later Mme. Peyrol received these two letters from By:

Your kind letter was most welcome, and I assure you, my dear Sis, I long to have you with me. We will work hard. We will get up early and go for a walk in the fresh air under the tall trees, where the sun plays in the sap of the boughs, shortening the big shadows as he creeps up the trunks still bathed with the fantastic vapours of the lingering fogs of night. There your sister sometimes fancies she can make out figures of giants and fairies, white-bearded Druids, St. Hubert-like stags with halos around their heads, in fine, all the nonsensical phantasmagoria that the imagination conjures up, to render some of our hours less purely animal than those of work, eating and drinking.

You know how often I get sick of everything, even while animated with the best intentions. You know, too, that my temper is none of the best. Well, just now, I am on the lookout for some new " valets," as our noble aunt would say; and it is that which is worrying me. So much so, indeed, that I have a good mind to make an end of all these nuisances, to blow out Margot's brains, so as not to have to sell her, and to prevent her being driven by brutes less noble than herself, and coming to a miserable old age. I have a great mind to eat up all my sheep, to have all my dogs shot, except Shorck with the mange, to leave my house as it is and to start off with nothing but my box of colours and a few articles of linen no woman can do without, not even savages. Bah! my dear Juju; the fit will pass. But I am really sick at heart in my little kingdom. How much sovereigns are to be pitied! And how necessary it is some mission should have been given to them here below by God or the devil!

I think of you in your little cottage with your fruit-trees, poor dear Juju. You haven't much luxury; but, at least, you are happy, I hope, whilst I, your silly sister, with my chicken's heart and my wilful mind, can't be happy; and yet God has given me the wherewithal. My dear old girl, man's only ills are of his own making. With this conclusion, I will ask you not to fret about me, for, after all, I have a large fund of philosophy. Much love to you. Kiss the bairns for me.

Here is the second letter:

We are counting on you for Saturday evening. I say we, because Mother Soup [1] is grieved to the soul when she prepares a meal and the visitor does not turn up. On the other hand, she is in a rage when the visitor does not announce his arrival before-hand, considering it a dishonour to have nothing but cheese to offer in a house that respects itself. In the meanwhile, Nathalie is starting off for Fontainebleau in order to buy—not ortolans, it is true—but, anyway " quantum suf." So, whatever the weather, you must come. If it rains, I will send the big carriage drawn by the valiant Roland to fetch you from the station. Conse-quently, we expect you to dinner on Saturday; and you must obey orders! Above all, don't let Hippolyte forget to go to the grocer's at the beginning of the Rue de Tournon, the Palace end, where he must buy for Mother Micas three tins of green peas at two francs a tin.

I hope Mammy will be coming soon to see my manor. We shall have a high feast when she does come. As for Tatan, she seems decidedly to be afraid of manors and forests. Hereupon, my dear children, I take leave of you both. Don't forget Saturday.

With few exceptions all of the letters of this group are written at By.

January 21, 1861, Rosa writes to Hippolyte Peyrol, Sr., con-cerning an application to shoot rabbits in the Fontainebleau forest, which, at this time, was imperial property. The permission was eventually granted.

I will answer you as Don Quixote answered Sancho. Truly, friend, our hunting and shooting is not yet the royal pleasure, but it may become the imperial one. Meanwhile, we mustn't be discouraged by a few rebuffs. Ahem! With those sentiments of

---

[1] Mme. Micas.

158

proud and noble ambition, the appanage of fine minds, the civil and domestic virtues that animate us, in spite of the general degeneracy of our times, when the tottering papacy finds difficulty in keeping on its legs—under these circumstances, my advice is, let us give chase, if only to drive away bad thoughts, and . . . fleas! Man —and, when I say man, I include woman—must strive against namby-pamby tendencies! Well, my dear old boy, the two little panels which I am doing are already promised. But I will set about something nice at once. It will be something I can do quickly, until a better opportunity offers. Good-bye until we meet.

Isidore received two letters, one dated August 2, 1861, and the other three years later. The first runs as follows:

To think that you have two sisters and have not remembered to write to them for a whole month! Ah! how indifferent men are and how little their nature disposes them to fraternal tenderness! Not even to come and spend a day with them! No doubt you are engaged in prodigious labours, and, like your sister, you are not content. But you, the male, to whom God has given moral vigour grafted on to physical strength, how comes it that you are living on airy projects?

My dear old boy, I am only teasing you a bit. What I hanker after is to do the teasing in your studio. Indeed, I really intend to go over and have a look round, in about a week's time. Juliette wants to embrace her chick-a-biddy. But we rusty old maids and old bachelors are free from all such wants. I shall see you soon.

The second letter follows:

I am replying at once to your kind letter to tell you not to ask Father St. Germain [1] if he is in need of money, for he has written saying he has a little. So it might hurt his feelings to speak to him on the subject. If you see him again, don't mention the matter to him. My object in writing to you was for you to

---

[1] Probably M. Leduc.

find out whether he was in want of anything. Since he is provided for, the matter can drop.

When next you come to see me, I can offer you the pleasure of a ride. I have just bought for two hundred francs Rossinante, thus yclept on account of his resemblance to the warlike animal of that name. However, in spite of his apparent misfortune, this old steed, which, by the way, is no other than the long-tailed, white woolly-coated horse that we saw in the Wolf's Gorge [1] the day we were there together, this steed, I say, has good legs. I tried him yesterday. When he has spent a month here he will look very different. But even now he gallops splendidly. So now you have the tip, you might run over—Sunday, for instance. I will undertake to feed you, mount you, and, if need be, give you a bed.

I am thinking of going to Paris in a week or so. I can't get there before, as I am waiting for my big canvas. I will bring with me the image of Castor made for you as a homage. When I arrive, I intend to go for a prowl at the " Ninevites " in order to see the old masters. Embrace everybody for me, and love to yourself. Your old animal of a sister.

The word " Ninevites " in the last paragraph of the foregoing letter is painters' slang for the rooms of remarkable Assyrian antiquities at the Louvre Museum and offers a striking proof of Rosa Bonheur's indefatigableness in the continual study of every side of her art-work; for it should be remembered that a favourite subject of the Nineveh artists was the royal hunt. As Salomon Reinach has well said: " The representation of animals—horses, dogs, lions—is the triumph of Assyrian art; Greek antiquity has produced nothing superior." These are " the old masters " to whom this modern, eclectic animal-painter goes for new ideas when she comes up to Paris for a few hours' visit.

The next seven letters to Mme. Peyrol are dated from 1864 to 1865.

---

[1] In Fontainebleau forest.

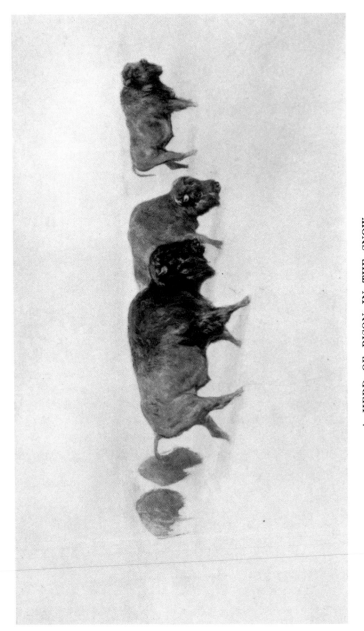

A HERD OF BISON IN THE SNOW.

1864: It is a long time, methinks, since we had a glimpse of each other. For the past week or ten days I have been hoping to run up to Paris. But I was given to understand that I might expect the Emperor's visit; so I have been cooped up all this while, and you know how little I like to be tethered. Besides, I have to endure the trying on of a dress with a train, and to be on the alert lest I am surprised in trousers and blouse; for I am trying to follow our good aunt's advice, who always laments my having abandoned the advantages of the more charming, graceful, and handsome of the sexes!

Blocked in, as I am, O Sis! I indulge in serious meditations on liberty, alternating these with divers tryings on of the aforesaid long dress; and I gracefully turn my head in front of the glass, so as to see myself behind, just like your boy René. Then, with my foot, I give the whole thing an elegant kick, in order to arrange the majestic train. Moreover, I have ordered a toque, in the Empire style, with a dozen tricolour feathers. So you can imagine, my rogue of a sister, how fine I must be in harness. Tell Tatan that her niece is even pretty! and that if I go to Court, I am likely to take the Emperor's fancy!

It's that scamp M. St. Germain who is responsible for the toque, pretending that I shall revive the fashion of his youth and that it would be a piece of clever flattery to the Court. The old man is a thorough courtier. You should have seen how he made me terminate my reply to the Duke d'Aumale, telling me I must run with the hare and hunt with the hounds, in order to obtain the privilege of inscribing in the Exhibition catalogues, together with my medals, " Mademoiselle Rosa Bonheur, Painter Extraordinary to All the Crowned Heads of Europe!"

Until such time as I can pay you a visit, dear old Juju, write me a line. It will give me patience to wait. The Duke of St. Germain sends kindest regards. Love to you all.

1864: I reply at once to yours to tell you that the decision [1] of the family council arrived just as I was writing to the Emperor's private secretary, M. Mocquart, to ask him what

---

[1] Counsel as to what Rosa should do with regard to the Emperor's visit.

I shall do. At present, therefore, I am in a state of expectancy.

My little René will be an artist, my dear Juju, a great artist. When I became his godmother, I prayed it might be so, in memory of his grandfather. Perhaps my prayer will be heard; for he loves the beautiful, as did our father. He is right to be fond of the world of flowers. It is the land of pretty dreams. I hope his good heart will help him to respect them on their stalks. It will bring him good luck.

As for Bichono,[1] he, too, will be a model man. You deserve, little sister, that God should bless your children. It is I, the old bully, that says so.

Kiss his Majesty, our brother, Pipon the First, and Marie.[2] The pretty Mme. Mondolot [3] desires to be remembered; her dog, too, with his cocked tail.

1864: I am going to reveal a secret to you which I beg you will divulge to no one. If you do, I will never forgive you. You mustn't even tell it to your husband. You shall share it because I know your generous mind, and I don't want to grieve Auguste, the rogue is so dreadfully susceptible.

Tatan is at Fontainebleau!

It was yesterday that I was favoured with her visit. Now don't be jealous, you inhabitants of Magny, for I am farther south [4] than you, and Auguste can get ready Tatan's room against the warm weather.

I wish you could have been here yesterday to witness a comical scene between M. St. Germain and Tatan. She read him some poetry she had composed when going to dine with Auguste. It simply made me ill trying to suppress my inclination to laugh, especially as M. St. Germain kept his face as solemn as a judge's.

I am doing my best to make up for lost time. But it is hard work at certain moments. Life is not always gay, and yet it glides away all too quickly.

---

[1] Nickname for her nephew, Hippolyte Peyrol.
[2] Mme. Auguste Bonheur.   [3] A friend of Mme. Micas.
[4] Aunt Elisabeth did not like the cold.

May 2, 1864: Yesterday was the opening day at the Salon, and yet here am I in By! My word! how I have stuck to my work! and I now have the joy of announcing to you that my fright of a shepherd is finished. I was getting afflicted with a stomach-ache of impatience. Now that it is going off, I seem to have thrown from my shoulders a mantle of lead, and feel quite merry again, although it's another daub that I have perpetrated! Well! one has to cultivate the philosophical mind, and I see none but those whose work is altogether bad, who are really content with themselves! So I hope still to be in the same frame of mind when I have painted my next picture.

I intend soon to go and take you to see the Salon. What interests me most is to know whether Auguste is well hung, and you, too; and whether Isidore, my heart's idol, has done well. I intend to work hard on my stags for Gambart, in order to gain time and to exhibit next year with Auguste.

I have had a visit from Mr. X. He is a nasty man, and a silly one into the bargain. And his cheek is amazing. But I have paid him back in his own coin. Let me tell you how. He came nagging me about those pictures. I was in a bad temper, but, out of politeness, I refrained from bundling him out. So we talked of some business that had been arranged by Hippolyte. Now, would you believe, old girl, that, although I told him I was doing it only for my brother-in-law, he was ass enough to propose I should treat with himself direct, fancying, no doubt, that he would gain by it, as well as I? The old fool! Well, I have just written him to say that these pictures belong to Hippolyte, and that he must treat with him.

I mean to paint my sheepfold and my horses for the next Salon. If my sheep are well done, Hippolyte shall do what he likes with them. As for the horses, they will be for Mme. X., as I promised. The big cows will be ready later, and these, too, must be bought through Hippolyte. In this way I shall have my little revenge on this impertinent fellow. Tell Hippolyte all this. Also tell him and Auguste to give some money to Tatan. I will write to her myself.

July 18, 1864: In spite of my wish to see you stay in the good country air, I am not sorry to have you nearer to me, since I can

often run over and pay you a short visit. Moreover, the hope of
having a glimpse of a nun's cap is an extra temptation, and if
these ladies were willing to admit me into their order, I might
possibly attain to the honour of being canonised! You know the
proverb, my dear Juju, " When the devil was sick, etc."; and
you alone know, too, your sister's perversity. So I can fancy
the grimace you will make on reading this.

I am pegging away, and yet the more I work the less progress
I make. Just now I am painting some landscape studies, which
allow me to hope that eventually I shall be able to excel all that
has been done in this style! I conjure up superb mossy slopes
where ants swarm and ferns fit to put in babies' cots and make
them strong. Poor Juju! how I miss you at these moments!
However, we will have a good time together next year, and, alone
with me, you shall paint masterpieces of vegetation under which
the amorous hen and the timid roe may come for shelter.

In my poetic strivings I am aided by M. St. Germain Leduc,
who, as he says, is " adorable " in his knightly attentions. The
Duke wafts a kiss toward your fair brow, my dear child, and I
also.

February or March, 1865: How sweet you are to your old
donkey of a sister! Just fancy, my dear Juju, I am virtue in-
carnate. As a proof of this, let me tell you, I have a box at my
disposal at the Lyric, where there is good music; and you know
how fond I am of music. Well, I could easily call for you and
go; and yet I resist the temptation in order to finish what I have
on hand. Since I last saw you, I have been working like a
nigger, from morning till night. So you may imagine how I long
for a little diversion, and the sight of a smiling face like yours,
little Sis.[1] But after the carnival we will sometimes go to the
Lyric.

Now, on Monday, I think of going over to meet you all, including Auguste and the children, who will no doubt be there to see the
carnival fat ox. Then, as Tatan will be one of us, I beg Mammy
to provide at my expense a truffled fowl, together with a Quillé

---

[1] At this time there was a momentary falling out between Nathalie and Rosa.

cake.[1] I want to offer a little feast. The thing must be done decently and in order; and, mind, there is enough for everybody of the truffles. And let there be the wherewithal to regale the youngsters, so that they may feel that they are really celebrating the carnival. And finally, let my aunt see that in our family we know how to preserve the respectable, time-honoured traditions of our ancestors!

Next, I will tell you, my dear Juju, that I have nearly come to the end of this letter, and shall, thereupon, return to the painting of my big stags, which work will be pushed on fast. I have just written to Pipon, as you told me he was a little under the weather. My letter won't do him any harm. I know my style always pulls him together. And yet how can one be merry? Eight months' snow and cold! One needs to be from Auvergne, not to be disgusted. I have smoked ten pouches of Maryland more than my wont. The country has been so dull. If this were to go on, I should have to think of moving. Well, good-bye, my dear Juliette. Love to the bairns. Shall see you on Monday.

May 19, 1865: The day before yesterday I had a visit from Prince Murat and his wife. They were nicer than ever. I promised to go and see them at the castle.[2] The Prince is intending to lend me some very handsome hunting hounds. If you and Isidore wish to profit by the loan, you may consider this as a hint.

Heartiest love to you, in which Mammy joins, as well as your little rogue René, who sends a kiss to his papa.

In writing to Hippolyte Peyrol, Sr., September 10, 1865, Rosa says, referring to the Legion of Honour decoration:

Will you oblige me by going to the photographer Bisson, as soon as possible, telling him that he has made me look like a worthy officer who has managed to get the cross—and the small-pox, too—on the field of battle, and does not seem pleased about it? Tell him that I consider the big cross peculiarly idiotic and

---

[1] Then the rage; a specialty of the confectioner of this name.
[2] Fontainebleau, where was the Court.

that I forbid his printing off the photos. As soon as I can do so, I will call on him and take the right sort of cross. Just oblige me as early as you possibly can.

And again, the following year, to M. Peyrol:

May 5, 1866: What the deuce are you thinking about to send us such a mongrel of a dog? Neither I nor Mother Micas is willing to have it. If we are to have a dog to stay here and be serviceable, I want him to be a good, handsome animal; otherwise, I had rather go without. I shall send you back your mongrel and you can do what you like with him, unless you prefer I should have him slain by the keeper, a task I would rather be spared. I am wondering if your sending us this sanctimonious-looking beast is not a little joke on your part.

I am just now waiting for a hat to go to the Salon, inasmuch as the one my milliner, Mme. Perrot, sent me was a fashionable horror. How I looked in it, I leave you to guess. So I postpone presenting myself in society until my head is decently covered.

I have just had a letter from his Majesty's secretary, which is couched in very kind terms.

Her next letter, written May 22, 1866, is to her sister:

I shall be going to see you soon. For one thing, I want to take a look at Dodore's sketches of lions. As for myself, I am back at work again, and, like a donkey between two tinfuls of bran, bustling about first with my horses, then with my bulls. I am going to paint a first sketch, and shall then summon a jury, impanelling you among the number. But I have no time to lose.

To her brother Isidore, Rosa writes the three following letters:

August 9, 1866: I have just written to Auguste, because you told me he was in the dumps, and that troubled me. I have been wanting each week to go and see both him and you. But I am so busy and the time is so short. I have had to interrupt my work on the horses on account of the rain, and for the last ten days have been in the studio doing what I can, until the sun shines.

I have good hopes that Auguste will receive his cross. This time, I shall be cut up, if he doesn't get it.[1] I am anxious to see your lions and your good self, for we haven't had a bout together for some time. However, I shan't be in Paris before the fourteenth. So till then, good-bye.

February 5, 1867: As I have been hard at work, it is some time since I have been in Paris. The last time I was there it was a business visit, and I didn't call at the Rue Hautefeuille, for when I once get among the family, I stick! I hear you are working at some horses and I should like to see what you are doing. But I am so busy! Just now I am fetching back some of my pictures from England,[2] and am painting away at my big canvas.[3] Anyway, I must escape one of these days in order to see you all and Tatan. When you write, send me the address of your modeller. Love to everybody. Your old Sis.

February 7, 1867: Dodore, you old cuss, I have just received your letter, which I could hardly read but which pleased me all the more as I'm in the same box as regards handwriting. However, I advise you, since you are fortunate enough to have Tatan with you, to ask her to give you a few lessons, if only to show you how to form your up-strokes.[4]

You old cuss! I asked you for the address of your modeller, and you haven't sent it. You forget, I have a masterpiece to get modelled, or else it will be spoilt, which would be a pity. So please send me this address, in the name of the pigs! I will arrange with him.

Peg away, peg away, my dear Dodore! You must produce us something fine in two months! As for your Sis, why, she is a body that hesitates at nothing. I work as I did at twenty, only there are so many things to do at once that I am like a donkey with

---

[1] But it was not till the following year that he was made a chevalier of the Legion of Honour.

[2] For the Paris International Exhibition of 1867.

[3] "The Thrashing," the large picture which she never finished.

[4] This aunt had been a teacher of French and writing.

twenty feeds of oats all around him, and trotting about to each of them in turn.

I have received a letter from Auguste. He's a nice cup of tea! It's rather late in the day to decide on a retrospective exhibition. I have just advised him to be quick and write to Herbert,[1] so as to get back some of his pictures for the Retrospective, and to keep the new ones for the annual Exhibition.

As for myself, I intend to keep to what I have already done, as you may see by the sketch given below and which was prepared by Gambart. It is he who has undertaken the needful, together with his faithful helper, the handsome Surville.[2] You will notice all my daubs are here and I am expecting others.

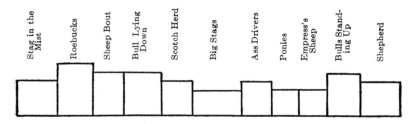

So much for the Retrospective. If the quantity can make up for the quality, all the better! I don't see why Auguste should not do like me, and put together his pictures sold by Herbert. Goodbye, my dear Dodore, and work well.

February 24, 1867, she writes to Hippolyte Peyrol, Sr.:

I have just written to M. Surville to fetch the frame of the " Sheep-fold," which is at your house, and bring it to me, as I wish to put into it the " Ass-Drivers," which I am engaged in cleaning. I got it back in a most dirty state, and the frame was all broken. Luckily I thought of the other frame, which is just the same size.

I expect you are worried about your exhibition, and poor Isidore, too. I hear his group is a vigorous one. No doubt it

---

[1] A Liverpool picture-dealer who had bought several of Auguste Bonheur's canvases.

[2] Gambart's Paris agent.

will succeed. It appears Auguste is contenting himself with the annual Exhibition. As for me, I am taking all the pains in the world to repair all my infirmities [1] which cost so dear. At times, I am afraid I have thoroughly diddled many sincere amateurs in art who buy pictures in order to make money out of them, yet without intending to be taken for dealers. Well, we shall see.

In the following August she writes to Mme. Peyrol:

Thanks for the good news. At last! He has it. Hurrah! Your brother is a chevalier of the Legion of Honour, too. I wish I could start for Paris at once and from there for Magny. But I can't. I am kennelled up here, waiting for Mr. Gambart and his better half, whom I can't run away and leave or tell not to come. Anyway, I shall be at Magny on Sunday, where we can all meet and drink to the health of the newly-made chevalier. Once more, thanks for your telegram. I shall see you on Saturday. Has your good husband got a medal? You might have told me, your old Sis.

At this time there was some talk of Auguste Bonheur being a candidate for a seat in the fine art section of the Institute of France. But nothing came of it.

At the end of her letter of November 3, 1867, addressed to Isidore, Rosa refers to this:

Tell this gentleman that I cannot receive him. I am at work, and am carrying on my studies. So it disturbs me to receive people. Besides, more than ever, I am disinclined to paint pictures to order. When I have been lucky enough to complete a picture to my liking, I shall exhibit it. But it bores me to death to have admirers. So get rid of your task by saying: " My sister does not wish to receive any one at her house; it disturbs her in her work." There, that's the end of the matter!

I hope, like you, I shall have the pleasure of seeing M. Pipon a member of the Institute, with his sword and his cocked hat. Love to you, my old philosopher.

---

[1] A favourite name for her pictures.

REMINISCENCES OF ROSA BONHEUR

July 24, 1868, Mme. Peyrol received this invitation from Rosa Bonheur:

The big girls [1] have written to ask me to go and see them, and brother Pipon sent me yesterday also a pressing invitation to pay him a short visit. To my great regret, I can escape but for a few days, and that only because I see the sun disappear, so that I can leave my horses. Moreover, it is the By fête on Sunday, which itself is enough to drive me away.

I shall start, therefore, to-morrow, Saturday evening, and shall spend Sunday in paying a visit to Ophélie. Then I intend to call on that old maid Dodore and carry him off, as well as you, for a few days at the sea-side. I shall make you both, willy-nilly, embark in a fishing-boat. So prepare yourself and Dodore also to be off on Monday morning. We must be at the station by nine, to catch the express. At three we shall be there. The ex's are my affair. So give the old sculptor a hint.

Our brother Germain arrived here yesterday morning, all ready equipped for his tour.[2] The pumps his mother had put in his knapsack to ease his poor tootsies from time to time were rather tight; so we have turned them into slit shoes, with a penknife. So, finally, the excursion will begin under the best auspices. Germain sends love. Good-bye till Saturday evening or Sunday morning.

Again, on May 31, 1869, she writes to Isidore:

I heard yesterday, through Mr. Gambart, my dear old Dodore, that you had gained a medal. That's what comes of being good and working. I am all the more pleased as I think you deserve it. I had a letter from Auguste this morning. He, too, is very pleased. While you are in the humour, peg away, my dear old Dodore. Life is awfully stupid. But we have got to live; and to live well, the best thing is to work. I am fond of moralising, and never miss an opportunity of having my say. It is Auguste who got me into the way. By the way, Auguste's mare is capital.

---

[1] Her nieces, the daughters of Auguste Bonheur.

[2] He was to walk through Auvergne, and thence, by rail, go to Spain and Portugal.

Only she hasn't much strength at present. I think I shall see you soon. Until then, good-bye and love from your old Sis.

From Rosa Bonheur's letters to Mlle. Elisabeth Bonheur, these two are quoted:

June 28, 1869: The present letter is in order to have the pleasure of asking you how you are. Tell me in your reply if you can wait for your month's money till July 4th, since I can't go to Paris before. If not, I will send it. On the fourth, I shall be with you.

The fine weather has come, but we shall have it hot, and when we don't have it hot, it is really cold. We no longer get the mild springs we had when I was young. The earth is travelling through some nasty cycles. I do believe, in spite of the free-thinkers, with their profundity and their divine gift of clairvoyance, that this general disturbance, this displacement of the seasons and many things besides, which were much better in the time of Dagobert, must be attributed to the fatal idea of burning the forests of Gaul, and, later, of getting out coal, which, through the great consumption of it, is altering the weight of the globe. Add to this the innovation of railways and steamboats, not to speak of the various manufactories and all the domestic chimneys, and all this ends in smoke instead of solid matter. The material is changed into spirit. How is it possible for the earth to keep its balance? Well, well! the oracles must needs be accomplished. The world must perish through the sun's fire; spirit must destroy matter, for the flesh killeth, but the spirit giveth life.

Good-bye, my dear Ophélie. Fondest love to you, my dear old solitary one. Enjoy the sunshine and the affection of your devoted niece.

August 15, 1869: Your letter reached me as I was getting up this morning, and delighted me, my dear old Tatan. I am a downright scamp, not to have gone to see you, all the same. Never mind, I will go soon.

It is true the heat we have had has something to do with this long absence; and, then, I am beginning to get like you. Provided

171

I know the members of the family are happy, that's the chief thing.

If fate had made me captain of a frigate, a brig, or an admiral's ship, I should have to support absence and all sorts of privations as regards affection. Well, reflect, my dear Ophélie, that envious Father Time is a rascally old joker who is never tired of playing tricks, that he sprinkles us with an infinite number of infirmities, and that we have to make haste, if we want to get through with our essential duties.

Anyway, I feel the need of seeing my brother's children, having recently seen those of my sister. When I go there, I will call on you. I am glad you saw Dodore receive his medal,[1] and I am pleased to hear of Mlle. Jacquemart's well-deserved ovation.[2] Much love to you.

In the spring of 1870 Rosa Bonheur had a falling-out with the Micases, and there had been some correspondence between her and her family about the project of Mme. Peyrol going out to By and renting a room in the village, which Rosa might use, in case of need, to take her meals in. The three following letters to Elisabeth Bonheur and Mme. Peyrol have reference to this domestic storm:

July 7, 1870: We have just had the boon of a mild storm, my dear Ophélie, which has at last given us a supply of good rain. I went and held my head under it like a duck, and, if it had been proper, I would have undressed. But there are men here, so I was hindered, as you may fancy. It was quite time the rain came, for we were all dying with heat. As for me, I was like a fish out of water.

You must know, my dear friend, that I have stopped taking my meals with the Micases. Without falling out, we have settled so as to be free reciprocally. This is the principal news, and I

---

[1] At this time the annual Salon awarded a unique medal in sculpture. Isidore Bonheur had received it in 1865, and he now received it again, which placed him *hors concours*.

[2] Nélie Jacquemart (Mme. Edouard André), the distinguished portrait artist. She received her second medal this year.

send it to you at once, as you are in my confidence. If my servants wish to poison me, it will be easy for them to do so at present. But they have no interest to serve by it, which is the best guarantee against any such thing happening.

Best love, until I see you, which will be one of these next days. Your affectionate niece.

July 18, 1870: This letter is to tell you:

> Pretty woman,
>   Coy and fickle;
> Trust her, no man,
>   E'en a mickle.

In other words, my dear little sister, I have changed my mind. I certainly won't prevent your husband's renting a little room in the country and making a kitchen of it. I have calculated that this would give me two—one for days of storm. I think I could even supply a fat sheep or two to be cooked in the fashion of the red Indians, and Germain shall be the cook. Peyrol has only to buy a crane big enough to bear the weight of a whole sheep, and then to roast it on a spit. Mammy shall baste the beast in its own gravy. As for me, I will do the eating. Meanwhile, I am training her son for the artistic glories of oil painting and my own desire is to urge him to do something for himself. In doing so, I wish his well-being; for man's first duty is to fettle for himself, a duty which is no child's play.

Crying a truce to nonsense, I announce to you, my dear little sister, that I have gone back to my friend's table, and am delighted with the result. Each may think what he or she likes. I shall keep my eyes on the scales of justice to console myself for the opinions of Peter and Paul who are at liberty to consider me a weathercock. I was born with a spirit of contradiction, and as the newspapers are very bellicose at present, I, on the contrary, am inclining toward peace, if only to show a little opposition. Thus, I offer to your eyes the appearance of equilibrium within my household.

When you come, therefore, you will find a welcome at my neighbour's table, if it suits you, and I hope it will; for you have had nothing to do with my caprices and the whims of my character, which is somewhat similar to Tatan's. This proves how much more nature is responsible than I in the matter, since I take after my aunt through my father. And it is not your fault, if you can't always overcome your nature. I find, indeed, that the old Adam is terrible in me; so I am quite ready to excuse others from time to time.

Thank the Portuguese aunt [1] for her pineapple, which was i'faith very toothsome. We had quite a feast. But I should have preferred seeing you eat it also, which, however, would have been difficult; for it would have necessitated my going to Paris or you all coming here, in order that all the members of the family might nibble a portion of it. But perfection is impossible in this nether world, which is why St. Paul says, " Marriage is honourable," but the unmarried state more honourable, sometimes.

And you, Mme. Geneste, since you have taken to gallivanting about, you will be welcome here with your big little sister, Mme Bonheur, second of the name; and I, too, shall be pleased to go and see you, but I don't know when. And now, to each and all of you, good-bye.

You see, my little Juju, that I am not sparing in the sweets of correspondence. I have my days for it. Such is my nature. Ah! here I am back at the beginning of my paper. So love to all, and believe me, your affectionate sister.

July 28, 1870: I am very pleased you should think I wouldn't be guilty of hurting the feelings of an old woman and her daughter, who is already quite enough afflicted with physical ailments and the disorders of her noddle. But one must not expect perfection in humanity and discernment is a rare gift, foolishness being often mingled with bad as with good sentiments. I note what you say about your not speaking to Auguste or any one else of my disagreement with the Micases, thinking it would not last. However, I may tell you, my dear little sister, that I have just the same character as the rest of you. I don't like people meddling

---

[1] Mme. Geneste, sister of Rosa Bonheur's stepmother, who had been living in Portugal since 1867, and who had come on a visit to her native country.

with my business in my own house, and I don't care a fig about what may be thought of my private affairs, into which no one has the right to poke his nose. I resemble Auguste in this respect. And I have always been careful not to obtrude where I was not wanted, holding that it is only fair each should be responsible for his own conduct. So from this you will see, my dear Juliette, that it is quite indifferent to me what people think, when I am myself conscious of acting for the best. You are right, Sis, to take the same view that I do in the matter.

Concerning an illness, she says on February 25, 1870, in a letter to Mme. Peyrol:

Don't worry about me. I am all right now, though I have been really unwell—mentally, however, rather than physically. I was so upset to see poor Nathalie suffer; and she has been very ill. Such a life is a veritable martyrdom. You may imagine, consequently, that I was not much in the humour to do honour to a marriage. I preferred not to go, although I am fond of my old Surville.[1] But I couldn't get in the right mood. Besides, I have annoyances of an artistic character. You know yourself what it is to be tempted to kick a hole through the canvas, just as I am now, in order to give more depth to my landscape. What a profession! How much better I should like to charge a body of men, sabre in hand, and so allay my rage, instead of having to fret and fume before a bit of canvas, and to see some one else suffer into the bargin.

At present, Nathalie is somewhat improved; so don't be anxious about me. I hope Mammy will soon be well also, and that the devil will get tired of substituting evil for good. Say your prayers, and let fly at him with some holy water! When I have finished the picture that causes my fits of rage, I will run up to Paris. In the meanwhile—love.

November 26, 1871, writing to Isidore concerning an art present which Mr. Gambart had ordered from him for Rosa:

---

[1] Mr. Gambart's Paris representative, who was getting married.

I have received a letter from Mr. Gambart that concerns you. I wanted to send it to you, but can't imagine where I have put it, just because I laid it aside carefully with this intention.[1] Anyway, I can tell you, all the same, what there was in it. He wants you to make your sketches of the proposed group and send them to him. I shall be only too happy to possess a fine bronze of yours. Later on, I hope I shall be able to repay the good fellow for his kind thought and for the friendship he shows me. All you have to do is to oblige us both.

On Sunday you will see my young guests and companions, Joseph Verdier and Germain. The latter has really a good heart. The former has told me things about him that please me immensely.

Now I present you with my homage and am off to take my soup. Endeavour to work with resolution and your sister will profit by it. If you are a good boy, you

> Shall have your brows with garlands bound,
> With angels hovering all around.

So says your old Sissy.

This note to Mme. Raymond Bonheur was written in July, 1872:

My dear Mammy, alias Mme. Bonheur, I send you a line by Germain, because I shan't be able to see you myself before I start to-morrow for the sea-side, where I intend to spend the week at Mme. Carvalho's. Let Germain come back here, after he has been to Magny and seen you, for he seems to be taking to his work. But tell him to say nothing to the Micases about my staying with Mme. Carvalho. If he were to, Nathalie would very likely go into a fit of rage that might be dangerous to her. I intend to stuff her up with a story of my being with Auguste and Marie, for I don't want to give her an attack of apoplexy. At her age, it would be bad for her. In the meanwhile, I am in the best of

---

[1] "Rosa had a prodigious memory for all that related to her art," one of her nephews writes me; "but in other matters she was most forgetful."

spirits; and, on my return, I will go and arrange with you about the rent for Germain's studio. Love to you, Juliette and the children.

From 1860 until this time all Rosa's letters have been sent from By. The next two, however, are written from Puys, a little bathing-place near Dieppe, on the English Channel. July 17, 1872, Rosa says to Isidore Bonheur:

I write to invite you, at the request of Mme. Carvalho, to come and spend a few days at the sea-side. Being alone, we are quiet and happy, and in conditions of freedom and simplicity that you are no less fond of than I. I should really like to see one of you accept the honour and friendship shown us by Mme. Carvalho. She evidently hopes to keep me longer with her by asking you to join me. I have just written on the same subject to Juliette; and if she can get away, you might come together, for there is room here for you both. Indeed, she would only have been too glad to have you all here, if it had been possible. Now, if you all refuse, it will vex me very much, since it will look as if an intentional slight were intended. Do come, and we can return together. Bring things for drawing and modelling; of course it wouldn't do to lounge about all day. There are animals tethered here, so you will be able to occupy your time. Reply at once, and tell me the day and hour if you are coming.

At the same time Rosa writes to Mme. Peyrol:

I am greatly put out that you can't share my stay with Mme. Carvalho, in a quiet little nook full of interesting things for your pictures; for there are heaps of rustic farms hereabouts. In fact, you know all this for you have been here. Mme. Carvalho, as well as I, is writing again to you. It won't be kind if neither you nor Auguste is willing to give her the pleasure of seeing you, especially as she shows us such a friendly feeling. As for me, little Sis, you know how much I love her and esteem her. If only you were to spend five or six days with her as I have, you would see how good and sincere she is, as well as intelligent.

I am just a little annoyed about that silly Nathalie. Perhaps I shall play her the trick, after all, of bringing her here, if I remain a few days longer; and I intend to stay as long as possible, on account of the friendship which I receive and reciprocate. Love to you and to all.

Back once more at By, she writes the following eight letters, one to Isidore Bonheur, the rest to Mme. Peyrol:

November 25, 1872: I hasten to reply to your letter to rid you of your gentleman. You have only to tell him I have nothing to sell at present. I have done nothing and don't feel I want to do anything; and, even if he were to come, I shouldn't upset my constitution in working for him. However, I suppose you are working, and, to tell the truth, I am too; but without the appearance of it. That is to say, I am working for my own satisfaction, as an artist. For, above all, I am an artist, and my aim is to paint a few pictures toward the end of my career. I, too, dream of glory!

It is splendid weather just now for landscape painting. Yesterday evening I went to have a look at the river which has overflowed. All the meadows between the Seine and the Loing are flooded and the effect is fine.

May 9, 1873: I see by your letter that the Salon is jogging along pretty much as usual, except that there are some budding artists to be met with by the way. In fine, it would seem that the average excellence of execution is higher and that there is a more general tendency toward photographic intensity. There is no harm in this tendency of the art world. Nor need we complain if, in some quarters, the art of painting is considered simply as a sort of pastime, for we know that it is not so easy as all that, alas! Just compare all those canvases in the Salon with the great conceptions of Rat Phaelle![1] And yet, all the same, little Sis, between you and me, this last-named gentleman hadn't a fine ideal

---

[1] One of those pointless puns that Rosa Bonheur loved to indulge in. She, of course, refers to Raphael.

of the Eternal Father, representing him with a white goat's ancient-looking beard! To depict God with the face of a poor old man is, to my way of thinking, the highest presumption and impiety. Moreover, to make him old and bearded is as much as to say that his immortality is decrepit, and that, tired with creating, he has grown gray at the task. Don't show my letter to the clergy. It might be the death of me!

July 18, 1873: I had been really thinking of going to Paris lately. But I have been unwell, partly on account of my age, and partly because I injured the calf of one of my legs in trying to cure a cramp with my whip. It was only yesterday that I began to walk again. I fretted myself to fiddle-strings, for I am not used to being cooped up.

Nathalie came back from Paris yesterday. She went on some business of her own, and also to pay Tatan's rent. I told her not to go up and see Tatan. If she had, Tatan, finding I wasn't with her, would have walked into her like fury and there would have been the deuce to pay!

You mention a trip to Puys. My present state of health will hardly allow me to give myself that pleasure, which would perhaps, however, do me good; for last year I profited a great deal by it. I was happy to be with Mme. Carvalho and her kind brother, M. Miolan, whom I miss.

Nothing goes on right when I can't carry out my ideas; and I don't care to work except when things are to my liking. The devil cannot conquer me, however. For the last three weeks he has been playing me his tricks, so that I haven't touched a brush. Consequently, I am like the bristling hair on the back of a mad dog.

I intend to go to Paris as soon as I can trot about again. In the meanwhile, love to you and Dodore. If you come over with your boys, you will give me much pleasure. Remember me to all.

August 1, 1874: You must own that you are lucky with your ugly duckling of a son, my little chickabiddy sister. He has more merit than a saint; not that I reproach heaven. But really, not to speak of the true deserts of your offspring, to which I must render justice, you are downright lucky. I have friends who are not in the same case. You must be pleased; indeed, I know you are.[1]

I am not quite up to the mark myself, and I am going to see if a change of air will do me good. I think of spending a week or so with Mme. Carvalho and am already dreaming of catching big-bellied fish.

As for my painting, I have turned my back on it for the moment. But that won't last long, unless I also turn my toes to the daisies!

I dreamt last night that Bordeaux was on fire! It is a sign of glory for that town!

March 5, 1875: I have not been able to answer your little letter earlier, my dear little sister, in which you thank me for my little fish, because I have just been a little upset in my health. But make your little mind easy, for my little stock of health seems as though it would leave me for some time longer on this little earth; and I am presumptuous enough to suppose that my little death would pain all my little friends, especially my little Sister. It is quite enough to have lost little Father Corot;[2] and I quite understand that his death grieved you, although you never saw him, since he died as a Saint Hypocrite, like nearly all the saints. I should like, I assure you, to live long enough to have this glory.

I see that you are pegging away, which pleases me on your account. I should like you to have a success this year with your sheep—and if only the gods will hear my prayers or rather my wishes, you will—and to make these idiotic judges fork you over a good medal. So set to, little Sis, and let them see what colour can do.

I see, too, you are desirous of coming to me in order to enjoy the charms of the fine weather. I quite understand it, little Sis, I quite understand it. Well, when you are ready to carry out this wish, just give me timely notice, for I have taken it into my head to have Mme. Carvalho with you. Mother Micas being ill,

[1] Young Hippolyte Peyrol had just taken his bachelor's degree.
[2] Born in 1796, he died in Paris on February 23, 1875.

we can't do this summer what we did last, as I intend to work and can't look after the house. At present, I have no housekeeper, and Nathalie has started painting. So the cooking is sure to suffer. This is why I want to kill two birds with one stone, and, while inviting two persons only, at most three at a time, get you to come at the date when Mme. Carvalho does me the friendly honour of spending a day or two here.

Much love, my dearest Sister, and work well until I have the pleasure of seeing you.

May 16, 1875: I hear your picture looks very well at the Salon, which gives me much pleasure, as you will quite understand. It seems Germain's pictures, too, produce a good effect. I am delighted, and hope his health is better.

August 16, 1876: I take up my pen again to-day, my arm now allowing me to write. Isidore must have told you I had a narrow shave of breaking my fore-paw, that of the off-side, while making a dare-devil leap with my horse. But, little Sis, the angels watched over me and I was held up in the void. The soul of our old Ophélie,[1] or of our mother or father—sex has no importance up above—or else of some long-dead friend, must have aided me.

I have done the proper thing. I have just written a letter to good old Marandon, who wanted to trot her casket over here, together with two or three young damsels, which would have made four, all told. I have told her that I shall be pleased to go and fetch the casket myself. You alone, my dear Sis, can understand how highly delighted and flattered I am![2]

I cannot tell you how grateful I feel to you for being willing to represent me in the Delaroche hemicycle at the School of Fine Arts, and on the arm of M. de Chennevières, who is a perfect

[1] Elisabeth Bonheur died in 1873.

[2] Mlle. Marandon, head of the Girls' Drawing School, over which Rosa Bonheur once presided, and her pupils, had designed a casket as a gift to the latter. But she disliked being disturbed at By. In the next paragraph reference is made to the commencement ceremonies of this same school, which took place under the chairmanship of the Marquis de Chennevières (1820-99), then director of the School of Fine Arts.

gentleman, if ever there was one. Now people will go and believe I am a charming little lady, fair-complexioned and shy; for your blushes must have been pink and youthful. I can quite fancy the scene, and the looks of the parents! What glory! as you say.

We've got the heat back again. There are storms all round, but not one here. So the forest has caught fire. We went yesterday evening to see the Solle valley [1] burning. For the last three days the work of extinguishing has been going on and is even now not quite finished.

Flirt my compliments all around. With love to yourself, your half-burnt Sister.

November 22, 1876: I am glad to hear your son finds favour in his colonel's eyes.[2] Colonels have long arms where men in the ranks are concerned. Last time I was in Paris, I caught a bad cold while sketching some costumes at the "Tapisseries," and have been rather poorly, but am better now. We were hoping to be in Paris again before this. But you know how quickly the days pass. When you come over, you mustn't be too much afraid of a tame tiger I have got from Marseilles, to make studies after.

On December 18, 1876, Rosa Bonheur writes M. and Mme. Ulysse Besnard, whose daughter Germain Bonheur married the following year:

It is with unfeigned pleasure that I thank you for the two fine pieces of porcelain which you have so kindly sent to me and my friend. It is not necessary for me to say how beautiful they are, for that would be simply repeating what everybody declares concerning your celebrated artistic ware.[3]

I learned yesterday from Isidore that Germain is much better. I should like to know that he is perfectly well and so sure to be happy in this poor life of ours. Let us hope that so it will

---

[1] A charming spot in the Fontainebleau forest.

[2] At this moment, Hippolyte Peyrol, the sculptor, was doing his year's military service.

[3] M. Besnard was a well-known painter on porcelain, as has already been stated.

be. It would be very sad to sacrifice for him a young girl, for such would be the case, unless he can be cured. I trust there is in store for them both, God being willing, only good and happiness.

In 1877 she wrote four times to Mme. Peyrol:

January 1: I am in such a hurry to finish my boars that I don't allow myself even the time to go out at present, and shan't go to Paris before they are done. Let me wish you a very

Kiki.

happy New Year. If you could come over, it would please me, and you would see how I have worked during these short days. To-day, no doubt, all the young people will be assembled at Magny, and everybody will be merry. Here, I have my accounts to make up, Christmas boxes to give, letters and cards to reply to; and, before going to Paris, I must, as I have already said, polish off these boars.

March 5: As I think of going to Paris soon, I shall be delighted to see what you are doing. Over here, I am pushing on my studies of a tiger's coat, in order to get rid of my hired animal as soon as possible. Poor Sis, I know how you love your painting and how hard you work; but you must get a little fresh air now and then.

It was a great satisfaction to me to learn that the amorous Germain is about to have his desires crowned by Hymen. The Ulysse family appear to be delighted, so that everything is for the best in the best of worlds, and we shall be able to enjoy ourselves at the wedding. Nathalie is making her little preparations already.

In haste, but with love; for the day is at its best, and the days are still short. Compliments to all, including the wedding folk.

April 24: I went to Paris the day before yesterday and came back the same day, so that I couldn't call and see you. My reason for going was to visit a sale exhibition of pictures that I wanted to look at. We shall return next week for another and for the Salon. Then we shall have time to drop in at Rue de Crussol.

If you feel inclined for a trip this year in the Pyrenees, I think we'll start in June or July; and you shall share in our doughty deeds, if your husband is willing to entrust you to us giddy-pates. Nathalie must take the waters at Eaux-Bonnes. We can make a few excursions without tiring ourselves and it will do us all good. While at Bordeaux, we will trot round to Verdelet, Quinsac, and Pessac.[1] Surely this will tempt you!

June 5: I expect you are wondering whether I shall soon have finished the picture I promised your husband. Well, I may tell you, little Sis, that I have made haste and that, in spite of a pretty bad attack of influenza and the pictures I had promised to finish for Gambart, yours is nearly terminated. The frame is ordered. I shall have it in six or seven days and will write when I send the thing off, unless you prefer to come and fetch it yourself. So you see, I haven't wasted my time.

As for our journey, I am afraid it will be delayed; for I must get that copy of the boars ready for Messire Gambiche,[2] and there is still something to be done to it. Moreover, I want to pay an-

---

[1] Little places associated with their childhood.
[2] A nickname for Mr. Gambart.

other visit to the Salon, which I haven't yet had leisure to inspect. The days run away so quickly! as you see.

Since we were not starting at once, I decided to have some work done in my wood. After hesitating a long time about getting rid of my rather untractable stag, I have just determined to have a trellis-work constructed in the middle of the wood and to make a little pond there, too, where will be installed hind and stag. It will be charming; don't you think so? Furthermore, I shall have the wall pulled down that separates the garden from the wood; and to complete the alterations, there will be a gravel walk all round the stag-park. When finished, you must come and see all my improvements.

In haste and with much love, in which Nathalie joins.

From Bayonne, on July 9, 1877, she writes to Auguste Bonheur, giving some account of the journey referred to in the preceding letters:

Here we are at Bayonne, as you see. We arrived last night, at eight o'clock, after spending five days at Bordeaux, where Juliette paid her devotions in all the churches, which we conscientiously visited. We found time to go to Quinsac and Cadaujac, crossing the Garonne in a little fishing-boat. I succeeded in finding my fig-tree and the tree under which mamma tried to make me read. Now it is a magnificent one. We drank some milk at the foot of Bel-Air, at a vine-dresser's, where I insisted on taking some soup with barley-bread in it, as in my childhood, with the vintagers. There were peasants of my own age with whom I perhaps played as a girl. In fine, I abandoned myself to all my childish reminiscences.

We went to Royan by steamboat. Really the Garonne is a splendid river! We must tell you all about this trip when we see you. The Landes we crossed, too, where, about Dax, there are some charming things suitable for our kind of painting, big oaks and most picturesque cork-trees, from under which one gets a glimpse of the Pyrenees.

Bayonne is delightful with its fortifications. You pass over drawbridges, which is just what I like. We are in an excellent hotel here and intend to leave our trunks while we make a few trips in the neighbourhood. If we find anything that tempts us, we shall do a little sketching.

Juliette looks in the pink of health. People take her for our daughter and we all three tuck in alarmingly. We are taking life easily and are enjoying ourselves so far. Although we are always on the jog, we don't get tired. Nathalie wishes to be remembered to you all. Much love to you and all, dear old Pipon.

P.S.—I had left room for Juliette to add a few lines, but the little minx, with her love of mystery, prefers a little letter of her own. Once more, love to you, dear old brother.

From the following note to Hippolyte Peyrol, Sr., in 1877, we get an idea of the busy life Rosa led at By and of her financial relations with Mr. Gambart:

Tell your amateur I can't pledge myself before the end of the year. The days are short and I haven't the time to do even a water-colour. Those I have are not for sale, being trials I want to use up later. As for a picture, well, I have some that are begun. But I can't neglect my stag any longer, inasmuch as I shall soon be in need of money; for I am obliged to settle bills for work that has been done to the place here. And as I already owe money to Gambart, I must finish him his stag and his ass's head, in order to ask for a fresh supply of funds. Otherwise, I should be stumped up, you see. I am sorry not to be able to do everything at one time.

Love to all, in which Nathalie joins.

In her letter to M. and Mme. Germain Bonheur, written in 1878 from Paris, Rosa Bonheur praises her two young Peyrol nephews:

My dear brother and nice sister-in-law, thanks to both of you for your good letters. I learn with joy that both of you are in good health, and that you, my dear Germain, are working well at your art. Yes, René has parts, and if he will work, I believe he will go far; and his brother is not less talented, all of which must please you. The latter is going to make your father's bust,[1] and if he does it as well as the one he made of Nathalie, it will be a good bit of work.

I have come to Paris to see the horse-show.

After returning to By, she encourages Germain Bonheur with this note:

July 5, 1879: I have read with much pleasure your good letter. Here I am, as you may guess, back home again, which is pleasant, because of the animals and the retainers living on my domains; because of the air of the woods and because of my trousers, which I always pull on again with satisfaction, like the young lads who don them for the first time.

I am glad to see that you have recovered from the fatigues of Paris and that you are preparing to take up work again. That's a good idea of yours to make a shepherd picture. Such a group is always charming and the picturesque figure of the shepherd, in the sun and in the rough ploughed fields, can be treated better than Millet does it. Man and beast produce a happy effect under such conditions.

Good luck in your work, my young brother. You can succeed, if you try. You are still young enough to secure a distinctive and honourable position in our field of art. Mark what I tell you. There will be more Bonheurs still.

On January 21, 1880, to Mme. Peyrol, in which is a reference to the celebrated Spanish political family of Silvela:

I write to you at once the news I have just received and which will be made public in a few days. I think it will please you. The King of Spain [2] has just conferred on me the title of Commander of the Royal Order of Isabella the Catholic. This title ought to be to your taste! I have just written to Auguste, and I fancy the son of his godfather, Auguste Silvela,[3] must have had something to do with it, together with the talent I believe I possess, for which last reason it may be hoped that the King of

---

[1] Ulysse Besnard.   [2] Alfonso XII.   [3] See pages 4 and 35.

Spain is not badly bestowing his commandership. I feel flattered, and so address the announcement, all hot, to every member of the family. Nathalie is as proud as the wife of an old soldier! We have a Castilian dignity!

To Auguste Bonheur she writes the same day:

I don't want you to hear from any one else the news Mr. Gambart has just announced to me—viz., that the King of Spain has just conferred on me the title of Commander of the Royal Order of Isabella the Catholic. It is freely offered and I accept it. It would be presumptuous not to and an insult to those that offer it. But my conscience is not quite easy. For as for being a Catholic, I can hardly say I am, and don't believe I ever shall be. However, I imagine that this honorary title in no way pledges me on that point, and I am flattered by the honour done me.

A short time afterward, April 11, 1880, to Mme. Peyrol:

Don't be anxious about my health. I have good news to give you. The doctors tell me I can start for Nice as soon as I like. We shall be able to sleep in the train, and at Marseilles, Mr. Gambart will come to meet us. I shall try to have a look at the harbour, for I am fond of seeing ships. I shall also have a peep at my lions, which I am longing to do.[1]

We shall stay only a week at Nice, as I have a good deal to do here and I don't want to keep Mr. Gambart there on my account. I shall take my little black colour-box with me; it will be enough for sketching a few impressions of palms, rocks and backgrounds. The annoying part will be the two or three visits and dinners, which I shall have to swallow. However, I shall clap on sail. When I return, I shall set to work on my lions.

This trip to Nice, she describes to Auguste Bonheur as follows, on April 16th:

---

[1] Rosa Bonheur generally visited the Zoölogical Gardens when she passed through Marseilles.

You will no doubt be pleased to have a few lines from me. I think I have done right to risk the journey, which we managed capitally. The sea-air seems already to have benefited me, and the change has calmed my mind.

About a dozen leagues beyond Lyons the scenery became most interesting. The Dauphiny mountains look quite the grand with their bluffs skirting the Rhone as you pass along to Avignon, Tarascon, and Marseilles, which last is a most amusing town. The port is superb. There I had a glimpse of some old sailing-vessels different from anything you will see elsewhere. They must be Spanish or ships from the coasts of Africa. I paid a visit to the Zoölogical Gardens, which are fine and well kept. I found my lion and lioness, who looked quite handsome. I kissed one of the baby-lions, whose father is named Nero, but doesn't belong to me.[1]

From Marseilles, here, you pass through mountains that run along the sea, wooded with pines. Though not very lofty, the mountains are exceedingly pretty with their varied forms, and there are little quaint sea-washed creeks where one might make some very original sketches. In the direction of Cannes and St. Raphael, which you pass to get here, I saw some fine landscapes, with shepherds and flocks of black and russet sheep, wild and picturesque in appearance. I intend to indulge in some tip-top studies, you shall see, my dear old Pipon.

As for this home of Mr. Gambart's, it is a superb palace. Everything is trim and neat, with palms, aloes and all sorts of tropical plants growing in the open air. As a background, there is the Gulf of Nice, quite like that of Naples, judging from the pictures I have seen.

She writes from By to Mme. Peyrol, on July 1, 1880, concerning the death of Germain, who had been ill since 1875, suffering from a heart disease, chiefly the result of the fatigues of the Franco-German war, in which, as we have already seen, he took an active part as a private soldier. His trouble grew worse with each attack:

---

[1] Rosa Bonheur had a lion of her own named Nero. See page 344.

So our brother Germain has gone from us, I suppose it was inevitable. But, like you, no doubt, I was painfully affected by the sad news arriving just when he seemed a little better. He has finished like a poor lamp that has no more oil; and his life could never have been very happy, like that of a man who is able to accomplish something. He knows now the Great Secret. And the justice of the Being that has determined life and death will know better than ourselves how to weigh his faults and his good intentions. Our father's soul, which was good, has asked to have back that of his son, which was vegetating; and, in this world, God allows many things to be done which will be sifted by his justice; for he alone knows how to weigh the good and the evil.

I have written to poor Mammy, who is the one I pity most. I could not attend the funeral service. Indeed, I should not have gone in any case, yourself and our brothers being there. I think it my duty to preserve my health for the talent God has given me. I must end my life in fulfilling my destiny. Emotion and fatigue might have brought on an accident, especially as I have been much tired by work and the great heat.

Writing to Auguste Bonheur from Nice, March 25, 1881, Rosa says:

Fearing you may have read in the paper about the fire at the Nice Opera House, I write in haste to tell you I was resting quietly at home when Nathalie came to fetch me to see the flames which seemed to reach the sky. From the casement-window of the studio we could see everything, heartbroken in the presence of the loss of life which we knew was happening. The cause of the fire was the explosion of the gas-metre. The performance had commenced, for it was just eight o'clock. All at once I saw the whole framework of the theatre fall in, swallowing up the unfortunate people who were inside and who must have been chocked by the smoke and gas without being able to save themselves. It is horrible. We are in consternation at the heart-rending accounts of what took place. The best thing is not to think of it. Mr. Gambart had a narrow escape. He was on his way to the theatre but had not got there when the fire broke out. I write, as I am

A FORAGING PARTY.

(By permission of Messrs. L. H. Lefèvre and Son, 1a King Street, St. James's, London, England,
proprietors of the copyright, and publishers of the large engraving.)

not able to telegraph, the office being crowded with people of the town. But you may make your mind easy on our account.

During her stay at Nice, Rosa wrote the following letters to Mme. Peyrol:

May 8, 1881: I am feeling very well at present and am trying to get on with my big lions, which are almost finished. They would have been altogether, had it not been for the attacks. If I see that I can't finish my picture here, we will pack up and be off in a few days.

It is getting warm here, but the sea-breeze is delightful. I find this part of the country admirable, and still more so now that the fields are at their best. The sky is pure and, from a height I have climbed, the glaciers of the Alps are as visible as if one were close to them. What splendid backgrounds!

Just fancy, the evening before yesterday, I was able to explain to myself something that had puzzled me all my life. When I was a child at Cadaujac, I saw one evening in a meadow a star that flitted before me and which kept on flitting, quite near the ground, as I advanced. Well, I was walking two evenings ago in the garden at dusk, when I saw to my amazement, first one gleam, then another, and, at last, Nathalie and I were surrounded with shooting stars. I caught one, a bluish-looking creature with a phosphorescent light on the hind part. This destroys the poetry of the phenomenon. They are simply fire-flies, just as in the colonies.

I long to see the Salon. I have read Wolff's [1] notice in the *Figaro*, but I cannot judge from what he says. I am inclined to believe, as you, that the Salon is a good one.

May 22, 1881: A line to tell you I am well, but tired with my efforts to finish straight off my big lions. I no longer know what I am doing. To work too much does no good. So I am bringing them back to By with me. We shall arrive about the 29th or

---

[1] Albert Wolff (1827-91), the distinguished Franco-German journalist and art critic.

30th. I begin to want to see a little painting, as also the phizzes of the family and friends.

The fire-flies are more numerous than ever. In the evening you can see these shooting stars by hundreds, on branches, in the meadows, and flitting over your head.

Returned to By, this letter is addressed to her sister:

July 19, 1881: How are you supporting this heat? You must be cooking, for even here we are really changed into fountains. All the liquid part of us is running away. If this continues much longer, we will only have our bones left! I can't touch my brush. My palette is as much water-colour as oil. I am going to write to Magny to see if they too are not stewing. However, it doesn't seem to affect my health. On the contrary, I am jubilating at my improved condition. But I can't sleep at night, and last night I saw the comet for the first time, between eleven and twelve. It is quite high now, showing by its tail that it is going toward the sun. I have also much observed the moon of late.

The next three letters are dated from Nice, and are addressed to her sister:

December 23, 1881: According to the astronomers, we enter winter to-day, and yet, three days ago, the sun was magnificent, and I took a fine walk in the mountain with my little pet dog. All the trees were green. The oaks still had their leaves, which were, however, as sere as in autumn. But as for the cork-oaks, they are as verdant as holly. The carob-trees, olives and heather are in flower. It all makes you think you are in the month of May, almost. The orange-trees have their flowers at the same time as their fruits, which, however, are not quite ripe. We are going to send you a small box of flowers.

We have been three times already to the theatre, like any vile revellers. The old Mammy is very well, and she it is who is going to make up your box of flowers. She gets on capitally with Nathalie, who, by the way, has the influenza.

Good-bye, little Mother Jub.

192

FAMILY LETTERS

January 25, 1882: I have another touch of the influenza. Yesterday I went with Mammy to see a little town perched on a rock, as also for a walk by the sea. The day before, we attended an evening party at Mr. Gambart's, where we didn't enjoy ourselves very much, as there were not many caricatures present. Many pretty women were there instead. Mammy had spread all sail and Nathalie was in her fire-coloured dress. Somebody relieved her of an eighty-franc Spanish mantilla, which she had left in the vestibule. As for me, such things please me about as much as twenty kicks in the back-side! There were fine dresses galore, decorations, and orders. Father Gambart was in plain black. He didn't wear his plumed hat and sword, as we saw him do on New Year's Day.[1] In the midst of it all, our one agreeable moment was when two artists sang, both having great talent, and charming me with their beautiful voices and expression. Mammy was proud to see me with my crosses and the Order of Isabella on my breast. I hadn't them all here with me in Nice, so that Mr. Gambart was obliged to help me out with his.

March 19, 1882: I quite recollect the picture in question from your description of it. Auguste is really the author of it. I had painted the little sheep and we both signed it. His name has been taken off, no doubt. The picture-dealers who are exhibiting it can change nothing. I am by no means vexed that the picture is considered mine. As the letter I have written them need not be shown and as they have repaired the mistake they made in exhibiting it without my permission as if it were mine—Peyrol may show them this passage of my letter and they can do the best to sell the canvas.

I have not yet finished my rain picture. I am letting it dry. Meanwhile, I am working at the one for the Tedescos,[2] which is progressing famously. I think I shall be able to get them both done within the fortnight, and afterward I shall do some mountain sketches.

---

[1] Mr. Gambart was the Spanish Consul General at Nice, and so had a uniform.
[2] The Paris picture-dealers.

193

REMINISCENCES OF ROSA BONHEUR

" Dear Mammy," wrote Rosa to Mme. Raymond Bonheur on the same day:

This morning I climbed up a mountain by the valley-route we took the first time in January. Yesterday I went for a stroll in our neighbour's garden, and found some picturesque olive-trees there; thence, I went on to the yew-lined avenue, where, between eight and ten, I started sketching, for you know I can't work in my studio in the morning.

I think Juliette wouldn't do badly to come down for our last five weeks here. She would get a taste of the country and it would do her good. Let her come and bring her paint-box. We can both do some sketching. I will be her brother instead of her sister. My breeches look quiet respectable in the mountain.

Nathalie is better and has taken to her painting again, which quiets her. We haven't been to the theatre since you left. However, we haven't felt the loss of it. The carpet on the staircase is laid; it is quite nobby. As I walk up, I turn round to see if there isn't a princess behind me. But on catching a glimpse of my feet, I am recalled to reality, like the peacocks who are taken aback on beholding their ugly extremities.

My health is very good for the moment. I wish your sister Marianne's were the same. Alas! we can never be entirely happy. First it is one and then another who has to suffer. Well, well, old Mammy, there are, after all, a few small consolations, and you will find in your old Zaza the heart of her brother Germain. I will be your daughter and also your boy. This I have sworn to myself.

Again from Nice, to Auguste Bonheur:

April 1, 1882: If I have urged you to come down here, it is because I want you to become acquainted with the finest country that you can see, especially at this time of the year, when Nature is at her best—mountains with a background of snow and, in addition, the real Virgilian landscape, flocks of sheep and goats, with shepherds in most picturesque costumes. Sea and mountain show up the olive-trees with a golden light over all, that is superb.

Anyway, I hope it is only a pleasure deferred and that some time or other I shall be able to doubly enjoy it, having you with me.

We have only one more month here and then we shall all see each other again. I shall be glad to go over to Magny with my old friend Nathalie, when I shall see your new horse, and you know that, like your daughter Juliette, I adore animals. Your old Derby is still capable of rendering you service; animals need us just as we need them. He must enjoy himself in the country.

I am very happy to find, my dear brother, that you care little for the grandeurs of this world. We have quite the same ideas on this subject, as on many others. We are not brothers for nothing.

As for my art, the older I grow, the more I love it. Were I to paint only daubs, it would make no difference. You see I am even more of a philosopher than you; and, as we neither of us do worse than other folks, we can afford to be open-minded and go our own way.

The three letters which follow are all from Nice and relate chiefly to a severe illness which afflicted Rosa Bonheur for a year or more, and which, as will be seen in the next chapter, Dr. Apostoli finally cured. The first letter is addressed to her sister and the second to Major Rousseau, the Fontainebleau military veterinary, whose name will occur several times in this biography:

March 5, 1883: I can write only in pencil, my doctor forbidding me to sit up. The attack has been a severe one. But thanks to the care taken of me, and the sympathy shown us on all sides, everything is going on well. I am looking forward to embracing you soon.

April 9, 1883: At last, I have the pleasure of writing to you myself, and I know how glad you will be to hear that I hope I shall soon be finally rid of the wretched ailment which has upset my life for several years. At length, I shall be as I was in my youth, free in body, as in mind. If I no longer have the strength I had at thirty, I trust I shall still have enough to enable me to work and go about as I choose.

195

April 29, 1883: Do kindly let me have a line about everybody at your house and at Auguste's. If you have any artistic gossip, send it on, for Nice is very quiet, and we lack news.

My health continues to improve, and I am getting back a little of my strength each day. However, in order to write to you, I have had to have the stove lighted behind my back. But already I have been for three short drives on the way to Cagnes, from where I walk a little by the sea. While driving the day before yesterday on this road, I met some superb-looking shepherds with goats and sheep. The whole thing was so exactly my style, that I should have liked to paint them on the spot. But the weather is so bad—no one ever remembers it worse—that our excursions have been wet ones. As I write, the rain is falling and there is a rough sea and a south wind. The best thing is to stay in the studio, where, by the way, I am just finishing my she-fox with her young ones; for I want to settle my pecuniary affairs with my landlord before quitting Nice.

I hope you are all well and that Dodore has taken to his old habits again. I am already making plans for next year, with the idea of procuring him the means to make some excursions, and mother Jub the means to paint her sheep, shepherds, and landscapes. I trust my health will enable me to do all this and you to see the country a little better than you have been able to do.

Love to all, not forgetting old Mammy, and hoping to see you all soon, I am, your affectionate sister.

A short stay at Marseilles, May 23, 1883, results in this letter:

You must be saying: What has become of my sister? But, as you see, I am at Marseilles. I broke the journey, so as not to tire myself and also because I have found some lions in the open air at the Zoölogical Gardens, which are under the management of M. Geoffroy-Saint-Hilaire. I go there from eight till eleven o'clock in the morning, and will probably continue doing so for the next four or five days. Then we will start for By again. I began this morning to make some rough sketches which I shall find very useful; for, as the animals are in the open air, one gets very different shades of colour than if they were caged.

Mme. Borriglione has made me a present of a Corsican female mufflon, which will probably have little ones at By. She must be there by this time.[1]

Just let me have a line here, addressed to the Mesdames Micas, Hôtel Beauveau. I didn't give my name at the desk. I hope all are well. I long to get back to my By home and also to see the Salon.

From By again, referring to the death of Auguste, which occurred on the 22d:

February 26, 1884: We are only three now, my dear sister, and, like you, I pray God will leave me my other brother and my sister. Dear Juliette, it is only in the grief of losing a brother that one realises what is the intensity of fraternal love. I will go to Magny as soon as I can, in a few days at the latest. But my poor friend has been obliged to take to her bed again, and I am much fatigued myself. However, I am getting on as well as can be expected. Yesterday, Dr. Apostoli applied his treatment to me and I saw that he has a kind heart, for he had tears in his eyes on hearing of the events that forced us to leave so suddenly.[2]

I have received a very touching letter from good old friend d'Eichthal,[3] from his daughter, Mme. Le Bret, and from M. Dusommerard,[4] whom I have just thanked.

In the beginning of March I shall surely see you. In the meanwhile, take courage and finish your pictures. Heartfelt love.

---

[1] See the correspondence with this lady, in Chapter XI, for a fuller account of this mufflon.

[2] See, in the next chapter, the correspondence with this physician.

[3] Gustave d'Eichthal.

[4] His father, Alexandre Dusommerard (1779–1842), was a distinguished archæologist and founder of the Cluny Museum, Paris, of which the son (1817–85), in his turn, became the custodian. But Rosa Bonheur's relations with him were in connection with his official direction of the fine arts of the Second Empire.

REMINISCENCES OF ROSA BONHEUR

Sunday, March 8, 1884: How the time passes, my darling Juliette! How many days have already gone by since we lost our brother! In truth, life here below is of little worth, and I hope that he not only lives in our affection, in our hearts, but that he has again found those affections which have preceded us beyond the bourn and which we in turn shall again find when freed from the miseries of this world. Meanwhile, we have consolation. I receive from my friends, both great and small, comforting letters. One long one from the kind Duchess of Saxe-Coburg-Gotha touched me exceedingly, not to speak of many others. No doubt it is the same with you.

We shall leave here to-morrow for Paris. We are to go on Monday, with Tedesco, to the picture exhibition at the Mirliton Club. On Tuesday, I have to see Dr. Apostoli. So it will be Wednesday before I get to you and to see the exhibition where you have your picture. I am so happy at your success, my dear sister. Much love to you.

May 5, 1884: I ask your pardon for being so late in replying, my good old Sis, but I am in the conception period of painting, and the days pass like lightning. I get up with the early worm and after dinner I nap and doze in bed. In this way I have burnt a pound of oil in a fortnight.

Just now By is like an ants' nest that somebody has stirred up with a stick. They are electioneering, and have spent the night at the polling-booths. There is a movement to oust the mayor. As yet, we don't know the result. There have been lots of amusing incidents.

Love to you, to Mammy, and to all the community.

Mme. Peyrol, who was sketching at a place near Fécamp, on the Channel, received this letter there:

July 8, 1884: I am so happy to know that you are in so nice a place to do what you want. You will find there subjects for pictures, studies, pure air, and quiet. Make the most of it, my good Juju, and paint us a good canvas which will knock into a cocked hat all our duffer animal painters who, as a rule, haven't many ideas in their heads.   Just now, I am pretty much in the same case.   The heat has been so intense for the last two days and the drought has parched up everything to such a degree, that I feel quite flabby-dabby.

The next group of letters comes from Nice.   The first one, which follows, is addressed to " My dear Juliette and all of you ":

December 16, 1884: You will have already heard from Dodore that we arrived here safely.   You have no doubt received his skits on our persons.   Your humble servant is wearing breeches; otherwise it would be too tiring, and not practicable with the lunch to carry, not to speak of the parasol spike, the stool and the case. I don't know what I should do if I had to lift up my skirts.   It amuses me to see how puzzled the people are.   They wonder to which sex I belong.   The ladies especially lose themselves in conjectures about " the little old man who looks so lively."   The men seem to conclude: " Oh, he's some aged singer from St. Peter's at Rome, who has turned to painting in his declining years to console himself for some misfortune."   And they shake their beards triumphantly.

Nathalie wishes to be remembered.   We three are getting on famously together.

The next letter refers to the visit which the Emperor of Brazil paid her:

February 21, 1885: Isidore, I trust, reached you yesterday at half past ten, and will have given you an account of the honours I have received.   I know, my darling sister, how pleased you must be to hear of them.   Every one here is so kind to me that I should be extremely sorry to leave Nice altogether.   Dodore must have told you also all about our excursions.   But we haven't much to show for them in an artistic way.   However, my chief object in getting him down here was to give him rest and change.   I should have liked to keep him longer, but I saw that while he was loth to quit me, he was anxious to take up his work again.

199

We have had the worthy Dr. Hubin [1] and his wife staying with us for some little time now, and I am delighted to be able to show him my gratitude. More than once he has got up in the night to come to my aid, and I cannot forget it. They will stay another two or three days, and then I go to work in earnest.

I hope you will succeed at the Salon. Here the exhibition opens to-morrow. I have seen only one of your pictures, which was hung high and in rather a bad light. I hope the committee will give you a better place.

It will be a year to-morrow since our brother Auguste was taken from us, and the anniversary is a cruel one. I shall be with you in thought at Magny. My kindest remembrances to poor Marie and my nephews and nieces.[2] Well, my poor Juju, we have only now to wait on God's will and to live as honourably as possible until it pleases him to call us to himself in our turn.

Another letter worth reproducing is addressed a few days later to Isidore, who is always for Rosa Bonheur "My dear old Dodore":

I am going to have my tea, for the sun is shining into the studio. You, I expect, are preparing in your little room to go down into your home circle. No doubt, by this time you have resumed your ordinary work and habits. As for me, I have not yet been out since you left. I work in the studio instead, peddling away at some water-colours, until such time as I can revisit Cape Ferrat and the mountain.

I have been to the Nice Salon. Juliette's picture has not been moved to another place, notwithstanding what I said. It looks very dark and really is rather sombre; but the position it occupies renders it doubly so. Mr. Gambart will try to get it moved. There are a goodly number of daubs in the exhibition. The best pictures are by Italians. They show much more progress than the French. I maintain my honour with my lion's head and my dogs. The sculpture is in a very fine room and is well arranged. I

---

[1] The By physician. See the correspondence with him in the next chapter.
[2] The widow and children of Auguste Bonheur.

am sorry Peyrol hasn't sent in anything of yours. Cordier [1] is the cock of the walk. He has some things that are poor enough. But two cressets, in bronze and onyx, are really good.

That is all the news from Nice. Now, I want to hear about my Juliette's picture and the figure chiselled by my sculptor nephew. Some of you must write me. It is difficult for me to write with my own hand to everybody. In the evening I get the miller's dust in my eyes, and in the morning I make water-colour daubs of lions, while waiting for an opportunity to get up to the mountain in order to paint a background.

Love from Nathalie and myself to my dear old Dodore.

Referring to her step-mother's illness, she writes, April 1, 1887, to Mme. Peyrol:

I was deeply grieved, my poor sister, to receive your letter, realising how anxious and troubled you all must be. Let us still hope for the best. The weather may get milder all at once, and you can let the poor Mammy have a little more air. To live in that room while stifling is terrible. When quitting Paris, I did not think of bringing her to Nice. But it would have been possible only before the early winter. Anyway, I do not give up hope, my good Juliette, and I trust I shall not need to undertake this sad journey, God willing.

Love to all and especially to our poor Mammy.

In a letter of a week later, written after attending in Paris the funeral of her stepmother, Rosa Bonheur says:

Just a few hurried lines to tell you I have arrived safely and without being too much tired. Here I am back at Nice. In four days, Nature has clad herself with flowers. It's quite wonderful. But I found the plains between Marseilles and Nice covered with water. They are much like big lakes, and the mountains are quite white. This makes the air fresher than in Paris.

It seems to me, as to you, that I have been having a painful

---

[1] French sculptor (1827-1905), pupil of Rude.

dream. My poor Juliette, I keep thinking of you all and of the aching void you will now feel; and I assure you I shall often be with you in spirit, and with *her*, too. However, I am resuming the work I had begun before going to Paris, and in a month we shall see each other again.

Love to all and to yourself.

While at Nice, an incident which she describes in this way, May 11, 1887, befell Rosa Bonheur:

I have a little adventure to relate to you. Just fancy! I have been arrested by two artillery soldiers and narrowly escaped being a State prisoner in the fortress just constructed at Cape Ferrat in lieu and place of the Telegraph.

I had started at seven in the morning, in order to go and take some small photographs of mastic-trees and other plants, when, on reaching the vineyard belonging to M. Polonnais, I found, by rare good luck, a most picturesque-looking shepherd, keeping a flock of goats each of which seemed handsomer than its neighbour. I halted and was soon engaged in an expressive pantomime with this Italian herdsman, tempting him with a shining franc-piece. He understood me, and telling him not to budge, as he was in a most charming pose—you know if one tries to make them pose, it's absurd—I hastened to fix up my paraphernalia. After taking two plates, I discovered that the sun had interfered with my lens. So, altering matters a little, while my shepherd remained motionless, I eagerly operated afresh.

Just then, two artillerymen came upon me from behind, and wanted to seize my camera and the plates I had already taken, under pretext that I had been photographing the fortress! In astonishment, I energetically defended my apparatus and frames; and, sticking them into my lunch-bag, I tried to explain that I would not give up my property. " Then show us what is inside," they said. I replied that they would see nothing at all, for, if I did what they asked, I would lose my photographs. But the Tommies did not seem much impressed by this truth. I then got angry, and they insisted that I must go with them to the fortress. Thereupon, my dear Sis, I intimated to them that they might convey me thither by making a palanquin of their arms, but that, climb up there on foot, I would not. Whence, embarrassment of the troops!

At this stage of the conflict, I noticed that I luckily had my red ribbon of the Legion of Honour in my buttonhole. So I assumed my most important and imposing mien and showed them the decoration, saying that in the presence of a member of that body, they ought to make the military salute. The troops were now quite out of countenance, while, more than ever, I blessed the memory of the Empress Eugénie. " Well," said the sergeant —it appears that my interlocutor had this rank—" if you are in the army, Madam, you will understand we must obey orders." Then I assumed the air of the Little Corporal before Horace Vernet's sentinel, and said: " My good fellows, I not only esteem you, but I will entrust you with my man-servant who shall climb up there, which would be painful to me at my age, and one of you will take him prisoner instead of me; and you will tell your superior officer to come and parley with me!"

Thereupon, Nathalie wanted to go up and explain everything herself, so that we might not lose our man-servant. This made me waxy again and I insisted on her returning to the carriage. As for myself, I shouldered my property, with the firm intention of holding it tight, while poor Auguste made the ascent with the main body of the army, and we, remaining under guard, were curious to see what effect would be produced. With my camera in one hand and the stand in the other, I marched toward the carriage in spite of the sergeant, who brought up the rear. Then, taking my seat in it at my ease, I began trying to upset the poor non-commissioned officer's mental equilibrium by explaining to him that there were photographic apparatuses with which it was possible to take a portrait of the moon in its minutest details; so that, consequently, I had only to climb up to the top of Mount Boron, without coming to Cape Ferrat, if I had wanted to betray my country; for, commanding the fortress quite well from there, I might, without his suspecting it, have photographed, just as in the case of the moon, all the details of the fortress and even made the portraits of the good fellows who defended it with such estimable zeal. My keeper had not got over his amazement at my narration, when, lo and behold! Auguste returned accompanied, not by an officer but by the same private soldier—a sign of victory! We were saved! We were free!

There, my dear sister, you have an incident wherewith to enrich my biography, for my life is lacking in stirring events of this kind! Now I am obliged, if I want to sketch at Cape Ferrat, to ask permission of the General in command. But as I shall be leaving Nice in a few days, my petition will be to next year's officer.

I couldn't help relating the story, as it seemed to me worth narration.

This letter of Monday, November 19, 1888, to Mme. Peyrol, is the last of this series dated from Nice:

As you see we are in Nice, having reached here at three o'clock yesterday. This morning it is magnificent weather and the sun is even deucedly hot. I don't know how many degrees there are, but my blouse and my chemise are enough clothes for me. My old friend has got over the journey pretty well. She is now in the garden. As yet, I have not set foot outside. Everything is in good order in the villa. Ratata [1] is in her fine cage out in the sun and is rolling herself in the hay. Gamine [2] puts on her lordly air as soon as she gets to Nice. My little bull-finch is just now singing his ditty, " Father Bugeaud's Cap," while Green Cocotte [3] is swearing in Spanish. You see I give you every item of news and now I am off to unpack.

The remaining letters of this chapter are written from By.

In a letter of January 21, 1891, to Isidore Bonheur, is the following paragraph:

I am spending my evenings in reading. Just now I am in the heart of Africa, on the mountains of the Moon; and if I were a male instead of being a female, and if I counted only twenty years in my pocket, I would go and make studies in that country.

---

[1] Rosa Bonheur's she-monkey. [2] Her dog. [3] Her parrot.

As it is, I travel on the map, following Stanley in his peregrinations. At night I visit the Dark Continent with my feet on the fender, and during the day I work at my sheep under the rock and smoke my cigarette whilst watching the snow fall, peeping out at what is going on over on the road.

My love to you, dear old Dodore, as to all.

Replying to her cousin, Mme. Lagrolet, Rosa writes, December 18, 1891:

I am always behind in everything, just like an old tortoise. But this morning I hold the pen instead of the brush. However, what really prevented me from writing to you sooner was that I had to make a sheep's head, for a young friend of mine, on a fan, which he doubtless intends to give to some nice girl. So I will do up his head in frills, and, while I have my hand in, I will make you a fan, too. My good friend George will hand it to you for me, when I will have the pleasure of presenting to you M. Georges Cain, painter, with as much talent as any of the others. You can give him a kindly reception, for he cuts a very good figure in a social way.

These two letters, addressed to Isidore Bonheur, belong here. The first is dated " By, Sunday evening, February 21, in the year of our Lord 1892," and runs as follows:

I have not replied to your letter earlier because I was half hoping to see you risk your life in a P. L. M. train,[1] in order to come and dine on board my vessel, the temperature being much milder and the snow having melted, so that my hull is no longer a black speck in the surrounding white. While smoking my pipe at my cabin port-hole, I cast a glance over toward Captain Bourdon's craft,[2] thinking that perhaps you had accosted his vessel before mine.

---

[1] The Paris, Lyons and Mediterranean Railway Company was once famous for its accidents.

[2] M. Bourdon, an amateur artist, was Rosa Bonheur's nearest neighbour. His former house and studio are still conspicuous landmarks at By.

I hope, my dear old brother, your cold is nothing serious. Just scrawl me another line, if only to help me while away the time; for I can't go up to Paris at this moment. I am sticking close to my lions, like you when you are getting to the end of some creation. At times, I go at it hammer and tongs, saying to myself: " Now, my little Rosa Bonheur, my girl, you have just produced a masterpiece! " And in this satisfactory state of mind, I long for the morrow in order to add a few more finishing touches. Then, when morning arrives, I could box my own ears! It's too red! It's too green! It's too light! It's too dark! " Come! We must alter all that, my poor girl! You are a confounded fool, all puffed up with pride! Let us make haste and remedy all that! "

So the days pass, the months and the years; for during this time the anchor has been weighed and the vessel scuds along. One needs to be wide awake. Now there's moon, now there's sun, and we revolve quickly.

When evening comes, I read the newspaper, which sends me into a rapture of wonder over my fellow-creatures' state of mind. Or else I make projections with my Diogenes lantern or touch up blue-paper proofs.

That's how the time is spent, my old greybeard, and that's why I can't very well desert my frigate, especially as my crew work better when I am personally in command, and also because I have promised Mr. Lefèvre [1] to deliver him my merchandise by the end of the month; and you know in the navy a man must keep his word.

March 30, 1893: I received your letter at 1.50 P.M. to-day. The sight of your writing, which is pretty rare, has the knack of pleasing me and putting me in a good humour. But verses addressed to your sister render me forsooth poetic myself, and, before the end of this letter, I will prove it to you.

And yet, at the present moment, I am anxious about my vessel. After wintering for long months, as you know, and being busy with steering by the compass, I am lying to, not very far

---

[1] Gambart's London partner and relative.

from Paris by the sea, and have given the order to my crew to up with the hammocks so as to have a regular clean-out before quitting my deck, as I hope to go and see the Fine Arts Exhibition, leaving Chicago [1] on one side, since I have quite enough of the North Pole.

So I am preparing at my leisure to get in a fresh stock of feminine attire, a task which always embarrasses me as it does you. Luckily, I have still some old uniforms which can serve under a new cape, and I have also the good fortune to have up my sleeve a pretty woman who desires to give me her elegance; consequently, with my umbrella and my catalogue, in the morning hours, I hope to see the 1893 Salon in peace.

I trust your cussed, dirty rheumatism will leave you alone and that we shall be able to do a little more water-colour painting after your trip to Magny, with René, too, if he is willing to come a-wooding in our company.

With this, accept my love, you, as also the other pilgrims of the Rue de Crussol.

To you I dedicate these rough-and-ready lines:

Brother, the woods are dry; but yet there is no saying,
In spite of the hot weather, when we shall go a-maying.
　　The mosses all are stunted grown,
　　The sunbeams turn the blossoms brown,
　　With nightly frost the fields are sown.
　　　The forest gives no longer shade,
　　Its ancient trees are vanished fires,
　　They are no more, those hoary sires
　　　Whose branches twixt each other strayed,
When Gallic swords were brandished, in battle-line arrayed.

　　Adieu, O sacred wood! adieu,
　　Forest that nursed the gentle dew,
　　Of all its first remain but few,
　　Nor these their pristine strength renew.

---

[1] Rosa Bonheur finally decided not to visit the World's Fair, though she did exhibit in the Fine Arts section.

And yet ere long the greenwood tree
Shall yield us its soft canopy;
And still along the sandy walks
We'll wander on in happy talks,
 With water for our sketches borne,
And other baggage, treasure trove;
And blithely onward will we rove,
And hear within the leafy grove
 The little warblers greet the morn;
Or else the humid places find
Where treads the timid-footed hind.

Well, well! in twenty years from now,
To this world we'll have made our bow,
And joining those who've gone before,
We'll be released from care and chore.
And if old Nick his wish avowed,
Of sticking me up on a cloud,
To travel round the Milky Way,
Think you that I should answer nay?
And if I could but glance around
The earth from thence, faix, 'twould be found
The rocks were but a dusty mound
Serving as a potato ground.
Troth! may they always keep their size,
Be royal praties, void of eyes;
Know nought of what by freedom's meant,
Its praises sing and be content;
And leaving many young behind,
Perpetuate their mealy kind.

'Tween now and then, old cup o' tea,
We shall have painted many a tree,
Mingling our talents, lad and lass's,
You with an eye-glass, I with glasses,
The which we'll try, when sketching's over,
Not to leave lying in the clover.

208

And now, my dear Dodore, ta-ta!
    Accept my Virgil, modern style,
To make you merry, tra-la-la,
Is my best wish, your old Za-za.
    It's good to laugh and stir the bile,
Since life itself's a jest, ha! ha!
This 30th of March, 1893, from ten till eleven in the evening.
Good Night!
R. B.

Rosa Bonheur's interest in her young nephew, the late René Peyrol, is indicated by these lines:

September 2, 1893: I see you like your trip. If I had been as young as you, I should have been glad to accompany you. I know very well the part of Auvergne where you are, having gone over it with my brother Auguste. We rode across the Puy Mary mountain, after sleeping at Falgoux. That night I remember most distinctly on account of the fleas. We returned by Apchon and Bort. I trust you will find nice subjects for sketching and motives for your figure. The cottages are often of a fine colour, with their old stones and whitewash. I shall be delighted to see what you bring back, especially as I believe you will get motives that are quite as good as those to be got in Brittany. It's not the same thing. I address my letter to the Rising Sun at Mauriac, thinking that will be your headquarters. Good luck and don't tire yourself all out. Love to you. I shall see you soon again at By.

To Isidore, " My dear old Dodore," she writes on January 14, 1894:

I haven't answered yours sooner, as from ten in the morning right till the evening, I have had sittings to the Marchioness of Grasse,[1] who is painting my portrait. Only the evening was free, and in the evening, while reading my *Figaro*, I would doze off over

---

[1] See in the next chapter the correspondence with this lady for an account of the painting of this portrait.

the news of the day. For this reason, I am all behind with my letters. There's a ream full of 'em I have not yet replied to. My friends must be thinking I have died without letting 'em know. But to-day being Sunday, all my household has skedaddled, which rejoices me exceedingly. I can't tell you how happy I am to be alone with my dogs. Your old sister.

To the same, three months later, " St. Vincent's Day, the day after St. Isidore's Day ":

You may come at five on Sunday. Céline will roast a leg of mutton, and there will be a pie for lunch. You see I was promoted to the grade of Officer in the Legion of Honour on Low Sunday, not long before St. Isidore's Day; so you are evidently mixed up in the thing, and consequently the reason for your coming out! Then again, Mme. Fould has sent me some more champagne and I shall sacrifice a bottle in your honour. The champagne is in the name of Prince Stirbey. Yesterday, M. and Mme. Georges Cain came to bring me some rosettes of the new decoration. So you see I am on as good terms with the nobility as with the clergy, and now I learn that I must show deference to the Republic by writing a letter of thanks to the Chief of State; at least, so says Georges Cain. It seems it's the proper thing to do. Indeed, I ought to have done it last evening. But I couldn't keep awake, and as the letter must be written in style, it is no easy matter for me. So, just to get my hand in, I begin with you, and the others will come after. Love to you. Your old rum 'un of a sister.

A propos of M. Hippolyte Peyrol's coming marriage, she writes Mme. Lagrolet, November 4, 1894:

I managed to sprawl myself out at full length, the other day, on the dead leaves of the forest, by getting my foot caught in a root. Nothing serious happened, though I am still stiff from this fall. If I am like this when my nephew's approaching wedding comes off, I shan't be able to attend. They will have to get on without my grandeur, but will not be less married on that account. By the way, I must look into my wardrobe to see if I have got my Sunday-go-to-meetings here, or if one-half of my gala harness is in Paris.

A short time afterward, to the same:

I accept your kind invitation to a simple family dinner, next Sunday, the 30th inst., St. Andrew's Day, when I will visit your new apartments, whose walls are hung with the fine engravings of Rosa Bonheur, that illustrious artist, of whom you have the honour to be the cousin.

My dear Cousin, I am now much recovered from that sprawl of mine on the ground, and am astonished, myself, that I got off so easily. But my poor lone tooth troubles me when I eat. So I must have a very strong desire to convince you of my affection for you all to risk myself on Sunday at your house with such a tusk. However, I think it ought to be left in its socket, for if I have it pulled out now, the gum will be too tender to do justice to Sunday's feast. Your affectionate and honoured cousin, Rosa Bonheur, of By.

A letter of May 10, 1895, to Isidore Bonheur, refers to his having been finally made a Chevalier of the Legion of Honour:

At last, my dear old Brother, you've got IT! Better late than never. This time the proverb is worth quoting. Thanks for the telegram. But the *Figaro* had already apprised me. I hope to see you soon and to drink a bumper in your honour with some champagne, if there is any left, which I trust is the case.

I have just come back from the Salon. It took me two days to get round it, and I wasn't sorry to be home again, for I had had enough, considering my seventy-four years. However, I shouldn't have liked to miss René's picture, which looks very well, although it is skyed. The Salon is a good one. There are some very fine things in it, and I shall return there as soon as I have rested my Shank's pony, who is a little bow-legged for the moment.

My love to you, my dear old fellow-horse, from your affectionate old sister.

The following brief communication is addressed to Mme. Lagrolet, December 11, 1895:

REMINISCENCES OF ROSA BONHEUR

I am in good humour this morning because, at last, I am giving the finishing touches to my " Horse Duel," which, unless I am greatly mistaken, I have made a success of, a deserved reward for all my efforts. I am going to receive fifty thousand francs for this rattling canvas, which I shall deliver over in a week.

October 9, 1896, she writes to Isidore Bonheur:

I have just come back from Paris, where I was obliged to go, having been invited by the Fine Arts Department to participate in the reception at the Louvre in honour of the Czar, where I thought I would see you, as you are a chevalier of the Legion of Honour. Strangely enough, there were very few artists present, but quite a lot of faces I didn't know. Having managed to get up to the scratch, I am now back home again and am not sorry.

I hope I shall see you soon, and with much love, my dear old Dodore, believe me as always, your old rum 'un of a sister.

A subsequent letter to Mme. Lagrolet says:

June 21, 1897: I found old Céline ill when I got home, and so I am obliged to do her work; consequently, I am attending to the birds, the dogs and the rest. This keeps me busy till the lunch hour. Then I have to superintend things, to write letters and to put up with interruptions at every moment. On top of all this, I have had a royal visit, and so, in order to put my best foot forward, I was obliged myself to polish up the floors and myself too, all of which has quite tired me out.

The " royal visit " referred to above was that of the then Princess and Prince of Wales, who, during a stay in Paris, went out to By, accompanied by Mr. Austin Lee, now Sir Henry Austin Lee, of the British Embassy. One of the party has said to me: " The great artist was much flattered by this attention, and, contrary to her usual practice, consented to pose for a photograph. In fact, she was much amused at the Princess insisting on photographing her in her droll attire."

212

On August 14, 1897, comes this information to Hippolyte Peyrol, Jr.:

I am pleased to hear you are all well, including your youngster. Here things are not too bad. I am recovering from a somersault I executed over the head of my mare Panther, who managed to spill me, my man-servant and my two dogs, and who broke his knees into the bargain. We were going down the Wolf Gorge road. The spill was not a very bad one. But, for a week, I felt like Don Quixote after he had been drubbed by the mule-drivers, not being able to move without being reminded of my sore places. So I resigned myself to take a short journey, in my arm-chair, as far as Timbuctoo of mysterious fame, after a previous one to the North Pole, with Nansen, in order also to refresh myself from the heat of my stove of a studio. With this exception, things are as usual at By. I shall be delighted to see you over on your return, and beg you to greet them all for me.

In response to a letter from Mme. Lagrolet, she wrote this note on August 14, 1897:

Thanks; I am in good condition, though I did recently turn a somersault out of my carriage. It is not the first one I have made and I hope I may make others without breaking my bones, for in this business I really have Bonheur (luck).

Again, to the same:

October 24, 1897: I have a mass of letters to write and I begin by addressing one to my cousin, with perfect confidence, since M. Jules Claretie, of the French Theatre and the Institute, has assured me that I write very well, though M. Borriglione, the Senator, was so discouraging on this point that my pride was wounded and my writing suffered in consequence.

To Hippolyte Peyrol, Sr., in November, 1897:

I have received a letter from that lady thanking me for Isidore's bronze and mine, and, in my turn, I write to thank you

213

for having pushed on and looked after the matter. Please let me
have the bill, for I know that at this period of the year one is
not sorry to receive what is owing. And I, as I like to keep my
affairs in order, am not sorry to settle my accounts, not wishing
to owe a cent to any one, according to my wont. If you can't
bring the bill over, send it, and I will find a convenient way of
paying it.

This gloomy weather makes me wild. At three in the afternoon, impossible to see at all. However, we are about at the end
of the fogs, which must make fret Dodore and all the brethren of
the craft.

I hope you are all well. For the last three weeks I have had
a proper sort of a cold in the head and on the chest, which hinders
me from going to Paris. Kindest remembrances to each and all
from your sister-in-law, Rosa Bonheur, who does nothing but
blow her nose and spit all day long.

Replying to René Peyrol, August 26, 1898, Rosa Bonheur
writes:

Thanks for your kind letter on my birthday. You must
excuse me if I am rather late in acknowledging it. But I have
been melting in perspiration—some sixty pounds or more I should
say I have lost—and have been obliged to fly from my two studios,
both the upstairs one and the downstairs one. I have been incapable of doing anything. One must be an American, like my
companion and portrait-painter, Miss Klumpke, to work when it
is 90° in the shade. It is only during the last two days that my
faculties as a painter and a writer have been somewhat restored.
Please thank all the family for me. It will save me writing and
so going to bed at eleven o'clock; for I was up at five, according
to my custom.

I am awaiting the pleasure of seeing you again, which is rare
enough now, like the fish. But I have only one room to offer
you, each in turn, as America has made an alliance with old Europe
and, in addition, is working to preserve for the family and for
France the portrait of your aunt, Rosa Bonheur.

At the end of May, in the following year, Rosa Bonheur died.

CHAPTER VIII

THE character of the correspondence of a good letter-writer changes radically in tone and nature with the character of the person or circle to whom the epistles are addressed. This is especially true when the writer is of a sensitive, artistic temperament. Striking instances of this fact are found in the letters of Rosa Bonheur, and some good examples of it are given in the present chapter.

The reader has already seen how Rosa Bonheur wrote and thought when dashing off letters to her brothers and sister. The family tie, always so strong in France, was especially so in this case, where all were bound together by a common love of art and where all were working to win ease and fame in the same calling. Love and affection are naturally the predominant note. " She always spoke of the various members of her family in the tenderest terms," writes M. Paul Chardin.

I would now invite attention to Rosa Bonheur's letters to her friends which are purposely presented in groups, either in order to bring out more clearly different sides of the artist's complex nature, or because it is chiefly one episode that runs through them. I begin with the long series addressed to the different members of the talented Mène-Cain families.

I

This remarkable group of artists consisted of Pierre Jules Mène (1810–79), a most prolific animal sculptor; his son-in-law, Auguste Cain (1822–94), a pupil of Rude, also a distinguished animal sculptor, several of whose best works adorn the parks of Paris; and the two sons of the latter—Georges Cain, painter, writer on art and archæology, and conservator of the Carnavalet Museum; and Henri Cain, painter and dramatist, whose wife, Julia Guiraudon, was a well-known singer of the Opéra Comique.

Henri Cain sends me the following note:

For fifty years Rosa Bonheur was the friend of our family. When we saw her come, it was a joy for us all, and when she died, my brother and I—all that was left of the family circle—felt very keenly her loss. It was at our house that she learned to know all those artists, from Troyon to Barye, whom she afterward got to like so much. They were made to feel as if they were in their own home as soon as they crossed the threshold of 19 Rue de l'Entrepôt, where lived my grandfather, my father and the rest of us. It was the hive. There they both worked, there all the family died, there we were both born. Through that old-fashioned drawing-room passed the first artists of France of the last half of the last century, and not the least of them was dear old Rosa Bonheur.

Rue de l'Entrepôt is a wide fine old street near the Place de la République, known in those times as the Place du Château d'Eau. The Mène-Cain home was a *hôtel* two stories high, with a nice garden at the back. The second floor front was given up to the two studios, one for M. Mène and the other for Auguste Cain, each having a large bay-window looking out on the street and filled with ivy and plants. In 1900 the house gave way to a tall modern structure, but the *hôtel* still standing next door somewhat resembles, as regards its street front, the old Mène-Cain house.

Mme. Achard, widow of Léon Achard, once a popular tenor of both the Opéra Comique and the Opéra, and the daughter of Le Poittevin (1806–70), the painter, thus describes the social life of the Mène-Cain circle:

The Mène-Cain dinners occurred weekly during the season, at first on Friday evenings but later on Wednesdays. Our hosts and hostesses were M. and Mme. Mène, their daughter and her husband Auguste Cain and the two sons of the latter, Henri and Georges, all the men of the household being sculptors or painters. Our family scarcely ever missed one of these dinners. My father bubbled over with fun, had an inexhaustible fund of anecdote and told good stories well; so his presence was much appreciated at these gay gatherings. Among the dozen or more other guests from the Paris art world, the most frequently seen there were Bellangé, Adrien Dauzats, Dubufe, and Bonnat. Gérôme and Rousseau also sometimes attended these dinners. But no representatives of the Barbizon group came, for neither the Mènes, nor the Cains, nor Rosa Bonheur, nor my father, for that matter, ever had anything to do with the Barbizon school. Rosa Bonheur was very friendly with Bellangé, who was a charming man and a great artist, and she of course knew his son, who was far inferior to the father as an artist and who was very pretentious. Rosa Bonheur would come four or five times during the season to these dinners, and as she always felt perfectly at ease with the Mènes and Cains, she appeared at her best on these occasions, when she contributed her share to the general gayety. The mannish touch in her attire and bearing added not a little to the interest which she awakened, and when, after the dessert, the ladies left the dining-room, Rosa Bonheur always remained behind to have a smoke with the gentlemen. Sometimes, however, she would suddenly come and join us in the drawing-room, and on one occasion she appeared, rather red in the face and somewhat agitated, when we teased her and asked what could possibly have produced such an effect, whereupon she answered: " Well, the fact is my hair really stood on end!" For the Mène-Cain dinners were a gathering of typical Parisian artists who did not hesitate to tell pretty crude stories on certain occasions, and " Gallic wit " is not often intended for children's ears.

Rosa Bonheur and my father were great friends. She often came to his studio, and was attached to him both on account of his merit as an artist, and because of his natural wit and his rattling way of telling a story. She would say to him at times, " Come, Le Poittevin, give us a yarn; tell us something funny." But she was not often at our own dinners. She was too far away.

When she came to the Mène's, she would often say: " Ah, mes amis, faut-il que je vous aime ! " For it is very hard to drag artists from their work, especially in the spring when the light is good. " These social duties are a great loss of time," Rosa Bonheur would say in chorus with my father; " for when we have begun any part of a picture, we want to do it as quickly as possible." And my father would add: " When I have a sky to paint, I like to finish it at one sitting; it is no good unless done all in one day. So on such occasions I turn the key on my studio door." Rosa Bonheur would applaud this sentiment.

Nor did we ever succeed in getting her to our home in Etretat, then one of the most characteristic gathering places, on the Channel, for Paris artists. She often promised to come but never did so, though the free and easy existence which prevailed there among the painters and sculptors would have been exactly to her liking, especially as most of those who then frequented that charming spot were her friends. The many gay episodes that happened in those circles would have found an ardent actor in Rosa Bonheur, who often laughed heartily over my father's graphic descriptions of these never-to-be-forgotten scenes.

Writing from Paris, June 7, 1854, to M. Mène, Rosa Bonheur says:

I don't know M. Bellangé's [1] address; so I can't send him my eagle direct, which, however, I will be happy to lend him. Please tell him so and send him it by your servant.

The following letter is addressed from Paris, in 1855, to Mme. Mène:

Nathalie tells me for you that some art amateur wants me to make him a drawing. But it will be impossible for me to undertake any new work between now and New Year's day. My head is full of subjects which I want to give birth to and which the devil keeps preventing me from bringing into the world. Now, if I spend the

---

[1] Hippolyte Bellangé (1800–66), the painter of French battle scenes.

few evenings that remain to us, before the coming of the dread day which gives us a year more, a year less, in trying to produce some small thing of my own, what time will I have left to set about bothering over, licking into shape and touching up, a drawing on which I should have to spend at least ten evenings, working myself blind? Try and get the idea out of that gentleman's head. His wishing to possess a sketch of mine would cost him more than it is worth.

Your devoted friend, whose desire it is to go and take pot-luck with you.

Again we find a large number of letters coming from By; the first in 1860, to Mme. Mène:

I have been commissioned by the Great Nana of China [1] to thank you a thousand times for the consignment you have been good enough to make her. This Great Chinese Screen [1] expresses to you, through the medium of my pen, running over with good things, and we in chorus express to you, the need we have of the appearance of the planet Hortensia [2] and her satellites in our part of the sphere, in order to settle up quietly certain accounts that are due. I need, too, the presence of the planet Cain, so as to be able to repair some bas-reliefs, which have been damaged in sundry places by the moon.[3] Now, just as the earth needs to be sprinkled by the rain, so I want Cain, along with a little plaster.

I have here another object which might interest the regard of that other star, whose hairy rays are silvered.[4] I can show him an elk which has just been sent me from America and which, though a female, is not without merit.

And finally, if you are honourable folks, come the day you like and send me a line the day before, so that we can round out properly the rotundity of your Serenissimi Majesties.

And now I, along with Nathalie, embrace all your planets.

---

[1] Nathalie Micas.   [2] Mme. Mène.
[3] A group of rabbits, by Auguste Cain, adorned the walls at the head of one of the staircases at By. The French peasants believe that the light of the moon cracks and deteriorates masonry.
[4] M. Mène.

There follows here a letter written, June 27, 1860, to M. and Mme. Mène:

I am not yet settled. But if I were to wait till my church [1] is done, I would deprive myself too long of the pleasure of seeing you. I therefore take the Liberty, goddess though she be, of begging you to come and see my domain. Don't refuse this honourable satisfaction to a brother, or rather to a sister, artist. (Put the last first in accordance with the rules of our mother tongue.) But be sure and write beforehand, so that Mother Micas may do things largely, for you know, everybody has a dignity to preserve; and remember that if you don't give us sufficient notice, you will get only a bit of cheese to eat. Yes, ladies, be considerate, and give us warning. In the meantime, love to all, male and female.

In a letter, dated 1860, beginning " My dear good Madam Mènichon," Rosa continues:

You must come out and see me some Sunday, otherwise you are no friends of mine. If the weather is good, we will go a-fishing or for a drive to Fontainebleau. We will try and have a good time and I'll do my best to give you one or two rabbits shot by my own hand. You see, my dear folks, I can't be here the day you mention, as I have got to go to Paris at that moment concerning my resignation of the directorship of the drawing-school and I can't put off this affair, though it deprives me of seeing you sooner.

Rosa sends these lines from By, " end of December, 1860, year of the assassination of Poisot,[2] and the chilblains," to M. and Mme. Mène:

My good friends Mène & Co.: I intended going bodily to see you, but the weather has been so beastly that so far I have remained pent up in my den and only pushed my nose outside for

---

[1] The new studio at By had a roof somewhat resembling a church.
[2] I can find no explanation of this reference.

an instant in order to go and say good-day to my relations. But I forthwith drew in my head again. However, once returned to the warmth of my domestic hearth, I was smitten with remorse and my conscience reproached me with not writing a line to old P. J. and Hortensia. As at bottom I am not a bad sort of soul, I hereupon take up this little quill, which our species make use of in order to send to friends at a distance all sorts of nice messages, and after dipping it in the customary black liquid, I convey to you in this way two big smacks.

As soon as you can, you must come and see me, as you promised to do, along with friend Le Poittevin. I send love.

A year later, to the same:

My old P. J. and my Hortensia Mène-las:[1] I hear that that simpleton, M. Gérôme,[2] has nearly got himself winged for the sake of a light-o'-love. It would have been a fine thing if he had deprived the arts of one of its first champions. Happily he is all right again. May it be a lesson to him and may he in the future prefer painting to women. It's much wiser and less deceitful. If you see him, my good M. Cain, tell him that I am very happy to learn that he is himself once more.

We find these autobiographical notes in a letter of 1862 to M. Mène:

I must tell you that I have forgotten all the details about which the society is asking for information. I have lost all my note-books and so I cannot tell what has become of my pictures. You know that I was born at Bordeaux in 1822, and was the pupil of my father. In 1845 I had a second-class medal. In 1847, my famous first-class vase, for my red oxen. Then there was my "Ploughing," and, next, my "Fair," which gained me admission to the Royal Academy of Amsterdam. Then a half dozen silver and bronze medals from smaller towns. These, dear friend, are the only details I am able to give you. My kindest regards.

---

[1] Doubtless, a pun on Menelaus (in French, Ménélas), a good example of Rosa Bonheur's proneness to indulge in far-fetched and irrelevant word-plays.

[2] French painter and sculptor (1824–1903).

REMINISCENCES OF ROSA BONHEUR

To Auguste Cain, Rosa writes, October 3, 1863:

I would have stayed to dine but I didn't wish to get separated at the station from my arm-chairs, which, though very worm-eaten, I am highly pleased with. We are now busy rubbing up the nails. Nathalie has found that the gilding is very good.[1] There are only three good legs on one of them, but, if some care is taken, you are safe enough. If your rump can't rest on this one, your eye can very agreeably. At present, I can think of nothing else but my chairs. If you want to please me, have a friendly sentiment for them, and, next time you call, don't feel cut up if I don't offer you one of these state arm-chairs, which I mean to reserve for kings, emperors, grandees, and devils. Love from all to all.

To " My dear friend, Mr. P. J. Mène ":

January 24, 1864: My whole day is devoted to my stags. In the evening, after dinner, the ladies read to me, not to the stags, till eleven o'clock, after which I am too lazy to write letters. And yet, I am going to do so to-night, for I want to get something out of you! Here is what I want. Do you happen to have a plaster stag for a study, either to lend or give me? If so, it would be a godsend to your friend, Miss Rosa Bonheur, a most distinguished artist, as you know. You might send the thing to 24 Rue Haute-feuille,[2] and I'll answer for the rest.

As regards the quails, they are in a cage. I am waiting for a warmer spell to put them in the aviary. There I can catch them more easily, when I want them, with a net; for, if I try to take them from the cage with my hands, they might hurt their heads and be made all wild. So in a short time I will loose them into the aviary. Then I mean to choose a fine couple for you, so that Mlle. Aroult can train them and give them more tractable manners.

Excuse me for sending you this letter without an envelope. But I haven't one left. I send it, therefore, quite bare, like the poor maiden Truth, who, since the beginning of the world, has been crouching at the bottom of a well, at least so people say, in

---

[1] "Very gout" in the original.
[2] The Peyrols and Isidore Bonheur lived here at this time.

company with the frogs, which are not without self-esteem since they have seen cows. If Truth would only put on an old pair of trousers or an old skirt, she might, nowadays, show herself a little, at least. I am not now referring to you artist people, who are not too much scared by the nude, but to a heap of dames and Johnnies who are.

Good-night, for I am half asleep. Love to you and the whole household.

Also to M. Mène, concerning the railway brake described in Chapter IV:

May 5, 1864: I am going to accompany Nathalie to Belgium to see about her affair. She is not well and I can't let her go alone. If you see any of my family, say nothing about my going to Brussels, for, you know, I am always between two stools. This is quite between you and me, my good old friend. You may tell Mme. P. J., but nobody else, please.

To " My Hortensia, much beloved and much respected wife of my much beloved and very good old P. J. Mène," she writes on June 4, 1864:

I am counting on you for Sunday, the 12th, St. Guy's Day, by the almanac, and on that well-known rascal, Eugène Le Poittevin, with his couple of towering daughters and that high-born lady, his wife. By the way, I saw at the Salon some drunken church bell-ringers, which pleased me very much. It is a long time since I have seen anything by this young old man Bellangé so fine and so successfully painted.

We noticed also an interior where the son [1] has imitated the father. In my opinion, the son would do better interiors and effects from nature, of some sort, than battles. As he is still young, he can make great progress. As regards the father, he always displays the same artistic temperament, and whether it be a Bellangé young or old, it is ever young, and full of feeling and strength.

---

[1] Eugène Bellangé (born 1837).

A word about " Narcisse." I discovered much talent in it.[1]

And finally I may say that I noticed at the Salon many excellent and fine things, which does one good; for it is a great pleasure to observe what our brother artists are doing. We left the exhibition dog tired, for this time we really saw things, as we were there from ten in the morning till four in the afternoon. That was long enough, was it not? to examine what was worth examining.

Try and read my writing. I embrace you with my whole tender heart, and I am yours for all eternity.

To " My good, old and dear friend," M. Mène:

October 13, 1864: As soon as I got your good, affectionate letter, I wished to thank you for its amiable contents and the kind remembrances of me which it announced. But before doing so, I wanted the box to arrive, which was mentioned therein and which I was most impatient to open. So, ever since yesterday morning, I have been sending three times a day to the station in order to learn if it had come. At last I have what I thought was a young lady, who, heaven forgive! turns out to be a man. In your letter I read " ewe " for " ram." The little bronze is on my table before me, as I write, and its light form is as agreeable as possible to look upon. He seems to ask for his mountains and shepherd-boy, and one of these days I will send him back to you in a mountain after my fashion. Thanks, my dear P. J. I embrace you on your two cheeks, and am always your old Rosa Bonheur.

Here are a few words addressed to Georges Cain, June 24, 1865, when he was nine years old:

One does not come into the world, my dear child, solely for one's own pleasure. You will find that out when you are big.

From her numerous letters to M. and Mme. Mène, six more are selected.

---

[1] One of the earlier productions of Vibert (1840–1900) with which he won his first medal.

To " My good old P. J., or, what is better, Friend Mène," she
writes on August 16, 1865:

I owe it to you who have recently given me a proof of your
friendship on the occasion of my decoration, I owe it to you to
inform you, my good Ménichon, that I have just received the
decoration of the Imperial Order of San Carlos of Mexico. You
see, I have no good ground for complaint on the score of honours.

I have not been able to finish my picture because I'm doing
several things over again with which I wasn't satisfied. I hope
you will come and see it and we'll have an excursion together to
the Long Rocher, which we have so often planned to make. In
a few days the forest will put on its fine autumnal tints.[1] You
could seize the occasion to give me news of our poor friend Bellangé, whom I often think of.[2] I would also like to divulge to
you some verses, so neatly inspired by your kind friendship for
Mlle. Bonheur and put to charming music by M. Bizet, the composer, whose acquaintance I had the pleasure of making at the
house of Mme. Carvalho. Julia[3] will sing it for you. I wanted
to bring it to you along with myself, but I was not able to carry
out my plan.[4]

Wednesday or Thursday evening, 1865: I went to Paris recently, but came back quickly, because my stags must soon go to
London. I have promised them to Gambart, and I shouldn't like
him to put me in the lock-up, or make me pay damages, like
Fourchet.[5]

I had the pleasure of seeing Mme. Carvalho for a moment last
evening, when going to hear the flute. But as I was afraid of dis-

---

[1] This sentence offers a striking example of Rosa Bonheur's peculiarity of not noting
time. "The hour of the day, the dates of the month, the seasons and sometimes the
years, were," her nephew, the younger Peyrol, writes me, "often quite forgotten by her."

[2] He died in the following year.

[3] The wife of M. Auguste Cain.

[4] M. Henri Cain thinks these verses were written by his father, who sometimes
indulged in rhyme. But neither Bizet's widow, Mme. Emile Straus, nor his publisher, M. Choudens, can find any trace of this piece of music.

[5] See the last paragraph of the following letter.

turbing her, I wasn't able to learn positively her day and hour. M. Carvalho said a few words to me that made me almost despair of having her with us. It appears that there are rehearsals for a first performance soon to come off. If she can't come, I shall be very sorry. But we cannot accomplish the impossible. Anyway, I must have you, my good friends, as I want to have a day's rambling on the Long Rocher, for lately I have been pegging away at a great rate, and have earned a little outing. And it will do you good, too.

Give me news of M. Bellangé. It appears that the poor M. Brascassat [1] is very ill.

Good-bye to all. Try to make out as best you can my hen-scratching. I shan't write it over again. Good-bye, ladies; good-bye, gentlemen.

1865: You must think that I have melted away or frozen to death in my manor, since the charming evening passed so pleasantly, thanks to the grace and kindness of Mme. Carvalho, to whom I want to send a little sign of my gratitude and some mark of my fraternal admiration, to speak artistically. But, my good friends, the devil seems to stand in the way. I do not think, however, that it is the same one who managed so well in plunging poor Faust down under the stage the other evening. No, for he sang very well, that Faust did. But whichever one it was, some devil, I feel sure, has got in at me with the wind through my big fireplace, which I had forgotten to close up, and has thrown an evil spell over the house.

I have felt a little indisposed, too. But, in spite of all this, I have managed to finish the little drawing for Mme. Carvalho, and other drawings, besides, bending over the evening-lamp, listening to the groaning forest, while I saw flit by crowds of shades. Among these was the white-robed Margaret, whom that old fool Faust so gallantly provided with a red necklace, before sending her up to heaven—all this for having loved her more than himself and for having changed his old wig for a so-well-employed youth.

---

[1] He died some two years later, in 1867.

While engaged in making these philosophical reflections, my old P. J., and you, my beautiful Hortensia, I have been waiting for a good wind from the direction of Crau [1] to come and warm my melancholy thoughts. This soft breeze has doubtless passed too swiftly over the chimney-pots of my dungeon. Perhaps it is well that such is the case, for I really have for the moment nothing light to put on, Mme. Perrot [2] evidently forgetting that in this forest I haven't the resources of Geneviève de Brabant. But if I were to tell you what she has made for me, that Mme. Perrot! Well, I will tell you all about it, but not write it. But, in the meanwhile, O Julia! make known to her my distress.

Good-night, my dear children. Send me news of your good selves and, at the same time, the address of the white Margaret,[3] for, once my little infirmity [4] under glass, I will launch it into space, praying that it may fall at the feet of talent.

I embrace you all before being dragged before the court of my canton.[5] Oh, if only they would do me the favour of providing me a justing-field and permit me to measure arms of courtesy with that Fourchet, notwithstanding the feebleness of the weaker sex, to which I am proud to belong, " Fourchet, you would receive the finest drubbing a gentleman ever got from a stick ! "

1866: I am pegging, pegging away, my dear old P. J., in order to finish Gambart's stags as soon as possible. When they are sufficiently advanced, I will ask you to come and see them, with the children; for they mustn't go without your having a glance at them. If they are terminated to my satisfaction or thereabouts, I shall have them back for the next exhibition, with something else that I am ruminating on. Anyway, Auguste and I are determined not to expose, the one without the other, and

---

[1] A plain near Marseilles sending off a warm wind.

[2] Rosa Bonheur's Paris dressmaker.

[3] Mme. Carvalho.

[4] The above-mentioned drawing.

[5] A Lyons collector was suing Rosa Bonheur at this moment, before the Fontainebleau courts, for non-fulfilment of contract, she refusing to deliver a picture which he had ordered. She lost her case, paid her fine, but would never give M. Fourchet his canvas.

coming to a mutual understanding as to what we shall expose. He will thus have his revenge for this year, while I will show nothing without my real friends being satisfied with what I intend showing. Thereupon, my love to you.

May 4, 1866, and it is freezing!

My good Mme. P. J., alias the Fair Hortensia, your husband, whom I had the pleasure of meeting at the Salon rambling about alone with a sentimental air, has probably told you that I forbade you—knowing that you were going to the theatre in the evening —to let anybody learn that I was in Paris that day. If you see Mme. Carvalho, there is no necessity of your hiding from her that I was at the capital. To her, I always tell the truth, for it is ever the naked goddess whom I prefer, as she is so beautiful. One reason why I did not make known to you my presence was because I could not attend a first performance in a travelling costume covered with dust. And then, I had to hurry back home, having so much to do here. If you like, you might come out, if you don't mind being bored a little bit in our company. But I must tell you that the political atmosphere here is somewhat disturbed at this moment. Mme. Micas is changing her minister of the interior with and without a portfolio, and, in a few days, I am going to overturn my cabinet, because the wind is too much in the war point. Within a fortnight, however, we expect to be quiet again, and my subjects—sheep, deer, stags, dogs, which swarm and are in a somewhat agitated condition on account of the coming of gentle spring—will then be enjoying a government that seeks to make them happy. Then, order ruling, we can bed and board you, whether you come a-horse or a-foot. Countess Micas and her daughter commission me to inform you that, though the times are hard, you shall not starve. Thereupon, dear Mme. P. J., suffer me to touch your rosy lips with my forehead so pure, and to remain, devotedly yours.

May 23, 1871: What the deuce can you be doing in the Paris of Father Duchesne? Can it be that you are mixed up in the Commune, my old Mène? I can't swallow that even if you told me so. I don't suppose you are a partisan of the artistic principles of Citizen Courbet,[1] who has some talent for knife painting, but whom I find heavy in every other respect. But then one can't have everything in this nether world.

Rosa Bonheur's affection for the Cains comes out strongly in the following series of letters from Nice. The first, written to Mme. Auguste Cain, May 6, 1888, contains these words:

We are busy preparing for our departure for the castle of By, thank God; for I am awfully bored in these fine apartments. I can't make any excursions or do any sketching, being obliged to stay at home, as we have had to send away our servants twice running. We have with us now only a coachman, whom a lady has lent us. You may judge, therefore, what sort of a government this household enjoys just now, for we are without ministers. Yes, we are like a king without a cabinet or a republic in a state of anarchy. We have a temporary woman cook, who would surely poison us if Nathalie didn't keep her eyes open and put her own hand to the paste. This female minister of the palate makes panadas spiced with nutmeg. Does my friend Cain, Sr., the great sculptor, who is pretty toothsome, know this kind of panada? Anyway, this will give him a rather fair notion of the quality of our Nice cooking just now.

To all these ministerial embarrassments in our own palace are to be added those of the town, which votes to-day for Peter or for Paul.

In the meanwhile, our trunks are packed and we are only waiting for the new ministers of the whip and the sauce-pan to quit this luxurious and boring spot, for us ourselves to go and see the Salon and the inhabitants of Paris. Best love from us two old fogeys.   ROSA BONHEUR MICAS.

December 28th, to the same:

Your husband is a naughty, impolite man to have told you that that fan is too fine for you. It forces me to disclose the secret.

---

[1] Gustave Courbet (1819–77), the distinguished painter, accused, but falsely, of having been instrumental in pulling down the monument in the Place Vendôme during the Commune, of which he was, however, an active supporter.

If I have had the pleasure of hatching this poor fan, he is the father of it. That is to say, saving your respect, he was the inspirer of it. However, I have the merit of having attempted, for your sake, a lighter and frivolous style of work to which I have not been trained and which is not in my nature. O Julia! I confess to you that it was not easy; so I am all the more happy that this ephemeral creation pleases you.

To finish up the year properly and to enter upon the new one in the same fashion, I must send my love to you and to the handsome Auguste. But, however, whether I do so or not, the solar system will go waltzing along. The worlds turn quietly in spite of everything, which fact should give our pride a rude shaking-up.

By the way, my dear Mme. Cain, if you chance to know Jules de Goncourt, please tell him for me that his poetic art, judging from the few glimpses I have caught of it, is stunning. Hurrah for the Ideal! It inspires one as does the " Jewess," the opera. And so, in the future, instead of painting animals head to the front, I'll present them t'other way about. Tell Auguste Cain he had better follow my example and be inspired by the " modern school."

The next year, on January 26th, she writes this letter, beginning " Hey-day handsome Auguste ":

I receive your amiable missive at the same moment when mine should reach you, expressing my thanks, notwithstanding the fact that you say it [1] is no good. I am going to try it to-day, at noon, alone with Nathalie, who is a little better, which puts me in good humour, I confess, my fine friend. And when one's heart is contented, your mouth is disposed to gormandise. If I find it a failure, I will frankly tell you so, and then you can try again.

And now to the real object of this letter. My dear sir and friend Cain, you write me about exposing at the coming international exhibition. But how can I do so? I have absolutely nothing

---

[1] A *pâté-de-foie-gras*, or something of that kind, prepared by Auguste Cain, who now and then tried his hand at the kitchen, as he was particularly fond of good cooking.

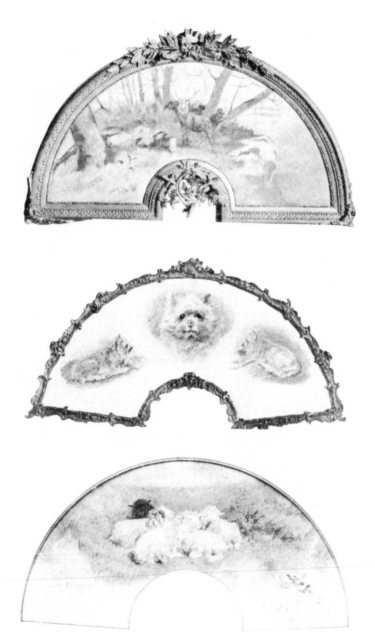

THREE FANS.

to send. And even if I had, how can you ask me to worry my soul in this era of puff and log-rolling? To-day, one lives from hand to mouth and labours simply to keep the wolf from the door. The fleeting years are the chief cause of all this, and exhibitions come and go like the years, so quickly that one sees, my friend, the nothingness of things. The only things that stand are the lions and the pâtés of the sculptor! But, for your eyes and beautiful hair, Auguste, there is nothing I would not do! So if there is a wish to do me honour, why then have your way.

In 1889, different friends, and the Cains among them, urged Rosa Bonheur to exhibit. But she herself was not particularly eager to do so. However, she asked Mr. Gambart to lend her for the purpose two of her best pictures which he possessed—a large deer and some boars. He consented to do so, on condition that he should have the hanging of the pictures. But Cain, who was a member of the jury, and the jury itself, would not consent to this. Thereupon, Gambart refused and Rosa decided not to expose. But the French Government sent to the retrospective exhibition of French art, one of the grand features of the art exhibit of the Exhibition of 1889, the "Ploughing in the Nivernais" and the "Hay-making," which belonged to the State.

August 21, 1893, finds Rosa back at By, where she writes as follows to M. and Mme. Cain:

Rosa Bonheur is a good-for-nothing. The heat has gone to her head, so that she requires a week in which to write a letter. Moreover, she's got more selfish than ever. She is ashamed to say so, but that's the truth. She no longer dares to show herself to her friends, the Cains, after the crime she has committed. The little griffon, which she got from some of her friends for Julia, arrived in the midst of the dog days. But it appeared so excited that Rosa Bonheur didn't dare to take it to No. 19 Rue de l'Entre-pôt, where there was nobody, being afraid the little fellow might have an attack of hydrophobia. Then, finding it so much to her own taste, this old hag has kept it for herself, thinking to find another less handsome for Julia! It has erect ears and a little stump of a tail that is rather funny. But it happens to be of the feminine gender, so that Julia could not take it out in Paris without being followed! I have asked my English friends for another one, which, I trust, will not, like this one, flee from velocipedes, thus forcing a-body to run after it and so get all in a sweat. You'd be sure to lose her and your reputation, too, which is another and my last reason for keeping her myself.

Love to all of you, men and women, and the whole lot.

To Mme. Cain:

August 26, 1893: Your rascally son Georges is continually leading me astray and corrupting my regular habits. He goes about the thing in a very clever way. First, he brings me into relation with illustrious men, and then throws in a few ministers of religion in the hopes of making amends for the distractions into which he has inveigled me.

I have chosen Wednesday, the 6th, St. Nicholas's Day, to dine with you. St. Barbara's or St. Ambrose's Day is for the Carvalhos, and St. Sabinus's for Grivot. I start from here, with your son, on St. Aurelian's Day, and he is coming back to me on St. Eloi's Day.

If, while I am with you, you care to offer me some after-dinner amusement, I've a mind to see one of Ambroise Thomas's operas.

I hope the little dog I gave you is quite well. Mine is doing admirably. And now suffer me, Madam, to deposit a kiss on your physiognomy, which is not so badly preserved, and allow me also to kiss my friend's papa.

To Georges Cain, Rosa writes on January 5, 1894:

I have just had a surprise visit that I ought to have appreciated and didn't—viz., that of a lady who chose the most inconvenient moment to come and paint my portrait. I was obliged to offer both to her husband and herself my rustic but loyal hospitality, with the result that, in spite of their discretion and perfect manners, I was completely upset in my habits. Into the bargain, I managed to catch a chill, which killed two days.

This will explain why I have not yet been able to thank the good M. Claretie for the charming article with which he has favoured me. To complete my misfortunes, I have no big envelopes for my note-paper.

To " Old Friend Father Cain," in January, 1894, was sent this mock telegram:

Would like line order have news about wife—Have just written Georges hoping have some that quarter—Am still public scribe—Hope resume brushes 1895—Am good humour this morning——

A month later Rosa writes at greater length to Auguste Cain:

I must tell you, as is my duty, that yesterday I had out here to see me my old brother Dodore. He came to give me the first inkling of the famous Legion of Honour decoration.[1] But, though the news is semi-official, it is not completely official yet, so I learn from Dodore. I have also received a very flattering letter from M. Ulrich, President of the Society for the Prevention of Cruelty to Animals, who offers me his congratulations. This led me to think there was really something in the rumour. But not having had wind of it from any other quarter, I am like a weather-cock. Any way, if you know nothing about it, you who are generally so eager to press to your fraternal bosom the great artist of animal painting, you, my old colleague, the animal sculptor, it wouldn't be nice of me to keep you in ignorance of this matter; for if you were in my place, you, with your friendship for me, would already have let me learn such a bit of news. So Nicolas, if you hear anything certain, be sure and communicate it to me. Your old Rosa Bonheur of the marble cross.[2]

Here are praise and criticism of Georges Cain's future wife:

April 14, 1894: Please forward the enclosed letter to your charming intended, Mlle. Ruffel, whom I thank for her nice letter,

[1] Rosa Bonheur was made an officer of the Legion of Honour for her exhibit at the Chicago World's Fair.
[2] The badge of the officer of the Legion of Honour.

which, between you and me, can only be reproached with one thing—it was so saturated with scent that it has given me a headache! While reading it, I was obliged to keep it at a respectable distance from my nostrils. Excuse an old friend for telling you this, my good Georges.

To M. Auguste Cain, she writes on the same day:

Forward the Old Guard! Cain, Sr., must march! So I beg him to kindly forward to the Grand Chandler's [1] the enclosed document, in conformity with the decree which requires the person, who is to be promoted to the rank of officer in the Legion of Honour, to designate a member of the order of a rank at least equal to that conferred on the said person, to whom is transmitted the insignia and, at the same time, the necessary powers to proceed to the reception of the said person. You see from this, M. Cain, that it is you, an officer, who must act, and that, in case of need, I can make people obey orders, whether they be young or old, male or female. So in order to carry out this program and also on account of his having a carriage, the handsome young Tedesco, my favourite, will call for you at your hostel at the hour when this sort of thing is done at the Place Vendôme.[2] And, furthermore, Rosa Bonheur must deposit the sum of 117 francs and 50 centimes. I must ask you to attend to this for me also; for, in the first place, I can't split myself up into two officers, and, moreover, my temporal disabilities oblige me to remain at my desk for two days longer, in order to reply to the congratulations which are being rained upon me, not to speak of the compliments of the unfortunates who've got their quiver full of children to make up for my having none, and who suppose that my wallet is lined for the express purpose of relieving their poverty.

As you cannot refuse the herein requested service, dear Nicolas, I entrust you with my birth-certificate, containing the verses my

---

[1] In the original, Grande Chandellerie, for Chancellerie, the administrative office of the Legion of Honour. One of those plays on words, so dear to Rosa Bonheur.

[2] The Minister of Justice has his offices here.

father wrote for his daughter in the year 1822.[1] I confide this paper to you. Keep it to yourself.

I have thanked the Minister and the Grand Chancellor, Place Vendôme. You understand all this.

Salutations and fraternity from one old guard to another.

And again, she writes him on May 18th:

I shall be very happy to accept the dinner invitation and to find myself in the illustrious society of my colleagues, with Gérôme, whom I have not seen since his prime youth and for whom you know my admiration; with Detaille so happily named, for he is the equal (*de taille*) of anybody; with Bonnat, the solid, and with Claretie, the well-beloved of old Rosa Bonheur; without forgetting the composer, Massenet. What a tony crowd, my old Cain! Compliments. But when one goes in for honours, one cannot get too much of it. So I am quite at your command, my dear sponsor.

To M. and Mme. Auguste Cain, she writes on May 23, 1894:

On Friday, at 12.30, I am going to see you with my nephew, Hippolyte, and I wish to tell you first why. He called on me to-day to show me the signatures of the great artists whom he had obtained in order to try once more to have my old brother Isidore decorated with the cross of the Legion of Honour. Isidore has no idea that we are doing anything of this kind. But I should be so glad to have him get the decoration. I therefore make it a point, my old friends, of announcing to you my visit for Friday, at 12.30, knowing that at two o'clock, my dear Nicolas, you are going over to the Salon to vote for the medal of honour.

Good-night. I am dead sleepy. Love to you both.

Writing May 12, 1895, she expresses her gratitude to Senator Borriglione concerning this same matter, as follows:

---

[1] Raymond Bonheur indulged in rhyme, now and then, as has already been stated. It is probable that he wrote, by chance, some verses on this birth-certificate, supposing it to be a scrap of paper.

Thanks for what you have done to help in finally making my brother Isidore a member of the Legion of Honour. I have a strong impression that you had much to do with it; in fact, I am assured that you did. The conferring of this decoration has been dragging on for ten mortal years. I am happy to know that at last he has it and to feel that I owe a part of this pleasure to you.

This letter of February 29, 1895, is to Georges Cain:

Don't come yet, my big Georges. It's just the weather to catch bronchitis; and for a man who is going to be married, it would not be very polite to cough and spit and wipe off the rheum of winter in the face of his pretty intended. So then, my dear and worthy Georges, stay quietly in Paris; get married without me, for I am not now capable of figuring in your procession, as, in the time when I was young, I attended the marriage of your mother with my old friend, your father. Knowing your great affection for me, I am sure you would not like to see me die of exposure to the cold. When you and your wife have definitely settled down in your home, at the end of February, and as soon as the small white flowers peep out in the woods, you must come and lunch with me for the sake of " auld lang syne." But not just yet, I beseech you; it would put me up a tree. I have not the wherewithal to send and fetch you from the station; my old mare is an invalid! I also; and we are not in a sufficiently good humour to do the honours of our country house. Moreover, my dear, good friend, I have just now been obliged to lie up in my room with a blistering plaster on my chest, and am ordered by my old doctor not to leave my chamber. My sole consolation has been to read the memoirs of Father Dumas, ten volumes running. What a veritable braggart he is! But what a good heart he has, and how justified the good Madame Dorval [1] was in calling him her big dog! The good man was so candid that he must have been fooled many a time without in the least suspecting it. And then, all this recalled to me my youth, back in 1830, the Saint Simonians, and the deuce knows what besides.

---

[1] An actress celebrated about 1840, who played parts in the elder Dumas's works.

Good-bye. I am awfully sorry it is impossible for me to go to Paris just now. I send you all my love—mother, brother, mother-in-law, mayor, bridesmaids, best man, men and women, and wish you all the possible happiness that can be wished by a true old friend. And you, Mademoiselle, allow me to send you my love as if you were Georges himself, and to share my old family affection between you both.

To M. and Mme. Georges Cain, she writes:

My dear Madam and friend Quinquina:[1] Thanks for your kind and affectionate note. I am pleased to tell you that I am all right again. My nose has stopped running. I have just seen my old Dr. Hubin, who is himself better, I am glad to say. So there is no need to be anxious on my account, and I am going to start again on the fans for the ladies. However, so far, I have been able to do nothing. The days are deucedly short and, in the evening, you are no good at all, my poor Rosa Bonheur, with your spectacles. Georges is a lucky soul to be able to see by the light of the lamp.

This being said, Madame and Monsieur, allow me to send you my love, while waiting for the moment to embrace you in person.

July 16, 1895, she again writes M. and Mme. Georges Cain:

I shall be glad to see you both. The death of Mme. Carvalho has been a great blow to me. My heart bleeds for her husband and son. How hard life sometimes is! Now and again I grow very discouraged with art as with the rest. Please give my love to your mother, my poor Mme. Cain, whom I found much changed. I trust in your kindness to her, dear Mme. Georges. Take good care of her, and believe me, both of you, your sincere friend.

" My dear Adolphe," [2] she writes to Georges Cain, December 27, 1896:

---

[1] For the explanation of this nickname, see the footnote on page 311.
[2] The appellatives in this letter are simply nicknames invented at the moment.

I cannot let the first day of the year 1897 pass by without sending you my good wishes. In doing so, however, I must be circumspect for fear of disturbing your wife's equanimity. Whenever I kiss you I notice that her eyes regard me doubtfully; and as I am a dame who kisses gentlemen unblushingly, and as your wife, O Adolphe, François, Anatole, Arles Cain,[1] seems to be somewhat susceptible, henceforth I shall kiss you only when there is nobody looking, and when you come to see me alone. Don't say anything about this to your mother, and don't show this letter to anyone. It is a new year's gift, Jules, for you.

Ah! what a time we used to have with the new year's wishes! There was the old Bellangé and the rogue, Le Poittevin. What a varmint he was! And the old clyster-loving doctor [2] whom we cut completely after the ball at which he appeared with a syringe in a basket and dressed up as an old woman! Your affectionate friend, Rosa Bonheur, Général de Baptiste.[3]

A little later, to the same:

I will ask you to kindly hand my letter to Mme. Réjane-Porel, as I don't want to address it to the theatre, which would hardly be proper. She wrote me a charming note, and, as usual, I am late in replying. You are, no doubt, very busy yourself, preparing for the Salon. You might, therefore, send your servant with my letter.

At last I am availing myself of a little quiet to do some painting. I have finished the water-colour for the good and illustrious M. Claretie, and a frame is being made for it. I am afraid I have taken too much trouble with my work and touched it up too much. Any way, there is a good intention in it. Tedesco will be so kind as to take it with my letter.

And how I enjoyed "The Candidate." [4] The end is a most

---

[1] Probably a pun on harlequin, *arlequin* in French.

[2] Dr. Gaide, who once attended a fancy dress ball at the house of M. Mène, disguised as a midwife.

[3] Georges Cain often addressed Rosa Bonheur as "General." As she has just been baptising him with a number of new names, she calls herself Général de *Baptiste*.

[4] A novel by Jules Claretie.

delightful bit of writing. The ceremony at Melun interested me exceedingly.

Concerning her domestic difficulties, she thus expresses herself, " Post haste, July 7th or 8th, year of grace 1897, to my good and old friend Mme. Cain, Quinconce " : [1]

" POST HASTE."

I have my hands full just now, for I have five servants to work for, feed, dress, and bed; and, as they are fed from the same kitchen as myself, they eat a great deal, in spite of the dreadful cooking of Louise, whose proficiency is not equal to that of the blond, stout, roguish-eyed Adèle, who served me so well during Céline's illness. The latter, by the way, is better.

At one time, it is my plate, then my glass, next the knife-rest, and at another time the knife itself which are missing, when the table is supposed to be set. If these domestic worries continue much longer, I may have to change the name, which the Thomery municipal council has given to the road passing in front of my castle. The Rue des Arts will have to be christened Rue de la Femme-sans-Tête!

O my Julia, henceforth you can make yourself easy, for, lonely woman though I be, I now have five friendly faces in my service, and a little girl in the bargain, though, I may add, she is no girl of mine! My old friend, I quite count on inviting you to spend a day with me, when my castle will be running broad-gauge again, if only to let you see it under such conditions. And

---

[1] Quincunx. A pun. Quin, in French, is pronounced like Cain.

now, Madam, I embrace you as always and am your old *ratapoil*,[1] first artist of France and Navarre.

An idea of Rosa Bonheur's philosophy may be gained from these words, dated December 31, 1897, to Mme. Cain:

The years pass, pass rapidly by, taking away from us those we love; and the longer we stay, the more of them we see leave us. You must know that the older we get, the more one thinks of the lost ones, and the more one loves them, because their little failings are forgotten and their good qualities alone are remembered. I often think of your handsome Nicolas,[2] who used to make me such nice *pâtés-de-foie-gras*. I have really been lucky in the choice of my sweethearts. But, wife, be easy in your mind, for I have never been the cause of anybody, either male or female, wearing a pair of horns!

To Henri Cain she sent the following note in September, 1898:

We have received, Miss Klumpke and I, your kind gift of the libretto. What especially touches me is my name encircled in a wreath drawn by Massenet.[3] What a feather in the cap for an old artist like Rosa Bonheur! I have just written him a few lines saying how grateful and proud I am. But I don't know his address. Please send on to him my letter, which is a fair specimen of my best style!

To Georges Cain and his wife:

January 1, 1899: How aggreeably surprised I was to receive at three o'clock the good news of my big Georges's admission to the order of knighthood! And so affectionately announced, too,

---

[1] A neologism. A word applied in ridicule to the extravagant supporters of Cæsarism or militarism. Littré.

[2] Auguste Cain had died three years before.

[3] The partition of "Cendrillon," words by Henri Cain and music by Massenet. When writing Rosa Bonheur's name on the fly-leaf of this copy, the composer surrounded it with a circle of laurels.

by telegram, with the hope of having you both here at last. When the welcome wire came, the Messrs. Tedesco were with me, and they were the cause of my delaying the letter I was intending to write you, to wish you a happy new year. I was not quite sure whether Monsieur de Carnavalet had not given me the cold shoulder since his appointment to the governorship of the historical monuments of the good city of Paris. Three cheers! Hurrah! Nothing of the kind! They haven't forgotten their old monkey who has been a friend of the family for three quarters of a century. So the new year, on the contrary, begins well.

I am making ready my broadest scimitar in order to dub, with its blade, Messire Georges Cain a knight, and to give him the embrace. Since his father was my godfather, I have the best right to be his godmother.[1]

Madame Marie, his spouse, it is a long time since I had the pleasure of beholding your face. I hope you will show yourself quite well again in my manor, and that you will do honour to the triumphal banquet we are going to prepare for you both; and that, at last, I shall be able to introduce you to the nose of the Lady of By, which is not of a form to displease you, believe me!

Send us word, therefore, in good time and my coach shall go to the station you fix. Wheel us over my handsome Henri,[2] if you can. Good-bye; love to you both, and may the year that begins to-day be a happy and propitious one for all. Indeed, it begins well, at least for your old friend from father to son.

Rosa Bonheur's gift for verse-making is evidenced in these lines to Auguste Cain, which may close this correspondence with the Mène-Cain family. They were sent in acknowledgment of a present whose wood was richly carved and decorated with brass nails:

> What a bellows! What a bellows!
> Oh, my friends! oh! what a bellows!
> For a bellows, like this bellows,
> Must be worth a tierce of bellows.

---

[1] See the letter on page 234.   [2] Henri Cain.

REMINISCENCES OF ROSA BONHEUR

From out thy brain, Augustus Cain,
It's very evident and plain
The bellows's drawing has been ta'en.
Blest be my lot, thrice and again,
To have such an Augustus Cain!
Conferred on me, it is a grace
Touching me in a tender place.
Wherefore his cheeks I do embrace
In fancy, till I see his face.

Now, changing themes, let me preface:
    I have a stale upon a broom,
Of oaken stem so strong and hale,
    That, if a pillar in my room
(My painting-room) should yield and fail,
The besom's stale would then avail.

Moreover, when the witches brew,
Astride it, up the chimney-flue
I could escape, flying with ease,
Safe wafted by the bellows's breeze.

But Nathalie will have to squeeze it;
    For, with such prim folks around me, please,
Myself, I'd never dare to wheeze it,
    Its wind has such a funny—sneeze.

I'll use it, then, to put behind
Me, when to visit I've a mind,
And turned towards Paris is the wind.
There, having all the distance coursèd
Upon the besom-stale aforesaid,
I'll come and all you people bless,
As should each proper sorceress.

This writ, my love to small and great.
How big it is, I cannot state.

II

M. Paul Chardin exhibited for many years in the annual Salon, and one of his pictures, the interior of a Brittany chapel, was bought by the State in 1873, and hung for a long time in the Luxembourg Gallery. He has illustrated several important books of travel and published illustrated articles on archæological and heraldic subjects pertaining to Brittany, where he has long had his country home. He is a corresponding member of the French Society of Antiquities. Gabriel Chardin, a pupil of Troyon and one of the Barbizon landscapists, was his cousin, but he is not related to Chardin, the celebrated painter of the eighteenth century, though he possesses some excellent specimens of his work. Rosa Bonheur exercised a strong influence over the development of the artistic talents of M. Chardin, and they were close friends throughout her life. Her favourite nickname for him was, as has already been pointed out, " Rapin," Dauber, or young pupil in painting. A tone of unusual sadness runs through all this correspondence

August 23, 1867 : One finally becomes so enervated and worn out by the things of this life, whether they affect one nearly or remotely, that unless one lets one's self drift, it is necessary to react against the laws of physical nature which each day deprives us of a little of those we love, and of ourselves, too, happily! One has to become, if not hard, if not selfish, at least tough, and to brace in order to go on to the end without allowing one's self to drop like a rag.

As for me, I must own that I am in the position of the old rat who, after sniffing about over hill and dale, retires, quite satisfied, to his hole, yet, in reality, somewhat sad to have seen the world without taking a part in it. So I shut my door in the face of all that is commonplace and keep only three or four sincere affections, after studying those who wished to do the same, a thing allowable to each; so that, after having chosen one's friends, one keeps those that please and neglects those that don't. Now, my good Rapin, you of course belong to the small number of those

I really like, and you will find me always happy to receive you but more and more buried in my small shell, with my door shut against the indifferent. For you, then, I will open it and for three or four other friends of my predilection.

I feel I am becoming more of a hermit than ever; not that I wish to reproach others or indeed myself. Still, willy-nilly, my life is spent in meditating and ruminating on society, and, at times, things appear to me the reverse of enchanting, almost always sad or entirely comic, according to the point of view taken. Yet, bless me! there is something good in everything, and the tendency is for this righteous feeling to grow. The essential is to see it. Though much disgusted with life lately, my friend Rapin, I have been setting to work again at my horses, during the last few days, so that the mornings go by more quickly than the evenings. After finishing the studies I am engaged on now, I shall continue with a big horse you have seen here. I mount horseback pretty often in order to divert myself a little. The horse is an old Arab mare that was once very handsome.

You must work, too. Your visit to my brother Auguste at Magny must have encouraged you. I am sure the more you know him the more affection you will have for him.

October 13, 1871: I am still pegging away at my stag whom I shall soon have finished. Afterward I shall have no lack of projects, the best of all being to be free from strangers' visits, in order to live in peace and do what I have in my head; for I have intentions that I feel strong enough to carry out in the face of everybody. I possess the nature of old boars and more and more I want to be alone. Now and again I work with passion; for, when I am not in the humour, I can't force myself. But at present, I feel I am at last going to set to work again at my pictures. My mind inclines me to it with more pleasure or with less indifference; and, naturally, I like to conquer.

I have been trying water-colour painting, and have just finished one which I think a fair success, after one or two failures. But I now see that, in this kind of work, one must execute boldly, at the first stroke, in order to produce the transparency effect so much sought after.

On this letter M. Chardin makes the following comment: " Rosa Bonheur went to a great deal of trouble in order to obtain this luminous transparency of leaves under a reflected light. This reminds me that when she once painted an easel-picture, representing a roebuck and its doe resting under an oak, in broad midday, she told me that to get this transparency she had prepared her foliage in very clear, almost white tones, or in very pale yellow, afterward glazing with greens. This picture was, I think, bought from her by the Empress Eugénie."

February 26, 1884: I share your ideas. Without the belief in another life, our present one, having no aim, would be an infamy. I believe in a divine justice that punishes the wicked and does not confound with rogues and brutes the souls of the true and noble. Life is fleeting. It is a trial for intelligent creatures, and, more especially, a field of battle on which courage is necessary. I realise it as you, yourself, have learnt to realise it, my poor friend.

It is now four days since my poor brother Auguste's death. Ah! how cruel it is, dear M. Chardin! Still, my poor brother has left us this consolation that he was always so good and so kind a father. Through his work, he has assured an honourable life to his wife and children. Moreover, we are left to take care of them as you, my good friend, those whom your dear wife has left you.

Commenting on the above letter, M. Chardin says: " About the year 1873 Mlle. Bonheur interrupted her correspondence with me. At this time her health was very unsatisfactory, and her character suffered in consequence. She became taciturn, almost unapproachable, seeking solitude and receiving no one, not even those she called her friends. She resumed her correspondence with me only in May, 1882, writing to me on the occasion of a death I felt keenly. An allusion to this event occurs in the above letter."

January 4, 1885: I am enjoying life this winter, being in a lovely part of the country, with a May climate. My brother Isidore is with me and we are both doing landscape, intending to put lions in; water-colouring especially, which pleases me and amuses me. Just now, we are making studies of carob-trees perched up in rocks that descend sheer into the sea. We ourselves are perched in the shade of these trees. That's our existence at present. We are here till the end of April, when we shall leave Nice for good, unless we decide to rent somewhere else; which means that we are to change our villa.

January 4, 1886: Here at By everything is still the same except the years that pass over our whitened heads. I am still surrounded with my animals. My old Nathalie and I love them more than we do three-fourths of our own species. I am at present making experiments on wild beasts. We are rearing a lion and a lioness which are gentleness itself toward us. The painting is going on as usual.

The forest is devastated more and more. In twenty years' time there will be nothing but sand, firs, and heaps of stones. But it is all the same to me, for I shall be in a better world, I hope, together with my old life's companion.

January 19, 1890: Since I have lost my friend,[1] I care for being nowhere else than here alone in my corner, where nearly all our life has been spent. I live on the souvenirs that surround me, just as if she were here, and I find it difficult to quit them. I occupy myself unceasingly, and the time passes quickly; nor do I regret to see it pass.

You mention the little horse given me by Colonel Cody.[2] I have no desire to get rid of him, for the good reason that he was given me and also because he is a splendid trotter, very free and very gentle. I take great care of him.

January 6, 1891: I am not working much. At present, I am gathering material in a desultory way. My solitude I am more attached to than ever, and would not exchange it for the glories

---

[1] Mlle. Micas.

[2] Buffalo Bill, whose "Wild West" was in Paris throughout the International Exhibition of 1889. "Rosa Bonheur attended the show several times," writes M. Chardin, "and studied the bisons and other animals, as well as the Indians."

of this world, which, in general, I consider very poor. I look out of my rat's hole just to see how the humanitarian geniuses arrange together again the systems which they have pulled down. Let us hope they will make the universe perfect. Meanwhile I shall be delighted to leave no one behind me, thank God; and with this thought, I hope to quit this world with a light heart and a clear conscience.

May 12, 1891: You see how much I have been afflicted during the last two years.[1] Now we are alone, my poor Isidore and I, alone out of the four. But we have reached the age when we can wait our turn without great fear, having seen those we love go before.

December 30, 1891: I muse a good deal, only half living in this world. I count the days that pass. They glide by and I am rejoiced at it. I live alone and like it best. If, perchance, I see a human being, I am bored the more. Painting still pleases me, especially when I begin a picture. Before I finish it, I find it tiresome.

January 18, 1894: I have not been able to answer your letter before, because I am sitting to Mme. de Grasse for my portrait, so that your old artist companion is not free except in the evenings, and then she is not much disposed to write after a day's sitting.

I have nothing on earth to regret leaving. Since my dear Nathalie has gone from me, the world is an object of indifference, and I look at everything as though I were seeing a play. The painting is jogging on so-so. My dogs are my surest friends. My old brother Isidore still works; it is the best thing after all.

July 9, 1897: It pleased me very much to succeed in a kind of painting that I had never cultivated, and the success is a sufficient reward.[2] On the other hand, since in this world there is always a

---

[1] Her sister, Mme. Peyrol, had recently died, and about two years earlier Mlle. Micas had passed away.

[2] M. Chardin had congratulated her on her pastels, then on exhibition at the Petit Gallery.

black as well as a bright side to everything, I will confess to you that I have had some disappointment following close on my laurels. My ship has run aground; in other words, my manorial dwelling has suffered a disaster. The helm had got out of order; by which you are to understand that Aline, my first lieutenant, has been ill. I paid off half my crew, and just now am a little less angry, for Aline is on her legs again, and I have at length succeeded in getting a suitable head-cook, whose superiority consists in forgetting to put salt in the soup. Still things are supportable.

After perspiring with writing a heap of letters of gratitude to praisers of my pastels, I have, happily, come to the end. I am certainly fond of praise, but much fonder of being quiet.

THE MARQUISE DE GRASSE PAINTING ROSA BONHEUR.

February 26, 1899: I have just come back from Nice, where I have spent ten or eleven days with Mr. Gambart, the Consul-General for Spain. Now that I am safely back, I am glad to be in my own house once more, far from the world, in the peacefulness of the woods. My new studio will soon be finished and will be ready by the end of March. As for the electricity, which will cost me more than five thousand francs, I shall have to wait a fortnight before it works properly. I have, however, a good light already. But the accumulators must be garnished in order to have the light for several hours in the evening. Then it will be superb to be able to do chalk drawings in the evening; and as I have got my head full of subjects which I should want a hundred years to execute in painting, I hope to be able at least to render them visible in chalks by means of the electric light. My health is getting better.

Just three months after this letter was written Rosa Bonheur died.

III

Mlle. Simonin Valérie graduated from the Paris Conservatoire, where she won the first prize in acting, joined the Odéon troupe, and then passed to the Théâtre Français, where she remained for four years. She then left the stage and married Gustave Fould, who was subsequently elected deputy, and whose father, Achille Fould, was cabinet minister for sixteen years under Napoleon III. By this marriage she had two daughters, Consuélo and Achille. Several years after the death of her first husband, Mme. Fould married Prince Georges Stirbey, of the distinguished Roumanian family of that name, in which country he played an important political part. The Prince has cultivated letters, and the Princess has shown talent not only on the stage, but in sculpture and literature.

Princess Stirbey writes me:

Travelling in England and Germany for some time after my first marriage, I lost sight of Rosa Bonheur, yet without forgetting her. She often formed the subject of my conversations.

But it was not until my two daughters, who had become painters, asked me to introduce them to her, that our relations were resumed. So we went to By, where we had a cordial reception, the warmth of which was at first somewhat dampened by etiquette. "You are a fine lady now," she said, laughing; "at present I must mind my p's and q's when speaking to you!" From this moment our intimacy was resumed as if there had been no interruption. She offered to advise my daughters, to give them the benefit of her experience, and to teach them what she herself had learnt in the course of her long career. This promise she carried out, insisting with so much grace that I accepted, and my daughters submitted their paintings to her inspection and criticism. Soon after the death of Mlle. Micas, wishing to alleviate my friend's great grief by giving her something to occupy her mind, I ventured to ask her if she would not allow my daughters to paint her portrait, a favour which she had hitherto refused to grant to other artists. A single likeness of her was extant, an old one executed by the second Dubufe, that in which she appears leaning on a bull. She accepted my proposal, and thus it came about that we spent three weeks with her at By, whither we returned on several occasions.

Mme. Consuélo Fould, the art name of the Marquise de Grasse, whose husband is a lineal descendant of the French admiral of the American Revolution, was born at Cologne in 1868. She studied painting under Léon Comerre and Antoine Vollon, and has exhibited since 1884 pictures depicting pleasing, graceful subjects, many of which have been reproduced in engravings in England, America, and Germany. She has received an honourable mention at the Salon, and one of her pictures has been bought by the Museum of Gothenburg, Sweden. She has written on art, and is the inventor of a process for drawing with damp colours which can be rubbed out like charcoal.

Mlle. Achille Fould, the second daughter of Princess Stirbey, is also a successful painter, and has long exhibited at the annual Salon. Speaking of the Fould portraits of Rosa Bonheur, she writes me:

250

My sister and I had long wished to know Rosa Bonheur—it was one of our childhood dreams—when my mother, who had not seen her old friend for many years, decided to present us. So we all three started for By, where we were cordially received. My sister and myself were both burning with the desire to paint Rosa Bonheur's portrait. She acceded to our request, and invited us to go and spend some time with her, sitting for us during three weeks every afternoon. Both of us did our very best to produce the true portrait, the one which should go to the Salon. Finally, Rosa Bonheur proposed with a smile that we draw lots for this honour. We did so, and I was the lucky one. When the work was well advanced, I returned to Paris to complete it, and then went back again to By for the finishing touches. Rosa Bonheur herself painted on my canvas the pictures she was at work upon at the time and which formed a part of my composition. This picture was exhibited at the Salon of 1893, and was bought for the Museum of Bordeaux, where it now hangs.

From Rosa Bonheur's letters to Princess Stirbey, Mme. Fould, the following may be quoted here:

In two letters to Mme. Fould in 1889 she says:

July 28: What touches me most in your last letter is the vivid recollection which you retain of my friend Nathalie. I am not so fortunate as you. I can see her only in my memory. So my thoughts on life are not very gay. I try to argue with myself and to take to my art again. But it is very hard work. However, to-day I thought of starting with my brush again. Thanks for what you say of my Pitchoun.[1] I myself am only a poor dog, little or nothing else. He joins me in sending you a good paw-shake.

September 3: For the last five months I have not felt in a mood to paint. You will understand what a struggle I have had and what strength is necessary to combat my low spirits, so that I can employ the short time that remains to me in this world in

---

[1] Bordeaux dialect for little.

executing, if I can, some paintings which I have in mind. It seems to me that this would be the desire of my friend, who was so proud of what I can do and who would advise me to so act if she were in reality near me. Thank your husband, who, like yourself, so well understood my Nathalie. Don't believe that I can ever forget this. It is only now that I am getting back a little of my soul which she carried away with her, but which is wholly hers for another life, if the Creator permits it.

" Dear and a thousand times kind and amiable Madam Fould," runs a letter written in 1889:

Since you ask me how I am getting on, I may answer you that I am living like my dogs. I am swallowing life as best I can. The days pass quickly. They go by, they go by! And I am not sorry, I can assure you. Only I am a mixture of dog and tortoise. However, on making a closer study of myself, it is the bear, I think, which predominates over the various other animals that I am. Dear Madam Fould, the Creator would really be the devil himself if he made us to live, love, and admire in order to annihilate us afterward like generations of bugs which swarm in the old houses of Nice, Auvergne, Brittany, and the Pyrenees, and which we clean people destroy forever without respite and without mercy, so that they have a tendency to disappear from the surface of the globe. What a gradation there is between living things! Why is it so? Is it because the Creator has so willed it? That's the question.

I am trying to sell my Nice villa, just like you. It would be too painful to me to go there alone, whereas at By I am accustomed to being alone.

Please remember me kindly to the Prince.

December 19, 1889: As your idea of me is that of a person who possesses beauty, genius, amiability and charm, I ask myself whether it is possible that I correspond to the description without knowing it. I look upon myself as a dog that has been playing a flute. Then I reflect and I perceive that we often attribute to others our own feelings and qualities. Ought we to fool ourselves by placing before us too fine an ideal? You and I have in our souls birds' wings, instead of crawling about like worms in a lubbering angler's bait-box. That's something. And Uranus is there to prove to us that we are a little better than the turkey.

"Dear and charming one," begins the next letter, which is dated January 1, 1890, and runs as follows:

It is you I mean, oh, my kind friend, Mme. Fould; for you see, I am only an old fogy. Why should I bring tears into the eyes of the poor old friends who are still in this world and are doing all they can to help me bear its woes? I owe them something for their good intentions and especially to you who have never neglected me for a single instant. For your New Year's gift, though the custom is no longer very swell, I can't resist sending you these verses, which come to me by inspiration.

> With thy suave lines, O charming bard,
>   Thou fain woulds't make me out too fair;
> My Demon, who's a cunning card,
>   Discounts the praise, nor turns a hair.
>
> Knowing thy heart, I have a proof
>   How good is all that dwells inside;
> Where, if the devil shows his hoof,
>   There's love to quickly tan his hide.

The original of these lines—the best I have found by Rosa Bonheur—is as follows:

> De tes charmants vers, O charmant poète,
>   Tu voudrais bien m'entortiller;
> Mon génie, qui n'est pas bête,
>   Le voit d'ici sans sourciller.
>
> De ton cœur, je sais reconnaître
>   La bonté en ce bon séjour;
> Si le diable est un peu maître,
>   C'est pour être rossé par l'amour.

REMINISCENCES OF ROSA BONHEUR

January 10, 1890: I am, I know, an old brute, dear and a thousand times excellent Mme. Fould. But your kindness would turn a wolf into a lamb. But, dear Mme. Fould, since I have lost my dear friend, nothing makes an impression on me. I have become like a stick of wood, metaphorically speaking, of course; for there are still people whom I love, and you among the small number. And I still feel able to throw off a few more little pictures, which will sell at least after my death.

June 26, 1891: Rosa Bonheur is a dreadful scamp! She makes promises and then doesn't keep them. Why? Because she is charming when anybody is with her—you yourself have said so— but so soon as she is alone, the old hag falls under the influence of her natural character. And then it should be taken into account that she is sixty-nine! Fatigue knocks her under. Very humbly this old donkey comes and begs your pardon, for she went to Paris on the 23d, starting in the morning and coming back in the evening, because she was expecting company on the 24th in her castle at By. Then weariness and the heat made her lazy. The old rascal of a Rosa begs pardon and thanks her friend, Mme. Fould, for the flowers found on the tomb of her friend Nathalie Micas, and takes the liberty of sending a kiss to the best of mothers and to her children.

June 18, 1892: I am at your service for Monday, the date chosen by your Excellency. I am quite ready to pose like an angel for the future glory of my Department and France, as well as for Art and the Magistracy, without forgetting the Clergy.

August 23, 1892: I do not know where you are at present, dear Mme. Fould, my grandmother, but I am receiving perfumes and liqueurs from the most reputed towns and manufactories through which you pass, escorted by my charming elder sisters, like three adorable nymphs wafted by the zephyrs of the north, I hope. For at By, the fires of Phœbus have turned us French into roasted potatoes, or, if you prefer it, into dried-up shavings —parched grass, perhaps, would be better. I hope we shall meet before dying and that you will be fresher than I who am, you know, much younger than you are!

I should advise you and the Prince, as you must be simply stewing at Royan, to put on your bathing trunks and squat down in the water, with a tent over your heads. It is the sole way in which anybody can live just at present. This is what Rosa Bonheur is doing, dear mamma, which prevents her from receiving the court and the town. Pardon me if the heat of the dog days has affected my head!

Greetings and fellowship, except for my grandmother, whom I kiss. Rosa Bonheur, in her castle at By.

September 24, 1892: I haven't written to you before, because it would have caused my genius a loss of time, better employed, doubtless, in the noble art of painting! My days being counted, I must use the precious moments in a way that brings in cash. But I must thank you for your poetry. Alas, I feel myself incapable of replying to you in the language of the Muses; so I fall back on simple prose, like the Bourgeois Gentilhomme, having but once felt poetic inspiration through you, which fact, however, ought to render you modestly proud.

I am occupied with more prosaic things, washing and combing the abundant head of hair which the gods have given me, brushing the last teeth which remain to me and which have to be treated with much care lest they too escape me, giving thought to this mouth which you find young and charming, to the pretty little ears, to the aristocratic foot inherited from the marchioness; in a word, doing all I can to prevent the lie being given to my kind attractive sisters, who cherish in their soul the poetry and ideal of a better world, just as does our dear and venerated grandmother in the spirit.

" Dear Mme. Fould, my thousand times kind Grandmother," she begins on March 2, 1893:

I shall expect you when you like to come. I can't lodge you, but I can offer you my rustic dog-kennel table. It will be an opportunity to cook a superb York ham and I have some excellent champagne and curried chicken. Céline will look after the rest.

I am delighted to learn that you have no further need of my head, for my hair cutter has clipped me a little too much, and that takes from me all my poetry. My Nathalie was always scolding me about it. But I must tell you that when I put on a lady's hat, it looks slovenly to see my hair poking out behind. And as I hope to be able to go to Paris after your visit, then your grandson will become your granddaughter.

I am very happy to learn that the masters Bouguereau, Comerre, and Haller [1] interest themselves in the great artist Rosa Bonheur, who certainly is not without talent and whose duty it is to apply herself as much as possible. This, in fact, is what your grandson is trying to do, in spite of years, winds, and tides, and with the aid of St. Pétronille.[2]

Allow your affectionate grandson to kiss you heartily, as well as my sisters, without forgetting the Prince—Father Prince—who often has the kindness to kiss my hands when we meet, though, egad, they are not always in a kissable state. But I beg you not to deter him in his good intentions and to thank the kind Father Prince, offering him my best regards.

March 19, 1893: Yesterday, very venerable grandmother, just at the end of the lunch offered to Mr. Lefèvre, a rich hamper reached me and I at once guessed where it came from by the truffle odour which you generally diffuse around you. I had it opened forthwith and Mr. Lefèvre looked at it so longingly that, i'faith, I thought it my duty to invite him to dinner, which invitation he immediately accepted with evident pleasure. We then went for a drive in the forest and talked a great deal about the portraits of Rosa Bonheur, we both blinking at each other with noses as red as American pipes.

My opinion is that a woman who overwhelms me with good things has designs on my life, truffles especially being extremely heating for artists. And then, there are all the other dishes you

---

[1] Gustave Haller was the art name of Mme. Fould.
[2] A virgin martyr of the first century.

try to corrupt me with, as Eve was tempted by the serpent. Happily, I am on my guard. But don't feel hurt, for I am, as ever and nevertheless, your most respectful grandson, dear master in the art of painting.

March 30, 1893: I send you, most cajoling grandmother, a letter received this morning from the *Illustration*. You will render me a great service by telling the writer for me that I have no wish to lend my studies for photographing. When I am dead, it will be quite time to dispose of them. At present I can still make use of them. If they were once published, it would look as though I were utilising other people's studies.

I send you a kiss with my pipe in my mouth.

May 9, 1893: Your grandson has a running nose and can't be frequented at present without danger. She is ashamed to have to make use of napkins to wipe her nose. Handkerchiefs are too small and, anyway, they are all in the wash! All this is one of the reasons why this miserable animal has not replied at once, as she usually does, to her good mother's letter. In the next place, the old beast, profiting of a little rest, is having her stables cleaned out and so is getting herself covered with the glorious dust of years, so that her head is really filthy, which gives her only a faint resemblance to the portrait of her painted at the age of twenty by her charming and aristocratic fellow-artist.

In answer to one of your questions, I must tell you, mamma, that at present I detest women folk. I now like only men, because I find them in general so stupid that it flatters me.

I kiss respectfully your hands and even your venerable face, in spite of the dust and dirt that covers mine, pardoning you for forcing me to interrupt my labours in order to write a letter of the kind that I can write only to you.

On June 26, 1893, a letter is addressed to " Mme. and Great Grandmother " : [1]

---

[1] In the original, this word is By-saïeule for bisaïeule, an untranslatable pun on the hamlet and château of By. Rosa Bonheur, as has already been seen, had a great liking for far-fetched playing on words.

As regards your artistic daughter who has not received the Salon honour, I give her the same advice as you yourself, dear Mme. Fould—not to fret. In matters of art, rewards are much like blisters on wooden legs—they don't affect much. That which proves something is doing one's best, regardless of consequences, especially when the exercise of one's art is not necessary for the getting of one's bread and cheese. If you have done about the best you can, you cannot do more. Sometimes both critics and flatterers have bad spectacles. There will always be some prophets one need not pay heed to. Tell that to my Little Sister, who is a brave girl.

From your only grandson in the spirit and great artist of horses.

August 29, 1893, Rosa writes to Mlle. Consuélo Fould:

I wonder why I inspire such fear that I am compared to a Japan elephant, while a Princess [1] compares herself to a tiny insect! I am obliged to pinch myself and to ask whether I am not perchance Jupiter himself without knowing it. Yet, deuce take me if I am; and deuce take you, too, with your gratitude and admiration. I believe you are making fun of me to my very beard, while you are the cause of my losing my time in manufacturing you witty letters.

You may paint my portrait, since it will give you pleasure. You may make me to sit as often as you like. For you, I will pose like an angel; and the sooner the better. Posterity will profit by it, and there will be glory in it, also.

I offer you my blessing with all the incense with which I am saturated, and beg you to receive, dear Mademoiselle, the tender homage of the illustrious Rosa Bonheur, who dares to touch with her old moustache your good and charming face.

To Princess Stirbey, October 7, 1893, she again writes:

Decidedly, mamma, you are the best of women, only you have got an artist's head. Twice, dear mamma, have you announced to

---

[1] Mlle. Fould was, as has already been said, the daughter of Princess Stirbey.

your unworthy grandson the approaching marriage of my kind and handsome sister, your daughter,[1] twice, in order, perhaps, to play some trick on me. So now, your pretty and highly honoured young boy will put on a collar as high as the column in the Place Vendôme. But, unfortunately, I have not been able to order a long-necked doublet, and now it is too late to do so. I have only an old pair of hose and my Sunday-go-to-meeting shoes. What I most regret is that I shall not be able to attend the wedding breakfast. Please thank papa for having thought of me. But you know, fine ladies and castles frighten me dreadfully.

As regards my posing again, thank you, mamma, for the request. Your artistic progenitor in the spirit, painter of animals by the grace of God and the agency of angels, is fond enough of you to pose once more even without the condition that you bring again, to his castle of the time of Charlemagne, some delicate dishes and juicy wines.

Greetings to all the company from your loving grandson.

Rosa Bonheur's correspondence with the Marquise de Grasse, which follows, is occupied chiefly with the portrait of the former painted by the latter.

November 26, 1893: Now let me offer you an idea which has suddenly occurred to me. The time of the year is not propitious to come into a house which is always rather damp when it hasn't been occupied for some time. As you are desirous of painting my portrait, I will go myself to your studio. In this way, you won't have to trot out here your painting materials and canvas. I can transport my person to your place two days running each week, which wouldn't put me out much; and you would thus have time to do my head. If another journey per week were necessary, I would undertake it willingly for a charming lady who is also a distinguished artist. Such is my plan, which simplifies everything. Please adopt it without ceremony if it suits you. When once the portrait is finished, or even before, if you prefer, you can send me the canvas and I will paint the dog.

---

[1] The Marquise de Grasse.

259

Thanks for your affectionate letter. You may present your-self at the gates of my fortress, either on foot or on horseback. My castle is open to you as well as my heart.

" Most estimable colleague and adorable big Sister," she writes on December 18, 1893:

On reflection I prefer you should come to me. But, excuse me, a week is soon gone. One in Paris and another at By in order to get over the fear of greatness, that makes two. I am at your disposal on and after Sunday, and, in fact, all the week following. You will have the shortest days of the year, and I shall be pleased to see how you manage. One more hint. If it should snow, you will find it difficult to get to By, and will risk catching a princely cold like mine. You assume, therefore, the full responsibility of colds and influenzas. After Sunday, I shan't stir from By. I remain, Madam, your slave to sit as long as you choose, Rosa Bonheur, artist, painter of animals from nature.

December 23, 1893: Your charming model will hold herself ready for you on January 3d, gracious lady and most honoured colleague, with her coat well brushed, although rather shabby, and her hair done up and beard trimmed. Don't bother about palette and colours. I will see that you have everything you need, and, in addition, I will behave like a real model of grace and modesty for three hundred and sixty-five days, if you wish.

Yesterday I saw Mr. Lefèvre, Jr., who brought me from Lon-don an admirable little bitch. We signed a heap of engravings. This time he was not able to call on you, being obliged to take the evening boat in order to reach London this morning.

Awaiting the pleasure of seeing you, I remain, with legitimate pride and a kiss for your husband's hand, as if he were an Auvergne woman, your little sister and first-class artist, with affectionate regards to you.

February 18, 1894: I received the photographs the day before yesterday, dear Madam and charming sister of the brush. They are superb and my heart is filled with joy. I shall obtain some

ROSA BONHEUR.

By Consuélo Fould, Marquise de Grasse.

magnificent enlargements, thanks to you. Thank your husband for his share in the work. I see you have found it difficult enough to do the touching up. As soon as I gain possession of this illustrious canvas, I will set to work on the dog's head in order to make it match the calf's head.[1]

In the meanwhile, believe me, with many thanks, your much flattered little sister.

To Prince Georges Stirbey, she writes on February 19, 1894, thanking him for a beautiful jeweled gift:

Last evening, toward nine o'clock, I was surprised to hear somebody ring at my gate, which is extraordinary at By, for at that hour absolute quiet reigns in my house. And now, this morning, I come to thank you from the bottom of my heart. My surprise has become glorified in reading your letter and in receiving from you, dear Prince Stirbey, this box, with my monogram engraved on it and holding the insignia of an officer of the Legion of Honour. I am profoundly touched by the affectionate letter which accompanies it and I now await with impatience the official moment when I shall have the right to embrace my Prince, who is, at one and the same time, my brother in arms and my honourable protector.

A letter to Princess Stirbey in February, 1894, runs as follows:

At last you are in favour again with your dear grandson, the great master and adorable damsel, Rosa Bonheur; for, since the Princess of Antibes[2] came and honoured me by getting me to pose, I have been without news from you, except on the occasion of the cross of an officer of the Legion of Honour diddled out of the Prince and brought to me at bedtime by my lord's secretary.

My graceful little sister is very fortunate to have had such a fine model for her picture. I am jealous in every way, as I myself

---

[1] A playful allusion to her own head in the joint work.
[2] A fanciful title for the Marquise de Grasse.

am condemned for life to paint beasts, the rumps of horses and
donkeys, and the horns of cows.

Mamma, I pardon you your temporary indifference, hoping
that you will, on your side, make allowance for the total lack of
bringing-up of her who is honoured by being your dear grandson,
in spite of her tricks of nature. I kiss your hand.

Quoting again from Rosa's letters to the Marquise de Grasse:

February 26, 1894: I write to ask, dear, charming and adorable Madam, if you are still stopped in your work and if I may
hope—to the great satisfaction of Mr. Lefèvre of London—soon
to illustrate, with my dog's head, your portrait of Rosa Bonheur.
I should also like to know if you would consent to receive a young
lady, a pupil of my sweetheart, Georges Cain, and allow her to
spend an hour in your studio so that she may paint from your
picture the colour of my face. By doing so, you would render
her a famous service and me also, for I don't want to sit for my
portrait again this year. I enclose with this letter that of
Georges Cain, which will give you the name of his pupil; and I
await your reply to learn whether you will submit to this intrusion on your artistic privacy. As soon as I get it, I shall write
to your rival, who will have a splendid opportunity of presenting
you with her compliments.

Remember me to your mother. I have not forgotten her kindness to me. I trust she keeps in the jar of her heart a little
affection for her spiritual child. Your old, very old and affectionate Rosa Bonheur.

March 19, 1894: I have just unpacked my portrait, or, rather,
your portrait. I expect to-morrow Sir Ernest Lefèvre. At last
it is dry, and I am going to set to work on the dog's head.

Since I saw you, I have had a great loss. My charming little
Daisy died while having some young ones. She has left me a
little bitch which I am rearing with the bottle. It will be a fine
creature, but resembles neither the mother nor the father, being
most like my little Gamine, whom the gods have doubtless deigned
to restore to me through the medium of my pet Daisy. Amen.

Good-bye, my dear and adorable big sister.

March 30, 1894: Pardon my being three or four days late in replying to your amiable letter, kind and adorable colleague. I have been and still am suffering from an eruption on half of my carcass. I may thank Jupiter for it, unless it is one of Venus's practical jokes, for just about this time she is busy everywhere in nature. In consequence, I haven't been in a very good humour, especially as maternal love—which has developed somewhat late in me—has just given me a terrible fright. I thought I was going to lose my baby bitch! But, O Universal Suffrage! my baby is well again, and my eruption is gradually disappearing, so that I am getting better-tempered, and honour you with my writing.

I commission you to write to Mr. Lefèvre and tell him the dog's head is nearly finished and is superb. It wants to dry a little before receiving the last touches. You must come, my dear colleague of the brush, and see this head. It will delight you, I hope, as much as the public.

April 6, 1894: My delay in writing means that I am just now done up, run down, worn out, quite muddled in fact, and I beg you won't come over yet, especially on a bicycle, for I don't want to see you completely lose your dignity at the very moment when I am trying to gain a bit myself. What I need is quiet. I can no longer distinguish what is good from what is bad. It must be softening of the brain! For what other folks find beautiful, I find ugly; and *vice versa*. It's a terrible malady, believe me, and pity me. But it won't last, I hope. Wait, therefore, till I am quiet. When I have finished my letters of thanks—the grave and the gay—and my pictures, as usual behindhand; when I have revictualled my money-bag, taken a few baths, passed the razor over the down on my chin—then it will be the time for you to come. Then I will write you and I hope we shall be able to give the embrace claimed by your husband. I'faith, if that happens, I shall be a proud woman, I assure you.

May 10, 1894: Dog's head finished at last; ground gave me awful trouble; mountains and valleys stood out and made holes when scraped. With what did you prepare those impastations?

REMINISCENCES OF ROSA BONHEUR

Not dry yet. Ought to have scraped them white. Did not dare. Dreadful medley. Will remain curtain of rock-work, and go down to posterity with Rosa Bonheur. So, blew Mr. Lefèvre up.[1] Arriving Paris 12th, to-morrow. Send you by gardener, box containing portrait so that may frame it. Only be careful. All not dry in dog's head. But wished to satisfy poor friend Lefèvre, make him open his mouth, wanting to carry off picture at last and really get hold of it. Not my fault; poorly, disturbed; wouldn't dry; as unfortunate as you, more unfortunate, even. Haven't seen the Salon. Am hankering to go, but got tooth-ache. No luck, but plenty of honours. Have made little rosette,[2] to spare you journey. Put on princely cross [3] to go to Chantilly,[4] and to visit President of Republic, happy man of Elysian Fields, dwelling of the gods.

August 21, 1894: You were quite right, distinguished artist and adorable big sister, in thinking that my genius has come down again from Mt. Blanc, or any other mount you may choose.[5] Here I am once more on the level ground, seeing my friends, brother and sister, descend into it, one after the other, and waiting my own turn for the final plunge. My philosophy grows larger and larger and surrounds itself with more and more charms, and I find there is no need to regret a sorry old carcass which fails me a little more every day. I think I must be bewitched and that some bad fairy takes a pleasure in making me lose my time. Every day that I see slip away worries me. My troubles are not those of the body but of the affections. I can't work quickly and I have the foible of not being able to do anything

---

[1] He gave a wrong measure for the picture, later perceived his mistake and sent the right measure. But, in the meanwhile, the picture was begun. So it was necessary to add a strip of canvas, and thickly impaste the seam, so that the joining might not be seen.

[2] As she had recently been promoted from chevalier to officer in the Legion of Honour, she changed the ribbon into a rosette.

[3] Prince Stirbey's diamond cross of the Legion of Honour, referred to in the preceding letter of February 19th, the cross being the full dress decoration of an officer.

[4] The home of the Duke d'Aumale.

[5] Rosa Bonheur had been visiting Switzerland.

264

when some one is behind my back. No doubt I shall never be tranquil until I am in the grave. From time to time I long to be there. I should like a fine funeral, with a large number of wreaths and a detachment of soldiers, since I am an officer.[1]

Remember me to your mother and to your dear other half.

Writing from her Paris *pied-à-terre*, on December 9, 1894, to Princess Stirbey, Rosa says:

You see that I am in Paris, at 7 Rue Gay-Lussac. So I have outrageously deceived you, O Mamma! But your affectionate grandson has been ill. However, she now writes to-day to let you know that, having recovered, she'll be glad to see you in her abode, if you like to come. If my two sisters wish to accompany you, I shall be happy to receive them, too. But the Prince, a little later, as I have only three arm-chairs!

Mamma, you will find me charming and looking younger; for I get to look younger as the years go by. A kiss to you all from your beloved and grateful grandson, Mademoiselle Rosa Bonheur, artist of the highest merit.

" Fair Madam, adorable lady, amiable big sister and colleague," begins the following letter to the Marquise de Grasse, dated March 9, 1895, from By:

It pleases me to think of you taking me for a wicked old beldam. The idea charms me and relieves me as being a punishment for my not replying to your favour of last month. Alas! yes, I have suffered from the ice-floes of the North Pole, where we have been wintering since I had the pleasure of your visit in Paris, where I had to lie to in the Gautier brig for nineteen days.[2] Here in my castle I have been down with influenza. But, at present, I am on

---

[1] It is customary for a half-company of infantry to be present in the street when the coffin of an officer of the Legion of Honour is put in the hearse. But, as will be seen at the end of this volume, when Rosa Bonheur died, she especially directed in her will that there be no military escort.

[2] Rosa Bonheur's Paris *pied-à-terre* was in the same house with the Gautiers, her neighbours at By.

the bridge again and am hard at work on my lions, which are to be exhibited along with the portrait your High-and-Mightiness has been gracious enough to paint. I promise you a glimpse at them as soon as the leaves begin to peep out on the lilacs, if you and your good man will then deign to lunch with me. I have no more of your Mamma's champagne to offer you, but Gambart's port is not bad. Georges Cain tells me Mamma is off on the spree at Nice. That's what I call doing it.

Love to you and kind regards to the other half of your existence.

The next month she sends a note to Princess Stirbey:

I am still hale and hearty, and it would need some poison in my broth to make me kick the bucket before my time. Providence has given me the wiliness of the fox, the prudence of the serpent, the strength of the lion and the wisdom of St. Anthony, which preserves me from my friends!

To " Dear Madam, adorable big sister, and much esteemed colleague "—that is, the Marquise de Grasse—she writes again a few days later:

I don't know why you should bow down in dust and ashes for not having thought of me earlier. My charming letter, forsooth! But it is much more charming to paint than to write letters. When I think what a worker you are and your sister, too, it makes me jubilate, for I see Woman marching on while the men fret and fume. Not all, however. There are still some knights of chivalry and your husband is of the number. I must confess I did not realise it at first, and I now see that I was most prodigiously mistaken.

You will come and see me, I hope, when May has brought out the leaves. But first I shall be taking a short trip to the south.

Two subsequent letters to Princess Stirbey run thus:

December 30, 1895: Your grandson was surprised, I can tell you, on seeing your Princess's crown on the letter you honoured me with to-day. For, as you are my mother, I am, therefore, a prince, which very much perplexes me. You ought to have told me so sooner, and then I should never have dared to call you mother. However, it would have been all the same; for if I hadn't considered you worthy of such a title, I would have begged the devil to carry you off in order that I should not be compromised by being found in low company!

And now, mother, I am going to bed, quieted down by these philosopho-pipic reflections on the grandeur of this world. I am a badly brought-up son, by the grace of God or the gods, as you like. But grandeur, or rather grand folks, has always awakened in me a certain respect, particularly since I have found, by reading the history of all nations, that the great have always been more unhappy than the small folks.

I send you a kiss, as well as one to my adorable sisters, and conclude since I have no more paper, your respectful grandson.

The next letter opens with a reference to a horseback accident which nearly proved fatal:

June 19, 1896: Here I am on my legs again and in a condition to be able to send you a sample of my scribble, which some people like and others don't. Your grandson, Princess, had a near shave, but the gods have been favourable to him and Rosa Bonheur will be glad to receive her kind mamma, but only after her return from Switzerland, two months hence. So have decided the gentlemen of the faculty.

As poor Gambart is moping to death all alone in the antique dwelling-place of William Tell, I am invited to hunt the chamois in his amiable society. This will rest me after the tribulation of artistic glory and will make it possible for me to have only this one old admirer to bore me. Along with the fresh air of icy mountains, I will get six weeks of tranquillity. On my return, I shall change into a woman of society and become once more the grandson of my dear mamma.

Answering the Marquise de Grasse, Rosa writes November 12, 1897:

Thanks for your kind letter. Your little sister and great painter of animals bears herself as well as the Pont Neuf itself, which, however, is not too new. As for art, I have long been animated with the best intentions with regard to it. Only our terrestrial ball turns so quickly that I, who turn slowly, don't know where to look first, with all the prodigiously fine things there are to see. Just now I am in a gestation period and need repose, which, however, it is difficult enough to obtain, as I am penniless and have to hurry up with some little masterpieces for the Tedescos, who receive them in all confidence.

Tell mamma she is confoundedly neglecting the great artist Rosa Bonheur. Yet I know my pastels gave her satisfaction, as well as you. Remember me to the family, my dear Madam, and believe me,

Your affectionate little sister in the holy spirit.

And again, January 4, 1899:

I was very glad to receive your letter and good wishes. So many things have happened at By during the last year or two that it would take me too long to relate them. I have had one or two bad attacks. But since I have had a colleague living with me,[1] it has brought me good luck. If you and your husband will honour my table with your company one of these next days, you will find me in pretty good health, but fallen off, alas! very much since you painted my portrait. I have sat again and am now sitting for my young colleague. But all my charms have disappeared since I sat for you.

I was not able to get a look at your artistic productions when I was at the last Salon, inasmuch as I had to run away to avoid being stifled under the roof of the hothouse where the arts of painting ripen. Methinks, however, that both you and your sister Achille are marching from victory to victory.

My best wishes for the Château of Bécon,[2] and affectionate regards to the whole lot of you, from your old Rosa Bonheur.

---

[1] The American artist, Miss Anna E. Klumpke, who, in the following May, became Rosa Bonheur's universal legatee.

[2] The home of the Stirbeys, on the banks of the Seine near Paris.

A note, dated January 26, 1899, to Princess Stirbey, runs thus:

A line simply to thank you for your gracious letter and to reassure you about my health, which has come back since I have found a kind, excellent friend who takes care of me and has cured me of my discouragement and misanthropy. I hope to introduce her to you one of these days.

Your Consuélo has made famous progress in her art, and as for Princess Achille, she, too, is getting tremendously clever with her brush. She's right to prefer art to marriage, which more often than not takes a woman in. However, I don't despise this natural institution among all animals, and so useful to men, who would mope to death without wives.

Our artist household is getting on very well. My wife has much talent and the children don't prevent us from painting pictures. What annoys me is to have to wear spectacles.

Awaiting the pleasure of seeing you, I remain, your old grandson who celebrates next March his seventy-seventh birthday.

A letter written to the Marquise de Grasse, May 19, 1899, just a week before Rosa Bonheur died, says:

I made a point of going to see the Salon where my portrait is exhibited, painted by my dear friend Miss Klumpke, and a small picture of my own which had not been very well appreciated in America. This picture had accompanied to America an early portrait, and now, like a boat disturbing a lake, it is creating a commotion of which my artistic vanity makes me very proud.

I was very pleased to see your picture. You have made great progress, and I am glad to be able to tell you so. Near mine, I also saw Achille's picture and I beg you will compliment her on it for me. I can't write much myself just now, as my eyes are weak.

You and your husband must come over and lunch with me one of these days. I shall be glad for you to meet my friend who does not lack talent, as you will have seen. With the portrait you painted of my amiable person, I shall remain, with a few years difference between yours and the present one, a historical character in the world of art; and that thanks to feminine artists, for I have never had a proposal of the kind from a man,[1] which somewhat humiliates me, especially at a moment when I am reaping a few laurels for my old age.

Good-bye, dear Madam. You will find my household a little better kept; and I hope you will like my dear colleague. Kind remembrances to your husband.

This note, addressed to me by Princess Stirbey, throws light on the letter and verses of Rosa Bonheur which follow it:

When my daughters were engaged in painting the portrait of Rosa Bonheur, she suggested that I also model her bust. But the time at my disposal was too short, and, furthermore, I was unwilling to trench longer upon her hospitality. However, as she admired my bust of " Modern Comedy," which I had sent to the International Exhibition of 1889, I made her an exact copy of it in marble, life-size, and, until her death, it remained in her studio. " When I am sad," she used to say to me, " I look at it, and then I laugh." To show her acknowledgment, she painted me a pretty picture which she sent me with some verses—an odd composition—both of which I still possess. Here is the letter from her which accompanied the verses:

I have had a terrible time grinding out these verses which follow and which are a description of the little souvenir I pray you to be kind enough to accept in exchange for the charming marble which ornaments my studio. I beg of you to pardon me if they contain some faults of French and if I do not write out for you a fair copy of them; for I have taken great pains with them just as they are. They come in well, too, right at the end of the year, though this never occurred to me when I was engaged in writing them. But this makes it possible for me to seize the occasion to wish you all three a happy New Year.

---

[1] Rosa Bonheur forgets the portrait by Edouard Dubufe, now in the Louvre, the first, I think, to make her features known to the outside world.

A STUDY FOR "THE HORSE FAIR."

THE REPOSING STAG.

LETTERS TO FRIENDS

When the fair Goddess of the day
Half drew the welkin's veil away,
The stag as yet in slumber lay,
Basking his limbs in sunny ray,
Within a fern-deckt, bushy clump,
From which peep'd out his pretty rump
In tints of purple, fire, and corn.
  But soon upon his list'ning ear
There fell the sound of distant horn,
    Warning the hunter's quest to fear.

His Goddess-planted antlers raising to the light,
Amidst the sunny haze he sprang upright,
Revealing all his noble curves and lines,
And showing ten, the number of his tines.
  The bark of dogs across the far champaign
Awoke repeated echoes nearer growing;
The stag was off, and like a mad thing going,
  Traversed the wood, ran over hill and plain,
As would have done the fly importunate,
Whose history I need not here relate.
The hounds, before, were baying in the wind,
Huntsmen and sportsmen followed close behind;
And to the wretched creature came the cries
Of those who sought his antlers as their prize.

The stag, still flying from his foes,
Wheels in his tracks and, doubling, throws
Them off the scent; then stops awhile
Amid his windings full of guile;
And as the moment is his own,
  For now the day is sweltering hot,
And they have left him all alone,
  He quietly seeks his resting spot;
And, since the sun will soon be set,
  The sportsmen turn their drooping heads
To home, where they the stag forget
  In suppers, quarrels, cards, and beds.

Meanwhile, the forest-denizen reflecting
On what the Fates intended him respecting,
Lay in his lair, and, from his panting nose,
A curling wreath of fiery vapour rose.
    Our friend now to Diana spoke and said
Some pretty words which I transcribe in verse.

    "Condemn'd, O Goddess, on this earth to tread
In staglike form, for sinning little worse
Than thy ancestress, Eve, who might not live
In Eden, as she was inquisitive,—
Mistress of my destiny,
I pardon thee!
But yet, if e'er thy sister Venus should
Transpierce me with her arrow in the wood,
Thou knowest that to take again, I'm fated,
The shape in which I erstwhile was created,
Losing my present nature, then and there,
Which I so long have been compell'd to wear;
These antlers very heavy are to bear.
So if, at length, my race should be no more
By Fate's eternal laws decreed before,
Becoming, thus, thy sister's friend, we might
    With what my ancestors could boast of horn
    And with all that which yet is to be born,
Make weapons for litigious folks to fight."

Dear Sculptor, smile and bend your eyes,
Without evincing great surprise,
Upon the lines I send to you;
But, as the Faun herself would do
Which you so kindly carved for me,
And whose sweet laugh and witchery
Console somewhat my solitude,
Deem not I bear ingratitude;
Forgive me if I am untaught;
    Receive my hero's counterfeit;
It is the image of my thought;
    And, should you find it incomplete,

272

LETTERS TO FRIENDS

Then friendship will it better make,
And prize it for the giver's sake.

IV

One of the oldest friends of Rosa Bonheur and her family was Joseph René Verdier. Toward 1844 or 1845 Raymond Bonheur went to Havre to do some art work, and there, at the house of Léon Charles, the painter, met young Verdier, who was studying under Charles. Raymond Bonheur was struck by the youth's talents, and advised him to go to Paris, where he would find better opportunities for the development of his artistic tastes. He followed this advice, went up to the capital, and became a pupil of Raymond Bonheur, his friend and a friend of his children. After the death of Raymond Bonheur, in 1849, Joseph Verdier turned toward Auguste Bonheur for art counsel, and occupied with him for a time a studio in the Rue de l'Ouest. Later he went to Sologne, and settled down in a home, which he owned near Blois, named St. Gervais, where he died at an advanced age in 1904, and which is still in possession of his family. " His style of painting," M. Hippolyte Peyrol, the sculptor, writes me, " resembles somewhat that of Auguste Bonheur." He devoted himself especially to landscapes where were animals. He exhibited for many years at the annual Salon, appearing there for the last time in 1878.

Jean Louis Joseph Verdier, one of the sons of Joseph René Verdier, was born at Ischia, Italy, about 1845 or 1846. His father wished him to enter business and, when he had graduated from the well-known Paris college, Ste. Barbe, sent him to Germany to learn the language. But the young man soon saw that he had no liking for commercial pursuits and entered the Paris School of Fine Arts, studying under Gleyre, as well as his father. He became a landscape painter, and visited, brush in hand, most of the French provinces. M. Hippolyte Peyrol, referring to him, writes me: " He was remarked for the sincerity which he showed

273

in rendering the colour and character of the scenes which he painted." He was for many years a regular exhibitor in the Salon, and died in 1895, " at the moment when he was at the height of a talent which was rapidly becoming that of a master."

Rosa Bonheur's letters to the Verdiers begin with that of April 21, 1869:

I am sure you will be pleased to hear that I am delighted with your son who is a worthy fellow and whom I am very glad to have as a companion in my sketching. What you will also like to know is that I am now certain he will have talent. I thought so when I saw his first attempts, and I have always encouraged him in the career he has chosen. He will be able, I believe, to make a reputation in landscape painting, notwithstanding the number of talented artists in this kind. What especially gives me hope for your son is that he is very simple and well understands that he must study nature ingenuously and honestly without stuffing his noddle with a heap of conventional ideas; that he must preserve his personal sentiment while seeking in others whatever may develop it.

January 3, 1879: An affectionate New Year's wish for 1879! dear kind Verdier and Halcott families. So the years pass! But as one gets older, one is a better judge of things and appreciates more fully old friends. The remembrance of the past becomes more lively and i'faith, I can't understand people who regret growing old. The mind then has more moral enjoyment. Love to you all.

January 4, 1880: How is the painting getting on? The cold has not stopped me. I do believe I grow more and more attached to my work as the years play their tricks on me. I am obliged to put on spectacles in order to finish details. But as there is always compensation in things, I find I see masses better. Anyway, I think I am making progress.

Is your son Joseph working? I saw some very good things of his at the last two Salons.

LETTERS TO FRIENDS

April 6, 1894, Rosa sends this message to Mme. Verdier:

Thanks so much for your kind, affectionate letter of congratulations on my receiving my new title of honour. All my best wishes are for you, dear Madam. How pleasant it is to call up the souvenirs of youth, when we used to go shooting! Now I am turned seventy-three and have only one tooth left wherewith to snarl at humanity. However, my honours console me and I have no reason to complain.

Two years later, to the same:

Thanks for the trouble you are taking to find me a married couple to take the place of the servants I am sending away. I give 150 francs wages a month, a winter and summer suit to the man and a New Year's present. He will have to look after and groom four horses, a big mare for the rough work, two small mares that I take myself, and a little Corsican stallion, a perfect gem, which stays in the meadow.

In summer, I go out from seven to nine in the morning; and as it takes time to groom the horses, one or two can be dressed down after coming in. There is little else to do, except cleaning the carriages, usually only one. The dining-room and dressing-room are waxed once a week. The staircases have to be brushed from time to time. The husband will have to go with the gardeners, about once in three months, to fetch fodder and oats from the station. So you see the work is not heavy for a man.

The wife will be in the kitchen with the other servants. She will have to feed four big dogs and help my chamber-maid, who has not a great deal to do either, but cannot mend much, as she is no longer young, and wears spectacles. The couple may judge for themselves, after what I say above, whether they wish to come or not. I must add that they will have to be tidy and neat, for I am sending the predecessors away because the man broke and dirted everything rather than keep the harness clean.

And after another interval of two years, Rosa writes twice to M. Verdier:

275

REMINISCENCES OF ROSA BONHEUR

July 11, 1898: I am at last going to resume my painting a little. Like you, I hardly ever leave my studio except for a drive each day in my little carriage and a short walk with my dogs.

September 21, 1898: I have just finished a picture which had to be ready for an exhibition in America. As I had promised it, I had to give all my time to it. So please forgive my delay in writing.

My health is good just now. I am thankful to say that a change has occurred in my life. I have found a charming friend, a kind lady of great talent and most distinguished family. I am happy and proud of her friendship. I will tell you all about it when we meet, for I intend to introduce her to you soon, when we pay you a visit. It will be only for two or three days, for we both have to work. Miss Klumpke is the lady's name. She comes from Boston where she was established. But we have decided to work together for the rest of our days. She has just painted a very successful portrait of me. I hope you will like her, and that Mme. Verdier will also. She is a good musician, which is a charm for me. In fine, my dear old friends, I feel quite young again, in spite of my seventy-seven years. I will write to you again, as soon as we can arrange our little trip.

V

Mlle. Delphine Gabrielle Keller, born in Paris in 1832, was one of the favourite and most brilliant pupils of Rosa Bonheur, who, in November, 1864, as director of the City Art School, handed her a diploma which entitled her to teach drawing and lithography. She was fourteen or fifteen years old when she first became a pupil of Rosa Bonheur. She used to roll the hoop with Isidore Bonheur, and knew well the Micases, father, mother, and daughter. Mlle. Keller has received several art honours and has been a regular exhibitor at the Salon for over forty years. She founded and directed for a still longer period a very successful drawing school, under the patronage of the Paris City Government, which has turned out many excellent drawing teachers. The walls of Mlle. Keller's apartment in the Rue du Bac are covered with fine specimens of her remarkable skill in lithography, the collection being especially rich in the works of " my Rosa," by which term of affection she always designates her old teacher and friend, some of whose letters here follow:

March 30, 1894: I am pretty well except for an attack of shingles. Do you know what that is? If you don't, ask a doctor. I assure you it is not at all disagreeable! It is very nice of you to congratulate me on having been promoted in the Legion of Honour à propos of the Chicago Exhibition. For a month past people have been felicitating me thereon and I have even received the insignia. But I am now waiting to be informed officially of the distinction before congratulating myself; for, like St. Thomas, I am of a doubtful mind.

Poor little wren! This is a hard world for a wee birdy not bigger than a flea!

August 16, 1894: During the past few days I have been so disturbed by birthdays, by visits, and by the devil and his train, that I have not been able to give you a day for your kind visit, for my time will still be taken up. I know that you prefer to find me in my ordinary tranquil state, so that we can go for a short walk in the forest with my two dogs and amiable self. I don't propose Monday, when I will have the extraordinary pleasure of having with me my family of kingfishers,[1] nor next Tuesday, when I have some one to lunch.

January 4, 1895: I am very late in thanking you for your kind letter. But the days are short and in spite of writing under the lamp-light, I don't succeed in getting leisure to employ my poor brushes. I'm in a rage about it. I send you my love, and Charlie and Daisy[2] join me in wishing you a little more tran-

---

[1] The Peyrols and her brother Isidore.

[2] "These two little dogs," Miss Keller writes me, "were always in Rosa's studio, and when she went out to drive in the forest, each was put in a basket and brought

quillity and health, especially; for courage you have enough of, poor little bird who ought to have been born in swan's down. The idea of your having come tumbling into this rough world! Well, one must put up with it and deem oneself lucky if independent. That, after all, is the best thing here below.

Kindest love to you, my dear Miss Keller.

August 16, 1895: Yes, try a little outdoor painting, but take care not to go into a lonely part of the Bois, for the environs of Paris are no longer what they were; there are so many black-guards in the suburbs now. If I mentioned the Jardin d'Acclima-tation, it was because this spot is well guarded, and in the morn-ing one is always quiet there. Nice little nooks and water abound, and I think you will find animals lying still, so that you can put them in your sketch.

October 27, 1895: I have the greatest esteem for you, my poor little wren, who have so much courage with your tiny musketeer's head. I note that you are becoming extremely smart with your blue note paper, when you write to Rosa Bonheur. But don't over-work yourself, you who are as big as a mouse, as fat as a match and as brave as a hare.

The great heat is long passed; but I am bewitched, my dear Keller. I can't get back to my oil painting, though I haven't gone to Paris for a long time, but remain at By like an old owl. I so much enjoy artistic glory and am so self-satisfied, that my genius, a lady very truly tells me, suffers considerably therefrom. Like you, I am obliged to see the days pass without my being able to touch my palette. As regards my health, however, tough enough I am in spite of everything.

I embrace my little wren, and hope to see her before the real cold sets in.

December 30, 1895: You are caught, Keller! It's I, this time, who arrive first, I hope, if the French post-office does its duty.

along. When the stopping place was reached, Céline's husband would take them down from the carriage, Rosa would call out: 'Let them go!', and off they would scamper in liberty."

So in this instance I am one better than my little wren, who must be having the devil of a time with such a lot of pupils. But we have to earn our living, however nice one may be, just as if one were a man of brawn.

I embrace my old Keller and heartily wish her good health for 1896.

October 28, 1896: In the matter of animals, I am happy to be your master and am entirely at your service to advise you. Poor little wren! You continue to give yourself the deuce of a trouble for those numbskulls of yours in general. But go on, all the same; for, sometimes, the good grain germinates and you have the conscience of having done your best.

August 22, 1897: You will indeed think I am getting old, for I am always behind in everything. Yes, I am an old tortoise and people in general vex me more and more, and especially fatigue me. I care little for this world, I assure you, notwithstanding the artistic honours and favours which have been bestowed upon me and which I consider all humbug. There, you have enabled me to free my mind!

December 30, 1897: I embrace you with all my heart, my dear good Miss Keller, and always remain your old professor of the Rue de Touraine [1] in 1855, and your friend for 1897 and 1898, while wishing you all possible good, as you deserve.

January 3, 1899: The fine arts are at a standstill at this season of the year. So, at this time, one must be a wren to keep on pecking away like Keller. Luckily, in spite of her little humming bird body, she has the energy of a lioness.

VI

Dr. Xavier Stanislas Hubin, born in 1815, was a graduate of the Paris Medical School, and practised medicine at Thomery,

---

[1] Now the Rue Dupuytren.

near Fontainebleau, for over fifty years, dying there on June 3, 1897. A few days after his death Rosa Bonheur wrote as follows to his nephew, M. Clouzeau:

"I cannot tell you how much Dr. Hubin is regretted in our region, where his goodness and nobility of character were fully recognised. As for myself, I cherish for his memory the greatest esteem and I feel the deepest gratitude toward him, for he saved my life twice."

As further evidence of Rosa Bonheur's gratitude to Dr. Hubin, we have these letters to him:

June 18, 1887: On returning from Paris we find your kind letter, dear doctor and friend, and we are very glad to hear that you have gone to Aix-les-Bains and are well enough to undertake the trip. We hope to see you come back well and in good spirits, as of yore. I am not a physician, but I feel sure that during the last long hard winter you must have found it cold and damp in your buggy, as you went about caring for your patients, always on the increase, at the expense of your own precious health. Dear Doctor, remember that you are no longer twenty.[1] I trust, therefore, that the waters, the mountain air, and, above all, the tender care of your good wife, will bring us back a physician stronger than ever before. I also count on Nice doing you some good next winter, when we shall tramp over the country together. In the villa stands the doctor's room and that of the doctress, of course, while you will have besides, Dr. Nathalie Micas, ever ready to discuss cases with you.

November 26, 1887, during one of Rosa's brief absences from By, she writes at Nice:

We got here a week ago last Thursday, and we have been very busy getting things in order in my fine villa. You will be glad to know, dear and good doctor, that I have been honoured with the visit of a fine sovereign *par excellence*, who won my esteem at first view. I refer to His Majesty the Emperor of

---

[1] At this time Dr. Hubin was seventy-two.

Brazil, who, as you know, is, besides his birth, a man distinguished for his learning, artistic tastes, and elevated mind. You, dear Doctor, who have a big heart, can understand what my emotions must have been on this occasion.

Forgive me for being behind in my correspondence. I can't write in the evening, as I am dead with sleep. My head falls over into the paper when I try to read a few lines of the *Figaro*, and I often find myself snoring over the sickening public events now passing in our poor France.[1] What makes me the saddest of all is to see the quarry made of the poor old President. What cowards we humans are! What happiness it is to be old so as to be able to light out of this world! Let us trust that God will pay some attention to our affairs and that He will once nore save France.

After such a fine speech, dear Doctor, I am going to go and have some breakfast!

This visit of Dom Pedro is also referred to in the following letter of the same date as the foregoing, addressed to M. Grivot, one of Rosa Bonheur's By neighbours, who was once a successful tenor at the Paris Opéra Comique, but who afterwards retired to Brussels, where he taught singing:

November 26, 1887: My studio is at length ready. But I had to wax it myself in order to welcome, as best I could, his sovereign Majesty, the Emperor of Brazil. However, I can confess I was well repaid yesterday by the kindness of this prince who conferred on me as much glory as an artist is able to receive; and I was very happy to once more meet with a proof of the great and noble simplicity of sovereigns so misunderstood by fools and ingrates. May God render them justice in this world. You will see, my dear friends, that I am still under the impression of my day, yesterday,

---

[1] The year 1887 was indeed a baleful one for France. General Boulanger's appearance on the political horizon threatened the existence of the Republic and incidents on the German frontier nearly plunged France and Germany into another war, while, at the moment this letter was written, President Grévy was being dragged in the mire by the wrong-doings of his son-in-law, and was even forced to resign in the following month.

and as I know you will be pleased, I express to you my inmost sentiments.

Just now, my old Nathalie is at market. Yesterday she was very proud of her friend, and said: "You know, now it's not masses at twelve sous that we owe!" She asked me to give her love to the good Pauline and her male half. In this, I join her heartily, and remain, your old neighbour and friend.

On December 31, 1895, she again writes from By to Dr. Hubin:

I send you, my very dear Doctor, as a New Year's present, a Chester cheese. Share it with me along with my affectionate and grateful good wishes for your continued health. Dr. Bonheur also sends a prescription—good wine, which, my good Doctor, you have in your cellar. Remember the proverb of the nations, Good Wine is the Milk of the Aged. I get on capitally on this diet. We have been having some scientific discussions, myself and my colleagues, and all advised me to follow this regimen, which agrees with me perfectly. It is only right that I should give you my views on this subject, though my aim is a selfish one, for I naturally wish to keep you on this planet as long as possible. Permit, therefore, your stupid old colleague to send you heartiest regards and to place this old cheese at your feet. Your old patient, Doctor Rosa Bonheur.

January 1, 1897: I send my very best regards and there is no necessity of my making any declaration of love. Sincerest wishes for this year and for many more to come. Stand firm, Doctor, by the grace of God and for our friends in this world. We will go over to the majority a little later. Good doctors are not on this earth for nothing. God helps those who help themselves.

February 21, 1897: Birds of a feather flock together. That explains our mutual sympathy and our liking for these crustaceans. I will take upon myself to properly introduce these poor animals into the palace of my jaws, with tears in my eyes and with all possible thanks to you for the good idea of sending them to me. I was breakfasting when they arrived. But I will devote my special attention to them at the evening meal. I am now engaged in giving my studio a thorough cleaning and so am eating only dust. Consequently, to-night, your crabs will be doubly welcome. Renewed thanks and best compliments, my dear old Doctor, the most esteemed of my friends.

Scarcely more than three months after this letter was written, Dr. Hubin was dead.

VII

The other physician who played perhaps a still greater part in the existence of Rosa Bonheur was Dr. George Apostoli (1847–1900). He was the son of a doctor and a graduate of the Paris Medical School. For ten years Dr. Apostoli was a military physician, but about 1878 he resigned from the army, and, devoting himself to the application of electricity to medicine, acquired a wide and richly deserved reputation. He was one of the founders of the Paris Electrotherapy Society, and established, in 1894, a monthly devoted to this branch of medicine.

The Paris daily, the *Gaulois*, of December 14, 1884, contained this item: " Rosa Bonheur, completely cured, thanks to Dr. Apostoli, of the painful malady which has kept her in bed for a whole year, left last night for Nice. ' I have just been given a new lease of life,' she said, in bidding good-bye to the friends who went to the station to see her off."

This cure is also mentioned in several of Rosa's letters to Dr. Apostoli, the first one of the series, written from By, running as follows:

June 28, 1884: I am very well. I think I am cured, thanks to you, dear Doctor. It seems to me that I had more than my share of misery. I am so happy to be able to take up my art again and to begin life anew, that is, to enjoy the country and to come and go at my ease. I can never express to you all my gratitude. But we must consider the practical side of the matter which interests every mortal who has not had the luck, or bad luck, to come into this world with a 200,000 francs' income. Give me the pleasure, dear good Doctor, to settle the matter of the honorarium before you start out on your journey. I have put aside some money for this purpose. I can never repay you for all you have done for me, and I trust that in the future I shall have the double pleasure of receiving you at By only as a friend.

A few days later:

I seize the occasion of Céline's going to Paris to hand you five thousand francs, which I indeed owe you, for, as I have already told you more than once, you have given me back my life. If I were rich, it is the double of this sum that I ought to send you.

January 7, 1886: Céline, on returning, tells us that she found you very ill in bed; that you cannot stir or lift your hands. We are very sorry to hear this. Knowing how much you like fresh eggs, we send you some, along with some grapes. If my poor friend Nathalie is too ill to come with me, I will go in a few days, and see you without her. This is the least an old woman can do to whom you restored life and strength, who owes you her very existence. She cannot forget it.

Hoping to have better news from you soon, I send my sincerest regards.

Writing January 7, 1886, to Major Rousseau, formerly chief veterinarian of the State Cavalry School at Fontainebleau, Rosa Bonheur says:

We have just heard from Céline, whom we had sent to Dr. Apostoli's, that he is very ill, in bed, and unable to stir. Happily his mother is with him. Will you kindly inform his friend, Dr. Fournier? If he could go and see Dr. Apostoli, I should be glad, as that would both please him and enable us to learn what is the matter with our good physician, to whom I am indebted for the health and life I now enjoy, in spite of my sixty-three years odd.

LETTERS TO FRIENDS

Rosa Bonheur's friendship for Dr. Apostoli, is further seen in these three letters to him:

January 31, 1886: Your nice letter made us both happy, both Nathalie and me. You must have suffered morally as well as physically, not being able to attend to your poor patients. But now the days are getting longer and this horrid winter is coming to an end. You will improve with the fine weather and soon be able to work again. But do be patient. We are going in to Paris soon, when we will see you and find you, I am sure, up and doing again. I am going to bring with me a little picture for Dr. Terrillon as soon as the frame is ready. So you see, I grub on and on, as does also my old friend Nathalie.

October 8, 1886: You will probably receive to-day a box containing a little picture representing some stags standing under the branches of a tree.[1] I have painted it expressly for you. I have long wanted to send you this feeble proof of my gratitude. But, though tardy, I now have that pleasure.

From Nice, March 8, 1887, Rosa writes:

I am a little late in sending you news from us. But we have been very busy since we got unpacked. Nathalie is so happy to be here and so enjoys the villa that she already looks better. As regards myself, I am as well as possible, and I also look upon myself with pleasure as a landlord. The truth is we really have a very pretty villa, and what a staircase! But you will see it all, I hope, good Doctor, and then you will be able to judge if we have so much to rejoice over, especially if a new earthquake is going to bring down about our heads these Parian marbles. But I have little fear. The papers have greatly exaggerated what has happened at Nice. Our earthquake, or seaquake, has been a small affair compared with that which occurred in Italy two years ago, I believe, and those that have happened in other parts of the world.

---

[1] This picture hangs to-day on the walls of the Neuilly home of Mme Saunal, niece of Dr. Apostoli.

VIII

Intimacy with the rich and great, who persistently sought her society, did not prevent Rosa Bonheur from cherishing humble attachments. Among these was one which she had inherited from childhood, and which, for its origin, carries us back to her father's youth. When a young man and still at Bordeaux, Raymond Bonheur's closest friend was Justin Mathieu, mentioned in the earlier chapters of this work, an artist like himself, but in miniature sculpture. Separated by the former's removal to Paris, the friends, after ceasing their relations, were brought together again through the agency of a mutual acquaintance named Duchemin, and, for a time, had a studio in common, where they not only elucidated many artistic works, but discussed lofty theories of social regeneration. It was in this studio, with its imitation rock decoration, that disdain of filthy lucre was occasionally carried to such an extent that coins were tossed into the rockery, where a fountain played, to be fished out later, when needed for material wants, by Rosa or other members of the family.

Justin Mathieu was a sculptor of considerable ability in his special field, and frequently exhibited at the Salon, where he obtained in succession a bronze, a silver, and a gold medal. Some four years younger than Rosa Bonheur's father, he married in turn and had two children, both girls, to the younger of whom Rosa Bonheur, being about twenty years the senior, became godmother. To this goddaughter and the elder sister Rosa Bonheur was ever afterward a faithful and loving protector. During the last year or two that their father lived his sight almost completely failed, and a small pension of twelve hundred francs was settled on him by the French Government. At his death in 1864 his widow was enabled to keep five hundred francs per annum of this, and to obtain four hundred more from the National Society of French Artists, of which her late husband had been a member. When she died in 1872, Rosa Bonheur endeavoured to secure the reversion of the pension for the daughters, but failed in her attempt. She then continued it out of her own pocket during the remainder of her life, and provided in her will for an annuity of twelve hundred francs to be paid to the two sisters.

Her affection for her goddaughter, Rosa Mathieu, is clearly shown in these three letters from By:

May 6, 1893: I write at once to thank you for your few lines. I am quite well now. Like almost everybody else, I had caught the amiable influenza; and I may reasonably hope to attain perfect purity, after enough nose-blowing and expectorating to fill my reservoirs, which, by the way, are empty. We shall be obliged to fetch our water from the river. The forest is at once frozen and burnt up. Everything in nature is awry. I wish somebody would get us rain either by prayer or an invention of science. I am not quite strong enough yet to go and see the Salon, but hope soon to have that pleasure. Till then, my love to you.

June 27, 1894: I have just turned up your letter of the 17th, to which I find I haven't replied. Please excuse me; I'm late, as usual, when letter-writing is in question. My health is good, on the whole, although at present I am much cut up by the assassination of President Carnot, whom I visited not very long ago. I was intending to go and see you in your new home. But so far I haven't been able to do so, as I am in a hurry to finish pictures that are promised and that I am hindered from completing by continual interruptions, which upset me terribly. I should like you to spend a day or two with me in the country. But no longer having my old friend with me, it's hardly possible. I shall be quite in a pickle soon with four men of my own family who will be coming over from Saturday till Monday, now that fishing has begun. I should prefer them to stay at an hotel, if there were one, which would not deprive me of the pleasure of seeing them, especially my brother. It is of little or no use having servants. Housekeeping and painting don't go together; and there are not the neatness and order here I should like. If you should be in want of anything, don't hesitate to tell me of it. Love to you both, and hoping to see you soon either here or in Paris, I remain, your affectionate godmother.

REMINISCENCES OF ROSA BONHEUR

August 19, 1896: Late again in writing. Thanks for your kind note. My health is not bad for an old woman of my age. I should like to see you, but am just now changing servants, which is always a nuisance. However, I could not help it. The wife I could have put up with; but the husband was a downright brute, not willing to stir a hand for anything. All my kitchen crockery is smashed. I am so disturbed in my work that I receive as little company as possible. Still, as I shall not be able to go to Paris for some time, I will ask you both to come over and spend a day with me at the end of September. Till then, my love.

IX

Some miscellaneous letters may now be given. From Paris, October, 1850, she writes to Gustave d'Eichthal:

I received your letter on my return from Ivry, where I went for two or three days to make some studies of horses which I needed.[1] It is now about a month since I got back from Ems, where the waters did me good. My brother Auguste has just arrived. He has been passing six weeks at the Castle of Valençay, where he has painted all the family of the Dukes of Valençay and of the Dino-Talleyrands.

In a note to Adolphe Yvon (1817–93), the distinguished French military and portrait painter, dated from By, May 25, 1863, we read:

Excuse me, please, for not having sent sooner my photographs. I am not perfectly sure that you can do much with them, but they ought to help some. The larger one represents Hungarian oxen and the smaller ones Roman oxen. As regards the studies, they will be useful only for the colour of the nose and eyes, for the coat is not the same and the hair is very long because of the

---

[1] A suburb of Paris, not the historic place. She then was conceiving the "Horse Fair."

climate. Please take good care of my photographs, as they are unique.

Kindest regards to Mme. Yvon.

To Mlle. Passy, the daughter of Antoine Passy and the sister of Louis Passy:

By, July 24, 1868: I wish to answer your questions about art, and in so doing we must be sure that we understand one another. Because you paint too black and too red is the very reason why I find that you imitate too closely the old masters. Now, since you yourself perceive that you produce a black effect that is too deadened, you mustn't be afraid of painting white what you see white, that is to say, not to make a yellowish white in order to give it a conventional warmth.

I am convinced that you can succeed in painting, if you will only work hard at it. It would be too bad not to make the most of your advantages. You should always pay attention to your professor, Roland, to whom you owe all you know. But above all, paint just what you feel and make things as *you* see them, particularly as it is quite true that our eyes, according to their conformation and colour, see things strong, vigorous, or pale and big. Then, too, it is the spirit within us which translates nature. This is what gives diversity and charm to each artist, the original-ity of each.

M. Paul Chardin makes this comment on this letter:

" It is odd that Rosa Bonheur appears to think that not only the conformation, but the colour of the eyes has an influence on the vision. She had queer ideas of everything."

Some fifty years ago this question of the human eye in its rela-tion to art was quite to the fore. It was asked whether the eye had always perceived objects just as it does to-day, with the same delicateness, the same precision, all the shades of the complete gamut of colours; or whether, in the course of the centuries, the eye had not evolved in growing more and more fine in its per-ceptions. Especially in the matter of colours had not the eye attained a degree of perfection which it did not possess and could not possess in ancient times? But it will be seen that Rosa Bonheur carries the subject still further in the foregoing letter.

To Frederic Korn (1826–96), a retired business man residing at Fontainebleau:

By, September 13, 1873: I am seizing the occasion to send you a cane-gun of mine. I would like to try it but I can't get the cartridge into the mouth of the barrel. The head is all right but the end is too big. When you go to Paris—but there is no hurry—will you please exchange this cane for one that will go better, if there are bigger ones? Or tell the gunsmith he must make me one with the mouth a little more hollowed out, so that the cartridge will go in easily. I have had made a little ramrod for cleaning the barrel.

To M. Grivot and his wife, she writes from By, on September 21, 1887:

Excuse me for being so late in replying to your kind letter. But, during the last few days, my time has been taken up with finishing pictures which I want to exchange for cash, and I have also had the agreeable society of Georges Cain, who is painting Nathalie's portrait. We have been going in for photography, too. I don't know whether you have already received our por-traits—me on the bench and the other pilgrim, Georges, admiring the wild snake-weed, which is none too luxuriant, festooned about your humble servant who is wearing the blouse, and all of which made that rascal Georges laugh heartily! Anyway, you shall have the portrait of the amiable pilgrim and that of the honest old man who is resting on your bench.

I hope we shall see you soon and that you will come and take pot-luck with us. We will certainly come and lunch with you, to wish you good-bye, before starting for Nice, Nathalie and I.

Kindest regards, dear Mme. Grivot, to you both.

To Major Rousseau, written from Nice:

February 7, 1885: We are doing water-colour sketches with my brother Auguste, who is a good companion for me. Nathalie is better. We return to her each evening, after being out all day. Next Monday she will accompany us, as we are going to sketch at a place where she can go without being tired. As for me, I climb up the goat-paths, and manage capitally.

She writes as follows to Mme. Borriglione, now a widow, but then wife of the French senator:

July 29, 1885: So you are at Mont Dore. Well, here at By, I have not had a moment to give to photography. All my time—and how rapidly it passes—is devoted to my big horses.[1] It is kind of you to think of me for the peasant types of the region where you are. But in Auvergne, a country which I have known for many years, there no longer exists any special costume. I think I saw the last of it some thirty-five years ago, in the Cantal. But if you can't find any picturesque peasants to paint, you can amuse yourself in making landscapes.

And a second time, five years later:

I have seen in my *Figaro* that M. Borriglione has been fighting two duels, and that, though he got scratched in the second, it is but a slight wound. I also notice that M. Saint Genest [2] has been attacking him. What a fine example of Christian charity all this presents! I would say to these foes of your good husband: " Embrace one another, my brothers, and taste the goodness of God and even swallow it." It is a long time since the sons of Father Adam have acted in this wise. The blood of Cain appears to be more in vogue just now on this terrestrial ball. It is getting more and more evident that the Almighty must come down and bring order out of this chaos here below. This will probably happen one day; for what ought to come about, does finally

---

[1] The large unfinished picture, which she was working on when she died.
[2] The pseudonym of Arthur Bucheron (1834–1902), the brilliant *Figaro* journalist.

come about, generally. Hypocrites get trapped, in the end, through their own evil ways. Nothing is lost sight of. Those who are responsible, suffer. People who do not keep faith cannot deceive the Creator, who is the grand judge. But enough of my poor philosophy.

With best regards to your good husband, who has so happily escaped, I am, yours sincerely.

To E. A. Gautray, dated from Nice, January 3, 1888:

You may say to those who inquire that I never paint such little canvases as this one of yours and that I do not wish to paint them, because of my eyes. So you will be the sole possessor, because of this, of a work of mine of these dimensions, which I trust, however, will not in the least lessen the merit which I tried to give it.

This series of letters may close with three to the Tedesco Brothers, the first being from Nice and the two others from By:

December 10, 1888: In regard to the horses in the moonlight, I think you had better have them mounted in white with a gold border, so as to gain in effect, the white margin to be from eight to ten centimetres wide. As to the " Don Quixote," it seems to me it will look well in the gold frame you have ordered. But if you have not yet had it made, perhaps dark garnet plush will be better.

April 28, 1898: I arrived home safely for dinner. After having again seen my picture, " The Duel," I write to say that I must insist upon this canvas being washed and varnished before it is further exhibited. Nor do I wish my portrait shown alongside of it, or anywhere else at the same time. I think that sort of thing in very bad taste. In Paris it would look like a cheap sort of advertising. I prefer to be let alone, especially as I do not need anything of this kind, and have never asked anybody for it. A thousand pardons for speaking thus frankly. Please convey this final decision of mine to Mr. Lefèvre, whom, I am sure, will raise no objection. I am going back to see the picture again when it shall have been varnished.

February 2, 1899: Since my return, I have been reflecting about the charcoal pencil sketch now at the Exhibition of Painters, which closes, so you told me, on March 10th. I have a chance to sell it, unless you wish to buy it along with the right of reproducing it, as I would like to have it nicely engraved. I want 20,000 francs for it, and before binding myself elsewhere, I give you the option on it. But I prefer to keep my drawing if you cannot give me twenty bank-notes of a thousand francs each, French money. I will decide what to do with the drawing after I hear from you.

It has often been remarked that a person's character may be judged of even more surely by the letters received than by those sent. Throughout her life, as we have seen, Rosa Bonheur enjoyed the company of male artists with whom she was on the most excellent terms of comradery. Their letters to her reveal a peculiar union of reverence for the woman and companionship for the virile artist. A few extracts from the correspondence of Paul Chardin will suffice to show this and will show it well. But it comes out in a similar way in all the letters I have seen, and especially in those addressed to her by the younger artists of her time.

Paris, October 11, 1862: Your kind letter found me, dear Mademoiselle, an invalid here. However, I shall be all right in a few days, and then I shall rush over to By with "arms and baggage" since you are good enough to have me. I shall be most happy if, as you lead me to hope, you were to paint from nature during the few days I shall spend in your beautiful forest. Your "Rapin" would profit by it, and come back to Paris a great artist. Your apologies as to not being able to turn your manor into a hostelry were really not necessary; for even had you wanted to do it, I should have refused peremptorily, although such a proceeding would be rather rude on a Rapin's part towards an illustrious General. I find you are already much too kind to me in allowing me to profit by your excellent advice and your amiable society. To ask for more would be presumption. You must know, great and venerated General, that you have to do with a Rapin who has learnt how to behave.

I have painted only six or seven water-colours, which I will bring for you to give me your opinion about them. When it rains, I will come and work in your hospitable manor. The hope of painting by your side and under your protecting wing cheers me, and if the doctor is willing, I shall start to-morrow. Asking you to receive my best thanks and the assurance of my devoted affection, I am your grateful Rapin.

I subjoin to my letter the description of " my animal," as you say, General. The Rapin modestly acknowledges that his trotter is not equal to those of the " Horse Fair."

Plouha, near St. Brieux, May 30, 1870: Just now I am dreadfully ugly, Mademoiselle, awfully like my portrait, in fact. The sea-air has turned my nice complexion to a liquorice colour. I look like a Florentine bronze, or better still, like an old skin pair of breeches. Good-bye. Believe me always your affectionate and faithful Rapin.

Paris, June 2, 1870: I thank you, Mademoiselle and dear General, for your kind wishes and advice about the *aqua fortis*, and beg to remind you, with my best regards, that I have a liking for my dishevelled hair, in souvenir of you and your name.

Apropos of Fourchet,[1] Mme. Darlly said, the other day: " If I were in Miss Rosa's place, I would take a big canvas and then I would paint, in a jiffy, a huge pig on a dung-heap, and under I would write: To Fourchet, Rosa Bonheur."

Good-bye, dear, good Miss Rosa. I send you my heartiest wishes for the success of your law suit, and take the liberty of adding to them a brotherly kiss, begging you to believe me, respectfully and affectionately, your Rapin.

---

[1] See page 227.

CHAPTER IX

THE forest of Fontainebleau, so closely identified with the artistic career of Rosa Bonheur, covers some 40,000 acres, has a circumference of about 50 miles, and is provided with roads and paths measuring, in all, probably 1,200 miles. The principal trees are oaks, which predominate, beeches, elms, and pines. The trunks of some of the oaks measure at least 26 feet in circumference. The forest was once frequented by perhaps 3,000 stags, roes, and roe-bucks, which are now, however, very rare and shy; by wild boars, the old males wandering about alone, and the females and young in groups; and by hares, rabbits, pheasants, and partridges. But to-day all this game has nearly disappeared. Though in late years I have walked, driven, and bicycled on many occasions in all parts of the forest, I do not recollect ever having seen even a squirrel.

In and around the forest of Fontainebleau were formed the greatest French landscape painters of the nineteenth century. The fame of Millet, Rousseau, Corot, Troyon, Diaz, Courbet, and Daubigny is associated with this spot, and many of them lived in the neighbouring villages of Barbizon, Chailly, Marlotte, etc. But none was more faithful to the forest than Rosa Bonheur, who was in almost daily communion with its animal life and its natural beauties during the long period of nearly forty years. Denecourt, " the sylvan," [1] was not more attached to Fontainebleau than was

---

[1] Claude François Denecourt (1788–1875), "French cicerone," Vapereau calls him might perhaps also be named the Thoreau of Fontainebleau. But he not only there

"the artist-recluse of By," who used to enjoy when translated to her this passage from Stevenson's essay on Fontainebleau:

One generation after another fall like honey-bees upon this memorable forest, rifle its sweets, pack themselves with vital memories, and when the theft is consummated depart again into life richer, but poorer also. Something, it should seem, had been forgotten. A projection of themselves shall appear to haunt unfriended these scenes of happiness, a natural child of fancy, begotten and forgotten unawares. If anywhere about the wood you meet my airy bantling, greet him with tenderness. He was a pleasant lad, though now abandoned. And when it comes to your own turn to quit the forest, may you leave behind you such another; no Antony or Werther, let us hope, no tearful whipster, but, as becomes this not uncheerful and most active age in which we figure, the child of happy hours.

The estival picture of the wood is the best known. But its hibernal dress is not less beautiful and characteristic. Rosa Bonheur well knew and well loved both. "Fontainebleau forest in winter," she once wrote, "is beauty in perfection, with its long avenues of pure untrodden snow, save for the small hoofs of the deer. Then there are the glimpses of the stags browsing in groups, their graceful bounding away when they catch sight of you, the lovely golden sunsets seen through the leafless trees, and the biting wind sweeping over all."

This sonnet, by an American poetess, can, with a single change, be most fittingly addressed to Rosa Bonheur and By:

> Not far from Paris, in fair Fontainebleau,
> A lovely, memory-haunted hamlet lies,
> Whose tender spell makes captive, and defies
> Forgetfulness. The peasants come and go,

---

buried himself from the world and sang the forest's praises in many a printed page; he also spent a large part of his own fortune in opening up its beauties to the public. "Next to my parents," Rosa Bonheur once said, "I owe most to dear old Denecourt."

ROSA BONHEUR IN THE GARDEN OF BY.

FONTAINEBLEAU

Their backs too used to stoop, and patient sow
The harvest which their narrow need supplies;
Even as when, earth's pathos in her eyes,
Rosa dwelt here, companion of their woe.[1]

Though these verses really relate to Millet and Barbizon, they describe equally well the little hamlet of By, which, with its hundred houses and its four hundred inhabitants, is situated on the northern edge of the forest, just as Barbizon is on the southern edge, the one quite the *vis-à-vis* of the other. In 1894 the municipal council of Thomery, the spruce village famous for its luscious grapes whose vines so prettily festoon the cottage walls and fronts, and of which village By is a dependency, gave the high-sounding name of Rue des Arts to the modest country road on which stood the homes of Rosa Bonheur and two or three minor artists. Among these was M. Bourdon, a painter, who was her nearest neighbour and whose name is mentioned here and there in the letters which will be found in this chapter. A local poet, enumerating the personages of the region, closes the list with these verses:

A côté de ces noms, une gloire récente,
 Chère à notre pays, trouve sa place ici.
De succès en succès, sa marche fut croissante;
 L'art, une fois de plus, compte un maître excellent:
 Dans un hameau voisin, Rosa Bonheur habite;
 Le nom nous dit assez ce que vaut le talent.[2]

The castle of By—villa or country house would be a more exact description—which Rosa Bonheur and the Micases bought in 1860, is very ancient. Its history goes back for at least a century before the discovery of America. The artist during her long residence made many changes in the old edifice, some of which

---

[1] "Mine and Thine," by Mrs. Florence Earle Coates.
[2] Huet's "Thomery Ancien et Moderne," p. 9. M. Huet was long the public school teacher of Thomery and when I met him some four or five years ago, he held a similar position at Melun.

are mentioned in her letters given in this volume, and before she died, the house was rendered rather comfortable. There was even a touch of spaciousness about it. The fine large studio was worthy of her fame, and to-day it is a touching spot to visit, filled as it is with so many interesting souvenirs of the dead artist, and just as she left it when she passed away, almost brush in hand.

Rosa Bonheur's grounds at By are in the form of a long parallelogram, and are to all appearances cut out of the very forest itself, the trees at the end of her property and those of the contiguous forest being of the same kind. In the wall, at the back of her grove, is a wooden double-gate, which opens directly into the forest, from which it is separated only by a narrow shady lane. Through this gate the great artist could get into the woods quite unobserved.

In order to take her almost daily drive of the closing years of her life, Rosa Bonheur would pass out by a narrower wooden door in the west wall that opened on to the neat little macadamised road running from By to the station—the Rue de la Gare—the municipality having had the bad taste to give the name of street, as has already been said, to the rustic lanes of its village suburb.

A few rods from this last-mentioned door begins, in the forest, the Route de la Fontte, a grassy avenue lined with fine oaks, beeches, and elms. This was Rosa Bonheur's favourite short walk. On these occasions, when she did not go far from the house, she would take with her dogs and monkeys. The latter—Boniface and Ratata—would run up trees, but would return on her calling them, and perch themselves on her shoulders. The only thing to disturb the silence of the spot and remind one of the near presence of the busy world was the occasional rush and rumble of a train on the Paris-Lyons Railway which skirts the western edge of the forest.

Turning to the left, Rosa Bonheur would enter the once famous but now abandoned Route de Bourgogne, and thence back to By by the same macadamised road on which she had set out. In this quadrilateral used to be some little ponds, now generally

298

dried up in summer, though they still contain water in winter, which added some variety to the spot. " Perhaps what makes me most regret their disappearance," said Rosa Bonheur during one of her last walks in this part of the wood, " is the way in which my dogs miss them; they never wearied wading in them and lapping up the fresh water with their hot tongues."

In her tilbury Rosa Bonheur took almost daily drives in the forest. In the summer she was an early riser, getting up at four or five, and being back from her drive by eight o'clock. In the winter she would go out at eight or ten, or in the afternoon. She never liked to miss this daily drive. It was rare that she returned from one of these drives without a new artistic idea or experience of some kind.

One day, not fifty rods from the Carrefour de la Pointe d'Iray, in the Route des Châtaigniers, Rosa Bonheur was driving when she saw a stag couched under the foliage, with the sun playing on him through the leaves. He remained perfectly still, though but a yard or two from the roadside; so that Rosa got a good long look at him. On returning home, she immediately made a study of this little scene, " which was an exact reproduction of form and colour of what we had been gazing at a few moments before," says her nephew, who happened to be with her on this occasion. He continues :

" Rosa Bonheur had acquired great skill in this art of photographing on her mind all she saw and then reproducing it faithfully with her brush as soon as she reached her studio. The forest of Fontainebleau, with its many natural beauties and surprises, developed her talents in this direction until she attained a really wonderful skill in this respect."

This same nephew recounts an anecdote which happened in the forest, and which illustrates the masculine energy of Rosa Bonheur's character. In the earlier days she would go out alone on long excursions, armed with a revolver. Later, when afflicted for a time with a painful disease, she was always accompanied by a man-servant, or a relative or friend. On one of these occasions

she was in her carriage with her nephew when he noticed her begin
to grow solemn and uncommunicative, and then to urge the horse
to the top of his speed, till they were rushing along the rough
sandy forest lanes in a really dangerous manner. Finally, they
reached the house, the horse, as well as driver and companion, all
worn out. Rosa Bonheur hurried right to her bed, and it was a
week before she could leave it. "She felt the dreadful attack
coming on," says her nephew, "but was too proud to let me,
though then thirty-five years old, know it. So she clung to the
reins, and, though in the greatest suffering, herself drove to the
very door of the house."

Not far from the By side of the forest is the Route de la
Curée, where Rosa Bonheur loved to drive because of the large
number of stags which used to be seen there. In this alley she
placed the scene of the picture, which, I believe, is in the United
States, of a party of huntsmen, with their dogs, standing in a
little grove of fine towering beech-trees. "It is one of Rosa Bonheur's best efforts," says her nephew.

Farther on in this same Route de la Curée you perceive the
striking Rocher Besnard, consisting of splendid big moss-coated
boulders half buried in the fern-covered ground, with lofty oaks
rising above them. So much was Rosa Bonheur enamoured of
this spot that she got the forest authorities not to thin out this
portion of the wood when the regular time came round for it to
be done.

On her more extended promenades Rosa Bonheur would leave
the Route Ronde at the Croix de Montmorin, pass around the
steep and sandy Rocher Brulé, and return home by the Route
Hallali; or she would do the reverse, and push on, by the Route
Ronde, to the wild Gorge aux Loups. The plateau between this
gorge and the road was, in Rosa Bonheur's day, far more picturesque and left more in a state of nature than is the case at present. The labours of Denecourt, the bicycle, the automobile, Cook
and his French imitators, and the construction of the narrow macadamised road from the Route Ronde, now bring crowds of visit-

tors to a spot once so unfrequented. A shed of a restaurant, with its rough board tables and benches, is a blemish, and Nature herself seems bent on doing what she can to render the place less attractive. The grand old oaks of other years are dying and rotting away, and are now mere wrecks of their whilom grandeur. The sandy soil does not grant them a long lease of life, and they begin too soon to die at the top. The beeches, on the contrary, appear to flourish. The severe winter of 1879, mentioned in some of Rosa Bonheur's letters found in this chapter, gave the *coup de grâce* to many of these noble trees, whose big trunks, gnarled branches, and wide-spreading foliage lent themselves beautifully to the artist's pencil. Their crests were not lost in the clouds, and the squat, sturdy mass came admirably into a picture. Rosa Bonheur was quick to feel this, and here she found congenial settings for several of her smaller paintings. But during recent years shabby birch-trees have been killing out the old stately oaks of the Gorge aux Loups. So Rosa Bonheur went there but little in the later part of her life, and used to lament the planting of so many unattractive pines, though she recognised the soundness of the reason given by the authorities—viz., to afford the soil time to recover its pristine strength, when, after a lapse of fifty years or so, her favourite oaks would again be planted.

Another change in the Fontainebleau forest also caused deep regret in the heart of Rosa Bonheur. I refer to the drying up of the ponds, which seems to be in course all over the region. She thought this waning symbolised the gradual decline of her own life. This disappearance of the water in the neighbourhood of the Gorge aux Loups removed still another attraction from that spot. In those earlier days, the Mare aux Fées, now scarcely more than a marshy hollow, contained shallow but limpid water, while its banks and the plateau roundabout were covered by a short, thick turf, in the midst of which rose up those healthy isolated oaks. At night the moon would light up the whole scene most beautifully, and then it was that Rosa Bonheur, hidden behind a tree or shrub, would lie for hours together, watching the stags who would come there from miles around in order to quench their thirst, and who, in the autumn, when in heat, would lock antlers and fight sturdily on the banks. Many were the studies of combating stags that Rosa Bonheur bore away in her mind from the Mare aux Fées, and transferred to canvas early next morning in her studio.

From this plateau, high above and beyond the deep gorge, you perceive opposite, lying against the horizon, Long Rocher. It is a steep and sandy road which leads to it, but thither Rosa Bonheur often went in her prime. " It reminds me of the Scottish Highlands," she used to say. " Perhaps another and powerful attraction," says her nephew, " was the permission, which she had for a time, to shoot rabbits there." Long Rocher, as has already been seen and as will again be seen farther on in the present chapter, is frequently mentioned in Rosa Bonheur's letters. It was unquestionably one of her favourite haunts, though, as her nephew truly says, " she had to the very end a warm spot in her heart for the whole forest and for everything in it—for its trees and lanes and animals which she knew so well."

Here may be given reminiscences bearing on Rosa Bonheur's life at Fontainebleau, written out for me by some of her old friends and relatives.

Henri Cain says:

One of Rosa Bonheur's greatest delights was to wander through the Fontainebleau Forest. She would start out early in the morning and would stop to sketch when she noticed a spot which took her fancy because of the colouration. You couldn't get her to come to Paris if she was in the midst of a study of this kind that especially pleased her. When captivated by her painting, everything else was secondary. She was carried away by her artistic dream. " I can't leave now," she would say to me; " the forest is too beautiful at this moment, flaming with magnificent foliage which is so soon to fade. Let me finish two more studies, and then I will go and look after my Paris affairs. In the mean-

EXTERIOR VIEW OF THE BY STUDIO.

FRONT AND COURT OF THE CHÂTEAU OF BY.

while, they must suffer, if needs be. What would suffer more than all that would be this poor Rosa Bonheur if she could not finish the sketch she is now engaged upon."

M. Grivot writes me:

I was Rosa Bonheur's neighbour at Fontainebleau. She was familiar with every nook and corner of the forest. During the fine season, her delight was to start at dawn in her tilbury, attended by her faithful servant, Stephen. Ensconcing herself in the wildest and most picturesque spot, she would hang her watch on a branch, place her revolver within reach, and then dismiss her servant, who came back to fetch her at an appointed time. During these excursions it was sometimes my happiness to accompany her.

At By, she used to get up as soon as it was light and would paint all day till night forced her to lay down her brushes. In winter she even sketched by candle-light. What bored her most was going to Paris, for it meant the discarding of trousers, smock, and felt hat, as well as the putting away of cigarettes, which she constantly smoked.

Mme. Lagrolet once said to me:

Walking and driving among the trees was an endless source of delight to her. It always seemed to put her in a sunny mood. Once when we were all out in a landau, she literally danced in the carriage; she was as gay as a small boy. At one moment she stood up, took off her hat, and bowed first to this tree and then to that one, to this big rock and then to that one, pretending to be the president of France and regarding these trees and rocks as citizens of the republic over which she presided. Sometimes she was a king and these were her subjects. They were cheering her and she would salute and reply to them. I can see her now, every moment rising to this tree or that one, and keeping up the fun for a long time and in a most witty fashion. When on foot, she would generally be in a less hilarious mood, and would become particularly sober when she happened to espy the foot-prints of deer, which she would bend over and study and then follow with the stealth and silence of an American Indian as painted by Fenimore Cooper; for she knew if she moved with care and quietly, she would come upon them and could study their movements at ease.

Mme. Renée Thirion, her sister-in-law—the re-married widow of Germain Bonheur—adds this curious touch:

Rosa Bonheur loved living in the forest, imagining, like a child, that she belonged to a tribe of red-skins; roasting the game she had shot in the open air, and enjoying this smoked meat.

Rosa Bonheur's relations, or rather lack of relations, with the Barbizon Group, is thus presented by M. Paul Chardin:

The fact is she had nothing to do with this art circle composed exclusively of landscape painters, if we except Troyon, Karl Bodmer, and Jacques—the three animal painters of Barbizon. Living on the opposite side of the forest, I doubt if Rosa Bonheur ever put foot in Barbizon, though one of her favourite stamping-grounds was Long Rocher not far away. She never spoke to me of the spot. She worked alone in her corner of the wood. As she did not paint landscapes, she needed but restricted motives to serve as frameworks for her animals, and these she could find within a stone's throw of her house. Rosa Bonheur knew too well the artistic temperament—extravagant, nervous, intolerant, irascible, and jealous—to have relations with any group or school. I do not know what the famous Barbizon painters thought of her. But I doubt if these artists had much of a liking for Rosa Bonheur, who, as I have already said, eclipsed them, perhaps, in precision, correct drawing, and the wonderful address of her touch. Her method of interpreting nature, diametrically opposed to his own, leads me to believe that Rosa Bonheur's talent could not have found much favour in the eyes of Troyon. I do not know whether she was personally acquainted with him. I doubt it, for I never heard her speak of him or of any other of the Barbizon group. I repeat, the Barbizon art colony was a coterie for which Rosa Bonheur could not have had much of a liking and where she could not have had admirers. In fact, she never had many artist friends at her By home. I recall only the Cains and Mène, Le Poittevin, the marine painter; Lavieille and the Verdiers, and perhaps two or three others.

Here belong a few letters touching more especially on life at Fontainebleau.

To Paul Chardin, Rosa Bonheur writes from By in 1865:

I have some more subjects to give you, supplied by a nice little excursion we had recently in the forest with Achard of the Opéra Comique and a few friends. We regretted you were not with us, as you would have been able to get something out of a lot of adventures that happened to us through a restive horse, whose mouth, as friend Mène said, was as hard as a footscraper. I showed the ladies Chardin's Tree, which has become quite a resort during our walks. Cain insisted on getting inside, and, with some difficulty, succeeded. But on coming out, oh, shocking! he could not show himself from every point of view; for his trousers were too tight, and the rest you will understand.

M. Chardin adds the following note to the above letter:

The tree alluded to, and to which Rosa Bonheur gives my name, was an oak of the Long Rocher and was the scene of the following incident: In the autumn of 1864 I had taken up my abode in the village inn at By in order to paint a series of sketches in the forest. I had chosen as one subject a clump of trees in the Gorge aux Loups, near the Long Rocher. This part of the forest being about seven kilometres from By, Rosa Bonheur was kind enough to place her carriage at my disposal, and each evening the coachman came about five to fetch me and my belongings. One evening, however, I waited in vain at the appointed place. But no carriage came; and as night had come on and I was afraid of losing myself entirely in the trees, I decided to look for shelter where I could spend the night. Prowling about in search of a friendly rock, I happened to knock my parasol against a tree which sounded hollow. I struck a match and by its light discovered a cavity inside the trunk, which was that of an oak, into which I managed to creep. Wrapping my plaid round my legs and ensconcing myself as comfortably as I could,

I tried to sleep. But the noise made by the stags who were belling around the Mare aux Fées and by the night birds who were perched above me rendered my efforts useless. One after the other, I heard the hours struck by the clock of Marlotte church, and I had just counted the twelve of midnight when I thought I saw a light glimmering at some little distance. Springing out of my tree-hole, I perceived two shadows in the proximity of a lantern which was moving away from me. I shouted, gave my name; the lantern now began to come toward me, and I recognised the man-servant and the cook of Rosa Bonheur, who, as soon as they heard my voice, began also to shout and to blow a horn. Soon, Rosa Bonheur herself arrived, kind soul, with an iron-shod stick in one hand and a hunting-horn in the other. Behind her came my village landlady, Mme. Girardin, and a number of the village inhabitants. They gave me an ovation; for everybody believed I was lying somewhere seriously hurt by the stags which were numerous in this part of the forest and were particularly aggressive at that season.

While returning to the village, Rosa Bonheur related to me the cause of the coachman's absence. Her brother Isidore, who had come over from Paris to see her, had fallen and sprained himself. The carriage intended for me had gone for the doctor. After the doctor's visit, Rosa Bonheur herself had started out to fetch me, but her carriage had been surrounded by a number of stags and she had been obliged to get her mare back to the stables as soon as possible. We arrived at By about three o'clock in the morning, and I was straightway conducted to the kitchen, where Mlle. Nathalie Micas, whose hobby was medicine and surgery and who was expecting to see me brought in on a stretcher with broken limbs, was ready to experiment her art on my person. Everything was prepared, even knives and saws for cutting, and, in the glow of the fire, shone chemists' jars and medicaments of the most varied description!

To Paul Chardin, " My good and worthy Rapin ":

By, October 15, 1869: I will tell you what I was saying to myself just now. Since All Saints' Day is near at hand, I was saying that about this time the famous Rapin used to come and call on his old General in order to go and sketch with her on the melancholy Long Rocher, both shivering with cold; then, in order to warm themselves at lunch time, they would descend into the Grotto, lighting a big fire that their varlet had gleaned wood for among the firs, at the expense of the State, and there toast their poor trembling bodies and blue faces; next they would stuff them-

THE GROTTO OF LONG ROCHER.

selves with enormous hunks of bread seasoned with good victuals and an agreeable cup of coffee boiled over the big fire; and finally, they would smoke an exquisite cigarette while chattering about everything that passed through their head and then return each to his seat to go on daubing masterpieces. Lastly, the good Rapin would come in the evening and stretch himself in front of a large fire that blazed in the big chimney of the studio, and there muse and smoke.

This time has already gone by, and my letter is to tell you that the years succeed each other with their varying experience, and that about this season I usually think of the old friendship between the Rapin and the General. Now the General's voice has become hoarser and more cracked, when she smokes in the morning. She gets up late and grows fonder of being alone like the solitary boar. But she nevertheless remembers her friends and was glad as always to receive a kind, affectionate letter from her worthy Rapin, accompanied with a pen-and-ink portrait, quite the thing.

How handsome my old Rapin is with his big hat in one hand and his umbrella in the other! It is an umbrella, isn't it? Alas for the ravages of Time! Why, he hasn't a hair left on his cranium, and his long ears are more visible than ever! And how pensive he looks!

Well! enough of this. Six pages is not bad, my dear friend; and my horse is waiting for me. But if one day the artist Chardin should have a mind to come over, I will introduce him to a friend who is working at some fine clumps of trees the Rapin once saw with me. The friend's name is " the old 'un," and this friend is painting at present some things that would interest M. Chardin, the landscape painter, who sees more than he can put on canvas, which is, however, about the case with all of us.

April 30, 1870, Rosa Bonheur replied as follows from By to Antoine Passy, who had written some humorous verses on the subject touched upon in this letter:

The Rapin is a wilful fellow. His friends know it well, and, anticipating what might happen, the good Rosa told him to beware of her stag, who, although the horns were only just growing again, could clatter with his front feet and drum smartly on the poor Rapin's hide. But the obstinate Rapin, not wishing to make a fuss, did not listen to Rosa and bravely entered the lists in all innocence and with no artifice. Rosa, however, had advised him to arm himself with a stout stick, as a measure of precaution.

Chardin began to sketch, smiling graciously the while. The stag, with a meek and mild air, approached, then suddenly reared and began raining blows on the back, belly, and nose of the Rapin who took refuge in the stag's trough. Thereupon, the stag, still more irritated by this invasion of his property, continued to drum on the victim with a vengeance. Just then, she whom the gods had appointed, flew to his help, thereby a second time saving his life, the first being his deliverance from the deep, dark forest.

UNDER THE SHADOW OF AN OAK.

CHARDIN'S ADVENTURE WITH A DEER.

FONTAINEBLEAU

Such, sir, is the sad story which I have artistically illustrated above for your private edification. Make verses if you choose. We are ready to reply to you, although in lines without feet, yet no worse turned for it. If this vexes you, why you must be vexed.

The three letters which follow were written to Mme. Peyrol in 1879–80, and show what Siberian winters were sometimes experienced in Fontainebleau:

December 10: In fancy I transport myself under your ice-covered windows, which must be opaque enough at present. I hope you are making your stove roar and that you will not be prevented by frost-bite from sending me news out of your winter-quarters. It's really as though we were making a journey to the North Pole. The newspapers have at last arrived and the trains are now managing to run again, somehow or other.

Bourdon goes out reconnoitring from time to time, and brings us back news with a nose as red as a radish. As for myself, I am fully occupied in trying to keep the animals cosey and snug, and have to potter about continually in the snow. There are places in the park where the snow comes up to the knees. In all my life, I have never seen it so deep. My poor stag lies in it, and the hind, who has a house, prefers to lie in it, too. A funny sort of preference! The poor little birds come and pick up the grains in the hen-yard, and, though the fowls stay inside, their crests and feet are nevertheless frozen. The river is frozen over; and, in spite of the sun, the thermometer stands this morning at zero, Fahrenheit, and to-night, from what I hear, it is likely to be four or five below. It's stiff!

Nathalie spends all her time in calking up the windows. We are so far safe and sound, except our poor Farino,[1] who must be dead in some corner or other, for he hasn't made his appearance the last five days.

December 16: What a winter! Just now, at mid-day, it is 5° Fahrenheit above zero, and last night it was 20° below. There

---

[1] A long-haired cat, which was white all over.

was a slight thaw, but it has begun to freeze again. The birds are dying of cold and hunger, and alas! women and children, too, of starvation. It is terrible. Let us hope the January sun will do something toward altering this state of things. But between now and then many will be dead! Write to me, since you mustn't think of coming over. There have been three railway accidents on our line, one very serious, at Pont-sur-Yonne. The switches were frozen.

Tell me if you can keep warm. Fortunately for us, Nathalie had our stove repaired before the cold set in; otherwise there would be no staying in the studio. Now it is very comfortable there, only we have to keep poking the fire up all the time.

Yesterday I opened a small casement to let in a bit of sun, and a little wren flew in, who was half starved. To-day, he is eating the flies along the window, quite perkily, warming himself between times and then perching on my pictures. Before long, I believe he will come on my shoulders. I hope everybody is well.

January 26: Thank God we have reached home. But it is impossible to give you an idea of what the country is like, after passing the plain of Lieusaint.[1] Every bit of wood in the forest is torn and mutilated. We were terrified to see everything bent and broken as if a dreadful tempest had swept over it. Not a birch is standing. The big oaks have part of their branches on the ground and many of them are cut in two across the trunk. Even the middling-sized ones that are not snapped in twain, are bowed to the ground and are covered with icicles. You will better understand when I tell you that a bit of hay is coated with nearly two centimetres of ice. My park is a regular thicket of brush-wood, quite impenetrable, and the tops of the trees are like a cane. To walk, you need to be shod on purpose, without clogs or shoes. To get here from the station, we had to risk being over-whelmed by falling branches as thick as your arm, which crashed down with their burden of icicles, deafening you with their noise. Indeed, in order to be able to walk at all, we were obliged to hold on to a handcart drawn by some people of the neighbourhood who

---

[1] That is, after leaving Melun and entering the Fontainebleau forest.

had come to meet us at the station. Last night the cracking
noises continued, and this morning the branches are still snapping
in the park. If this doesn't stop soon, nothing will be left but
the trunks of the trees. Bourdon is in despair because his birches
are all destroyed. The telegraph wires are down and the poles,
too. And yet, in spite of it all, one can't help admiring this
veritable fairy-land. Just imagine the branches all in limpid
crystal, and, as they are bent to the ground, they make an infinite
number of crystal grottoes. For there are a good four centimetres of ice round the little branches, and festoons on the
telegraph wires. In fact, no such phenomenon has ever occurred
before within the memory of man. At last it is thawing, and as I
write, I hear the sound of falling icicles.

The following note to Major Rousseau, written at Nice, April
9, 1883, gives quite another view of the forest:

You must be very happy, dear M. Rousseau, to be able to
take your rides with your son, in the crisp morning air, when the
woods are all in leaf. It is so invigorating in the forest! I shall
perhaps meet you sometimes in my tilbury, with my big black
horse, who is improving wonderfully, is growing stronger and
becoming firmer in muscle, it seems to me. So I am going to take
him out every morning.

The autumnal forest effects were frequently not less impressive,
as is seen by the two letters which follow. Thus, Rosa Bonheur
writes to Auguste Cain, " my old friend and illustrious sculptor,"
on November 5, 1892:

I thought of going to Paris this week. But on Thursday,
while making a morning round in the forest, I noticed a tint of
colour on the last leaves of the trees, which are so beautiful this
year, that to-morrow, Sunday, I have planned to go and make a
water-colour sketch to regale myself. Now, if it does not interfere
with your plans, my old Cain-quina,[1] I would like to ask you
to let me go and lunch with you rather on Thursday next, when

---

[1] A play on quinquina, or Peruvian bark, advertised in the French newspapers and
on the city walls.

I shall have satisfied my hankering after this natural effect. Fontainebleau is so beautiful this year. Some seasons it is not so. I suppose it is because we have not yet had any frost. So tomorrow I will go and make my sketch, if it does not rain too much. Kindest regards to both.

A short note, written next day to Isidore Bonheur, runs thus:

I am starting after lunch, my dear old brother, in order to make a little water-colour sketch at the Gorge aux Loups or rather at the Mare aux Fées. You can't imagine how beautiful the last tints of the leaves are this year. I intend to work in my gig and there is room enough for two. Even if it rains, it will be possible to paint all the same.

You are an old rascal to portray your sister with her spectacles on, when you don't wear any yourself. Nevertheless, it is a good likeness.

To-morrow I have friend Cain to lunch.

Your old Zaza and fellow student.

The " gig " mentioned in the foregoing letter is thus described by Mme. René Fouret, wife of the Paris publisher, whose summer residence has long been at Fontainebleau:

One beautiful November day, when a warm sun was melting the hoar-frost of the night, I was bicycling between Marlotte and Montigny, when I noticed a sort of little shepherd's wagon, a kind of cabin on four wheels, which was standing in the middle of a field. Two horses attached to a plow and driven by a farmer were going forward and back before the cabin. Much puzzled by this odd sight, I stopped and went nearer, when I perceived that one side of this strange vehicle was all in glass, behind which, protected from the cold air, sat Rosa Bonheur, brush or pencil in hand, sketching the moving man and animals. Not many months afterwards, the grand artist was dead.

This anecdote shows not only with what care Rosa Bonheur studied all the details of her art, but that she never felt she had learned all there was to be learned.

THE INTERIOR OF THE BY STUDIO.

ROSA BONHEUR IN HER STUDIO.
By Achille Fould.

FONTAINEBLEAU

A few years ago was formed in Paris a society called the Friends of Fontainebleau, whose object is to protect the natural beauties of the forest. This was always one of the constant cares of Rosa Bonheur, as we have already seen more than once. However, another example is given in these words addressed in 1895 to Georges Cain:

I thought you would like to know that yesterday I went with the forest ranger to have a look at the ground in question. All the gentlemen interested came to my house and were most polite. You will have the credit of having saved one of the few remaining bits of the threatened part of the forest, for it is you, my dear Georges, who are the real preserver of this spot. All I did was to ferret it out and conduct you to it.

This series of letters devoted to the charms of Fontainebleau may close with this note written one April morning to " My good Mme. P. J.," Mme. Mène:

Easter Day, I have promised to spend at Magny-les-Hamaux, that festival each year being devoted by me to my nieces. But why couldn't you come out Sunday week, for instance, which would be the 23d, Saint Quosimodo's Day, a good saint, i'faith, whose name I find very pretty? But why need I give you a day? You've simply to drop me a line the day before you arrive, in order to find some capital cabbage soup waiting for you. If you could stay over night with us, I would take you a delightful walk in the moonlight. I've spent the last three nights almost entirely in the forest. This evening I am returning to the Mare aux Fées, where I am going to try to reproduce an admirable effect of the moon reflected in the water. You hear the owls and frogs having a concert, and then the stags come down to drink. If that tempts you, I am at your service.

In 1901, as has already been stated, a permanent memorial to Rosa Bonheur's lifelong association with the beautiful forest of Fontainebleau was raised by Mr. Gambart in the heart of the town. The inscription on the pedestal of the monument reads:

REMINISCENCES OF ROSA BONHEUR

"The Chief Works of Rosa Bonheur, Painter and Sculptor."

Over this inscription is a bronze copy, in high relief, of the Younger Peyrol's bust of Rosa Bonheur. On the other three sides are bronze reliefs, executed by Isidore Bonheur and the Younger Peyrol, of the "Horse Fair," "Ploughing in the Nivernais," and the "King of the Forest." The magnificent bronze bull crowning the pedestal is from Rosa Bonheur's original, enlarged by her brother and nephew. All the labour in connection with the casting and putting together of these various bronzes was performed by the Elder Peyrol. This monument, therefore, is a remarkable and appropriate exemplification of the art genius of the Bonheur family, erected in the spot which was a perpetual inspiration to the most gifted member of that family.

CHAPTER X

THE first fighting of the Franco-German conflict of 1870–71 began in August, 1870, on the Rhenish frontier. Before the end of the month Bazaine was shut up in Metz, and at the beginning of September Sedan had fallen. This closed the first phase of the war. The second phase opened with the declaration of the Republic on September 4, 1870, followed by the siege of Paris, which lasted from September 15 to January 28, 1871, during which period the War in the Provinces was carried on with varying results until the end of February. In the month following the peace with Germany, on March 18, 1871, the struggle commenced between the French Government, fixed at Versailles, and the Paris Commune, with the Germans encamped hard by looking on. This civil war lasted until the end of May.

During the War in the Provinces there was not a little fighting in the immediate neighbourhood of Fontainebleau, and the German soldiery even invaded the forest and disturbed the quietude of the village of By itself. The Prussian headquarters in that region were at Moret. Several of the leading citizens of Thomery were held as hostages in Fontainebleau prison, and the requisitions in money, kind, etc., amounted at Thomery to nearly forty-five thousand dollars. From the Carrefour Montmorin nearly to Thomery the Route Ronde is paved, and it was felt that the town would be safer if these paving stones were pulled up and the road left sandy and muddy. So this was done. But later, the German military authorities forced some of the leading citizens of Thomery to replace the stones. The work was of course badly done and the road is rough even to this day. Over it Rosa Bonheur used frequently to pass on her way home from a drive in the forest. " So I always have the war with me," she would sometimes say, as she went jolting over the uneven surface.

Though Rosa Bonheur's property did not suffer, her brother Auguste was not so fortunate. " The Germans occupied his country home," M. Hippolyte Peyrol tells me, " and utterly ruined the interior of the house. The drawing-room was converted into a stable. The drawers, taken from the tables, were used as mangers, and the iron bedsteads as hay-racks. The furniture was split up for firewood, and the house itself was nearly burnt to the ground. In March, 1871, when my uncle and I returned to Magny, about all that was left of the building was its four walls."

Several of Rosa Bonheur's friends or neighbours have given me interesting bits of their reminiscences concerning her thoughts and acts during " the Terrible Year," which, with the letters that follow, throw a curious side-light on the crisis and on her character in a stormy period that tried men's souls. There can be no question that Rosa Bonheur rises fully to the occasion and displays a patriotism and a fearlessness worthy of any man. In fact, at the height of the danger, her family feared, and with reason, that she might imperil her life by some overt act. Let me give here some of these proofs that Rosa Bonheur not only dressed like a man, but conducted herself like one when the occasion demanded it of her.

Paul Chardin writes me:

Rosa Bonheur had a fine character, at one and the same time proud, independent, and full of self-sacrifice and heart. To such a nature, the unhappy Franco-German war was a terrible blow, and all the more so because she was brave and loved France. On this noble patriotic artist it had a really heart-rending effect.

During the Prussian occupation, the ten-antlered deer with whom I had a battle described elsewhere in these memoirs, also showed himself to be a real patriot. One day some German officers in full-dress uniform came from Fontainebleau to visit Rosa Bonheur's studio. But on their arrival, they found the doors closed against them. They insisted, however, in going round the park, which the gardener did not dare to hinder. On reaching the stag's paddock, the officers were desirous to get a nearer look at the animal; and, in spite of the gardener's warning, they opened the gate and went in. As soon as he perceived them, the stag rushed toward them, and leaping into the middle of the pool that was his drinking-place, he splashed the muddy water all over their fine uniforms. This protest of the ten-antlered stag was a great joy to his mistress.

Consuélo Fould writes me:

When the Prussian troops arrived in her neighbourhood, Prince Frederic Charles, in order to show Rosa Bonheur that he admired and respected her talent, sent her a safe-conduct. But she, indignant that she could be supposed capable of accepting a favour from an enemy of France, tore up the paper in the presence of the officer who bore it, and informed him that she felt in honour bound not to allow herself to be treated any better than the humblest peasant of her village.

In the foreground of the picture by Horace Vernet, at Versailles, representing a cavalry charge during the Crimean war, is Captain Charmeux at the head of a squadron of hussars, his long, fair beard floating in the wind. It was the Charmeux family that, in the middle of the eighteenth century, began the cultivation of the celebrated *chasselas* grapes, now the wealth and the originality of the region round about Thomery. His son, M. Paul Charmeux, the horticulturist, gives me this striking statement:

At the moment of the war of 1870, my father, a retired captain of the army, organised, among the older inhabitants, a sort of home guard. Rosa Bonheur joined the company, and more than once did I see her at that time, with her gun over her shoulder, march and drill with her male neighbours. Of course, her men's clothes made this all the easier and more natural.

Her neighbour, M. Grivot, says:

During the dark days of the war of 1870 the Prussians were camping at Champagne, a small village separated from By by the Seine. One evening Rosa Bonheur induced an inhabitant of her neighbourhood to go with her, and both spent a fair amount of powder and shot in firing at the enemy's sentinels. The next day the Prussians crossed the Seine and entered By, some officers even coming into her courtyard. "Here are the keys of my house and cellar," she said to them; "you may do what you like there. As for my studio, I absolutely forbid you to cross its threshold."

Henri Cain writes:

In 1870, when the Germans invaded the Department of the Seine-and-Marne, Rosa Bonheur assembled in the courtyard of her country home all those from the region roundabout whom she knew to be good shots and bold poachers, with the intention of putting herself at their head to go and defend the crossing of the Seine at the foot of the By hill. But her more prudent neighbours finally dissuaded her from such an act, by pointing out to her that the village might be burnt in retaliation, without the nation gaining anything. So with her heart boiling over with pent-up rage and weeping like a child, she was seen to return to her house, where she shut herself up and went almost mad with chagrin and sorrow that she could not fight on the river's bank.

Her old and faithful servant, Céline Rey, gives me this anecdote:

Two or three German officers stayed at the By home while the enemy was in that part of the country. They ate with the Micases; Rosa Bonheur took her meals in her studio and would never sit at table with them.

On one occasion a score or more of Prussian soldiers appeared at the gate bent on requisitioning. Rosa Bonheur happened to be downstairs, in the kitchen, and immediately went out into the courtyard to parley with them.

"What do you want?" she asked, sharply.

" Moutons," several of them mumbled, with a strong Teutonic accent.

" I have no sheep, nor anything else to give you; you may have a drink, and then you had better be off," was the bold reply.

" A little woman got up as a man to frighten us," they whispered; and the uncommonness of the act and the bluntness of the refusal seemed to please and disconcert, at the same time, these troopers, dominated by the sentimental strain which I have been told is inseparable from the German character. So they threw off the proffered wine and rode away without their " moutons," while Rosa Bonheur, satisfied at her diplomacy, smiled and went upstairs to her studio and her work.

This chapter may close with some of Rosa Bonheur's letters written at this period, which are replete with evidences not only of her bravery and love of country, but contain several examples of that odd capriciousness, that humorousness and even levity, which often seem so out of place and remind one of the similar breaches of good taste of which Lincoln was frequently guilty during the dark days of the American Civil War.

To Mme. Peyrol, on March 18, 1870, from By:

These war rumours disturb me and I have no time to lose, considering the work I have on hand; for the drought and the impending conflict, which won't be favourable to art, urge me not to lose my time and cause me to wish not to incur expense. And as there are some things about which I do not change, I have resolved to execute what is in my mind—viz., to paint my animals and then eat them, one after the other, so that if the Prussians should come, there will remain nothing for them!

" Shortly before the war was declared," Paul Chardin writes, " Rosa Bonheur asked me to procure her a certain number of books, such as Pluvinel's ' Royal Riding School,' for its costumes, and Joinville's and Froissart's ' Chronicles,' which she wished to know. Several of the works being rare and dear, the news of the

22   **319**

declaration of war caused her to change her mind, as will be seen by the following letter, addressed to me ":

By, July 19, 1870: Please don't buy those books I asked for, unless you have already done so; for in these sad times we must all think only of how to economise. Nobody can tell what may happen. If you have bought them, all right; but if not, stop expenses all along the line. Act for me as you would for yourself. We are to have stirring times, and events will move rapidly when once the war gets underway. My poor Rapin, all we can do in our corner is to work at our art and to pray God that the conflict will soon be over.

July 28, 1870, Rosa Bonheur writes Mme. Peyrol from By:

I am seriously uneasy about this deuce of a war, and, just like a sailor who anticipates bad weather, I intend making sacrifices, and shall throw overboard all that might embarrass me. In other words, I mean to economise. So my animals will soon be having a lively time; and afterward, I shall take a little more leisure, and you will see a little more of me. Now, I must make haste. So good-bye. Love to you, to Dodore, and the small fry.

In much the same mood she wrote to Paul Chardin, August 6, 1870:

Like you, I've got my head full of this plaguy war which won't be very favourable to the progress of the fine arts. So I see I must be prepared to make sacrifices, and, before winter comes, the animals that ministered to my pleasure and professional wants will have to hop off, as they say in society and court.

I have no more wish to paint than I have to eat sweets. But reason tells me I must work. Unfortunately, what I do is ill-done. I paint nothing but daubs, and that's the truth. I have discarded, somewhat, water-colours, in order to take up again with studies of the animals I intend to have killed, one after the other, so that if the Prussians should come, they would not be able to find anything besides old frames coated with concentrated linseed oil that has become rather rancid through age.

I have had some places in my manor undermined, and am going to mix in a vessel a certain quantity of picrate and gun-cotton, with a train laid to a spot where I shall only have to apply a match, in order to have the pleasure of blowing up the turrets and towers I have indulged in during times of peace. My good Rapin, if we have to resort to extreme measures, come to By. If your tenants are no longer willing or able to pay you, that is all the more reason for you to come. Then we will escort to Paris old mother Micas and big Nathalie. From there, we will go armed with our fowling-pieces and cover the retreat to the capital of my brother Auguste's family, and once there, we will engage in the defence of the city or we will do ourselves the pleasure of getting our heads broken, for want of something else to do. Till then, let us go in for painting somehow or other. That will hurt nobody.

These letters to Mme. Peyrol deal still further with Rosa Bonheur's feelings at this time:

By, August 16, 1870: Like you I am not at all pleased at what is taking place, for war is of course never so agreeable as peace. But as there is nothing better to do, I have quietly and philosophically returned to my labours. My argument is that it would be stupid to waste days which each dawn diminishes by one; and, if Fate ordains we should perish sooner rather than later, well! the time will have been more beneficially employed than in lounging about and doing nothing. Alone, I could not save my country, even were I able to defend her in arms. If I had been a young male, I should have left for the front long since; and Germain [1] has done no more than I should have done in his place. Now, my poor Sis, nobody can tell what will happen to him, and he must be ready for everything, even to kill and to die, if necessary. I hope, however, that he will get off, like many others, with a little playing at war; for I confess I have great

---

[1] Germain Bonheur was in MacMahon's army and was made prisoner at Sedan. He subsequently escaped and returned to Paris before it was quite invested. Joining the militia, he served, as has already been told, all during the siege without wound or illness.

confidence in the affair not being so serious as some people imagine, and that, in spite of all, we shall gain a few little victories, which will put everything to rights. That is my opinion of the situation, and that is why I am working quietly.[1]

As for our poor Aunt Ophélie, I am very much afraid her earthly campaign is nearly at an end, for I, too, find her much changed lately.

God bless you, my poor Sis.

By, August 18, 1870: Both last night and this morning I was tempted to set off and take Germain the shoes he wants. But I reflected that I might have a journey for nothing, if he has started as he wrote; and another parting would be still more painful. If he falls, he will fall for the common defence, and so, for us. He will fall as others have already done. If he is not yet gone, kiss him for me. If he is garrisoned in the forts, he will not have much time to go and see you. Write me about him. If there is a chance of meeting him, I will run over to Paris. Tell Mammy to be easy about her son.

When I think of it all, I assure you I would go to the front, if I believed I could make myself useful in picking up the poor wounded. But there are stronger than I for the work, and if we should be reached by the invasion, I shall do my best, I give you my word. We are quite decided to throw in our lot with the inhabitants of these parts, and if we have to fly, I shall beforehand run all the wine out of the cellar, break all the bottles, burn the fodder, and kill all my remaining animals, including the horses, except the two we should want for our flight. They would only have the house left to burn, and that would not help them much. Perhaps even, I should have first polished one or two of them off with my own hand, if the opportunity offered, at the risk of receiving a sugar-plum, which would not be the worst of deaths after all, and would be better than suffering like a martyr at a slow fire, as I should suffer if I were to see foreigners the masters in our land.

But Juju, my dear, this will not happen; and in my heart,

---

[1] The day this letter was written the disastrous battles around Metz were raging.

I pray God, who is the only ruler, for us. Have confidence, Sis, and for the rest, let His will be done. I have just received this morning's news. It allows me to hope we shan't see the enemy here or at Paris. Don't fret, my dear Juju; for I am persuaded this sad war will soon be over, if we give these rascally Prussians a good drubbing, which we can't fail to do. That's my opinion, little Sis.

As for our brother, I hope he will have good luck, which will probably be the case, since I don't think he will be obliged to expose himself. I trust that those who are at present risking their lives for us will be victorious and save us. But if we have our share in the common trouble, let us remember there are families that have two and even three members at the front. Already some have the grief of losses suffered. Reflecting on all this makes me firmer and ready for anything.

Much love to you; and if you have news about Auguste, let me know where he is.

By, August 29, 1870: I sent you a line in haste last Wednesday or Thursday to try and make you easy on my account, for it seems people were already saying in Paris that the Prussians were here. I told you I should soon be going over to Paris or would write. But, my poor Sis, I have been so busy carpentering, packing, reading the papers and helping the Micases to hide those of our treasures that the enemy might appropriate, that we have only just finished the work. Now, I am going to resume my painting quietly; and if the Uhlans come, I'll ask them if they don't want their portraits painted to send to their wives and mothers, since I hope not many of the poor devils will return to their homes. If they march to besiege Paris, all the peasants of the neighbourhood are quite determined to hunt them down or to wait and oppose them, not to mention that they will find neither fodder, nor flour, everybody having made it his duty to destroy or conceal everything. They can burn the region if they like, but that won't do them any good, and if they go about in small parties, not many of them will remain in our country places when they find there is nothing to pilfer. So make your mind easy, and don't trouble about me. I should not like to abandon the Micases, and I could do no good in Paris. Send me news about Auguste and Germain. My heart's love to you, dearest Sis, for I love you well. Love to all, and don't fret more than you can help.

Rosa Bonheur's activity at that time is further evident in a letter dated from By, August 29, 1870, to Paul Chardin, in which she says:

I have only just sat down, having been on my feet since morning. For the last three or four days I have been working at the packer's trade. Moreover, I have been inspecting all sorts of pulling down and building up. In fine, we are now ready to receive the Prussians in a proper way. They won't find much that will serve them. All my painting studies are in safe hiding, and everything else to which I attach any value. So don't trouble about me, my good Rapin. I am not in a funk; and now that everything is safely put away, I am going to resume my painting as tranquilly as Baptiste, to use the expression employed among the people, whom I have always been fond of in spite of their defects. I cannot, however, excuse them for one defect—viz., being stupid enough to let themselves be led like beasts to the slaughter-house by scoundrelly sovereigns.

To further reassure Juliette, she writes from By, on September 1, 1870:

Do send me news about Germain, as soon as you get any. From what you write, he must be at the front. I trust he will come back safe and sound.

We poor women, as you well say, should do no good in trying to defend ourselves. We should only expose ourselves to pillage. This task must be performed by men, who run the risk but who also reap the glory. Alas! what else can we do except submit to the inevitable?

I note that you advise us to fly. It's a cowardly thing to do, and yet I had almost resigned myself to it when good news arrived, news which I had been expecting, for I had argued in this way. These princes, I had said to myself, must be very stupid not to see that they will be stripped of all they have, if they continue to march on Paris. God must punish the wrong acts of those who would inflict such evils on this poor earth. I have faith that this will happen, because I firmly believe in the justice of God, although I don't go to mass and don't believe in all the stupid inventions of men. So I am continuing to work at my painting while waiting for developments, and am filled with hope that the good news will be confirmed.

Let me beg of you not to worry about me. It isn't the Micases who are keeping me here. It's the calculation I make of what is likely to happen. So far, I am convinced that it is better to remain quietly where I am without incurring useless expense. Indeed, it wouldn't do to leave the house to be ransacked perhaps by French pillagers. We have hidden all that we attach any value to, and for the rest, we must let things take their course.

If all goes well, as I trust, I shall run over to Paris and see you one of these next days.

And also to Paul Chardin, on the same day:

Make your mind easy, my good and worthy Rapin, your General in painting is no baby, nor yet so hare-brained as you suppose; and she is ready to assume the responsibility of everything she does. She has no intention of exposing her own life, and much less that of a poor old woman or of an old friend, who gets easily excited.

FLEEING FROM THE PRUSSIANS.

I have already told you how I had concealed all the things I considered valuable, so well indeed that the devil himself would be clever if he succeeded in profiting by them. There's nothing but my manor that can perish by the flames. To tell the truth, I was half inclined to blow it up at the beginning of the war, for I was then expecting the coming of the Prussians. But now it seems, they are turning back; so I shan't be able to satisfy my hankering to see a fortress blown up.

With a view to our personal security, I had studied and followed on the map of France the march of the enemy; with my compasses, I had counted the days that separated us from the Uhlans, and I had divined what they would do in order to get through our lines. I then formed two plans. One consisted in getting myself appointed captain of the By national guard and heroically defending the place if the Prussians should turn out to be only four or five strong, in order to have people speak a little about me in History. My second plan was to fly at the critical moment.

In the first plan, I had contrived and perfected a sure way of fortifying ourselves. It was to go to the mayor and say to him:

" Mr. Mayor, you must get a hundred casks and put them in rows at the various approaches to the village. We will all get inside and, sticking the ends of our guns through the bung-hole, we might maintain a continuous firing on the Uhlans before they have time to recognise us."

Now, if what people say is correct, this heroic defence will be unnecessary. Anyway, if things should become serious, and I find they are quite serious enough already, I may tell my dear Rapin, in order to make him less anxious, that we have prepared everything quietly and in order, with a view to flying from here, if we are invaded by anything more than four men and a corporal. We should all be off, and, travelling slowly, we should, if need be, go to America, with all the animals we care for. Indeed, how could we part with our parrot and leave him to be roasted by the Prussians, perhaps by the King himself! No! I had rather die than abandon to them a single creature.

While Nathalie was seeing to my sketches, I was occupied with an important task—viz., that of concealing the deeds, papers, and valuables of Mme. Micas. In fact, I did this so well that I defy anybody whatsoever to discover the hiding-place. If we should perish, it would be a secret forever.

Now that everything is put away, I have gone back to my study of the sheep, whose numbers are diminishing every day.

But this is not my only loss. While engaged in writing to you, I have let go by a fine effect of sunlight!

God grant the Prussians may not return and that all may go well! But if, after everything is said and done, we are called upon to die, well, we'll die!

Two subsequent letters to Paul Chardin run thus:

By, September 5, 1870: I am as sad as it is possible to be over the dishonour of our poor country. It makes me wild with grief when I think of all that has just happened, and that a town so noble as Strasburg has been destroyed, after its resistance, simply because it has shown itself more honourable than those which have submitted to their shame.

My mind is irrevocably made up on one point, my dear Rapin; I intend to leave France. Death alone will prevent me. I don't know what will happen in the next few days. I shall do the best I can until the opportunity for starting offers itself. But the Micases and I cannot, without a little preparation, go off and leave everything, being surrounded as we are by our servants and animals.

I was counting on a better issue of events, and in my last letter to you, my brave and worthy Rapin, I even joked about the situation. But now I see that France is lost, and, in my opinion, she is disgraced forever; for public favour has changed too often, and I can no more swallow this card-board republic than I could the earlier one of 1848, especially as I now have the discernment that comes with age together with its real, honest independence.

Although we cannot fly directly, we shall manage it somehow, and—my mind is quite made up on this point—we shall quit France as soon as possible. You are a good and honourable man and you will quite understand the feelings that actuate me.

By, September 10, 1870: I shall not follow your good advice to fly from here. On the contrary, I want to stay here until the war is nearly ended, when it is my fixed intention to go and settle in Belgium. If France becomes Prussian, I will never live in it; but if she should be a durable republic or empire, I might come back later. I am quietly awaiting the Prussians, and in order to receive them courteously and with more dignity, I shall put on my full evening dress and wear the cross of the Legion of Honour, which was attached to my breast by the Empress herself, in recognition of a life of work which, by God's help and my own efforts, has enabled me to escape from poverty. There! that's just what I mean to do, my good friend, M. Chardin.

If I meet with brutes who try to insult unprotected women, well! I shall let myself be killed by the hirelings of that stupid man, William the Protestant, who, in order to impose his will and overthrow a single man, has had his own people massacred and ours, too, without perceiving that the policy which has urged him on to obtain this glory is the same as that which caused Henry IV, the Protestant, to be assassinated, and which has also destroyed in France the Protestant aristocracy, which was the most liberal, the most enlightened, and the most honest of all. But God's hand is in it, and he always punishes with a reference to the crime. He knows how to humiliate princes who commit low actions for selfish reasons. You see, everybody has his own way of looking at things. This is mine.

In closing, let me embrace you fraternally; for, if we are destined to depart this life, you may be killed on the ramparts of Paris, as I and the Micases may be assassinated here. It depends on what happens shortly. But if we are left here in peace, I repeat that I shall carry out my intention of going to live in Belgium, or elsewhere, if another place pleases me more.

The following letter to Mme. Peyrol, written at By, September 20, 1870, was received only on February 17, 1871:

I am still without any news from you, my poor dear sister. I quite understand the reason, for it must be difficult to get in and out of Paris. However, I still go on writing to you. Perhaps my letter will reach you sooner or later. I now regret you didn't all come and take refuge here, since the Prussians passed all around us without coming near. The fact is that we are in an exceptional position here in our little domain, on account of the bridges having been blown up; and they were no doubt afraid to come over to us through the forest. We saw them at Champagne, just opposite; and when I went with Etienne [1] to watch the blowing up of the Valvins bridge, just at that moment the Uhlans arrived, on their way to Fontainebleau, where it appears the good Prince of Prussia intended to establish his headquarters. A few Uhlans, whom I was able to get a glimpse of with my field-glass, tried to cross the Seine and were nearly drowned. However, the river being low, some of them got across and were made prisoners at Fontainebleau.

So now, I have beheld these terrible Uhlans, with their horses which look as though they had Arab blood in them. Men and horses are dying with hunger and fatigue. Wherever they passed in large numbers, they ravaged, being angry at finding neither inhabitants nor provisions. But when they were in small detachments of nineteen or twenty, half of these poor wretches were only too content to be made prisoners. Some of them wept when they saw the children, who no doubt reminded them of their own. They march because they are forced to, and foresee that Paris will be the death of most of them; for, alas! there will be a good deal of blood spilt yet.

Only fancy, my poor Juju, the country looks magnificent during all this time. The weather is splendid, the forest is peaceful, and only the chirping of the birds is heard. What a contrast! Afar off, we hear the booming of the cannon. But since this morning, they have been silent, and now my anxiety is all about Paris. If you write me, don't fail to post the letter. I know there must be already a large circle round the forts. But there should be breaks here and there, nevertheless. The enemy cannot possibly be everywhere. As soon as ever I can manage it, I shall go up to Paris in my tilbury, accompanied by my servant; for I cannot believe this siege will last. The more I reflect, the more I feel our enemies are attempting the impossible. But even if I could go to Paris now, it would hardly be right to leave poor old Mother Micas, who can't stir. When the war is over, we will see about it.

I have thought a good deal about poor Tatan. I am going to write to her. Poor woman! Poor old aunt! Who knows

---

[1] Rosa Bonheur's man-servant.

whether I shall see her again! Well, well, it's fate! I none the less hope she won't die before I can get to Paris.

Auguste might have written me and given me his address, and as he is not shut up in Paris, his letter would have reached me, I am sure. As for me, don't be uneasy. So far, I have had the good luck to be able to stick to my work, finding nothing better to do. Let us have confidence in God and pity toward men. I long to see you, my dear Juju. Kiss poor Isidore for me. Much love to you.

"My good Rapin," writes Rosa Bonheur to Paul Chardin, November 1, 1870:

Nathalie has written you a letter which she has put into a bottle and thrown into the river. But I am much afraid that the poor bottle has got stuck to the bank or been broken against some bridge. We shall try to-day a surer means of asking you for news. I think this letter will reach you. We are exceedingly anxious about the fate of our friends. As for ourselves, we haven't yet seen a single Prussian, and I have been going into the forest for the last five or six days, since I have found some pretty huts to paint, which the people of our village had built to take refuge in, in case the enemy had come this way. In these late autumn days, the forest is very beautiful, which makes me think of the time when we used to make studies together at Long Rocher, with our fingers tingling with cold.

"The above letter, written on tracing-paper, is unreadable in parts," says M. Chardin, "and it is with the greatest difficulty that I have been able to make it out. To it was joined one from Mlle. Micas, whose bottle never reached me. These two letters were brought me by the Tours courier."

A letter from By, to Auguste Bonheur, who had retired, with his family and the two sons of his sister Juliette, to La Vandée, dated December 10, 1870, is as follows:

I received your letter the day before yesterday. It took ten days to come. My mind is fairly easy on your account. I quite

understand how anxious you must be about the others, in spite
of the news you send me. Direct information concerning them
I have not had for a long time, as I am now in the midst of the
invasion. For several days, we have heard the cannon booming
all around us, but are quite ignorant of what is the result; nor
can we say what will become of us. Up to now, however, we have
not suffered, except in mind. I fill up my time; and, in this
respect, am better off than you. Moreover, you must have a
great deal of expense, and without being able to earn anything.
With all your family on your hands, it must be a difficult thing
to live. I can't help thinking of Juliette. What a time she
must be having! I think, too, of old Tatan, who is no doubt
worrying. Poor old woman! I did not leave her enough money.
But surely Juliette will go and see her often. I don't know
whether this letter will reach you, but I trust so.

At the end of January, Paris surrendered and there was an
armistice of three weeks. Rosa Bonheur immediately sent Etienne
and the horse Roland with a wagon-load of provisions for her
relatives; in fact there was a perfect stream of trains and wagons
pouring into the starving capital. The following letter to Mme.
Peyrol was written about this time:

I am contriving to send you a basket in which you will find
a leg of mutton, a chicken, and a bit of cheese. I wanted to
present you also three sacks of potatoes and one of my sheep
whole. But I must wait, for you have no idea of the crowds of
people everywhere who are trying to express packages. And then
again, the charges are one hundred francs and the agents will give
no promise that what you commit to their care will ever reach
destination. Now, I can't send Roland off again just yet, but
I will do my best to do so at the first opportunity. By the bearer
of the things just mentioned, I am forwarding to you a little box
containing two hundred francs, for I am afraid you are penniless.
I myself have had to borrow to get you this money, for I, too, am
without a sou. Tatan must try to make last the two hundred
francs I sent her, for I don't know when I shall have any more cash.
Tell her to be patient. I hope I shall be able to make it up to

her for these bad times. Yet, my poor Sis, I am very much afraid the arts won't flourish for long months to come, either here or abroad. God grant, however, that matters in general may mend; for otherwise, what will become of us? Well, we must leave it to Him. My conscience tells me that I have acted all right.

If I can go and embrace you all, I will do so. But for the moment, you can't imagine the difficulties there are with the trains. Let us hope it will be more practicable in four or five days. I have forwarded the letter you sent addressed to Auguste, but I don't know whether it will reach him, as we are at the Prussians' mercy —slaves as much as we can be.

Much love to you, my poor sister, as well as to Isidore and all the household.

Four similar letters to Mme. Peyrol follow:

February 4, 1871: I am exceedingly anxious about you and the others. Yesterday I tried to send you a line and a leg of mutton by one of the men occupied in the carrying service. I am now profiting by the kindness of another good fellow. Try to let me have a line in return, and do your best to leave Paris, if this is possible, and come here. I know nothing of what is taking place. There are all sort of rumours. As for my going to Paris, myself, that appears to be out of the question. Otherwise I should have attempted it long ago. But anyway, I would have done no good in Paris, having no money, while here I could live on credit. If you will send me word to the effect that you can escape, I will go and meet you as best I can. Dear me! I don't know what to do. Love to you and poor Isidore and to all.

February 6: According to Auguste's last letter, dated January 15th, your children and the other relatives with him are all well. We send you what provisions we can. May God grant these misfortunes will soon be over. You must have had my last letter asking you to come here if you could. But I suppose it is hard for you to do so as none of you want to be parted. I have no money myself, so I can't offer you any, and I am quite aware how dear everything must be. All this makes me very wretched.

We are guarded by a few Prussians at Moret, Melun, and Montereau. The postal service has stopped and no money orders or checques can be sent or received. So Mme. Micas will soon be in the same mess as myself—i.e., with an empty purse.

There are fine days in store for us unless the scoundrels that dishonour France are soon ousted. Well, if we want to live without reproach, we must expect to suffer the more. The virtue of men has brought us to a pretty pass, from which it will be difficult to extricate ourselves except by a miracle, seeing that generosity doesn't walk about the streets, any more than it sits on thrones. Meanwhile, I thank the God of Battles that we have had no victims in our family, while so many are suffering and mourning for lost ones.

February 18: I am going to try and send you a haunch of deer which will be a feast for you. I have had it cooked, so that, if it should not reach you, it may not be spoilt; for just now, with meat so dear, it would be a pity if it did nobody good. For three days before the deer was killed, I was making sketches of him. I hope you will find the haunch a good one. A piece that I dined on was excellent, splendid meat and covered with fat. I am always trying by hook or by crook to send you provisions, which, judging from your letter, will be most welcome. The worst of it is that we can't send much at a time, and, as I have told you, even some of the things we send never get to you and come back to us. None the less, we mean to keep on trying. By the way, along with the haunch, you will find two dozen eggs and two boxes of grapes.

I have had a letter from Auguste. All are well. He tells me he had been thinking of going to Paris, but I see the poor fellow feels the same as Isidore, and I quite appreciate their sentiments; for like them, though I want to embrace you, I experience an insurmountable repugnance to pass through the enemy's lines. It appears that all sorts of vexations are inflicted on those who do pass. So I prefer to await the turn of events a little longer.

You are quite right to have taken up your painting again. It helps one to forget, if only for a moment. No one knows better than I what courage is needed to do this. I have worked nearly all the time, and have put together a number of studies wherewith to paint pictures later. As to painting any at present, this would be quite impossible for me, because I would have no heart in it. But I think I have got material to produce some fairly good ones when I can start once more. I have often worked under the impression that I should never live to finish them; for, if the enemy had come and annoyed us here, I was quite determined not to stand it, I assure you. To tell the truth, they haven't done much harm in our vicinity; a few insults and requisitions are the worst things that have happened. Still, there might have been a rumpus if these things had gone on.

It is heartrending to see our poor, beautiful France in the hands of enemies, who have been able to conquer her only by a shameful superiority of numbers—eight or ten to one, and who have been aided by the ignominious treachery that has caused some of our brave, betrayed one's to blow out their own brains; for, had we not been deceived and encouraged in our divisions, nothing could have vanquished the French race. But God knows where the hypocrites are, and they are revealed in spite of the pains they take to throw on others the responsibility for the harm they have done. History has already branded their names in letters of blood in the popular feeling, and their tricks are at present thrown open to the light of day. The more they try by underhand means to conceal their crimes, the deeper will they sink into the mire of shame that will overwhelm them in the near and far future.

You cannot imagine how all this has made me suffer and how I am still suffering through anxiety. Such things cannot be expressed in words, and the mark they make remains for life. But I find some comfort and thank God for it, that He has been so kind to us all through in preserving those who are dear to me, whether relatives or friends.

I am going to try and get a little money through good Mr. Gambart, who is always ready to act as my banker; and, as soon as possible I will pay Tatan's debts, and will help you, too, as best I can. Much love to you and Tatan and all the family.

March 1: I have just found another messenger, who is leaving for Paris in an hour's time. By him I am sending this

334

letter and two hundred francs, as I am afraid you are short of money.

I am much worried, for there are sad rumours abroad concerning Paris. The least insolence on the part of the Prussians may produce terrible consequences. You would have done better, all of you, to take refuge here, where we can live on what the soil yields and where we can defend ourselves, if this cursed war should go on. There is still time to make up your mind. Tatan could be brought, too. You could try the rail or I would send Roland for you. You might bring all your paraphernalia. Anyway, do what you think best. Perhaps you are freer from anxiety than I, being better acquainted with what is taking place.

I am concerned about many people in this wretched Paris, and should like to see them here, even if we had only potatoes to eat. I fear famine may return if the town is shut up again. If there are Prussians to be dressed down, it could be done just as well from here as from the capital. It will be terrible this time, for every one will be exasperated, and I believe that, in case of revolt, the German's blood will be mingled with ours; but there will be much more of theirs. The longer the crisis lasts, the greater the evil will grow. Misfortune will quicken the Gallic blood that still remains in the people's veins, and even without their leaders, the masses will rush to the assault and will overcome all obstacles.

My poor, dear sister, I only hope I am mistaken; and my most fervent wish is that nothing may happen and that this wretched peace may be signed. Otherwise there will be a general rising, which will prolong the misery.

Reflect and decide according to circumstances. Much love to you and all.

Writing from By to Isidore Bonheur, March 31, 1871, at the moment when the Commune was entering upon its most violent period, Rosa says:

A friend who has arrived from Paris, and who is returning this evening, has just informed me that things are taking a very bad turn in the city. I therefore write to urge you to come here, and to bring some wax with you. I have tools and even some recumbent plaster models which you might amuse yourself in finishing. If you prefer to go and stay with Auguste, do so, but don't stay in Paris. You may be forced to serve in the National Guard. Take my advice. It will render me so much easier in mind.

" My dear Rapin," she begins a letter to Paul Chardin, written at By, August 10, 1871, and continuing:

It is already some time since we have had the rascally Prussians on us. But, the day before yesterday, at Villeneuve St. Georges,[1] I had a closer view of them. I had indulged in a drive from Paris to the place just mentioned, for which I had been hankering for some time. Thinking I would lunch there, while waiting for the train that was to take me to Thomery, and so avoid the heat and arrive back home just in time for dinner, I entered the inn which seemed the cleanest. But lo and behold! there were a lot of Prussian officers. I politely said to the good inn-keeper's wife that I should infinitely prefer eating at her table, as she was just lunching in front of her counter. So I was soon installed in her company, eating my omelet. I quickly discovered that the worthy dame was as inquisitive as her class usually is, and eventually I had to tell her where I came from and where I was going. In the end, we found out that she was the daughter of one of my friends' nurses, and I was treated in consequence with every honour.

Perhaps this chapter cannot more fittingly end than with the following comment, by M. Chardin, on the foregoing letter:

As her letters abundantly show, Rosa Bonheur was very patriotic, and the misfortunes of France went to her heart. The civil war, which followed the German invasion of the country, increased her anguish and grief, yet without abating her energy and her passion for work. On May 10, 1871, Nathalie Micas

---

[1] A town about half way between Paris and Fontainebleau

wrote to me as follows: " Rosa is sometimes very poorly on account of the sad events through which we are passing. But she has never shown more energy. She is now preparing canvas and colours to go and paint studies in the forest. Painting is her only consolation."

CHAPTER XI

BOUGUEREAU once said to me, speaking of his early friend, Isidore Bonheur:

I have often noticed that animal artists are always tender and kind-hearted. I suppose this comes from close association with dumb beasts. This, too, was the side of Rosa Bonheur's character which generally showed itself to me in my contact with her.

And Jules Claretie has written me:

Rosa Bonheur once said to me: " To be loved by wild animals, you must love them." She adored La Fontaine and the good Cherville.[1] On one occasion when I visited By, I praised her for offering such a noble example of a retired life which was not an abandonment of the world at the same time; whereupon she answered: " Well, no, not exactly an example that has anything noble in it. The most that can be said is that it has got to be a habit. I deserve no praise for leading this life. I need the society of no one. I care nothing for the fashionable. What can the world do for me? A portrait painter has need of these things, but not I, who find all that is wanted in my dogs, my horses, my hinds, and my stags of the forest."

In collecting the materials for this work, I soon found, as was natural, that the section devoted to Rosa Bonheur's relations with

---

[1] The Marquis de Cherville (1821–98), who was much admired for his writings on animal and country life, many of which first appeared in the Paris *Temps*.

338

the animal kingdom grew more rapidiy than any other, and finally reached such proportions that it called for a chapter by itself. This is the chapter we have now reached, and here, more than else-were in this volume, I propose allowing the story to be told by Rosa Bonheur herself, in further letters, and by her friends in the reminiscences which they have kindly written out for me. I begin with the latter.

Hippolyte Peyrol, Sr., in the manuscript memoirs already quoted, says:

In one corner of the early studio of the Bonheur family in the Rue Rumford was a sort of closet, where was kept a goat which we children used to take out to graze in the Monceau Plain, now covered with busy streets and big houses. He was a real play-fellow to us. Later, when this goat died, his place was taken by two lambs. He often took part in our games, and, when we started out, would caper down the five flights of stairs, with evident pleasure. On these occasions, our favourite game was hide and seek and the goat actually participated. In that part of the Plain were a large number of water or gas pipes lying on the surface of the ground. They were our delight, as they offered fine hiding places. We would disappear into them like rabbits into their burrows, and it was funny indeed to see the goat spring from one pipe to another and look into the ends in order to see in which one we were hidden.

Behind the easel of M. Bonheur, in this studio, was a large-framed landscape, which he had exhibited at the Salon. Kiki, an uncaged squirrel, set to work one day to gnaw the cord, when, suddenly, the big canvas, frame and all, came down with a crash on the easel. Fortunately for M. Bonheur, he was absent at this moment, and only the picture was hurt. Henceforth, the squirrel, who was a charming tame little animal, had to be deprived of his liberty, much to Rosa's regret. He was put in a cage and removed from his favourite nest, which he had made in the hollow leg of a plaster cast of a woman, where he was very comfortably installed and where he always had a little store of provisions which he ate at his leisure.

Near her paint-box in this studio, Rosa Bonheur had a well-filled bird-cage, for, throughout her life, she loved these charming winged creatures and, during her declining days at By, often aided her faithful domestic, Céline Rey, in taking care of them.

In 1846 Rosa Bonheur made her first trip into Auvergne and brought back with her some quails, which she let loose in her chamber, the windows having been first covered with a wire screen. In order that the birds should be as contented as possible in their captivity, she arranged for them, in one corner of the room, a miniature garden with grass, heather and wild flowers, gathered by us in our walks. She used to enjoy seeing them frisk about the apartment and then take refuge in their garden. So satisfied was she with this first experiment that she decided to give liberty also to her caged birds. But at the end of a few days this experiment had to be abandoned as the whole room was kept in a continually dirty state. The fact is that if her father had let her have her way, Rosa would have turned this Rue Rumford house into a veritable menagerie.

Rosa Bonheur took the best of care of animals and was as much affected at seeing a dumb beast suffer as she would have been at the sight of a suffering human being. I recall, for instance, that, when we were living in the Rue Rumford, a basket of provisions, which had been sent us, was found to contain a live duck, that had to be killed for the spit. Rosa would let nobody but herself touch the bird, saying that she knew how to despatch it with the least suffering to the victim. So, armed with a hatchet, she cut off the head with one vigorous blow. But when the headless fowl, convulsively flapping its wings, began to fly about the room, the young girl was so moved that she nearly swooned and was ill the whole day.

Mlle. Keller relates a similar incident:

One of her horses had to be killed, for some reason that I forget. In such cases—I recall two—instead of leaving the matter to one of the two veterinarians whom she knew at Fontainebleau, she would do the disagreeable work herself, giving as the reason that she would see that " the poor animal suffered as little as possible." Though she was strong and brave at the moment of performing the unpleasant duty, it unnerved her afterward, and I have known her to feel the effects of this during three or four days.

Mme. Demont-Breton furnishes this anecdote in this same connection:

One day as we stood in front of the enclosure where one of her deer was browsing, Rosa Bonheur said: " My poor hind! Come to me, my poor old creature! You are very wretched, you are indeed! with your abscess over your left eye and your rheumatism in your right leg! Just look at her. She can hardly walk. She drags a twisted foot. And yet I have not the courage to kill her on account of the pictures I have painted of her or with her. I have fetched my gun twice to free her from her troubles. But then she looks at me with the only eye she has left and I carry away my gun again. Her male companion I shot because he had become dangerous. They are friends, don't you see? They have worked with me. I owe them half of what people are pleased to admire in my pictures. So they have to grow dangerous before I can bring myself to kill them. And yet it grieves me to see this one suffer."

Prince Georges Stirbey points out a delicate distinction which Rosa Bonheur made in this matter:

She was, indeed, very fond of animals; but here we see a strange contradiction in her nature. Though she adored them, when she saw them suffer or getting old, she had them killed, if they belonged to her. This last condition should be noted, for when the Countess de Moltke, wife of the Danish Minister to Paris, left her an old dog to care for, Rosa Bonheur nursed it till its death. She would put out of existence her own decrepit pets, but on no account would she treat in this same way an animal confided to her!

Mme. Lagrolet probably refers to this same animal in the following communication:

Her love of animals was intense and showed itself in many ways. I remember, for instance, that she had a very old dog which was blind and half paralysed. She was very careful of him and said to her servants: " If ever I find that that dog dies from lack of care, you will all leave immediately." As soon as the dog heard her voice, he would rush to her. My husband has seen her take a lion in her arms; a lioness put her paws on her shoulders and kiss her; and all the time, Rosa Bonheur did not show the slightest signs of fear. Sometimes when one of these beasts was lying at her feet and she wanted to get up, she would push him off with a vigorous kick exactly as if she had to do with a dog. I recall her two dogs Charlie and Daisy, long-haired animals, whom she used to put through a series of capers and tricks, ordering them about with a whip with a piece of paper attached to it.

M. Peyrol continues his souvenirs as follows:

Among other animals which she had in her Rue d'Assas studio were a big black he-goat, which she named Canfranc, a village in the Pyrenees, and an otter, both of which she had brought back from a stay which she made in those mountains. This otter was the despair of Mme. Micas, for he had the bad habit of leaving the water—Rosa had installed a tank for him—and getting in between the sheets of Mme. Micas's bed, so that all the bedclothes and even the mattress would sometimes be wet through. So Rosa was finally forced to restrict the animal's freedom.

To this studio returned one day a dog which she had given to a friend residing at Rambouillet, whither it had been taken by rail. The affectionate animal had come back all the way—some thirty miles—which deeply touched Rosa, as an evidence of fidelity, and also astonished her not a little, as an example of rare sagacity.

Much has been written about Rosa Bonheur and lions. Many of the things said are false and some are exaggerated. But the plain truth is sufficiently astonishing. Take, for instance, this touching anecdote related to me by Mme. Demont-Breton:

ROSA BONHEUR'S LOVE OF ANIMALS

Rosa Bonheur once told me the story of her two young lions. The male died first, quite young, of a disease of the spinal cord. But the female lived long enough to become attached to her mistress. " She was tender and as faithful as a dog," said Rosa; " sometimes she would stand on her hind legs and put her front ones on my shoulders in order to caress me more easily. But she fell ill of the same disease as her brother. I nursed her as if she had been a human being, going to see her and to comfort her several times a day. Once I found her so weak that I said to Georges Cain who was there: ' My poor lioness can't move; she is going to die.' A few moments later, I heard a velvet-soft step down in the hall. I went to see what it was, and found that it was my lioness, who, though dying, had made an effort to see me again for the last time. She knew I had gone upstairs. She heard my voice and had crawled on to the stairs in order to reach me. I went down a little way and she stopped. When I came to her, I took her in my arms and stroked her. She lay back and looked at me like a person who thinks, and died thus gazing on me. I believe in the good God and in his Paradise for the just, but I do not approve of everything in religion. For instance, I find it monstrous that animals should be said to have no soul. My lioness loved. She, therefore, had more soul than certain people who do not love."

Mlle. Keller relates:

I remember arriving at By one day when Nathalie, who was the first person I met, told me that Rosa was with the lions. " What! with the lions? " I exclaimed. " Yes," she answered; " come and see." So I went, and there in a wagon like a cage, separated into two parts, I found Rosa on one side of the dividing bars and the young lions on the other. She had on leggings that reached to her knees and gloves on her hands. She had me go up beside her and then told me how to feed wild beasts without exciting them. These lions were let loose later in an open courtyard where Rosa could sketch them. They gradually became very tame, so that their mistress, whom they were evidently fond of, could caress them.

343

REMINISCENCES OF ROSA BONHEUR

Jules Claretie writes me:

One day Rosa Bonheur had to be separated from her lion Nero. The horses which were to pull the wagon to Paris trembled with fear at the odour of a carnivorous animal. Nero himself was sad as if he divined that he was to be separated from his mistress. While his cage was being boarded up, he turned an enquiring look, with his yellow eyes, on Rosa Bonheur, and when the wagon began to roll away, those eyes filled with tears. The poor beast was taken to the Garden of Plants, where an ophthalmia soon set in and he became quite blind. Rosa Bonheur once visited him there in his public cage, and calling out " Nero," the faithful lion recognised her voice, sprang to his feet and tried to discover his old mistress.

M. Grivot once said to me:

At one time Rosa Bonheur had a complete menagerie in her home: a lion and lioness, a stag, a wild sheep, a gazelle, horses, etc. One of her pets was a young lion whom she allowed to run about and often romped with—a source of continual alarm to me. She used to laugh at my fears. But I confess I was easier in mind when this leonine pet gave up the ghost. Had he survived much longer, I believe some accident would certainly have befallen my old friend.

Henri Cain has said to me:

Rosa Bonheur adored animals. I remember seeing in her grounds at By, stags, mouflons, wild boars, and other large animals, while among the smaller ones were young lions and lionesses, which finally became pretty large, however, though they continued to be nice and gentle; and they all, great and small, moved about in perfect liberty. I recall how, on one occasion, Nathalie and Rosa doctored an ill lion during a whole month, performing operations of a most intimate character, caring for him just as she would have cared for a child. It was most touching to see the poor animal lick Rosa's hand when she was relieving his pain. She was like a regular hospital nurse at this time, and was deeply

344

afflicted when the poor beast died in her arms, looking tenderly into her face.

Dogs and birds she always had in large numbers. She was often literally surrounded with bird-cages and took personal care of their inmates, even cleaning the cages and preparing herself their food. During the nest-making season, she would go the rounds of the garden to see that no cats were prowling about, armed with a small gun, in order to inspire them with fear. But the worst she would ever do to them was to shout "Scat!" And then, when they slunk away, she would stand in admiration of their graceful movements.

Several of her friends dwell on Rosa Bonheur's interest in and knowledge of horses. Thus, M. Alexandre Jacob writes me:

Rosa Bonheur's passion for animals is so well known that it is almost superfluous for me to allude to it. This passion, it is true, had its caprices. While, perhaps, horses were her especial favourites, she sometimes transferred her affections to other species. There would be a period during which lions were in favour, then boars, then stags. One stag, Jacques, remained with her to an extreme old age. Among the guests of her miniature zoölogical gardens was an eagle. For twelve months she kept three wild horses presented to her by an American gentleman, and named by her Clair-de-lune, Andrès, and Apache, respectively. One of these involved her in an accident in which she had a narrow escape of her life. Indeed, her accidents with horses were fairly frequent. Right up to the very last, she insisted upon driving, and in several of her spills she managed to get considerably bruised. Of course, when she mounted horseback, she disdained a side-saddle and rode as a man.

Mme. Achard says:

Rosa Bonheur rode very well, and always astride. She had a mare that she was very fond of, that was very friendly with her and came to her whenever she called. It would rear up, put its hoofs on her shoulders and actually kiss her. It would take a piece of sugar from her mouth so gently as not to touch her face. When the mistress went to her room, the mare would follow, going upstairs and putting its head through a little window in the dressing-room and then stand and stare at her with a pecu-

ROSA BONHEUR AND HER SHETLAND PONIES.

liarly pleased expression in its intelligent face. When the feeling of curiosity and friendship was satisfied, the animal would turn around and walk quietly downstairs again. The performances of this mare were really extraordinary.

Rosa Bonheur also had some rather wonderful little ponies which would run around you like dogs, when you took a walk in the woods; and if you held out a bunch of flowers, they would come up and eat them in a perfectly docile manner.

Paul Chardin has much to say about Rosa Bonheur's love of horses. Thus, he writes me:

She liked horses as much as she did dogs, and every day, when her work was done, she harnessed or mounted her old mare Margot. However, she never cared for thoroughbreds and never studied them. Country horses were her favourite subjects for painting. The following letter from her to me should be read in this connection:

By, June 28, 1868: My poor Rapin, I hear you have had a fall from your horse. I advise you to sell your mare, which, one day or another, will break your neck. Although you are a good horseman, you are too often absorbed by your studies of nature, and then, neither you nor your servant can give your mad beast enough exercise. What she wants is at least ten leagues a day. I know her. Buy a good little animal of the old French stock, either from Limousin or Tarbes, or else a Norman half-blood; and don't bother with your old race-hacks who are always on wires with their greyhound legs and body. Man is not built for riding on greyhounds, but on horses that are shaped in proper proportion, supple in their movements, graceful under the bridle, without any dare-deviltry. That's my opinion, anyway.

In 1869, replying to a letter I had addressed to her from Brittany, she wrote:

I am acquainted with the Carhaix race of horses, as I have been in those parts; and you know, my Rapin, that I have an eye for the various races of horses, animals that I am quite as fond of as you are, which establishes one more resemblance between us, excepting always the moustaches, the ears, and the height.

With advancing years, Rosa Bonheur's taste for riding horseback grew less, and at the end of 1869 she wrote me about a martingale she had asked me to get her for her saddle-horse:

However, there is no need to hurry, since I am not much in the humour for riding horseback at present. I feel weaker and much older, my good Rapin; and I am not sorry, for I am still more morally than physically tired of life. I ask no better fate than to quit this world, only I should rather like, before letting go of art, to make her feel something of bit and bridle. Anyway, I am very weak.

Writing from Nice, January 4, 1885, to Major Rousseau, Rosa Bonheur says:

I may tell you, since we are speaking about horses, that M. de Montgomery, who, I believe, is still living at Fontainebleau, wanted to give me his magnificent black horse, Solferino. The animal is of Russian origin, and you must know how celebrated his beauty is. I did not accept him as a gift, but I hope, on my return, to make studies of this animal.

To the same, from By, May 27, 1885:

I have just written to my brother-in-law asking that the bronze representing a horse, which I shall have the pleasure of offering as a prize for the officers' race, be finished as soon as possible. I think that a good idea of yours to call it the By Prize and not the Rosa Bonheur Prize. The latter would have been somewhat childish and, at the same time, pretentious. You forgot, however, to tell me the date of the race. But I don't fancy this need be put on the socle.

These notes about Rosa Bonheur and horses may end with this curious letter addressed, from Nice, in 1882, to her brother Isidore:

Thanks for your kind letter, my dear old Dodore, to which I reply at once in order to tell you to change nothing in your horses. The hack always starts from the right, for the simple reason that, like us, the right side of horses is always the stronger. In a state of nature, it is always to the right that the gallop bears. Ask any one who has to do with horses, except a hostler, if this is not so. Or, still better, write to M. Rousseau, the military veterinary, or, which is even still better, go and see him at Fontainebleau. He has always been expecting to see you and has spoken of you to the chief riding-master of the military school there. The riding-school is open every day. Go and sleep at M. Bourdon's at By and make an appointment with M. Rousseau. There's no difficulty.

Your old Zaza to her old Silly-billy.

ROSA BONHEUR'S LOVE OF ANIMALS

Rosa Bonheur's interest in animals comes out strongly in the following series of notes to Mme. Borriglione. The first two, from Nice, run thus:

May 11, 1883: I have received, as you must know, the fine mouflon you were good enough to give me. I installed her last evening and I think she passed a good night. I have just visited her and she appears to me to have a gentle disposition. She is quite willing to be caressed. I think we will become good friends, and once at By, she will have a happy time of it. Unless I am greatly mistaken, and I sincerely hope I am not, she is going to have little ones; for I should like to have them to paint. I feel sure that I could eventually get them as tame as little lambs. I have given the future mother some green herbs, which she seemed to enjoy. In a word, dear Madam, you have caused me great pleasure in sending me this animal, which I have so long desired to have. I shall find it much nicer to paint than the chamois, which, however, are also very fine. By the way, the men who brought her would take nothing.

May, 1883: As you are kind enough to invite us to dine with you before we leave for Paris, we will come at 6.30 and bring Niniche [1] with us.

I can't express to you all the pleasure you have given me in sending me this Corsican mouflon, an animal I have so long desired to possess, so as to make studies of it. It is such a charming animal to paint, perched up on its rocks.

Writing from By, she continues:

May 26, 1885: The mouflons, man and wife, still get on nicely. The first is mild and tame, which is not always the case with those gentlemen. The two together make a very charming household and are certainly as happy as possible. They have grass to eat and it is a real pleasure to watch them. They will be of great use to me, for I am still possessed of the idea of going to Corsica some day in order to sketch the rocks of that country,

---

[1] A favourite dog.

so as to be able to give local colour to the pictures which I wish to put them in.

July 29, 1885: The mouflon and his wife get on nicely together. They are both very gentle. As soon as it gets warmer, I intend to make their portraits.

January 4, 1886: This year we will spend but a little while in Nice, for the bringing up of two lions takes much of our time. We find them more frank, more grateful—these wild beasts—than are most human beings.

January 19, 1886: We are kept here by some art work which I wish to finish and also by the bringing up of the two young lions, which are veritable darlings. If we go this winter to Nice, we will bring them along with us in the train.

May 8, 1886: My good lions welcomed me and Nathalie home again from Nice, and here I am amidst all my animals once more.

May 20, 1888: Ratata [1] is in liberty on the roof and in the garden. In the evening, she comes home and does up my hair. I think she takes me for an old male of her kind. Gamine [2] is lording it over Bellotte [3] and Ulm.[4] She makes them accept her as the favourite of their mistress, just like an old house servant.

The following series of notes to Major Rousseau present still another view of Rosa Bonheur's intimacy with animals:

November 25, 1880: I have bought in Paris, from M. Rivière, two horses that I should be very glad to show you. One of them is for my carriage. It is a colt that will want a good deal of care for some time, I think; and is rather big, as I like horses. The other is a stallion which has gained a great many prizes as a fine specimen of draught-horse. I had him from the stud-stables

---

[1] A favourite monkey.   [2] A very small short-haired slut.
[3] A much larger yellow basset slut.   [4] A big Danish dog.

of the State, and intend to use him chiefly as a model. But as he is very quiet, he will do for domestic work.

During visits to Nice, she sends him the following notes:

March 11, 1881: My servant, Céline, has written to me about the trouble given by my little bitch Bellotte. I think she is going to have pups, the father being Charbonnier. I am rather pleased than otherwise, as the little ones will be a good mixture, and may turn out good shooting-dogs, with keen scent, both of them.

March 27, 1881: The manager of the *Farm Yard Journal*, M. Manger, wrote me a few days ago that he had another chamois to send me. [He had already sent her one which reached By in a dying state.] I wrote back saying that orders had been given for its reception. M. Manger has written me another very courteous letter to tell me that he will send some one with this animal to By. If you have a moment to spare, I should like you to see it.

April 27, 1881: I have just heard from M. Manger, who announces the arrival of the male chamois he had promised, to replace the other one he sent and which reached me, half dead. I think he is an honest man, who himself was taken in. As you kindly promised to examine this one, I let you know at once of its arrival. I enclose the letter, stating the price—416 francs. The other cost me 500 francs, which I have of course lost. Now, the essential thing is that the animal should be in good condition and not too wild. Please keep the letter, for I shan't pay, this time, until the chamois is definitely installed, safe and sound, in my park.

February 25, 1882: Thanks for attending to my old Pastour. The silly old dog would do much better not to trouble his head about that little minx Bellotte. I hope Céline and Etienne will stop her nonsense and shut her up in a kennel on a water diet. If she is to be allowed a gallant, only one pup must be kept.

December 26, 1882: Here we are and somewhat rested. I hope my old Nathalie will be able to get up to-morrow and enjoy

24   351

the beautiful, mild weather we have here. As for me, I am already up and doing. To-day, I intend to give an airing to my horse, who arrived here in good fettle. The oats at this place are white, but very big, and contain a good deal of meal, so that twelve litres do the horse as much good as fourteen of the nasty small oats gaffer Etienne buys me. Then, at noon, I get the hostler to give him a certain affair which feeds horses well, and, after, some hay and chaff, as usual. With that, he is ready to dance.

The mouflon referred to in the next note is the same as that mentioned in the preceding correspondence with Mme. Borriglione:

May 17, 1883: We are preparing for our departure, along with my horse and a female mouflon. I want the latter to be taken out of her box as soon as she arrives, as she is sure to be tired and will have little ones soon, I believe. We may stop over at Marseilles for a day or two. I should be very much obliged to you also, my dear M. Rousseau, if you would kindly superintend the arrival of my horse at Fontainebleau and see if he has been in a good box, as I am paying for first-class accommodations for him.

Major Rousseau writes the following comment on the foregoing letter:

On arriving, the mouflon sprang out of the box and, falling upon something pointed, was badly wounded in the chest. The whole of the right lung protruded from its cavity. The animal was wrapped up in wet towels and, two hours later, I was able to wash the lung with spring water and put it back into the chest cavity, completing the operation by a suture. Six weeks later, she gave birth to a fine little male mouflon.

Here may be given a collection of letters, each written at By, from Rosa Bonheur to various friends of hers, all of which refer, almost wholly, to her animals or her ideas concerning animal life. The one, addressed January 2, 1861, to M. Mène, the sculptor, is first given:

ROSA BONHEUR'S LOVE OF ANIMALS

My worthy old and good Friend: I have just received your portrait of my little Wasp. Nothing could give me more pleasure. You are indeed the nicest of men and of friends. I suppose you know that I have lost the poor little original, whose body I have laid away in a corner of the garden. So does everything pass away. I have kept one of her pups. But it is not the same thing, my friend, it is not the same thing. So your gift becomes doubly precious, and on account of its pretty dedication, too.

A happy New Year and lots of good health. Love to all.

To Joseph Verdier, June 26, 1882:

Thanks very much for your kind invitation to go and see you at your mill. We will write later on about that for just now I am taken up with my chamois or Pyrenean izards. I have two females that have each a little one, and I am perhaps the first person who has obtained such a result with tame chamois. I am consequently making studies of the little ones. They are charming creatures.

To Auguste Cain, in 1885:

I wanted to write to you sooner to tell you that the villainous little parrots, which you have been kind enough to give me, have arrived in perfect health. The sight of the verdure has given them matrimonial ideas and I write to ask you to have me made a small nest, as soon as possible. I have a big cage that I have put them in temporarily. By the way, if I remember rightly, your cage is a brass one. If you haven't ordered mine, I should prefer an iron one, but of the same shape and size as yours. The plumage of my pretty little creatures has become most beautiful under the influence of the air, no doubt. They may fly about as they please. When you come, you will see what good care I take of them.

You know that the soup of friendship and the rabbit of fraternity are always awaiting you. So come without ceremony, whenever you feel inclined.

You ask me the price of my drawing. It is 2,000 francs. It is now at the picture framer's.

REMINISCENCES OF ROSA BONHEUR

A note of April 9, 1892, to M. Grivot, runs thus:

My poor little dog is dead. I feel very lonely without her, as she was a souvenir of my dear Nathalie and was also my little companion during my walks. Alas! I can't bring her back again, and so I shall have to bear the loss.

To Georges Cain:

April 27, 1897: My gardener has found a nest of blue-headed tom-tits, such as you want. He is waiting for the time when the little ones can be best taken.

Of these tom-tits which were reared by Rosa Bonheur only three reached Paris. One of these, M. Cain tells me, died very soon; the second lived for two years, and the third flourished for a long time thereafter. "It was very pretty, very lively, quite a little glutton, and very choleric." Concerning them Rosa wrote these two letters, one to M. Cain and the other to his wife.

June 15, 1897: I see by your card that you are installed at the Carnavalet Museum, where this letter will doubtless find you. Let me tell you, my dear friend, that, notwithstanding my success in Paris [1] and the enthusiasm it has aroused, life is not all rose-coloured at By. Just when I want my servants most, Céline is ill, and has been so ever since the pastel exhibition conferred the artist's laurels on Rosa Bonheur! So I've got not only to answer letters of flattery and cards written in heroic style, not only to return visits of ceremony, but to think of my birds from four o'clock in the morning till ten in the evening, and to look after my dogs who are neglected by my man, Jules. In my studio, it is stiflingly hot. I am done up, tired to death, worn out, and cannot reply to so many people at once. That's why I have not written to you sooner.

Now I want to ask you why my fine Georges has become a tom-tit fancier—a hobby more suitable for a pretty woman. What

---

[1] An exhibition of her pastels at the Georges Petit Gallery.

a funny idea to take a liking for birds of this kind! They are hard to rear and a good deal of care is required in feeding them; otherwise they soon die. I should like to know if you have any cages that would do for three blue-headed tom-tits and five black-headed ones. There must be two cages or else they would kill each other. Let me add that, Céline being in bed and the house upset, I cannot receive any one just now, but can send you the birds. I will tell you when you must give them fresh paste, for the German paste is not sufficient, and it would not do to let such dear little birds starve. Renew the paste twice a day; give them some milk sop; then mix the bread dipped in water with chopped meat that has been cooked. Occasionally a little salad will be good; but keep it fresh, or you will kill the poor wee birdies. I am going to let people suppose that I have gone to the sea-side, so as to be able to remain quiet at By. Write to me, therefore, if you want your little birds, who have got their first feathers and will soon be quite pretty when autumn comes. Your old Rosa Bonheur, first rate artist and a friend of birds.

July 7, 1897: I am still up to my eyes in writing letters of thanks for the congratulations I have received, and have besides to get the house straight, which wanted cleaning on account of the moths. As soon as I am a little quieter, I shall request the honour of receiving Sire Marie Louis XIII,[1] and my Lord, the Curator of Carnavalet de Sévigné.[2]

Are the little birds dead yet? Anyway, I treated your dear Céline[3] as well as I could, so that she might be kind to my nursling, only one of which, by the way, has a blue head. I have no mind to rear any more tom-tits to please your husband.

Love to you both.

---

[1] Rosa Bonheur had found in a treatise on equitation, by Pluvinel, a portrait of Louis XIII which much resembled Mme. Georges Cain.

[2] Georges Cain was curator, as has already been said, of the Carnavalet Museum which occupies the house formerly inhabited by Mme. de Sévigné.

[3] Georges Cain's servant, who went to By to get the birds, and not to be confused with Rosa Bonheur's servant of the same name.

REMINISCENCES OF ROSA BONHEUR

To Mme. Lagrolet, February 5, 1894:

I am quite well myself, though I have just had a fresh affliction. I have just lost my nice affectionate bitch. She died after an operation the veterinarian was obliged to make, because she had a dead little one inside her body, which poisoned her. The whole affair has caused me considerable sorrow, and for the moment your cousin is a dog's nurse. I am bringing up on a bottle a little pup of this same unfortunate mother, and I spend the night giving it milk. Here you have one of the results of being a great artist who cares nothing about the grandeurs of this world, and who finds, unfortunately, that the human race generally is not worth as much as the dumb animals. If we did not have good friends here below, it would be a real bit of good fortune never to come on to this earth, where, by the way, a people finds amusement in watching the procession of the queen of the washerwomen after having cut off the head of a true queen.[1] Such a people is very ill; is, in fact, going to the devil! In the meanwhile, I am a dog's mother, and, what's more, I hope to save my daughter.

The following group of notes, some of them without date, addressed to M. or Mme. Joseph Verdier, all touch on Rosa Bonheur's shooting proclivities. The first, dated July 31, 1859, is as follows:

I have a little service to ask of you, if it can be granted, that is, if you have not got rid of your dog. I am going to spend a few days shooting with the Paleys. Could you lend me one of your dogs for these few days? You know I shall take care of the animal and not run it so as to make it thin. I might have borrowed young Mr. Penn's bitch, but she is just going to have some little ones. As for my own bitch, somebody stole her from me in Paris. I will answer for your dog, as I shall have it in leash.

---

[1] The reference is to Marie Antoinette and to the present Mardi Gras carnival, when the chief attraction of the procession is the young washerwoman who has been chosen by the other washerwomen as their "queen" for this fête.

She continues the correspondence:

August, 1859: Nellie is with me. She arrived all right, but is a little out of her element and in the dumps. She none the less made a good meal and is going to sleep on my rug. I hope that with a few caresses she will soon be at home. Don't trouble about her. She shan't leave me. She won't stay long and I will write to you the day I start her off again. Nathalie is going to look after her as well as I, so you may be sure she will be better cared for than if she were my own.

August 16, 1859: I suppose you have received my letter in time. But I repeat that it is on the 17th that Nellie leaves. I will bring her by the through train. Be kind enough to meet her at Blois. Thanks once more for lending me the fine, dear creature.

To Mme. Verdier:

My sister is coming to spend Sunday with me and will be commissioned to tell you by word of mouth how much I regret not being able to bring my gun and massacre all your husband's game, to get your brother to give me some music, and, in a word, to come among my kind old friends.

Again she writes these two notes without date to M. Verdier, this time from By:

Could you find me a small dog, male or female, for coursing rabbits? My dogs are no good and I want to get rid of them. If one of your neighbours had one to dispose of, or some game-keeper, it would be cheaper than buying from a gamekeeper here, in spite of the journey. You might address the animal here to the care of M. Peyrol, who would go to the station and get it.

You are a good friend. A thousand thanks for complying so readily with my request. I shall be delighted to have the dog from the worthy M. de Belling.[1] I want to do a little more shooting,

---

[1] Master of the Hounds of the Forest of Russy hunt, near Blois.

for I peg away at my work and don't get enough exercise. So I intend to have one afternoon's outing each week, to keep from becoming too heavy, my tilbury being somewhat favourable to stoutness.

And finally, August 15, 1863, to Mme. Verdier:

Tell your husband I have just received a letter from Dr. Lacorbière of the Papal States, which convinces me the poor man is quite losing his wits. He wants me to be painted by his side with my brothers and M. Verdier, in hunting costume and on horseback, with the Master of the Hounds, de Belling. Does he wish to offer to the Holy Father a picture of a meeting of papists, under the protection of St. Hubert? I shall keep the letter, which deserves to be framed.

Henri Cain writes me as follows concerning Rosa Bonheur and the chase:

She used to say that she loved hunting and shooting, but she never profited much by the Imperial permission to shoot over certain preserves of the Fontainebleau forest. She had her shooting traps and she would kill a rabbit now and then. She had her beagles, just as we have our pet dogs, chiefly for amusement. But she really never did much hunting or shooting for the simple reason that she adored animal life, and the idea of killing anything was repugnant to her very nature. While it is quite true that she enjoyed following the hounds, she never carried sport to an excess. She would sometimes talk of her prowess as a huntress, but I do not remember ever having seen her fire a gun, and yet I knew her from my very infancy. In 1870, however, she was quite ready to shoot a Teuton!

The friends of Rosa Bonheur do not all agree in the matter of her taste for cynegetics. Some, like M. Henri Cain, would have us believe that she could say with Shelley:

> No bright bird, insect, or gentle beast,
> I consciously have injured, but still loved
> And cherished these my kindred.

This, however, is not strictly exact, as the reader has already perceived both in this chapter and in other parts of this book. " I have killed a rabbit and a barn-door owl who was imprudent enough to walk out in the sun," she wrote one day to M. Grivot. She sometimes carried her love for the chase even into the smallest details. Her nephew, whom I have so often quoted, writes me: " Rosa Bonheur had some ideas of her own concerning her hunting traps. Thus, she wished to have sole care of her heavy hunting boots. She would always grease them herself, declaring that ' nobody else knew how to do it thoroughly and properly '; and then she would add: ' In the chase, as in many other things, " Style makes the man." ' "

M. Peyrol then continues:

Rosa Bonheur had a passion for shooting. During the closing years of the Second Empire, she was given a special permit to shoot over a large section of the forest, not far from By, for rabbits. Within a sandy triangle, covered with oaks, pines, and thick heather; and bounded by the Route Ronde, the road from Fontainebleau to Moret, and the Route de Sorgues, with the Croix de Montmorin at one corner, the Croix du Grand Maître at another corner, and the Carrefour des Sentiers d'Avon in the middle, here Rosa Bonheur at a certain period of her life would shoot two or three times a week, from the beginning of September to the end of November. With her dogs Caressant, the gift of the Count d'Armillé; Ramoneau and Ravaude, the son and daughter of Caressant, Rosa Bonheur would spend hours at a time, generally accompanied by her brother-in-law, my father, both eagerly on the lookout for rabbits. Occasionally a deer or a pheasant would come within range, and it required not a small effort of the will to let them go untouched; for the Imperial permit allowed her to kill rabbits only. She was a good shot, and generally returned to By with a bag of seven or eight rabbits. More than one of the present inhabitants of Thomery and By will tell you that their fathers were the shooting companions of Rosa Bonheur.

To Hippolyte Peyrol, Sr., Rosa Bonheur wrote on September 13, 1866:

I am forced to announce to you the disagreeable news that we no longer have the right to shoot in the forest. Yesterday the old brigadier came with this yarn, to wit, that the ranger now grants only the shooting with setters. I told him he might go to the devil, and begged him to say as much to the ranger, his men, and the dogs, too. Thereupon, I folded up my license and sent it back to the general secretary with a line of thanks in my fashion. So you see, my dear brother-in-law, we are stumped. I am sorrier for you than for myself. Anyway, my fine gun is hung up until next year, when I intend to hire a shooting box for the three of us. So now when you come over, you will have to prowl about the common until something better is available.

Her cousin, Mme. Lagrolet, presents the other side in these lines:

I do not think she really cared very much about shooting. It was a subject I never heard her speak about. Whatever liking she had for it was largely due to the fact that it took her into her beloved forest. Ah! for that forest of Fontainebleau, for that her heart was always warm.

Mlle. Keller relates this anecdote:

Rosa Bonheur was unquestionably a good shot. I remember one day being out in the field across the road from her grounds, when suddenly off went her gun so close to me that I started. " Don't fear," she said to me, smiling; " I haven't killed the little wren," as she nicknamed me. It was a wild rabbit at the other end of the field that she had hit.

M. de Pétigny de St. Romain, son of the Member of the Institute and French historian who died in 1858, gives me this description of one of Rosa Bonheur's favourite hunting-grounds:

Of all the meets in the neighbourhood of Blois, the best for the onlooker, who wishes to get a good idea of a deer hunt, is that of the Croix Pineau, in the forest of Russy. In the middle of this large open space—this carrefour—stands a white sign-post which gives the names of the eight forest roads radiating from this point and leading to the neighbouring country seats, Beauregard, Clénord, etc. These roads run, as far as the eye can reach, over a perfectly flat wooded plain. Consequently, a person standing at this sign-post during a hunt can, with the naked eye or by the aid of a field-glass, see pass eight times the stag, the hounds and the huntsmen. So Rosa Bonheur, wishing to study the movements of the fleeing deer, the pursuing dogs and the leaping horses, could not have chosen a better spot than this Croix Pineau Carrefour, whence could often be seen, at the end of the chase, the stag taking refuge in the Beuvron River in front of the Château of Clénord, a stirring sight which must have suggested many fresh ideas to the grand artist.

I very well recall, though it happened a half century ago, the first time Rosa Bonheur, attired in her masculine costume, came to hunt with us. At the dinner which followed, but which she did not attend, M. de la Corbière, the President of our Society, drank to her health and said he felt sure that the day's sport was to live in some form or other. I am, perhaps, the only survivor of that memorable meet, which, by the way, was a most brilliant one in every respect.

The picture is completed by this note on another hunt sent me by Mme. René Fouret:

Toward the end of her life, I was present on one occasion at a meet in Fontainebleau forest at the moment of the kill, when I noticed there Rosa Bonheur attired in a black velvet skirt, a sack-coat like a man's of the same material and a dark felt hat. Her white hair cut short, and her dark, lively piercing eyes, made an impression on me that I have never forgotten. She was indeed " the Diana of Fontainebleau."

CHAPTER XII

OTHER MENTAL AND PERSONAL TRAITS

I PROPOSE giving in this closing chapter conversations, memoranda, and letters from the friends of Rosa Bonheur, all bearing on her mental and personal characteristics. In so far as possible I leave the stage entirely to them, and though, now and then, the same statement is repeated, I have thought it best to let the documents stand as written. Furthermore, I feel certain that the reader, after perusing these various and varied reminiscences, will shut this volume with a pretty thorough and exact idea of the appearance, mind, and tastes of Rosa Bonheur.

An external and material thing contributed largely to the notoriety of Rosa Bonheur. I refer to her assuming masculine attire. Yet here, as in so much else published concerning her, there was a good deal of exaggeration. Thus, M. Louis Passy writes: "Much has been said about Rosa Bonheur wearing man's dress. Now, curiously enough, I cannot recall ever having seen her so attired. When she came to Gisors she always wore a sort of Brittany costume. Even at By, the only masculine garment in her get-up, as I remember her, was a kind of sack-coat. When I was there, she always had on a skirt, just like every other woman." And the elder Peyrol adds: "Rosa Bonheur at least was not coquettish. Provided she had a decent and comfortable gown, she was satisfied. She cared nothing about jewels, and would have given all the finery in the world for an animal that she wanted." M. Eugène d'Eichthal's recollections do not differ much on this point from those of his fellow member of the Institute, M. Louis

Passy: "When we were children, my sister and myself, Rosa Bonheur often dined with my father and mother, and, after the meal, she would draw pictures for our amusement. She was then dressed in a perfectly plain skirt and a sort of dark blouse. Her hair was worn just like a boy's, and I always remarked that in her studio she looked still more like a young man." "When Rosa Bonheur went to Paris or out in society," M. Paul Chardin explains, "she always put on woman's clothes, which consisted generally of a black silk gown and a rather long cloak of the same material. On grand occasions she would sometimes display all her orders on her breast, which made one think that she might be some great general or high functionary." Her cousin, Mme. Lagrolet, adds a few particulars: "Her shirt was more like a night dress, with its unstarched collar and cuffs. She used to say that starched collars and cuffs worried her. I always remarked that she seldom wore gloves."

The elder Peyrol explains as follows how it was that Rosa Bonheur began to don masculine garments:

When engaged in painting the "Horse Fair," she went often to the Paris Tattersall's of that day. Then were repeated the same disagreeable experiences as at the slaughter-houses in the earlier period of her career, and, as she could not hope to find a second Father Emile, the thought occurred to her to assume man's attire. Her strong face and short hair lent themselves to this disguise and its trial proved a complete success. Rosa was everywhere taken for a young man and no attention was paid to her comings and goings.

A short time before this, she had met at a friend's house M. Monval, the Police Commissioner of her ward, and she asked him to aid her to obtain a regularly authorised permit to wear male attire. He made the necessary application to the Prefect of Police and it was granted. Thenceforth, Rosa Bonheur dressed as a man almost continuously at home and when she went out on horseback, though in the streets of Paris she wore a gown.

A fac-simile of this permit is given on the next page.

PRÉFECTURE DE POLICE.

PERMISSION
DE TRAVESTISSEMENT.
(renouvellement)

Paris, le 12 Mai 1857.

Taille 1 m. 10 c.ᵐ.
âgée de 2 ans
Cheveux *châtains*
Sourcils *id*
Front *ordinaire*
Yeux *bruns*
Nez *ordinaire*
Bouche *moyenne*
Menton *rond*
Visage *ovale*
Teint *ordinaire.*

Signes particuliers :

Signature du porteur.

NOUS, Préfet de Police,

Vu l'ordonnance du 16 brumaire an IX (7 novembre 1800);

Vu le Certificat du Sʳ *Cazalis, Docteur* demeurant *en médecine de la Faculté de Paris,*

Vu en outre l'attestation du Commissaire de Police de la section du *Luxembourg,*

AUTORISONS la Demoiselle *Rosa Bonheur,* demeurant à *Paris, rue d'Assas,* nº *32,* à s'habiller en homme, pour *raison de santé* sans qu'elle puisse, sous ce travestissement, paraître *aux Spectacles, Bals et autres lieux de réunion ouverts au public.*

La présente autorisation n'est valable que pour *six* mois, à compter de ce jour.

Pour le Préfet de Police,

et par son ordre,

LE SECRÉTAIRE-GÉNÉRAL,

LE CHEF DU 2ᵉ BUREAU
DU SECRÉTARIAT-GÉNÉRAL.

POLICE PERMIT FOR MALE ATTIRE.

364

OTHER MENTAL AND PERSONAL TRAITS

Henri Cain writes:

Rosa Bonheur worked in her studio attired in a large blue blouse, trimmed with narrow white braid, which was slightly open at the neck, while the sleeves were drawn tight around the wrists. She generally wore trousers of a dark-reddish shade, made large and loose, from the bottom of which you could just see sticking out her little feet; for Rosa Bonheur had extremely delicate hands and feet. Her hands, which were well formed and agreeable to the eye, were just suited for jewels, but her fingers were always without rings. She was very proud of these hands, the only bit of coquettishness I ever saw in Rosa Bonheur.

When, in the evening, she went out for a promenade in the forest, when she came back and sauntered about through the fields of By and Thomery, the peasants returning from their day's labour would bow to this " little man with his fine white locks," who somewhat resembled, but in miniature, dear old Corot.

Sometimes persons foreign to the region, who chanced that way, would ask: " Who is that little gentleman whom everybody is bowing to? " And the reply would come: " That little gentleman, why, it's Mademoiselle Bonheur." And all the country roundabout adored her.

Rosa Bonheur was a woman full of energy, and men's clothes on her were on the right person, for she had a stout heart.

Joseph Verdier writes:

On one occasion Rosa Bonheur had come to visit me at Cour-Cheverny for the purpose of being introduced to Miss Charlotte Halcott, the daughter of an English officer, Major Halcott, whom I was about to marry. It was in the spring, and I proposed a drive to the ladies. " All right," said Rosa; " I will put on my man's dress and be your coachman, so that you can chat to your betrothed undisturbed." On our return, I set the ladies down at some distance from the house, so that they might gather flowers, while I went an errand. In the evening, Rosa and Miss Halcott went out again together, the former still in her male attire. The next day, Mrs. Halcott received a visit from a lady of the neighbourhood, whom she knew, and who came to tell her how exceedingly improper it was for an engaged young lady to allow herself to be accompanied out by another young man and especially one of handsome appearance!

On another occasion, after my marriage, when Rosa Bonheur was riding out with me, but this time in lady's dress, we happened to meet a gentleman friend of mine. He remarked in fun: " Mme. Verdier is unwise to let you two ride out together. In her place, I shouldn't be tranquil." " Oh, my dear Sir," replied Rosa Bonheur, whom the banter by no means offended, " if you only knew how little I care for your sex, you wouldn't get such queer ideas into your head. The fact is, in the way of males, I like only the bulls that I paint."

Consuélo Fould tells this anecdote:

One day in Paris, Rosa Bonheur was arrested by a policeman who, noticing her short hair and her free and easy air, was sure he had to do with a young man dressed as a woman. So he started to take her to the station; and as he was rather rough, Rosa, indignant, gave him a blow that made him all the more certain that he had a male in his clutches. The poor fellow was crestfallen, indeed, when, a few minutes later, the police magistrate berated him for his stupid error and dismissed the artist with a thousand apologies.

To Rosa Bonheur, masculine dress was simply a convenience, and, sometimes, a necessity. When working on one of her large canvases, and perched on a ladder, it certainly was a convenience; and out of doors, it was often a real protection to her. With her, there was no posing in the matter.

Rosa Bonheur's pronounced fondness for tobacco was sometimes looked upon as another masculine trait in her character. On this subject Mme. Lagrolet writes me:

She generally confined her smoking habit to her own studio, though when my husband offered her a cigarette at our house, she would accept it. She used to make her own cigarettes in a little mould. When conversing in her studio, she would often be engaged all the time rolling them. Even when she was as old as seventy-five, I have seen her sitting up on the side of her table, in a négligée position just like a young man, with a smoking cigarette in her hand. Her pretty little foot would then slip conspicuously out from under her trousers, which did not seem to displease her; for the truth is she was proud of her small feet and hands.

Benjamin Tedesco relates this anecdote:

Rosa Bonheur was an inveterate smoker of cigarettes. One summer's day, arriving in Paris from Fontainebleau, at ten o'clock in the morning, she hired an open cab and began making some calls. I was with her. At eleven o'clock she exclaimed:

"I can resist no longer. I haven't smoked for three hours. Give me a cigarette."

"But it won't do to smoke in the streets," I answered.

So she ordered the driver to pull up the cover of the cab, and when this was done, lifted up her skirt, beneath which were her men's trousers, and was soon enjoying her smoke.

Princess Stirbey has always preserved this note which she once received from Rosa Bonheur:

Many thanks for your kind letter of yesterday evening and the good tobacco which you have so thoughtfully given me to replace the stock which your presence and my gossiping made me leave on the way. I have not lost by it and I thank you once more.

The visitor to-day to the By studio is shown Rosa Bonheur's smoking materials, and the half-used box of cigarettes lies there just as it was left by the dying artist.

Rosa Bonheur had many spiritual and refined tastes. Tobacco and trousers were offset not only by painting and sculpture, but also by a marked fondness for music and literature, and, at least in her younger days, for dancing. The faithful Céline Rey declares that "Rosa Bonheur sang very well," though she had no trained knowledge of either instrumental or vocal music. Her nephew, Raymond Bonheur, himself a composer of no mean merit, well says on this point:

My aunt was exclusively attached to her art; her unique care was an attentive and passionate study of nature. Everything else in her busy life had simply the importance of a relaxation. In the department of music, about all that can be said is that she was a close friend of Mme. Miolan Carvalho, and that she frequented in her younger days quite assiduously the old Lyric Theatre, where she used to meet Gounod and the other composers of that time.

Mme. Achard gives further details on this subject, as follows:

I never heard Rosa Bonheur sing, though I know she liked music very much. Mme. Carvalho, for instance, who was a joy to her, was very much loved in the Mène-Cain household, and when she was to be there, Rosa Bonheur was generally invited at the same time. Though the latter always had a tendency not to go out, she never declined these invitations, as she knew Mme. Carvalho would sing during the evening and she would have an opportunity of hearing her, without exciting the jealousy of Mlle. Micas, who, in the last years of her life, caused Rosa Bonheur much annoyance in this way.

It was her love for music which drew Rosa Bonheur toward my husband, who was an accomplished artist, who sang well, was ten years at the Opéra Comique and four years at the Opéra. But it was through the Mène-Cain circle, who knew the father of my husband, that Rosa Bonheur got acquainted with the latter. In fact, we had both met her before our marriage and independently, so that after our union, she felt still more friendly in our society, where her musical tastes received a new and greater development.

At this period, Grivot played only in operettas, though he, too, finally reached the Opéra Comique, where he remained for a long time. He also had much talent and Rosa Bonheur was especially drawn to him because he was her neighbour at By.

Rosa Bonheur enjoyed the theatre, as she liked everything that was bright and artistic, and so she took a special pleasure in the society of her operatic friends—Carvalho, Archard, Grivot, and others whose names escape me. It was association with them which not only kept alive but greatly strengthened her taste for things musical.

Though Mme. Achard seems never to have heard Rosa Bonheur sing, Rosa Mathieu appears to share the opinion of Céline Rey, for she says:

One thing that always appealed to me and pleased me in Rosa Bonheur was her voice. It had a thrilling resonance which has remained in my memory with perhaps more vividness even than her features, which, however, I recollect so well. It was exceedingly musical in tone, and I may mention in this connection that Rosa Bonheur was passionately fond of music.

I remember hearing that long before she went to live at By, she had gone one evening to a Paris theatre to a performance of " The Magic Flute," I think. In her absent-mindedness, and with her thoughts more intent on the approaching pleasure than on her toilet, she arrived at the play-house in her painting blouse, and was only made aware of the fact by some audible protests of her neighbours. But, instead of being put out of countenance by the discovery, Rosa Bonheur contrived, by certain flashes of her fine eyes and the absorbed attention she continued to pay to the music, to so impose upon the protesters that they left her in peace till the end of the performance.

Mr. Gambart, like Mlle. Mathieu, admired Rosa Bonheur's voice. In his manuscript memoirs occurs this passage:

It was during the stay in Scotland in 1856 that, for the first time, I heard Rosa Bonheur sing; indeed, as far as my memory serves me, it was the only time. We were at Glen Falloch and were walking by the lake, after a day's work, amidst the evening gloaming. Her voice was really very fine and she used it with great effect.

Mme. Lagrolet and M. Henri Cain both agree in declaring in the same words that " Rosa Bonheur liked modern music," the former adding: " Her mother used to sing very well, and it was the delight of the daughter in later years to hear once more those old songs of her younger days, ' Pauvre Jacques,' for instance, being a special favourite."

REMINISCENCES OF ROSA BONHEUR

Henri Cain says:

Rosa Bonheur liked music—when there was " a tune to it."
But anything with a tendency toward Wagnerism she had no
taste for. She would try to understand it, however. One evening we went to the Paris Opera House to hear " Walkyrie," if I
am not mistaken. But she sat through only two acts. She felt
that it was beyond her. Mozart she adored; so too Schumann
and Beethoven. Among the composers of her own time, she especially admired Gounod and Berlioz. Massenet enchanted her. In
fact, every time I went to see her, she, who never asked a favour,
would say: " Do bring me something of that captivator! " So
I got in the habit of carrying her a partition of her favourite
composer, whenever I went to By, and she used to get friends to
play it for her, evidently enjoying it. In the closing months of
her life, Miss Klumpke, who has, I believe, considerable musical
talent, used often to play for her.

In the matter of Rosa Bonheur's literary tastes, M. Paul
Chardin says:

Rosa Bonheur delighted to dip into old chronicles, ballads, and
legends, and I remember her being so struck by an ancient Breton
legend that she made several crayon drawings based on it. The
title of it was " Lez-Breiz." She had read the story in the
" Barzaz-Breiz," or collection of popular songs of Brittany, published by the Viscount Hersart de la Villemarqué in 1867. Lez-
Breiz means Hip of Brittany, the word hip being taken in the
sense of support, and was applied as a surname to a legendary
hero of this country.

Most of her friends knew of Rosa Bonheur's fondness for
" Don Quixote." Her love for the old chronicles and the old
romances of chivalry was only equalled by her admiration of Cervantes. She must have read this masterpiece often, for she would
speak of it with evident pleasure, would recall certain anecdotes
from this celebrated story, would dwell on the hero, with all of
whose adventures she was evidently well acquainted. I remember having seen in her studio at By several crayon sketches sug-

gested by these adventures. Among others, there was a Don Quixote tilting against the windmill.

If, however, I may be allowed to criticise so great an artist, it seems to me that this kind of artistic work was not natural to her talent. In my opinion, Rosa Bonheur had not the faculty shown, for instance, by Decamps in a similar kind of work also inspired by Don Quixote, of giving to her characters a typical physiognomy and a peculiar stamp calculated to bring out each individuality. The same defect, I think, exists in her painting of people, even when they appear in her animal pictures.

Alexandre Jacob says, on this same subject:

One thing that always struck me during the conversations carried on in Rosa Bonheur's studio was her habit either of sketching or modelling while she was talking, and this without either the conversation or the artistic work suffering. The subjects were various, as the hostess disdained nothing that was discussable. It is true that occasionally she ventured out of her depth, her knowledge in some matters being in an inverse ratio to her genius in painting. It would be a mistake, however, to suppose that Rosa was not a well-read woman. Her reading was wide and in some cases deep. In all that concerned her art, she devoured information. Out-of-the-way books also she now and again drew inspiration from, notably Ossian, which suggested a picture quite in the Ossian style. Cervantes she possessed almost by heart. Books of anatomy were, of course, familiar to her. Books of travels she was fond of. Books of science she dipped into a good deal, though intermittently. And from this book knowledge, as well as from her own experience, she gathered materials of conversation. Willingly indulging in the lighter vein, sometimes cracking pretty broad jokes, she insisted on others keeping within the limits of decorum, and was quick to take exception if any one of her guests presumed to overstep them.

Concerning Rosa Bonheur's dancing accomplishments there seems to be less unanimity among her friends. Though Céline Rey declares that "Rosa Bonheur was a most graceful dancer

371

and enjoyed it very much," Mme. Achard is less positive. The latter says on this subject:

I remember a fancy-dress ball at the Mène-Cain home to which Rosa Bonheur came dressed as a gipsy and Mlle. Micas as a Pierrot. Though I was a mere child on this occasion and was soon put to bed, I recollect very well how Rosa Bonheur appeared. She looked and acted very funny. Mlle. Micas was far from pretty and wasn't bad as a Pierrot. That evening, Rosa Bonheur danced a fancy step to amuse herself and to keep up the part she had assumed, but I never saw her really dance. Though at the Mène-Cain dinner-parties, the young people often started an impromptu hop, I do not recall Rosa Bonheur taking part in it. However, I would not say that she could not dance, only that I never saw her do so.

The contributions which I have received touching upon Rosa Bonheur as an artist are, naturally, many and not the least valuable of this collection of reminiscences. I give below the principal ones, some of them slightly abbreviated. Taken together, they cover about the whole subject of Rosa Bonheur's gifts and defects as an interpreter of animal life.

Léonide Bourges writes:

In my childhood, my father's picture dealing was only in a small way. His business was that of linen merchant and the pictures he bought were frequently paid for in kind. Some of his first transactions with the Bonheur family were of this nature. He bought one of the very early productions of Rosa Bonheur, a canvas representing some cows near a mill, together with a willow and a kingfisher. The execution was stiff and had but little promise of the artist's future perfection. A later picture painted in the forties, before her great success, however, representing a large ewe with her lamb, was a fine bit of work. My father kept it for some years and finally sold it to a wholesale butcher. " I don't understand much about art," said the latter, when purchasing, " but I know a good sheep when I see one." Two later pictures, one representing three small donkeys, the other

OSSIAN RECITING.

MAC.

some sheep, were admirably painted, there being little or no sky in them and the artist's power being concentrated on the animals. Rosa Bonheur's skies, by the way, do not harmonise with the main part in her pictures, and detract from them rather than adorn them. I consider that Rosa Bonheur's perfection consists more in her drawing than in her colouring. One example of this is marvellous, "A Bison Fleeing Before a Forest Fire." With instinctive sympathy for a similar quality in a brother artist, Rosa Bonheur was especially fond of Gérôme's work, and often praised it.

Louis Passy:

Rosa Bonheur never said much about art. She worked more than she talked. When you spoke to her of the great painters, she never advanced any special opinion of her own in regard to them. She was not a great traveller and never studied profoundly. She knew but one book—Nature. Her eye and mind were centred only on what she saw. I never heard her express an opinion on other artists. Though she may have had some taste for music, she knew nothing about it. She was first and last an artist, a painter to her finger tips.

Mlle. Keller:

Though Rosa Bonheur led a secluded life at By and met comparatively few of the artists of her time, and these but rarely, still it should be remembered that during the early years of her career, which were passed in Paris, she lived in continual contact with several of the great painters and sculptors of modern France. I recall, especially, the frequency of the presence of the famous David d'Angers in her studio in the Rue d'Assas, his own studio being almost next door, in the same street. When he was there, general conversation was indulged in. But Rosa Bonheur, as a rule, had a way of saying to her artist friends, when she was at work and they were looking on, " Well, what do you think of this? " She would listen quietly to the opinion or criticism, but whether she afterward acted upon what was said is not so sure.

But Rosa Bonheur's talent was not confined to the painter's

brush; she could handle the sculptor's chisel with dexterity, and, what is less generally known, was clever with the lithographer's pen and pencil. I have a lioness's head which is firmly done and which I saw Rosa Bonheur draw and lithograph. She often did this with sheep and other animals. She had a high opinion of this process because of the many advantages which it offers in the reproduction of paintings, making it possible to interpret the character of the picture, to render its modelling with vigour and without dryness, and to bring out the qualities of the artist while, at the same time, the individuality of the lithographer is preserved. She often preferred, for certain subjects, lithography to engraving.

Rosa Bonheur would frequently discourse with me in this way on art subjects while she was busy working. She talked well on art. Her ideas were common sense personified. There was nothing hazy and sentimental about them, and the picturesqueness and quaintness of some of her expressions gave a stamp of originality to what she said that went home and abided with those who listened. You felt that she not only knew what she was talking about, but that she knew how to express what she knew.

Mme. Virginie Demont-Breton:

Here are some interesting scraps of conversation which I had at different times with Rosa Bonheur:

" Circumstances do not allow all women to combine the various necessary elements of happiness. In my case, it has been art which has monopolised my existence. I owe to it my greatest enjoyments and the consolation of the troubles I have had to endure. I have always been happy with my lot. But no one more than I better comprehends that to be a wife and mother as well as an artist must be complete bliss. To have been able to bind one's heart in love and yet to preserve liberty of thought and of mental creation are the realisation here below of the fairest dream."

" Who is the fool that made me laugh lately by writing in some important newspaper or other, that women have no imagination? I wonder at the critics who have never produced anything

374

and yet assert such things with so much confidence. Imagination! Why, I could have furnished them with a little, if the article were saleable; but I should have taken good care not to, on account of the bad use they would make of it!"

"My conscientiousness has sometimes been a drawback to me; I have now and again overdone each blade of grass."

"When I work, I try to satisfy myself, and I endeavour to do so that God in whom I trust may not be too displeased with the way in which I understand him! When one lives alone with the Creator, one has such modest pretensions as these!"

Henri Cain:

Rosa Bonheur studied animals both in books and from life. With my grandfather and father—both animal sculptors—she worked hard and for many years in the Paris Garden of Plants, where is a zoölogical collection. She also possessed many histological drawings, and was fully aware of the fact that an artist, who would paint or sculpture animals, must carefully study the skeleton. She used to say that, in order to draw correctly animals in motion and to catch their true movements, one must know what was under their skin; otherwise your animal will look flabby. "It will be a mat," she once said to me, "rather than a tiger."

Rosa Bonheur was not only an exceedingly intelligent artist, but a very conscientious and hard-working one. It should be borne in mind that each of her fine masterpieces was the result of a most extraordinary amount of preparatory labour. If she wished to put a lamb in the corner of a picture, she would first make perhaps a dozen separate studies of lambs. Whenever she had a painting to do, she would always begin by making very careful preliminary studies. She believed in honesty in art and ever desired to keep very close to nature.

Consuélo Fould has revised for this volume these views which she published in part at the time of Rosa Bonheur's death:

Rosa Bonheur had a most open and cultivated mind. She kept herself informed concerning all literary and scientific books bearing on art and visited all art exhibitions of any merit. She studied the movements and tendencies of the various schools, which she appreciated at their true value and judged with indulgence. She was ever ready to give full credit to all that was good in them and to find an excuse for what was bad. It was only with humbugs that she had no patience, with those Barnums who have recourse to eccentricities in order to influence public opinion, or with the style that happens to be in vogue and which captivates the blasés. I have often heard her dwell in a most luminous manner on the great harm done the contemporary school by this pushing of originality to an extreme. She was always ready to lift up her voice against the habit of filling the Salon, some years, with either *pleins-airs* or *clairs-obscurs*, as the case might be, according to the whim of the jury on admission. After the success of Puvis de Chavannes, she would come back from subsequent exhibitions all out of sorts with the sub-Puvises who thrust themselves on the view.

Rosa Bonheur used to say: " Every kind of painting can have its masterpiece. It is foolish to try to form all artists in the same mould. There was a time when it was held that Delacroix's work was not pretty enough, was not sufficiently refined in its drawing, and now they are ' turning down ' Greuze and Watteau simply because these two masters are found popular with the professional copyists and the trade."

Rosa Bonheur never wearied in praising the old masters and, in connection with them, would dwell on the material care which should be bestowed on every work which was to be considered as one's best. In support of this assertion and to show that she practised what she preached, she would place before me studies which she had painted fifty years before, on which she had noted the colours used in order to see what effect time had on them from year to year. Her own observations of this kind were supplemented by those of her father. So when she stood before certain canvases of the Louvre, she could assert that the lower parts, such as the ground, had been strengthened by this or that colour, often looked upon with disfavour to-day but then much used, as the chromes, for instance. She held in horror every kind of liquid or siccative, which has a momentary effect but loses its strength with time. She would cover her sketch with colours, leaving no trace visible of the pencil lines. She would say: " How can you get delicate effects if you have charcoal underneath? " She would put on the colours thick, sometimes giving the first coat two years to get dry. Then she would return to the work, using her colours generously, but without much oil, and once more let it dry.

Rosa Bonheur's attention to details extended even to her palettes. Some she kept very clean, while others were coated with many layers of various pigments, so skilfully treated, that, after the lapse of a few years, the surface of the palette presented the glossy and jasper appearance of marble. She laid great stress on these palettes, for they absorbed the oil and made it possible for her to better judge certain effects.

Nor did she neglect her brushes. I have seen Rosa Bonheur clean her paint-brushes with special care, different brushes receiving a different treatment, and she could obtain extraordinarily fine touches even with the antique ferrule brush.

After what has just been said, it will be understood why Rosa Bonheur made would-be purchasers of her pictures wait so long for canvases which seemed practically finished. Dissatisfaction with her own work or the fact that the drying was not completed was sufficient ground for her not to hasten the delivery of a canvas. A money offer could never hasten her. She would dispose of as many pictures as would furnish her the funds she was in need of, and then, as soon as she had some ready cash on hand, she would return to her studies. She pursued this course to the very end of her long life. It is the secret of the continual advance in her artistic powers right to the moment of her death. Nobody has an idea of the treasures in her collection of studies, the result of half a century of labour. She would part with none of them. " There I judge myself," she would say; " I compare what I do now with what I did in the past and I try to keep up to the mark." This excessive modesty, which is so rare among painters, was a special characteristic of her genius. She dreaded the thought of a possible decline and would sometimes find comfort in this reflection: " Have you not noticed that women, much more so than men, do not, as they approach the end, let their artistic work fall below their highest level? Look at George Sand, and so many others; their best productions are their latest ones."

Ernest Gambart writes as follows, in his manuscript memoirs, of these studies:

In 1874 I called at By, on my way to Spa, to ask Rosa Bonheur if she could not let me have a few of her sketches which she had made as studies for her pictures. I wished to add them to my fine-art collections. Although her practice was to dispose of none, she made an exception in my favour, and, after an examination of her treasures, she consented to part with some. The chief among these were sketches of a beagle, a wild-cat, an ass, a ram, a badger and a wounded eagle. Moreover, she insisted on making pictures of them by surrounding each with a landscape. The ram bears the dates of 1860 and 1874; the ass, the same two dates; the wild-cat, 1854 and 1874; the badger, 1855 and 1874; the beagle, 1847 and 1874. The ass has since been engraved by William Henry Simmons [1] and the beagle and wounded eagle by Joseph B. Pratt. All these animals are life-size. Later, I received an old donkey and, in 1880, an Arab horse and a brown horse. They, too, have been engraved by Simmons.

Rosa Bonheur's Paris apartment was decorated with six studies of dogs painted, in 1879, from the finest specimens of Viscount d'Armaillé's kennels. Each was signed by her. These sketches I had long coveted, and in 1890 she gratified my wish by giving them to me.

In this same year, Rosa Bonheur executed for me a large sepia and crayon drawing of the " Horse Fair " based on a photograph of the original. Before this, in 1876, I was fortunate enough to receive from her a large picture representing a herd of wild boars, and, in 1878, the " King of the Forest " (a stag). These two canvases, over two yards and a half by nearly two yards, were considered by her as her masterpieces. They were much admired at one of the exhibitions of the Antwerp Royal Academy and King Leopold bestowed on their author his order, which, until then, had never been given to a woman.

[1] 1811–1882.

Mr. Gambart's memoirs contain this interesting history of the "Horse Fair":

A great deal has been said in newspapers and art periodicals about Rosa Bonheur's great painting. I take this opportunity to give the facts in their simple truth.

The picture had been exhibited in Paris, at the 1853 Salon, and had come back to the artist unsold. In 1855, I paid a visit to Mlle. Rosa, and found her busy at the reproduction of her picture on a smaller scale, and occupied with several other things. For instance, I recall that she had a Bearnese mounted on a mule who was acting as a model for a picture she was also intending to paint, representing some Bauricaires crossing the Pyrenees. It was at this moment, if I am not mistaken, that I invited her to come over to London with her friend Mlle. Micas and to go to Scotland, where she would find ample material for future pictures.

After the closing of the 1853 Paris Salon, the "Horse Fair" was entrusted to the Society of Artists of Ghent for exhibition in that town, where it had a great success, but whence it also came back unsold. In the spring of 1854, I expressed to Mlle. Bonheur the desire to buy it from her. At that time, it was in Bordeaux, her native town. Her preference was that the municipality should purchase it for the city museum, and a price of 12,000 francs had been mentioned, at which the town authorities might acquire it. But she said to me that if the canvas came back to her again, she would let me have it. However, she could not let it go to England for less than 40,000 francs. I unhesitatingly accepted the bargain, and it was agreed that the picture should be mine, unless sold to Bordeaux. As the picture was back in her studio again in the following year, I told Mlle. Bonheur that I wished to take it at once, in order to have it in my 1855 exhibition, and that I should like to have it engraved by Thomas Landseer, the celebrated engraver and brother to the painter. She was delighted at the idea of the picture being engraved and said to me:

"I have asked you 40,000 francs for my picture, although in France I cannot get 12,000, and I am pleased at your consenting to my terms. On the other hand, I don't mean to take undue advantage of your liberality. How can we arrange matters? Let us see. Well, the picture is very large and it will be difficult to find a place for it in an engraver's studio. Besides, you want to exhibit it. Wouldn't it be better for me to paint you a smaller copy?"

I of course agreed to this proposal, and she continued:

"Well then, I will give you this copy into the bargain, and so my conscience will be clear. I shall be able to say that I have sold my canvas for 40,000 francs, and you won't have been too much fleeced!"

We now had to decide upon the scale of the reduction. We ultimately agreed that it should be a quarter of the original size. Thus I would have two Horse Fairs; one for my exhibition, and the other for the engraver. Mlle. Rosa set to work at once, and delivered me the copy as well as the original in June 1855.

Without loss of time, I placed the smaller canvas in the hands of Thomas Landseer, who began forthwith to engrave it. Whilst he was so occupied, Jacob Bell (1810–59), the well-known English patron of art, happened to see the picture and wrote me, expressing a desire to buy it for the purpose of including it in a collection of pictures by the celebrated animal painter, Sir Edwin Landseer. The offer he made was 25,000 francs, which I accepted.

As for the large picture, which was exhibited in the Pall Mall Gallery, its large size probably prevented its finding a purchaser, in spite of the general admiration it called forth; and, moreover, at this moment, the reputation of the artist was still in its dawn. Not till towards the close of the exhibition, did a bidder present himself, Mr. Wright, an American, who offered me 30,000 francs, leaving me free to retain possession of the painting for two or three years and to continue exhibiting it in England and America. He paid down 10,000 francs earnest-money, the balance remaining over until delivery. Subsequently, Mr. Wright claimed a share in the profits of the exhibition, so that when my agent handed him over the picture, he paid me only 13,000 francs. Thus, the two paintings—the larger and the smaller—brought me only 48,000 francs. However, the sale of the engravings had been very profitable, and the exhibition of the original established the artist's reputation on such a secure basis that her following pictures were able to command high prices and were bought up immediately when finished.

When in 1871, after retiring from business, I was preparing to settle at Nice and to form a private gallery of paintings, I wrote to Mr. Wright, offering to buy back the " Horse Fair " for 50,000 francs. But he did not accept my proposal. Later on, he became involved in some business difficulties and sold this masterpiece to Mr. A. T. Stewart, head of the great New York dry-goods store. On the death of this gentleman, there was an auction sale of his gallery, and the " Horse Fair " was bought by Samuel Avery, acting on behalf of Cornelius Vanderbilt, who presented it to the New York Metropolitan Museum. The price paid at the sale was 250,000 francs.

On the death of Jacob Bell, the smaller painting was bequeathed, with his other pictures, to the British National Gallery. As soon as Rosa Bonheur heard that her painting had become the property of the English nation, she decided to make another copy, on the ground that the first was not sufficiently good to figure in such a famous collection.

Although this second copy was painted without the aid of the original, or other guide than the engraving and her numerous study-sketches, it turned out to be a fine work, indeed a second original. When it was finished, Mlle. Bonheur requested me to offer it to the authorities of the National Gallery in place of the other. But, while they appreciated the artist's delicacy of feeling, they were unable, as trustees of Jacob Bell's legacy, to dispose of what he had bequeathed, or to make any exchange. This second copy, therefore, was at my disposal, and Mr. MacCornel bought it for the sum of 25,000 francs. Before parting with it, I had asked Walter Goodall [1] to propose to Mlle. Bonheur the painting of a miniature water-colour. This she also made and it became the property of Mr. Henry W. F. Bölckow (1806–78), the great Middlesborough manufacturer, who paid 2,500 francs for it, and who had a fine modern gallery.

Finally, to make this history complete, the photographer Cal-

---

[1] The water-colour painter (1830–89), brother of Frederick Goodall, R.A., and Edward Goodall, the line-engraver.

desi produced, in 1855, a fairly large but very faint proof on two sheets carefully joined together. This I sent to Mlle. Bonheur that she might utilise it for a sketch that should help the engraver in the course of his work. This sketch was begun, then laid aside, then taken up again, and remained in the artist's studio until 1890 —a period of thirty-five years—before it was finished. Later, it was hung in my Nice drawing-room, under Dubufe's portrait of Rosa Bonheur.

Thus, there are five Horse Fair pictures—the large original in the New York Museum; the first smaller copy that served for Thomas Landseer's engraving, which is now in the National Gallery of London; the second smaller copy, which forms part of a private collection in England; the small water-colour at Middlesborough; and the drawing of which I am the fortunate possessor and which is always greatly admired by the many visitors who come to see my collection.[1]

I ought to add in connection with my London exhibition of French art, mentioned above, that though it was opened by the Queen, accompanied by Prince Albert, and was a success from the start, it was not till June, however, when I received the " Horse Fair," that the exhibition became a veritable triumph. Both press and public praised it most highly, and the Queen having expressed a desire to see it, the picture was sent to Windsor. This, of course, increased its popularity and the small gallery was thenceforth thronged with visitors bent on seeing the wonderful canvas.

Hippolyte Peyrol, Sr., gives these additional particulars concerning the " Horse Fair ":

In 1848, Rosa Bonheur exhibited her large picture of the " Red Oxen of Cantal," based on studies made during her trip in Auvergne and on sculptured cattle made especially for this canvas, and which still exist. This was the last important work executed at the studio in Rue Rumford. When, at the end of 1848, her father

---

[1] Mr. Gambart's collection was dispersed by a public sale in London, in May, 1904, a year after his death.

was made director of the Girls' School of Design, Rosa took the studio at 56 Rue d'Assas, where was painted the " Plowing in the Nivernais," now in the Luxembourg Gallery. There she remained till 1851, when she took another studio in the same house, which studio was built especially for her by the father of Mathieu Meusnier, the sculptor. It was in this studio that the famous " Horse Fair " grew into being. The foregoing pictures naturally led up to this grand masterpiece, for which she made many studies during a long period of time.

Whilst engaged in evolving the " Horse Fair," Rosa Bonheur made the acquaintance of M. Dailly, the director of the Paris Omnibus Company, who gave her permission to utilise their horses for her studies. As her studio at this time was divided into two parts, the studio proper and a sort of stable annexed thereto, it was very easy for her to make use of the horses which M. Dailly so kindly put at her disposal. In addition, she also went to the company's stables themselves, which were then not far away, in the Rue Stanislas, and also found much help at the Paris Public Horse Market.

Prince Georges Stirbey says on the same subject:

Just after President Carnot, the first of the French Chief Magistrates to spend the summer at Fontainebleau, called on Rosa Bonheur at her By studio, the thought occurred to me, as a friend of his father, to request an audience and then to beg of him to bestow on the distinguished painter the rosette, the second grade in the Legion of Honour.

" She has ceased exhibiting at the Salon," objected the President; " and sells in America everything she paints."

" That is quite true, Mr. President," I answered; " but the reason for this is that the French Government declined the ' Horse Fair,' after ordering it. An inspector of the Fine Arts Department, who was entrusted with the examination of the various paintings and sculptures ordered by the State, reported that he was surprised that such a difficult work had been put in the hands of a woman, that it was a bad picture as it stood and recommended several alterations in it. Rosa Bonheur got wind of this adverse report, and naturally indignant, called on the Minister of Fine Arts.

"' If you wish it, Sir,' she began, ' we can annul the contract.'

"' No, Mademoiselle,' the Minister replied; ' there are only a few little changes to be made and then it will be a perfect picture.'

"' As to my making any modifications in the plan of my work, why, Mr. Minister, that is utterly out of the question. I again request and request firmly, that my contract with the State be cancelled.'

"' Well, if you insist upon this, Mademoiselle, then let it be so.'

" This, Mr. President," I continued, " is why the ' Horse Fair' adorns a New York Museum instead of being in its rightful place on the line in the Luxembourg Gallery, why Rosa Bonheur sends so many of her works to America, and why she should receive another recognition of her talent from the French Government, which on this occasion treated her so shabbily."

President Carnot was evidently struck by the justice of my request, for, a short time afterwards, at the moment of the Chicago World's Fair, he signed the decree nominating Rosa Bonheur to this new dignity.

Princess Stirbey adds this comment to the statement of her husband:

This affair with the inspector was always kept secret by Rosa Bonheur and her near friends. Check though it was, it was a grand step in the direction of her final artistic success. However, it wounded her deeply, so deeply that she lost hope for herself in France, her native land, where she is still less known than in England and the New World.

Apropos of the above anecdote of Prince Stirbey, M. Peyrol, Jr., says:

It is a mistake to say that the " Horse Fair " was ordered by the State, though an effort was made to offer it as a gift to the head of the State. The picture of Rosa Bonheur really ordered by the State was that called " Haymaking in Auvergne," the sketch for which was submitted to the Minister of Fine Arts for approval. But when the Superintendent of Fine Arts, Count de Nieuwerkerke, saw at Rosa's studio the " Horse Fair," he expressed the wish to take this canvas in lieu of the one which had been ordered and at the same price, " in order," he said, " to present it as a gift to the Emperor." Rosa Bonheur answered as follows: " It is the ' Haymaking ' which was ordered and it is the ' Haymaking ' which will be delivered in due season as agreed. It is quite natural that you should wish to make the Emperor a present, but not at my expense. If I should decide to offer His Majesty a gift, you may rest assured that I will act myself without any intermediary." The upshot of the matter was that Rosa kept the " Horse Fair," which in 1855 was sold to Gambart, and the " Haymaking in Auvergne," when finished, was delivered to the Minister of Fine Arts.

But Prince Stirbey's story is interesting even if more or less apocryphal, for it was told to President Carnot as true and evidently produced an effect on him.

Henri Cain thus refers to another canvas:

As was the case with all her great pictures, Rosa Bonheur carefully thought out the " Wheat Thrashing," that immense unfinished canvas which still covers one side of her By studio. I remember it always in an incomplete state. Not many months before her death, she said to me one day: " You must come out and help me with that terrible sky, which is a hard job. I fear I haven't the strength to do that part of the work." It was one of her last wishes to finish this grand picture, and Miss Klumpke, if I am not mistaken, laboured on the ground and sky, while Rosa Bonheur confined her attention to the large group of horses which compose this canvas. It is nearly done. She died while almost at work on it. I have heard it said that one of the reasons why she was eager to finish it was in order to win with it the grand prize at the Exhibition of 1900. I doubt this. Anyway, Rosa Bonheur never bothered about any prize whatsoever. She worked for her own pleasure. I never heard her say: "I am going to exhibit in order to have this or that recompense." Such a thought was not in keeping with her character. She always felt that she had already been honoured beyond her merits. She was in everything simplicity and humility itself.

Before leaving this subject, of Rosa Bonheur's art, I may add that she did not fully approve of Stevenson's definition that " art is first of all and last of all, a trade." She agreed more with his statement that " the business of real art is to give life to abstractions, and significance and charm to facts." But above all she applauded this sentence of her favourite author, George Sand: " Art for art's sake is a vain word. But art for the truth, art for the beautiful and the good, that is the religion that I seek for."

Paul Chardin thus touches upon another side of Rosa Bonheur's artistic talents:

She did not have the temperament of the true caricaturist who often has a funny side to his character. She, on the contrary, was serious, meditative, and had too high an idea of art to seek out in nature the ridiculous side of things. Frequently she liked to philosophise, and when she indulged in joking, it was by fits and starts. At such times she became a real *gamin*, and would often employ language which it would not do to repeat. But it cannot be said that she had that turn of mind which gives caricature its special stamp. The few caricatures by her which I have seen are overstrained, and do not at all present the typical side of the persons whom she would make fun of. And the mottoes under the drawings are generally lacking in real wit and are frequently far too broad.

The basis of caricature is the exaggeration of the striking and typical sides of the individual. Rosa Bonheur, who was so clever in getting the expression of animals, never seemed to me to grasp the physiognomy of human beings. Thus, in the Passy Cravat,[1] the caricatures of the persons whom she there painted bear no

---

[1] See the citation from M. Chardin which follows this one.

special characterisation. Without being told who they were, it would be difficult to recognise any one of them. The nack of catching likenesses is a gift in itself. Some of the greatest painters did not possess it, whereas mere daubers are sometimes endowed with this talent.

Rosa Bonheur would have succeeded far better in caricaturing animals than men. The perfection of life, individual expression, and character which she was always able to give to her oxen, stags, dogs, and cart-horses are more or less absent from her human figures. Her painting of them was heavy and insignificant; one cannot help the impression that her interest was concentrated upon the animals. Perhaps I ought not to register this impression as being more than personal to myself. At any rate, I have felt it in contemplating all the pictures in which it is possible to make the contrast, as, for instance, the " Ploughing in the Nivernais " and the " Horse Fair." The bipeds are squat and clumsy, with faces that have no psychological differentiation, whilst the quadrupeds are without exception individual creations right through from skeleton to artery and nerve, with eyes full of life and fire. In fine, Rosa Bonheur has produced comparatively few canvases in which human figures are added to her animals. But I may quote, perhaps, two others illustrative of the preceding remarks, both being hunting subjects. In the one, are to be seen some dog-keepers and whippers-in grouped round a fire and enveloped by mist; in the other, some huntsmen in Louis XV costume seated near a relay of horses. The animals are of course masterpieces, but the men have the defects I have pointed out, especially those in the Louis XV costume, who are not at all like those of that period.

But this same defect is found in other animal painters. It seems to me that Horace Vernet, so neglected by the artists of to-day, stands almost alone in his power to paint equally well men and horses, giving each a distinct and marked physiognomy. So in this shortcoming, Rosa Bonheur is in a large and distinguished company.

Returning to the subject of caricature, M. Chardin goes on to describe a most curious series of travesties in which Rosa Bonheur and her circle participated—the Passy Cravat.

REMINISCENCES OF ROSA BONHEUR

In the sixties I often went to By and made long stays in the little village tavern. Every evening after dinner, I would go over to Rosa Bonheur's and finish the evening in her studio, both of us sitting before the burning logs in her big fireplace. I would generally find her smoking a cigarette, with her beagle, Ramoneau, and her Scotch terrier, Wasp, lying on a larger deer-skin at her

Wasp.

feet. The room was dimly lighted by the fire and a single lamp on a table in one corner. It was the moment of repose after a long day's work. Rosa Bonheur, always so silent and meditative when engaged in painting, now gave free rein to her imagination and generally monopolised the conversation. She would touch upon all conceivable topics, ranging from subjects for future pictures to questions of philosophy. Sometimes she would interrupt the gravest discussion with an unexpected sally or some schoolboy prank. It was in one of these skylarking moods that she gave vent to the idea of the illustrated Passy Cravat. On this occasion, the Micases had had to go up to Paris, so that Rosa Bonheur and I were quite alone at By. Then it was that she was especially apt to give free play to her mirthfulness. She

388

considered us both young rogues ready for any wild tricks. Mlle. Micas was her Mentor and she herself, mine. I, too, was her Rapin and she my General. So she proposed that we begin this series of caricatures.

M. Antoine Passy was a deputy and a member of the Institute as is his son, M. Louis Passy. He often wore when in the country cravats covered with flowers. He had sent us a rhyme in commemoration of my night adventure in one of the trees of the Fontainebleau forest. "Let us give him some nonsense in return," exclaimed Rosa Bonheur on one of these autumnal evenings of 1864. The idea was immediately taken up and agreed to; she went to a closet and got a large piece of sheeting which she stretched over a table and marked off in lozenge-shaped spaces. Then, during the following evenings, all those present at the house were invited to fill up the spaces with original caricatures. So we set to work—Rosa and Isidore Bonheur, Mlle. Micas, and I—to daub the future cravat with pictures in water-colour.

Here is the translation of the rebus which forms the border of the cravat: "Cravat of Honour awarded to M. Antoine Passy, Member of the Institute, by the inhabitants of By, made under the direction of Mlle. Nathalie Micas."

Here is the description of the caricatures in the different lozenges based on notes furnished me by M. Chardin and the surviving persons—the Elder and Younger Peyrol—therein depicted:

Central lozenge: Nathalie Micas with her parrot and surrounded with all her attributes. On a big book in front of her is this title: "Essays on the Yam." She used to cultivate this edible plant. On the pot near this book is this inscription: "Micas's Pomatum for the Eyes." Mlle. Nathalie Micas had great pretensions in medicine, as we have already seen, and declared that this particular pomatum, which had been handed down from generation to generation in her family, was a sure cure for everything. On another pot we read: "Canned Tomatoes." Under the drawing, Rosa Bonheur, its author, has written these words: "Postulant Member of several Agricultural, Medical,

Artistic, Culinary, and Hydraulic Societies." Sticking out of her pocket is seen the head of a syringe, which she used frequently among the animals.

Lozenge to the right: Rosa Bonheur has painted herself at her work and surrounded by several of her pets, her two dogs, Ramoneau and Wasp, being especially conspicuous. This is the inscription under the drawing: " An Illustrious Friend. 1861. R. B."

The lozenge to the left: Mlle. Micas as Hamlet, holding a skull in her hand, with the inscription " Not to be," being a continuation of the inscription of the adjoining lozenge. It is the work of Paul Chardin.

The first lozenge on the upper line: " Tout By " means all the persons then at the Château of By. The French is pronounced like the first two words of Hamlet's soliloquy " To be," which suggested to M. Chardin the " Not to be " of the adjoining lozenge, though it is probable that Rosa Bonheur, who made this lozenge, had in mind quite another play on words, for the figures are walking on a loaf of bread called " Pain bis," this second word being an old French one signifying brown and pronounced like By. The figures on the extreme right of the drawing are Rosa Bonheur and her brother-in-law, Hippolyte Peyrol, Sr., out shooting with two beagles. Behind them, in the order named, are Mme. Micas, Mlle. Micas, Isidore Bonheur, and Juliette Bonheur (Mme. Peyrol). Isidore's leg is bandaged on account of the accident described in M. Chardin's souvenirs given on an earlier page. The two children are Hippolyte and René Peyrol, and the figure between them represents M. Chardin.

The next lozenge is entitled " La Vieille Poule," or old hen, the nickname given to the painter Octave Roland, who had a holy horror of vipers, which then abounded in the Fontainebleau forest. This lozenge was the work of Paul Chardin, with the exception of the frog, which is by Rosa Bonheur.

The lozenge in the lower left-hand corner: Mme. Micas is represented in the act of serving out soup. She used to preside over

THE PASSY CRAVAT.

the kitchen and table at By. The inscription on the tureen is " Universal Suffrage," because the dish resembles the urn in which ballots used to be cast in the early French elections. Paul Chardin is the artist.

The next lozenge is also by M. Chardin and represents his battle with the stag, which occurred a short time before and which was described on a preceding page of this volume. " L'Intrépide Rapin " means the Brave Dauber.

In the little triangles are a devil in a bent sitting position, by Isidore Bonheur; some ducks, by Mlle. Micas; a sauce-pan with rabbits sticking out their heads from it, by M. Chardin; a bat, frog, two rats, a dragon, etc., all by Rosa Bonheur, and in the lower left-hand angle, the monogram of M. Antoine Passy.

Rosa Bonheur is also the author of the various figures at the intersection of the dividing bands—a sun, moon and comet, a pocketbook, a heart transpierced by an arrow, an allusion to Nathalie's sentimentality, and a pair of spectacles and their case, alluding to the trade by which the Micases made their money.

I now present a collection of reminiscences descriptive of various sides of Rosa Bonheur's mind and character.

From Paul Chardin:

Rosa Bonheur's welcome was always frank and hearty. Her chosen friends she treated as real companions without ever assuming an air of superiority. The dominating qualities in her nature were honesty, candour, and uprightness. Her opinion she always expressed in plain, even blunt language, and without beating about the bush. She consequently had a peculiar horror of flatterers and hypocrites. This rougher side of her character often inclined her to fits of unsociableness which made her shut her door to all without discrimination. But this roughness was only skin-deep and did not affect her heart which beat most tenderly for relatives and friends, causing her to devote herself entirely to them. In everything she was courageous and valiant, capable of sudden, energetic decisions without ever fearing for herself. Still

391

sometimes she failed to use a needful discernment in the resolutions she made, and occasionally she allowed herself to be led away by ill-considered caprices. There was a shy dash in her nature. She did not accept new friends easily and was very circumspect before making a move in that direction. She opened her doors only to a few tried companions. The fact that she was a woman artist and that she became famous early attracted the attention of the inquisitive. She was their victim on more than one occasion and had a horror of such people. She liked solitude, meditation, and felt free only in the company of those whom she had known for a long time and whom she was perfectly sure of. In such surroundings she gave free rein to her thoughts and to bursts of gaiety which sometimes ended in real tom-foolery. Her open, cordial ways rebuffed all backbiting. But she knew too well the bad side of humanity not to be on her guard. With her deep and scrutinising eye she would read a newcomer through and through, and her first impression was ineffaceable. She held in particular aversion the complimentary fashionable man, with his adulation and his insipid talk, and he could be sure of a reception similar to that always reserved for the pushing reporter. To them she always preferred the peasant or the uneducated man of the people.

Frank and communicative with the people of the working class—the populo, as she called them—Rosa Bonheur was just the contrary with those who approached her with the intention of studying her and spying out her habits, especially where this intention was a mercenary one. The professional journalist found no favour in her eyes. If he rang her bell and were recognised, he was certain to be refused admittance. On one occasion she happened to find herself in company with the brothers Goncourt, who, endeavouring to make her talk, showed their hand too plainly. Rosa Bonheur immediately assumed a reserve that baffled their attempts, and, there and then, she took a dislike to them.

Georges Cain confirms M. Chardin's statements:

Despite her apparent gaiety, Rosa Bonheur possessed a serious and meditative nature. She was fond of solitude and would often escape from the trammels of society. This attitude was doubtless fostered by her deep aversion to flattery. As a woman artist who was still young when celebrity and fame came to her, she had constantly to be on her guard against a crowd of syco-phants and adulators. Here was one of the reasons of her peculiar dislike of reporters as well as of other inquisitive persons.

Here are the details of this Goncourt incident mentioned above, as given in a letter from Louis Passy to Rosa Bonheur and in her reply, both written at Paris in June, 1859:

Dear Miss Bonheur: I am going ask a favour of you. I am in a fix, which I hope, with your usual kindness, you will try and get me out of. My friends, the de Goncourt brothers, whom you don't care much for, I believe, are living at present not far from you, and they ask me for a word of introduction to you. For many good reasons, it is difficult for me to refuse their request, or rather, I am writing them that I have told you of their com-ing and that they may call. The rest I leave to your discretion and complaisance.

Dear Mr. Louis: I perfectly well understand your position, and though I don't at all like to receive the Goncourts, I will do it, and here is my letter for them. Don't worry about the rest. I know too well the ways of the world, and what I owe myself, to let them perceive my real feelings for them.

Commenting on the above letters, which he found in the vast mass of correspondence of the Passy family at Gisors, M. Paul Chardin says:

Rosa Bonheur, if I am not mistaken, first met the de Goncourts at Gisors in 1859, when they were visiting the Passys, Jules de Goncourt, the younger of the two brothers and the only one who had any real talent, having been a school-fellow of Louis Passy, both of whom were brilliant students. This letter shows in the most affirmative manner the profound aversion which Rosa Bon-heur always manifested in my presence for journalistic reporters and indiscreet visitors. She divined that the object of the two brothers in wishing to see her was purely one of curiosity. She felt that they were trying to study her close at hand in order to divulge her idiosyncrasies in their novels for the amusement of a public always craving for new things; in a word, to do with her what they did, with the most unpardonable indiscretion, with a certain family which received them in perfect confidence. Many novelists have been guilty of this sort of thing. If Rosa Bonheur honoured me with her most unreserved friendship, it was largely because she knew she could count on my discretion; so she hid nothing from me.

Mlle. Léonide Bourges:

Rosa Bonheur's reserve with strangers and her dislike to society arose from her timidity of character. When, as Principal of the Girls' Drawing School at the beginning of her career, she was called upon to make a speech at the awarding of the prizes, she was finally obliged to abandon the attempt, so great was her agitation. When she had passed fifty, she said to me one day: " Do you know, even now I cannot quote a price for a picture ordered, without blushing? "

As illustrative of another characteristic trait, in a manner connected with the preceding, I may mention that, in a catalogue of one of the first Salons at which Rosa exhibited, she was said to have been a pupil of Léon Cogniet (1794–1880). This was not correct. Rosa Bonheur was a pupil of her father. To him alone belonged the honour of discovering his young daughter's genius and fostering it. This mistake was never publicly rectified, and Rosa was reproached with having allowed another to usurp the honour due to her father. But it appears that Léon Cogniet had written an amiable letter to the young artist, in which he said how proud he should have been to have such a pupil. Rosa's reply to those who blamed her was that she could not bring herself to write the disclaimer after so kind a letter " from such a distinguished artist."

Princess Stirbey has this to say of Rosa Bonheur's retiring disposition:

394

She would probably never have been a member of the Legion of Honour if the Empress herself had not thought of driving over to By and decorating her *manu propriâ*. We had no little difficulty in securing for her the second grade in the Legion, for, during the previous years, she had not made a single effort to push herself in any way. Shut up at By, she sent her work to the picture-dealers, who disposed of nearly everything she painted, outside of France; or rather, the picture-dealers had to go to her retreat to get what they sold. She even turned her back on the annual Salon.

Mlle. Rosa Mathieu has this to say of Rosa Bonheur's quick temper:

When she settled at By, I was often invited over in my girlhood to spend a few days with her. On one of these occasions I was a witness of one of my godmother's characteristic outbursts of petulance, when interrupted in her work and surprised in her costume. We were both in the stable, where Rosa Bonheur was engaged in sketching a cow that had been sent her from Bordeaux. In addition to blouse and trousers, the artist was wearing clogs stuffed with straw. Suddenly Céline came to announce that the Duchess of Valencia, a relative of the Empress Josephine and the wife of the Spanish Marshal Narvaez, was in the drawing-room with Nathalie Micas entertaining her, and was asking for Mlle. Bonheur.

" May the devil fly away with her ! " my godmother exclaimed, as she followed Céline.

I afterward learnt that on entering the vestibule, clogs in hand, and before she could escape upstairs to change her attire, the Duchess spied her through the drawing-room door, which was nearly wide open. Thereupon, Rosa Bonheur made the best of an embarrassing situation and retained her male costume during the interview.

" You might just as well have come with me," she remarked on rejoining me in the stable; " the Duchess might have given you some oranges ! " a reference to the well-known fruit of Valencia.

REMINISCENCES OF ROSA BONHEUR

Mme. Lagrolet writes:

Rosa Bonheur was of a very generous disposition. She used to say:

" When I invite guests to my house, I wish to receive them with the largest hospitality possible." She was to the end wonderfully young in all her movements and thoughts; full of anecdote, very gay, liked slang, was, in fact, as the French say, a true *bout-en-train*. But it was her marked spirit of generosity that always made the deepest impression on me.

Let me give a few examples of this large-heartedness in Rosa Bonheur. I begin with this communication from Joseph Verdier:

One evening she was dining with me and some friends. Among the latter was a young lady recently married, who related to us an account of the furnishing of her house. All the rooms were finished except the dining-room; for this last, her husband could not, for the moment, give her the money, and she was compelled to hold her little receptions in her sleeping-room. After dinner, Rosa asked me for a large sheet of drawing paper, and while we were talking and she herself smoking a cigarette, she sketched a delightful hunting-scene, which she signed with her full name. Then, under cover of a general conversation on music as tea was being served, she approached the young wife and said to her: " Take this picture to Tedesco, on your return to Paris, and he will give you at least fifteen hundred francs for it. Then you will be able to furnish your drawing-room."

Ernest Gambart says in his manuscript memoirs:

In connection with the study-sketches so jealously treasured by Rosa Bonheur, I may relate an incident that deserves to be more widely known.

In 1867, Rosa Bonheur became acquainted with Mme. Carvalho, the talented singer, who was a frequent visitor to By, and whose brother, at the time I am speaking of, had gone into picture-dealing, most of his orders being for Bonheur paintings. After two or three years of business, he became involved in pecuniary difficulties, to the grief of the two ladies. Thereupon, Rosa Bonheur conceived the generous idea of helping him by a sacrifice of these study-sketches. So, sending for me she said:

" Mr. Gambart, you have often told me that these sketches were valuable. You even once mentioned a sum so considerable that I could not believe you were speaking in earnest. Well, to-day I want to raise money by them. How much do you think I could sell them for? "

Knowing the purpose she had in view, I felt that it would be useless to try to dissuade her from carrying it out. So I said in reply, that if five hundred thousand francs were sufficient, I would place this sum at her disposal within three days. She asked me whether I was not running a risk, and wished to know how I would get back my money. I told her that though retired from business, I should request my nephew Lefèvre to have them sold by auction, when I was sure their value would be found to exceed the sum I offered. Overjoyed, she hastened to tell her friend that the requisite money was found. But, after all, it was not necessary to make the sacrifice. It was discovered that the brother's liabilities amounted to twelve hundred thousand francs, a sum that was quite beyond Rosa Bonheur's power to raise. Indeed, the brother of Mme. Carvalho, while appreciating the generosity of the offer made him, refused to accept it; and, by a happy combination of genius and luck, contrived to extricate himself from his embarrassment. So Rosa Bonheur was able to preserve her loved sketches, the record of her forty years' artistic labour.

Benjamin Tedesco:

Like so many other artists, she never seemed to know the value of money. We were driving out one winter day, when she was struck with pity at the sight of some poor people who, insufficiently clothed, seemed to be shivering. Thereupon she said to me:

" Here are a thousand francs. Give some to those poor persons and distribute the rest among your charitable institutions. It grieves me to see people suffer whilst I am warm and well fed."

REMINISCENCES OF ROSA BONHEUR

Alexandre Jacob:

Rosa Bonheur's character presented some strange contrasts in money matters. In household expenses she would often criticise petty items, now finding fault because too much bread was eaten in the kitchen, now because the washing-bill was too large. From such little parsimonies, a casual observer might have deemed her stingy, near, miserly, etc. Nothing could be falser. Generosity, even prodigality, was far more natural to her. When she gave presents, they were costly. Nor was this done in order to be spoken of. When the fancy took her, she would spend without inquiring whether it was prudent. The possession of moneyed wealth seemed to bore her, for she would not unfrequently stuff bundles of bank-notes in any handy hiding-place and forget all about it, so that, after her death, more than one of these hidden treasures came to light in the general overhauling. The wise overseer of her fortune, as long as she was spared to Rosa, was Mme. Micas, not Nathalie, who was quite as much inclined to careless spending as her friend; and the fortune Rosa Bonheur left was certainly largely due to Mme. Micas's prudent and restraining influence. In this respect, as in so many others, Rosa Bonheur resembled her father, whose indifference to " filthy lucre " was so great that he would throw his money on the floor to lie in the litter of his drawings, and Rosa relates having had to fish out from under this artistic rubbish the five-franc piece necessary for the day's lunch.

At times, however, Rosa Bonheur could show that her own prodigality by no means implied looseness in financial arrangements, when the apparent obligation was on her side. On first visiting Nice, she stayed at Les Palmiers, Mr. Gambart's villa. As the climate suited her and she decided to make annual stays of some months in the place, Mr. Gambart built a very pretty villa which Rosa occupied and furnished, the Villa Africaine. But he refused to accept the rent which Rosa persistently offered, he deeming it an honour to have her near him and considering himself more than paid by her pictures which he had sold. On account of this refusal which continued, Rosa Bonheur finally had a sharp dispute with Mr. Gambart, at which I was present, and finding him inexorable, she quitted him in a veritable huff, removed from his villa and went to live in one of her own building, for which I supplied the plans. But still a neighbour of his, she afterward became reconciled to him.

Hippolyte Peyrol, Jr.:

A certain well-known picture of Rosa Bonheur was given by her to a picture-dealer for 40,000 francs. Some time later this dealer went to By, complained that he could not dispose of the canvas, and insinuated that he found the sum he had given for it too high. Thereupon, Rosa Bonheur invited him to come with her immediately to her lawyer's, where she had drawn up the necessary paper refunding him the 40,000 francs, and then exclaimed: " And now, take the picture, too! " After her death, the heirs tried, I believe, to recover these 40,000 francs, but with what success I cannot say.

On another occasion Rosa Bonheur sold to the Tedescos a picture for 20,000 francs, for which they found a purchaser who gave 53,000. Thereupon, they proposed dividing with her the large profit. But to this very honourable proposal she replied characteristically: " No; I considered it worth 20,000 francs; you bought it at that price, and you alone should profit by the business."

Mlle. Keller has this to say of Rosa Bonheur's simplicity:

When I was quite young I studied at one of the city art schools where Rosa Bonheur came once a week to criticise our work. She would enter the room without any ostentation, attired in a short black jacket, a green or brown dress—these were her three favourite colours—and a white straw hat, trimmed with green velvet. This hat she would toss on to one of the empty chairs and then begin her inspection. I admired her from the start and resented the mockery of her which her plainness awakened in some of the pupils. She seemed to feel my admiration of her, for on more than one occasion she suggested that the other pupils take me as a model of intelligent industry, if I may be permitted to say so. She was a hard worker herself, and nothing so endeared anybody to her as labour.

She disliked to attract attention in public. When we visited the Salon together, I was always careful not to pronounce her name. The last time I was at the Salon with her, we met the then Under Secretary for the Fine Arts, who addressed her in rather a loud voice, and forthwith quite a crowd began to follow her. She noticed it and quickly moved into another room where she was unknown.

Alexandre Jacob writes as follows concerning Rosa Bonheur's love of fun:

About the year 1873, when I was nineteen and a student of the architectural department of the Paris Fine Arts School, I was a frequent visitor at Rosa Bonheur's house, accompanied often by my fellow-students, who came to our country home, also situated at By. On one of these occasions we had a famous pancake-making which occurred, above all places in the world, in Rosa's drawing-room. It was her idea, and we enthusiastically set to work on this particular Shrove Tuesday, and, having spread sheets over whatever was spoilable in the parlour, we made our pancakes and eat them on the spot, Rosa Bonheur doing her share of the consumption.

Indeed, Rosa Bonheur lent her countenance with a good deal of zest and enjoyment to jokes in the cooking line. For instance, Mme. Carvalho's brother, M. Miolan, officiated more than once in the kitchen, with the result that the dining table was adorned with dishes more sightly than appetising.

With a mild propensity to practical joking, Rosa Bonheur gratified it mostly by means of her art. Perhaps the most notable example of this was the cravat or handkerchief—it might have been either—which she presented to an old acquaintance, who was addicted to copious snuff-taking.

M. Peyrol, Sr., writes:

Rosa Bonheur was a woman of great resolution. What she had made up her mind to do, she would do without feebleness or

PLOUGHING IN THE NIVERNAIS.

fear. In this respect she differed from the vast majority of her sex. If necessary she would have defended herself from attack from any quarter. Cowardliness made her indignant. She could say, as in the old couplet:

> Cet animal n'est pas méchant;
> Quand on l'attaque, il se défend.

She had a passion for heroic actions; and yet, at the same time, there were very infantile sides to her character. As I have related elsewhere, she, at twenty-two, still played horse with her brother Isidore, and it would not have taken much to get her to participate once more in one of those tournaments which occurred sometimes in the studio in the Rue de la Bienfaisance, when, with her companion Edmund Dervas, she would arm herself with her father's maul-sticks and palettes, which served as lances and shields, and when, like the real knights of the Middle Ages, there would be battles royal in which the canvases on easel and wall generally suffered the most.

Like all celebrities, Rosa Bonheur was the theme of many false anecdotes. In fact, I was once invited by an American periodical to prepare a collection of true stories concerning her, which I did with the aid of the members of her family. I am able to give the rather curious genesis of one of these apocryphal tales in the words of M. Paul Chardin, who wrote me, in August, 1905, from the Château de Keraval, in Brittany, as follows:

I thought for a moment a few days ago to have discovered a new fact concerning the grand artist, when one of my friends who lives near me told me he had an anecdote concerning her. "Yes," he began, "for you know she once came to Tréveneuc," a hamlet not far from here where is a fine castle whose park stretches down to the sea-shore. I knew that Rosa Bonheur had been in Brittany, but in the Finistère region, and she never spoke to me of having been in my part of the province. "Here is what happened," continued my friend: "One day while she was painting on the beach, the village priest of Tréveneuc came to watch her work and entered

401

into conversation with her. As he was short-sighted, he leaned over her shoulder the better to observe what she was doing, which so annoyed her that she determined to get rid of him. So forthwith she began painting in a group of naked bathers of both sexes whom she represented as dancing on the beach. This had the desired effect, and the indignant ecclesiastic beat a hasty retreat." Rosa Bonheur enjoyed indulging in tricks of this kind, but she would not have gone so far as that; so I immediately doubted the authenticity of the anecdote, when suddenly my memory recalled the episode which gave rise to this idle story. I remembered that some ten years ago there came to Tréveneuc a woman artist attired somewhat fantastically, who was always accompanied by two big dogs. She was said to be Spanish and was named Mlle. Arosa. Arosa easily became Rosa, and Bonheur was quite as easily added. This is the way in which anecdotes are often manufactured out of whole cloth.

On May 18, 1899, Rosa Bonheur came to Paris on a business visit. The weather was exceptionally chilly. She drove about in an open cab and caught cold. A day or two later she returned to By, not feeling perfectly well. On May 21st she took to her bed. On May 24th the family was informed of her illness, at first by letter and then by telegraph. During the night of the 24th to the 25th she grew rapidly weaker, and the pulse became so feeble during the day of the 25th that it was evident that her end was near. " At 10.30 that same evening," says her nephew, Hippolyte Peyrol, who was present at her bedside, " the sufferer's life was quietly extinguished like a lamp without oil."

On the morning of Monday, May 29th, a simple service was held in the neighbouring Thomery Church, attended chiefly by the peasants and village folk in whose midst Rosa Bonheur had so long lived, honoured and beloved. Not the least touching and characteristic incident of the sad day was the evident grief of the faithful dogs of the defunct, cooped up in the court-yard, when the procession started for the church. Nothing would have moved their mistress more deeply than their fidelity to the end; for had she not once said that she " generally considered the canine race more humane than inhuman humans "?

In the afternoon of this same beautiful spring day a second service was performed in the chapel at the Père Lachaise cemetery, Paris, where the hearse, preceded by a car laden with wreaths and bunches of flowers, arrived about five o'clock; and the sun was low when the body was finally laid to rest in the Micas vault, beside the two old friends with whom Rosa Bonheur had lived so many long years, in fair weather and cloud. A rule of the Legion of Honour prescribes that a member be accompanied to the grave by a military escort, and French custom calls for speeches over the remains of a personality. But Rosa Bonheur naturally preferred that both of these distinctions be honoured in the breach; for soldiers and orations would have been quite out of keeping in anything that concerned her.

In the spring preceding Bouguereau's death he one day said to me:

" I went to Rosa Bonheur's funeral with a little speech in my pocket which I intended to read. But when I got to the cemetery I learned that it had been decided that no remarks were to be made at the tomb."

Later, the widow of Bouguereau—Elizabeth Gardner, of New Hampshire—herself an artist of acknowledged merit and an old friend of Rosa Bonheur, gave me the manuscript of this inedited estimate and eulogium, which may fittingly close this volume. It runs as follows:

For many years, a warm friendship has bound me to the Bonheur family. Among the women of her century, the position of Rosa Bonheur has been unique. Among contemporary painters, her place has been in the front rank, with the masters. The beginning of her career was beset with difficulties. The family was not rich and the children, who had imbibed artistic tastes from their excellent father, were many. The study of animals, always attended with difficulties, was particularly so in the case of a young woman. The fame which, for fifty years, has encircled the name of this talented artist, has been heightened by the mysterious charm which surrounded this woman, painter of wild and domestic animals, living retired from the world, among her dear models—virile, energetic, original, but modest and good. Yet, brushing aside all the many legends that surround her, the fine talents of Rosa Bonheur support the closest criticism.

Thus, the applause with which her first important canvas—"Ploughing in the Nivernais"—exhibited at the Salon of 1847, was received, was due to no previous popularity. The artist was then almost unknown. This painting, so true to nature, so well drawn, so carefully modelled and so harmonious in colour, at once established her reputation as a great artist. To-day, that work has its deserved place among the best pictures in the Luxembourg Gallery, but in the near future it will represent in the Louvre the school of French animal painters, along with the works of Géricault, Brascassat, Troyon, and Van Marcke, to mention only the dead.

The "Horse Fair," a more imposing picture and more full of movement, was first seen at the Salon of 1853 and was praised beyond description.

But these artistic triumphs served only to increase the efforts of Rosa Bonheur to make herself worthy of them. She was unaffected either by flattery or by the enthusiasm of others for her work. Though her artistic life was passed amidst various phases of the modern schools, she ever remained true to her own conceptions of art and acted only upon her own inspirations. The conscientious and sober stamp given to her first efforts characterised all her art work to the end. Though her pictures be many, her studies are almost innumerable. There was no sign of vanity in her. The faithful worship of nature made her modest. When the aim is high, one can only approximate success and this success never gives birth to pride.

One of the most cherished recollections of my life is the visit which Rosa Bonheur paid me a few weeks before her death. She, who so seldom paid visits, did me the honour to come one day unexpectedly to my studio. During those short moments, what reminiscences of the past were called up! What recollections of friends who had disappeared forever came back to us! What a friendly talk we had on art, its shortcomings and its true mission!

This woman, so charmingly simple, was the only one of her sex who had the right to display on her breast the rosette of officer of the Legion of Honour. Though seventy-seven years of age, she told me of the return of health and strength, of her desire to work on and of the joy that she felt because it was so. She left me with a gay " Au revoir! "

Rosa Bonheur was a grand and valiant artist, a true and charitable friend, whose lifework is beautiful and will not perish. Her soul was good and, like her art, immortal!

INDEX TO LETTERS

INDEX TO LETTERS

GENERAL INDEX

409

DATE DUE

OCT 1 1 1993	